Adversarial Machine Learning

Adversarial Machine Learning:

Attacks, Defenses, and Emerging Strategies

By

Jaydip Sen

Cambridge
Scholars
Publishing

Adversarial Machine Learning:
Attacks, Defenses, and Emerging Strategies

By Jaydip Sen

This book first published 2026

Cambridge Scholars Publishing

Lady Stephenson Library, Newcastle upon Tyne, NE6 2PA, UK

British Library Cataloguing in Publication Data
A catalogue record for this book is available from the British Library

ISBN: 978-1-0364-7441-6
ISBN (Ebook): 978-1-0364-7442-3

Dedicated to my beloved mother, Ms. Krishna Sen,
whose unwavering love, constant encouragement, and enduring strength have always been the greatest source of inspiration and support in all my academic and scholarly pursuits.

Jaydip

TABLE OF CONTENTS

ABOUT THE AUTHOR

Jaydip Sen has over 27 years of experience spanning research, teaching, and industry. Over the course of his career, he has been associated with several reputed organizations, including Oil and Natural Gas Corporation Ltd., Oracle India Pvt. Ltd., Akamai Technologies Pvt. Ltd., Tata Consultancy Services Ltd., National Institute of Science and Technology, and Calcutta Business School. He is currently serving as a Professor in the Department of Data Science and Artificial Intelligence at Praxis Business School, Kolkata, India. His research interests include security in wired and wireless networks, intrusion detection systems, secure routing protocols for wireless ad hoc and sensor networks, trust- and reputation-based systems, privacy issues in ubiquitous and pervasive computing, the Internet of Things, machine learning, deep learning, large language models, and adversarial machine learning. Prof. Sen has edited 18 volumes and authored more than 263 research publications in high-impact journals and refereed conference proceedings. He has also contributed 28 book chapters to volumes published by internationally renowned publishing houses. In addition, he has authored three books in the area of machine learning in finance. He has been listed among the top 2% of scientists worldwide every year since the inception of the ranking in 2019, based on studies conducted by Stanford University. Prof. Sen serves on the editorial boards of three prestigious international journals and has been a member of the technical program committees of several reputed international conferences. Prof. Sen is a Senior Member of both IEEE and ACM.

PREFACE

The extraordinary progress of artificial intelligence and machine learning during the last decade has transformed the technological landscape across a wide spectrum of domains including healthcare, finance, cybersecurity, autonomous systems, intelligent transportation, social media analytics, and natural language processing. Deep learning architectures, particularly transformer-based language models and convolutional neural networks, have achieved remarkable success in tasks that were once considered extremely difficult for machines. Systems based on models such as BERT, RoBERTa, GPT, ResNet, and Vision Transformers now exhibit near-human or even superhuman performance in language understanding, image recognition, decision support, and predictive analytics. However, alongside these impressive achievements, an equally important and rapidly growing area of concern has emerged: the vulnerability of machine learning systems to adversarial attacks.

The field of adversarial machine learning encompasses both adversarial attacks and adversarial defenses. On one hand, attack methodologies are developed to identify weaknesses in machine learning systems and to understand how models respond to carefully designed perturbations. On the other hand, defense strategies aim to improve model robustness and resilience against such manipulations. The dynamic interaction between attack and defense mechanisms has created a highly active research ecosystem involving optimization theory, deep learning, cybersecurity, natural language processing, computer vision, explainable AI, meta-learning, and robust statistical learning.

While adversarial attacks were initially explored in the domain of computer vision through gradient-based perturbations, the field has expanded rapidly into natural language processing and multimodal learning. Text-based adversarial attacks introduce unique challenges because natural language is discrete, structured, and semantically constrained. Unlike image perturbations, even small textual modifications can easily alter meaning or grammatical correctness. Consequently, modern adversarial NLP research has focused on designing perturbations that preserve semantic fidelity, contextual coherence, and linguistic naturalness while still deceiving deep learning models. Simultaneously, image-based adversarial attacks have become increasingly sophisticated, extending beyond simple pixel perturbations to transferable attacks, universal perturbations, adversarial patches, and physically realizable manipulations.

The chapters in this volume present a comprehensive exploration of adversarial machine learning from both theoretical and practical perspectives. The book addresses adversarial attacks and defenses across natural language processing and computer vision, with a particular emphasis on transformer-based language models and deep convolutional neural networks. The discussions integrate methodological foundations, algorithmic developments, experimental evaluations, and practical implications of adversarial robustness in modern AI systems. The work combines research-oriented depth with implementation-focused analysis, thereby making the material useful for both academic researchers and industry practitioners.

Chapter 1 titled *Adversarial Machine Learning: An Introduction* presents the conceptual foundations of adversarial machine learning and discusses adversarial attacks and defenses in both text and image domains. The chapter examines white-box and black-box attacks, textual and image perturbations, real-world adversarial risks, and emerging research directions including multimodal adversarial learning and robustness in large language models.

Chapter 2 titled *Strategic Text Disruption Using a Modified Word Saliency Approach* introduces the Modified Word Saliency-Based Adversarial Attack (MWSAA), a context-aware framework for transformer-based NLP models. By integrating contextual embeddings and semantic similarity constraints, the proposed approach generates coherent and semantically faithful adversarial examples with high attack effectiveness.

Chapter 3 titled *Refining Text-Based Adversarial Attacks with Saliency, Attention, and Semantic Similarity* presents the SASSP framework, which combines attention-guided saliency with semantic similarity preservation to generate natural and contextually coherent adversarial texts. Experimental evaluations demonstrate high attack success rates with minimal perturbations across transformer-based NLP models.

Chapter 4 titled *Optimizing BERT Adversarial Attacks through Projected Gradient Descent* proposes PGD-BERT-Attack, an enhanced adversarial framework that integrates Projected Gradient Descent into the BERT-Attack pipeline. The proposed approach introduces adaptive perturbation strategies guided by gradient information and semantic constraints, resulting in improved attack effectiveness and linguistic fluency.

Chapter 5 titled *A Dynamic Ensemble Framework for Defending against Adversarial Perturbation* presents an adaptive ensemble-based defense mechanism for NLP systems. The framework combines model diversity, input-aware dynamics, and adaptive aggregation strategies to improve adversarial robustness against attacks such as TextFooler, PWWS, and BERT-Attack.

Chapter 6 titled *Meta-Learning Framework for Robust Ensemble Defense against Adversarial Attacks* introduces the Adaptive Meta-Learning for Robust Ensemble Defense (AMRED) framework, which combines ensemble learning with meta-learning principles. Using Model-Agnostic Meta-Learning (MAML), the proposed system dynamically adapts to evolving adversarial patterns while preserving robustness and computational efficiency.

Chapter 7 titled *Dynamic Contextual Perturbation for Adversarial Text Generation* presents a framework for generating contextually coherent adversarial texts at the document level. By integrating contextual embeddings, saliency analysis, and semantic similarity preservation, the proposed approach achieves high attack success rates with low perturbation ratios and strong transferability.

Chapter 8 titled *Comprehensive Analysis and Defense Strategies against Adversarial Attacks on Image Classification Models* investigates adversarial vulnerabilities in convolutional neural network-based image classification systems. The chapter analyzes the effects of FGSM and adversarial patch attacks and evaluates defensive distillation as a strategy for improving adversarial resilience.

Chapter 9 titled *Effective Defensive Strategies for FGSM and PGD Adversarial Attacks in Image Classification* presents a hybrid defense framework that combines adversarial training with convolutional autoencoder-based preprocessing. Experimental evaluations on MNIST and Fashion-MNIST datasets demonstrate significant improvements in classification robustness against FGSM and PGD attacks.

Chapter 10 titled *Hybrid Defense Strategies for Enhancing Adversarial Robustness in Image Classification* proposes a layered defense framework that integrates adversarial training with input transformation techniques such as resizing, cropping, compression, and noise injection. Evaluations on the CIFAR-10 dataset demonstrate that the proposed ADRT framework substantially improves robustness against FGSM and PGD attacks while preserving clean-data performance.

Although the chapters in this volume cover advanced concepts in adversarial machine learning, every effort has been made to ensure that the discussions remain accessible and self-contained. The relevant theoretical foundations, methodological principles, and algorithmic concepts are introduced in sufficient detail to support readers from diverse academic and professional backgrounds. While some familiarity with machine learning, deep learning, and artificial intelligence may be beneficial, readers are not expected to possess highly specialized expertise in adversarial learning before engaging with the material.

I am sure that this volume will serve as a valuable resource for anybody interested in understanding adversarial machine learning and the security challenges associated with modern artificial intelligence systems. However, the primary target readership of the book includes advanced undergraduate and graduate students, doctoral researchers, and faculty members in the fields of artificial intelligence, machine learning, cybersecurity, natural language processing, and computer vision.

I express my sincere gratitude to all those whose support and encouragement have contributed to the completion of this work. I like to thank the editorial and production teams of Cambridge Scholars Publishing, UK, for their cooperation and assistance throughout the publication process. My family members - my mother Ms. Krishna Sen, my wife Ms Nalanda Sen, and my daughter Ritabrata Sen - have always been the greatest sources of inspiration, motivation, and strength in all my academic and scholarly pursuits. Their unwavering encouragement and support have made this work possible. Finally, I hope that this volume contributes meaningfully to the growing discourse on adversarial machine learning.

Jaydip Sen
Praxis Business School
Kolkata, INDIA

LIST OF FIGURES

LIST OF TABLES

CHAPTER 1

ADVERSARIAL MACHINE LEARNING: AN INTRODUCTION

Introduction

Artificial intelligence (AI) and *machine learning* (ML) have revolutionized varied domains, from healthcare diagnostics and financial forecasting to automated customer service, autonomous vehicles, and cybersecurity (Esteva et al., 2017; He et al., 2016). As these systems become embedded in mission-critical applications, concerns regarding adversarial vulnerabilities have surged. Within *adversarial machine learning* (AML), malicious actors craft subtly modified inputs designed to mislead models into making incorrect predictions (Szegedy et al., 2014; Biggio & Roli, 2018). Such manipulations threaten the reliability, integrity, and safety of AI-driven systems (Huang et al., 2011).

The two most studied modalities in adversarial ML are *text* and *image* inputs. While image-based adversarial examples were the first to attract intense scrutiny due to their visual demonstrability (Goodfellow et al., 2015), the rise of large language models in *natural language processing* (NLP) has revealed significant vulnerabilities to adversarial text attacks as well (Alzantot et al., 2018; Jin et al., 2020; Zhao et al., 2018). This is especially significant given the discrete and structured nature of textual data, where maintaining semantics and syntactic correctness while introducing adversarial perturbations is nontrivial (Ren et al., 2019; Morris et al., 2020).

This chapter presents a comprehensive overview of adversarial attack and defense strategies in both text and image domains, detailing motivations, taxonomy, seminal approaches, real-world relevance, and future research directions.

Text-Based Adversarial Attacks

Challenges of Textual Adversarial Examples: The generation of adversarial examples in natural language processing (NLP) presents unique challenges that are distinct from those encountered in image-based attacks. *Unlike images, which are composed of continuous-valued pixels, text data is inherently discrete*, comprising words or characters arranged according to the rules of grammar and syntax to express semantically coherent thoughts (Zhang et al., 2019). Even minor alterations in text can lead to substantial changes in meaning, grammatical correctness, or overall fluency. Therefore, crafting adversarial perturbations in text requires not only the ability to fool a machine learning model but also the finesse to preserve the linguistic integrity of the input (Liang et al., 2018; Ebrahimi et al., 2018; Ren et al., 2019). Any deviation that renders the text unnatural or unintelligible risks being easily identified by humans or failing to achieve its adversarial objective. This constraint greatly complicates the process of designing perturbations that are both effective and imperceptible (Morris et al., 2020).

Another complicating factor in adversarial NLP is the *use of word and sentence embeddings*. Modern language models embed rich semantic and contextual information into high-dimensional vector spaces, capturing complex relationships between tokens (Devlin et al., 2019; Mikolov et al., 2019). Perturbing a word in this embedding space can result in changes to its syntactic role or semantic connotation, making it difficult to control for subtlety (Wallace et al., 2019). Consequently, adversarial text generation must walk a tightrope between misleading the model and maintaining readability, fluency, and semantic coherence (Alzantot et al., 2018).

Taxonomy of Attack Strategies: Adversarial text attacks can be classified along two principal dimensions: the nature of access the attacker has to the model, and the granularity at which the perturbation is applied. From a model access perspective, attacks can be either white-box or black-box. White-box attacks assume full knowledge of the model's architecture, parameters, and gradients. This allows attackers to directly optimize perturbations using backpropagation or gradient-based techniques (Ebrahimi et al., 2018; Li et al., 2020a). With access to internal representations and loss functions, white-box adversaries can compute which tokens contribute most to the model's prediction and selectively perturb those inputs. In contrast, black-box attacks operate without insight into the model's internals. These adversaries only have access to input-output pairs and must therefore rely on query-based methods, score approximations, or substitute models to guide their perturbations (Jin et al., 2020; Papernot et al., 2016b). Black-box scenarios are more reflective of real-world deployments, where proprietary models may only expose APIs rather than internal mechanics.

Another layer of classification arises from the *level at which the perturbations are introduced*. At the *character level*, adversarial attacks modify individual characters through insertion, deletion, substitution, or transposition (Gao et al., 2018). These minimal modifications are often designed to mimic common typos or intentional misspellings that preserve overall readability. Examples include replacing a character with a visually similar symbol or introducing repeated letters. *Word-level perturbations*, on the other hand, focus on replacing entire tokens with synonyms, homophones, or semantically related terms (Alzantot et al., 2018; Morris et al., 2020). These substitutions are often guided by lexical resources such as WordNet or contextual embeddings that ensure the replacement fits both the meaning and grammar of the original sentence. Word-level adversarial attacks often rely on search or optimization strategies to select replacement tokens that preserve semantics while misleading the classifier (Zang et al., 2020). At the *sentence or structural level*, attacks manipulate entire phrases or sentence constructs (Iyyer et al., 2018). This could involve *paraphrasing*, *rearranging clauses*, or *inserting/deleting sentences* in a way that preserves coherence but introduces enough variation to confuse the model. These higher-level perturbations are especially potent against models that rely heavily on contextual understanding.

Representative Text Attack Techniques: Several landmark techniques have emerged in the literature that exemplify the effectiveness and creativity of adversarial attacks in NLP. One of the most cited approaches is *TextFooler*, which operates at the *word level* by identifying and replacing important tokens based on their saliency with semantically similar alternatives (Jin et al., 2020). The method ensures that meaning is preserved while targeting the words that most influence the model's output. Another influential technique is *TextBugger*, which employs a *hybrid strategy of character-level* and *word-level modifications* (Li et al., 2019). By introducing subtle spelling variations or typographical errors, it deceives classifiers without altering the sentence's perceived meaning. Other methods have adapted gradient-based optimization techniques, such as *Projected Gradient Descent* (PGD), to the discrete nature of language (Waghela et al., 2024f). These approaches approximate gradient steps in embedding space and then map the perturbed embeddings back to valid tokens through nearest-neighbor or decoder mechanisms (Wallace et al., 2019).

In addition to gradient-based attacks, *saliency-driven techniques* compute token importance scores based on model sensitivity and direct perturbations toward the most influential components (Li et al., 2019; Waghela et al, 2025; 2024g). Some methods also use *paraphrasing strategies* via pretrained encoder-decoder architectures to produce syntactically diverse but semantically equivalent adversarial examples (Iyyer et al., 2018). These models generate alternative phrasings that shift the model's attention or mislead its contextual inference mechanisms.

Defense Mechanisms against Textual Attacks: The rising sophistication of text-based adversarial attacks has spurred the development of a wide range of defense strategies aimed at enhancing model robustness. One of the most prominent defenses is *adversarial training*, in which the model is exposed to adversarial examples during the training process (Miyato et al., 2017). By learning from both clean and perturbed data, the model becomes more resilient to future attacks. Although adversarial training has proven effective, it is computationally intensive and often struggles to generalize across different types of attacks or perturbation strategies (Zhou et al., 2019). Another common defense involves *input sanitization and correction*. These approaches apply preprocessing techniques to normalize the text, correct spelling errors, or filter out tokens likely to be adversarial. By cleaning the input before it reaches the model, these methods aim to neutralize potential threats at the source (Pruthi et al., 2019).

In addition to input-level defenses, some strategies focus on regularizing the model's learning process to improve generalization and robustness. Regularization techniques may incorporate robustness-aware loss functions, embedding smoothness constraints, or dropout mechanisms to prevent overfitting to specific token patterns (Zhai, 2020). Ensemble learning also serves as an effective defense by combining predictions from multiple models, thereby reducing the likelihood that a single adversarial example can mislead all components simultaneously (Tramer, 2017). More recently, researchers have explored causal intervention frameworks, which attempt to identify and correct inconsistencies in the semantic structure of adversarial inputs (Zhao et al., 2022). By applying principles from causal inference, these approaches aim to disentangle spurious correlations from genuine causal relationships in the data.

Explainable AI (XAI) techniques play a dual role in both interpreting model behavior and detecting adversarial manipulations. By analyzing attention weights, feature attributions, or heatmaps of model focus, XAI tools can highlight discrepancies between normal and adversarial processing

(Wallace et al., 2019; Rebeiro et al., 2016). Unusual shifts in attention or unexpected model confidence can act as red flags, triggering further scrutiny. Detection-based defenses use these interpretability cues to flag suspicious inputs for review or rejection. Finally, *certified defenses* seek to provide formal guarantees of robustness under defined conditions. In the case of text, this often involves certifying the model's prediction stability under bounded token-level modifications. Techniques such as *randomized smoothing* or discrete certification over the embedding space are used to bound the model's output variation and offer theoretical robustness guarantees, although they remain limited in scale and applicability (Jia et al., 2019).

Overall, the field of text-based adversarial attacks and defenses continues to grow rapidly, driven by the dual pressures of adversarial innovation and the need for model robustness. As NLP systems become more deeply integrated into critical applications, from sentiment analysis and machine translation to legal document parsing and conversational agents, the importance of understanding and mitigating adversarial vulnerabilities cannot be overstated. Advancing this field requires not only the development of more resilient models and smarter defense mechanisms but also a deeper understanding of the linguistic structures and cognitive principles that underpin human language processing.

Image-Based Adversarial Attacks

In recent years, deep *convolutional neural networks* (CNNs) have achieved remarkable success in image classification, object detection, semantic segmentation, and other vision-based tasks. However, these models are highly vulnerable to adversarial attacks: carefully crafted perturbations applied to input images that cause the model to make incorrect predictions while remaining imperceptible to human observers. The underlying cause of this vulnerability lies in the high-dimensional and overparameterized nature of deep models, which makes them sensitive to inputs that deviate slightly from the data manifold. Even a minuscule change in a few pixel values can cause dramatic changes in the model's output, despite the altered image appearing visually identical to the original. This fragility is especially concerning given the increasing integration of vision systems in high-stakes domains such as autonomous driving, facial recognition, medical imaging, and surveillance (Goodfellow et al., 2015; Madry et al., 2017). Ensuring the robustness of CNNs against adversarial attacks is, therefore, a critical requirement for deploying trustworthy and safe AI systems in the real world (Carlini & Wagner, 2017).

Taxonomy of Attack Methods: Adversarial attacks on images can be broadly categorized into four methodological families: (i) *white-box gradient-based attacks*, (ii) *black-box attacks*, (iii) *universal perturbations*, and (iv) *physical-world attacks*.

Among the most studied are the *white-box attacks*, where the attacker has complete access to the model's architecture, weights, and gradients. Notable examples in this category include the *Fast Gradient Sign Method* (FGSM) (Goodfellow et al., 2015), *Projected Gradient Descent* (PGD) (Madry et al., 2017), and the *Carlini and Wagner* (C&W) attack (Carlini & Wagner, 2017). FGSM was one of the earliest and simplest attack techniques, designed to generate adversarial examples by perturbing the input image in the direction of the sign of the gradient of the loss function with respect to the input. It requires only a single gradient computation and is effective under certain norm constraints, particularly the L_∞ norm. PGD extends FGSM by applying it iteratively while projecting the perturbed image back into a bounded ε-ball around the original input to ensure the perturbation remains within a fixed norm. It has since become a standard benchmark for evaluating the robustness of vision models. The C&W attack, on the other hand, introduces a more advanced optimization framework that minimizes a specially designed objective function under L_0, L_2, or L_∞ norm constraints. This method can generate perturbations that are even more imperceptible and harder to defend against than those created by FGSM or PGD.

In contrast to white-box attacks, *black-box attacks* assume that the attacker has no direct access to the model's internal parameters. Instead, they rely on either *transferability* (Papernot et al., 2016a) or *query-based mechanisms* like *Natural Evolution Strategies* (NES) (Ilyas et al., 2018). Transfer-based black-box attacks exploit the observation that adversarial examples generated for one model often transfer and remain effective against different models with similar architectures or training distributions. By training a substitute model and crafting adversarial images on it, attackers can deceive a target model without having to know its internals. Query-based black-box attacks take a different approach. Here, the attacker sends multiple queries to the target model and observes the output, such as predicted class probabilities or logits. Based on this information, the attacker approximates the model's gradients or decision boundaries using methods like *Natural Evolution Strategies* (NES), *bandit optimization*, or *finite-difference approximations*. These attacks are especially potent when query budgets are generous or when models expose rich output interfaces.

Another significant line of research in image-based attacks involves *universal adversarial perturbations*. Instead of crafting instance-specific perturbations, these attacks aim to compute a single, universal perturbation vector that, when added to any input from a given dataset, causes misclassification across a wide range of inputs and classes. This approach reveals a more alarming fragility in neural networks, namely, that there exist small directions in input space that consistently induce incorrect behavior regardless of the specific content of the image. Universal perturbations challenge the assumption that attacks must be tailored to individual inputs, and suggest that global vulnerabilities exist across the entire feature space learned by vision models (Moosavi-Dezfooli et al., 2017).

Physical-world adversarial attacks take adversarial research out of the purely digital domain and into tangible settings. These attacks involve crafting physical artifacts, such as stickers, printed patches, or specially designed 3D objects, that cause machine vision systems to fail when captured by cameras. For instance, small adversarial stickers placed on a stop sign can cause an autonomous vehicle to misinterpret the sign as a yield or speed-limit sign. These perturbations must be robust to environmental factors such as changes in lighting, angle, distance, and camera resolution. A notable technique in this domain is *Expectation-over-Transformation* (EOT), which generates adversarial examples that remain effective under a distribution of transformations, thereby ensuring their robustness in real-world conditions (Athalye et al., 2018). The ability of adversarial perturbations to persist in physical settings raises serious concerns for the safety and reliability of AI-powered systems operating in open environments.

Landmark Techniques in Image Attacks: Over the past decade, several landmark techniques have emerged that define the trajectory of image-based adversarial research. FGSM and PGD, as discussed earlier, are foundational gradient-based methods known for their simplicity and effectiveness. They serve as the basis for adversarial training and robustness evaluation. The C&W attack introduced more sophisticated loss formulations and optimization strategies, pushing the boundary of how imperceptible and effective an adversarial example could be. Other important techniques include *DeepFool* (Moosavi-Dezfooli et al., 2016), which aims to find the minimal perturbation needed to cross a classification boundary, and the *Jacobian-based Saliency Map Attack* (JSMA) (Papernot et al., 2016a), which constructs targeted adversarial examples by perturbing a few pixels based on saliency scores. These methods focus on generating adversarial samples with high success rates under tight norm constraints. Universal perturbation methods, such as those proposed by Moosavi-Dezfooli et al., further demonstrated that one can construct dataset-wide perturbations effective across multiple images and classes (Moosavi-Dezfooli et al., 2017). In physical-world settings, EOT enabled the creation of adversarial inputs that remain robust under a wide range of real-world transformations, significantly raising the bar for what constitutes a realistic attack.

Defending against Image Attacks: To counter these threats, a variety of defense mechanisms have been developed, although most remain imperfect. One of the most widely studied and effective defenses is *adversarial training* (Madry et al., 2018). This involves augmenting the training dataset with adversarial examples, thereby teaching the model to correctly classify both clean and perturbed inputs. While adversarial training significantly improves robustness, it also comes with high computational cost and sometimes reduced accuracy on clean data. Moreover, models trained against specific types of attacks may remain vulnerable to others, particularly if the attack method is not included in the training process.

Another class of defenses focuses on *input preprocessing and transformation*. These techniques apply various filters or transformations to the input image before feeding it into the model, with the goal of disrupting or removing adversarial perturbations. Examples include JPEG compression, feature squeezing, image quantization, random resizing and padding, and bit-depth reduction. While some preprocessing methods can reduce the success rate of simple attacks, they are often ineffective against adaptive attacks that are aware of the defense pipeline and optimize perturbations accordingly.

Gradient masking or obfuscation has also been proposed as a defense mechanism, wherein models are intentionally designed to make gradient information less useful or misleading. However, research has shown that most gradient-masking defenses are brittle and can be bypassed by carefully crafted adaptive attacks (Athalye et al., 2018; Carlini & Wagner, 2017). This has led to a consensus that gradient obfuscation should not be relied upon as a standalone defense strategy.

More rigorous approaches involve *certified defenses*, which provide formal guarantees of robustness within specific perturbation bounds. Techniques such as *randomized smoothing*, *interval bound propagation*, and *convex relaxation* are used to bound the model's output under small input changes, allowing one to make provable statements about a model's resistance to adversarial inputs (Wong & Kolter, 2018; Cohen et al., 2019). Although certified defenses offer stronger assurances than empirical methods, they often apply to limited model types, suffer from scalability issues, and typically impose restrictions on model architecture or input size.

Detection-based defenses offer another layer of protection by attempting to distinguish adversarial examples from clean inputs (Metzen et al., 2017). These methods rely on statistical tests, density estimation, or auxiliary classifier networks to identify anomalous samples that may be adversarial. For instance, some models use hidden-layer activations or output distributions to detect distributional shifts caused by adversarial noise. However, as attackers develop adaptive strategies, the reliability of detection mechanisms also comes into question.

Finally, *feature denoising approaches* insert specialized modules into CNN architectures that are trained to remove adversarial perturbations at the feature level rather than at the raw input level. These denoising blocks clean corrupted activations within the network, enabling subsequent layers to process more stable and robust representations. Models such as *Denoising ResNet* (Xie et al., 2019) exemplify this approach, showing improved resilience to various attack types without sacrificing standard accuracy.

In summary, image-based adversarial attacks reveal deep vulnerabilities in neural networks and pose significant challenges to the development of reliable and safe AI systems. While many attack and defense techniques have been proposed, the adversarial landscape continues to evolve, driven by the arms race between attackers devising new perturbation strategies and defenders developing increasingly sophisticated countermeasures. The study of adversarial attacks in vision systems is not only an intellectual challenge at the frontier of machine learning but also a practical necessity for ensuring the trustworthiness of AI in the physical world.

Cross-Modal Comparison and Combined Insights

As adversarial machine learning matures across both the *natural language processing* (NLP) and *computer vision* (CV) domains, a nuanced understanding of the similarities, divergences, and synergies between adversarial attacks and defenses in these modalities becomes essential. Although the data representations in NLP (discrete textual tokens) and CV (continuous pixel values) are inherently different, several common principles underpin adversarial phenomena in both domains. Exploring these shared underpinnings, as well as the unique challenges each domain presents, reveals new directions for robust model development and cross-modal learning strategies.

Common Themes across Text and Image Domains: A key theme unifying adversarial strategies across both text and image modalities is the principle of *optimization via gradients*. In the image domain, the continuous nature of pixel values naturally lends itself to gradient-based optimization. Attackers can easily compute gradients of the loss function with respect to the input pixels and use techniques like *Fast Gradient Sign Method* (FGSM), *Projected Gradient Descent* (PGD), or *Carlini-Wagner* (CW) to craft adversarial perturbations that maximize classification error while maintaining imperceptibility (Goodfellow et al., 2015; Madry et al., 2018; Carlini & Wagner, 2017). Conversely, in NLP, where inputs are comprised of discrete symbols (e.g., words or subword tokens), direct gradient-based optimization is not straightforward. To address this, researchers often operate in the embedding space, a continuous vector space where words are represented as dense vectors, and approximate gradients with respect to these embeddings. Some methods also leverage *surrogate gradient techniques* or use *score-based heuristics* to identify influential tokens for substitution or deletion (Alzantot et al., 2018; Ebrahimi et al., 2018; Iyyer et al., 2018; Joulin et al., 2017). Thus, despite the modality differences, both image and text attacks revolve around the central concept of exploiting model gradients to navigate the input space toward misclassification.

Another unifying concern is *perceptual imperceptibility*, the requirement that adversarial modifications remain undetectable to human perception. In image-based attacks, this typically means ensuring that the L_2 or L_∞ norm of the perturbation is below a certain threshold, so that the modified image appears visually indistinguishable from the original. Popular attacks such as FGSM and CW explicitly constrain perturbations within small norm-bounded spaces to maintain this imperceptibility. In text-based attacks, the concept is more complex. Since textual inputs are read and interpreted semantically, maintaining the meaning, grammatical correctness, and naturalness of the adversarial example is essential. This leads to constraints such as preserving sentence semantics (often evaluated using cosine similarity in sentence embedding space), avoiding syntactic errors, and ensuring that replacements do not make the sentence illogical or ungrammatical. Although the perceptual channels differ, visual vs. linguistic, the goal in both modalities is the same: to subtly alter inputs in a way that deceives the model without alerting the human observer.

Adversarial training is another widely adopted defense strategy in both CV and NLP. In its basic form, adversarial training involves augmenting the training set with adversarial examples, forcing the model to learn representations that are robust to input perturbations (Goodfellow et al., 2015; Miyato et al., 2016). In image classification, adversarial training using strong attacks like PGD has been shown to substantially improve robustness (Madry et al., 2018). In text-based models, adversarial training is more nuanced due to the difficulty in generating high-quality adversarial examples that satisfy linguistic constraints (Joulin et al., 2017). However, recent methods incorporate adversarial word substitutions or paraphrases during training to improve robustness (Yoo & Qi, 2021; Jia et al., 2019; Zhu et al.,2020). Despite its effectiveness, adversarial training suffers from several drawbacks in both domains. It is computationally intensive, especially when strong attacks are used during training, and it often overfits to specific types of perturbations, reducing generalization to unseen attacks. Moreover, designing universally effective adversarial training strategies remains an open challenge, particularly in cross-modal settings.

Recent progress in adversarial machine learning has highlighted the importance of semantic similarity, adaptive perturbation techniques, and ensemble-based methods for strengthening both attack capabilities and defensive robustness. A substantial body of research by Waghela et al. and Sen et al. (Waghela et al., 2024a–g; Waghela et al., 2025; Sen, 2024; Sen & Dasgupta, 2023; Sen et al., 2023; Sen & Waghela, 2025; Koley et al., 2024) has been instrumental in advancing this field. Their work introduces linguistically informed, context-sensitive attack methods that leverage saliency mapping, attention mechanisms, semantic similarity metrics, and Bidirectional Encoder Representations from Transformers (BERT)-based embeddings to produce adversarial examples that retain syntactic fluency and semantic fidelity. On the defensive side, they investigate ensemble learning, meta-learning, and hybrid architectures to enhance model resilience. Notably, their contributions span both textual and visual classification tasks, offering broadly applicable strategies for designing adversarial systems that maintain semantic coherence while enabling adaptive defenses transferable across diverse models and application domains.

In both image and text domains, *evaluation metrics* serve as the primary mechanism for assessing the success and stealth of adversarial attacks. Common metrics include *Attack Success Rate* (ASR), which quantifies the proportion of inputs for which the attack successfully alters the model's prediction. In images, this is often supplemented by perceptual similarity metrics such as L_2 norm or L_∞ norm, *Structural Similarity Index* (SSIM), or *Peak Signal-to-Noise Ratio* (PSNR) (Goodfellow et al., 2015; Dong et al., 2018; Wang et al., 2004; Hore & Ziou, 2010). In NLP, semantic similarity between the original and perturbed texts is commonly measured using cosine similarity in embedding spaces like those provided by *Universal Sentence Encoder* (USE) or BERT-based encoders (Devlin et al., 2019; Cer et al., 2018). Additionally, metrics like *Perplexity* (to capture fluency) and syntactic error rate are used (Ebrahimi et al., 2018). Another important consideration is *transferability*, the ability of adversarial examples generated on one model to deceive other models. Transferability has been studied extensively in both domains, with varying results depending on the similarity of model architectures and training data. High transferability signifies broader vulnerability, making it a critical factor in evaluating attack potency.

Distinct Challenges Unique to Each Modality: Despite these shared themes, adversarial machine learning must confront domain-specific challenges that arise due to the *fundamental differences in data representation*. In the image domain, the input space is continuous and high-dimensional, which allows fine-grained control over pixel perturbations (Goodfellow et al, 2015). This continuity facilitates powerful gradient-based optimization and makes adversarial example generation relatively straightforward. In contrast, the text domain is inherently *discrete*, composed of tokens like characters, words, or subword units (Joulin et al., 2017). As a result, direct gradient application is not possible. Instead, perturbations must be carefully designed to respect the tokenization structure, vocabulary constraints, and grammatical rules (Ebrahimi et al., 2018; Ren et al., 2019; Li et al., 2019). These requirements make text-based attacks more complex, as each perturbation involves not just altering the input but ensuring that it remains valid and meaningful to a human reader.

Another critical challenge lies in *semantic preservation*. In image attacks, the requirement is typically that the perturbed image appears visually similar to the original. Minor changes in pixel values, even if semantically irrelevant, are acceptable as long as they do not cause visual artifacts. However, in NLP, the semantic content, the meaning conveyed by the text, is paramount. Adversarial modifications that change the sentence's intent, tone, or information content are considered invalid. Therefore, NLP attacks must balance the need for effective model deception with *semantic fidelity*, often by relying on synonym substitution, paraphrasing, or syntactic reordering.

The *feasibility of black-box attacks* also differs between the two domains. In vision models, output scores or class probabilities are often available, enabling attackers to use *score-based* or *gradient-free optimization methods* such as *Zeroth-Order Optimization* (ZOO) or evolutionary strategies. These methods can estimate model sensitivity and craft effective perturbations even without access to internal gradients. In contrast, NLP models often return only discrete class labels or confidence scores, and do not expose internal token-level decisions. Moreover, due to the combinatorial nature of text and the cost of querying models with multiple variations, *query efficiency* becomes a major bottleneck in black-box text attacks. These differences demand specialized attack strategies and highlight the need for domain-aware black-box optimization methods.

Synergies and Hybrid Research Directions: The convergence of NLP and CV in multimodal AI systems, such as image captioning, visual question answering (VQA), and generative multimodal models, opens new frontiers for adversarial research. One promising direction is the development of *multimodal adversarial attacks*, where perturbations are introduced in more than one input modality simultaneously (Gao et al., 2018; Yin et al., 2023). For example, in a VQA system that takes both image and question as input, attackers can subtly alter the question wording and pixel-level features of the image to jointly mislead the model (Xie et al., 2019). These *cross-modal attacks* introduce new challenges in crafting perturbations that preserve coherence within and between modalities while maximizing model deception. Multimodal adversarial research has the potential to reveal hidden vulnerabilities in integrated AI systems that are not apparent when evaluating each modality in isolation.

Another exciting area is the *transfer and generalization of adversarial examples across modalities*. This includes understanding whether adversarial patterns learned in one modality (e.g., perturbations that affect image-text models) can be translated or adapted to another modality. For instance, if an attack on an image-text alignment model (like CLIP) succeeds through visual perturbation, can similar manipulations in the textual descriptions yield comparable results? Studying *cross-modal transferability* not only improves understanding of shared vulnerabilities but also helps in developing *unified defenses* that operate across multiple data types.

The need for *unified benchmarks and evaluation platforms* is also becoming evident. Currently, most adversarial robustness benchmarks are modality-specific, focusing exclusively on either image or text datasets. However, the rise of foundation models and multimodal transformers (e.g., GPT-4, Flamingo, Gemini, etc.) demands evaluation frameworks that can assess robustness holistically across text, images, and even audio or code. A cross-domain adversarial evaluation suite, encompassing datasets, attack implementations, and metrics, would significantly accelerate progress in understanding and defending against adversarial threats in a unified manner.

Finally, *explainability and interpretability* emerge as powerful allies in the quest for robustness. In NLP, attention mechanisms and attribution methods like LIME (Ribeiro et al., 2016) or SHAP (Lundberg & Lee, 2017) offer insight into how models arrive at decisions, helping to pinpoint which tokens or phrases are most influential. Similarly, in CV, saliency maps and gradient-based attribution tools visualize regions of the image that drive predictions. Integrating these interpretability methods into adversarial defense can provide *early warnings* about suspicious input manipulations or serve as regularizers during training to improve robustness. Moreover, explainable models make it easier for humans to detect adversarial behavior, especially in high-stakes domains like healthcare or finance.

Real-World Implications and Applications

The implications of adversarial attacks on machine learning systems are not merely theoretical or confined to controlled laboratory settings; they have increasingly significant consequences in real-world applications that affect human safety, social systems, privacy, and economic stability. As AI becomes more deeply integrated into critical sectors such as healthcare, transportation, finance, security, and communication, the demand for robust and trustworthy models becomes paramount. Understanding how adversarial vulnerabilities manifest in these domains is essential to anticipating risks and designing effective mitigation strategies.

In the healthcare sector, the stakes are particularly high. Medical imaging models used in radiology, pathology, or dermatology often rely on convolutional neural networks (CNNs) to detect anomalies such as tumors, lesions, or irregular patterns. Adversarial perturbations, even if imperceptible to the human eye, can cause these models to misclassify malignant tumors as benign or fail to detect critical symptoms. This can lead to delayed or incorrect diagnoses, compromising patient outcomes and eroding trust in automated diagnostic systems. Beyond images, adversarial text attacks can also disrupt clinical decision support tools, which rely on natural language input such as physician notes, patient histories, or triage chatbot interactions. A slight alteration in terminology or phrasing, crafted to exploit model vulnerabilities, could result in inappropriate prioritization, incorrect alerts, or misinterpretation of symptoms, potentially endangering lives.

Autonomous vehicles represent another domain where adversarial attacks pose significant safety risks. These vehicles rely on sophisticated perception modules that integrate multiple sensor modalities, such as cameras, lidar, radar, and GPS, to make navigation decisions. Image-based adversarial attacks, such as adversarial stickers placed on stop signs or speed limit signs, can deceive visual recognition systems into interpreting a stop sign as a yield sign or vice versa (Eykholt et al., 2018). Such misclassifications may cause traffic violations or, in the worst case, accidents. Similarly, adversarial manipulations targeting multilingual or multilingual-capable sign-reading modules, especially in areas with international signage, could exploit translation-based weaknesses, further complicating decision-making in navigation systems. Attacks on sensor fusion systems, which combine signals from multiple sources, can result in inconsistencies or contradictions in environmental understanding, undermining the vehicle's ability to respond to dynamic road conditions effectively (Wang et al., 2023).

The financial domain, particularly in fraud detection and risk assessment, also faces growing exposure to adversarial manipulation. Machine learning algorithms are widely used to analyze transaction histories, credit reports, and natural language descriptions of financial behavior to flag anomalies or detect fraudulent activity. However, these models can be subverted through carefully crafted perturbations in input data. For instance, an attacker could subtly manipulate the text used in transaction descriptions or modify the structure of a loan application to escape detection while maintaining a superficially legitimate appearance. Automated chatbots employed by banks or fintech platforms, which provide support and perform KYC (Know Your Customer) checks, may also be susceptible to adversarial textual inputs that bypass intent recognition or mislead the system into granting unauthorized access or approving questionable transactions. In such environments, even a single misclassified instance can lead to significant financial loss or data breach.

Adversarial threats are equally relevant in the realm of digital content moderation and information integrity. Social media platforms, news aggregators, and online communities rely heavily on automated systems for detecting hate speech, spam, misinformation, and other forms of harmful content. These systems typically analyze both textual and visual content using classifiers trained on large-scale datasets. Adversarial attacks on these classifiers can allow malicious actors to circumvent detection. For example, toxic or hateful messages may be rewritten using word substitutions or syntactic obfuscation that bypasses keyword-based filters while preserving the offensive meaning. Likewise, adversarial image modifications—such as slight alterations to memes, propaganda images, or deepfakes- can evade visual classifiers trained to recognize inappropriate or deceptive content. As misinformation continues to evolve in sophistication, adversarial manipulation represents a potent tool for disinformation campaigns, making it harder for platforms to uphold standards of safety and accuracy.

Speech-based interfaces and voice-activated systems form another frontier vulnerable to adversarial manipulation. With the growing adoption of voice assistants such as Siri, Alexa, or Google Assistant, as well as enterprise applications that rely on automated transcription and voice-to-text processing, the possibility of injecting adversarial audio has become a critical concern. Adversarial audio samples are designed to sound benign to human listeners but transcribe into misleading or malicious text when processed by *automatic speech recognition* systems (Zelasko et al., 2021). When such adversarial transcriptions are fed into downstream NLP pipelines, such as command execution engines or virtual assistants, they can trigger unintended actions ranging from setting calendar events to unlocking doors or placing unauthorized orders (Hussain et al., 2021). These threats become even more insidious when combined with physical world scenarios, such as playing adversarial audio over public speakers or embedding it within multimedia content, effectively creating a new class of imperceptible, remote-access vulnerabilities.

The real-world impact of adversarial attacks is not limited to these sectors alone. Any AI system deployed in the wild, whether in education, legal tech, cybersecurity, journalism, or scientific research, must contend with the possibility that its input can be manipulated by adversarial actors seeking to exploit weaknesses. For example, in online examinations or automated grading systems, students might use adversarial text modifications to trick grading algorithms. In legal document processing or e-discovery tools, slight adversarial changes in terminology could lead to incorrect legal interpretations or missed evidence. In cybersecurity, malware classifiers could be evaded through minor modifications in code or metadata that confuse static and dynamic analysis engines.

As adversarial machine learning continues to expose the fragility of otherwise high-performing models, these real-world applications underscore the need for robustness to become a core design consideration, rather than an afterthought. It is no longer sufficient for AI models to perform well on benchmark datasets in controlled environments; they must demonstrate resilience to manipulation, ambiguity, and noise encountered in dynamic, high-stakes settings. Only then can AI systems be trusted to serve humanity in its most sensitive and impactful domains.

Future Research Directions

The domain of adversarial machine learning is evolving rapidly, and future advancements are likely to emerge from a diverse set of challenges and opportunities across attack methodologies, defense mechanisms, evaluation strategies, multi-modal integration, and theoretical foundations (Xu et al., 2020). As adversarial robustness becomes a necessary consideration in real-world deployment of AI systems, especially in high-stakes applications, there is a pressing need to explore next-generation research directions that can address existing limitations and anticipate emerging threats.

Enhanced Attack Techniques: One of the most promising frontiers in attack methodologies involves developing enhanced adversarial techniques that *target complex and linguistically diverse scenarios*. Traditional adversarial attacks have primarily focused on English-language models. However, the increasing adoption of AI systems in multilingual and code-mixed environments necessitates the design of adversarial attacks that can effectively operate in non-English contexts or across code-switching data (Das et al., 2021). This shift presents unique challenges as synonym databases and word embeddings vary significantly across languages, and linguistic structures may differ in syntax and morphology. Attacks in such environments require not only language-agnostic strategies but also culturally and contextually sensitive perturbation mechanisms.

Another crucial area lies in *extending adversarial perturbations beyond single-sentence inputs to document-level or discourse-aware settings*. Most existing techniques target isolated sentences or short snippets, neglecting the broader coherence and discourse structure present in larger texts (Li et al., 2021). Future attacks may span multiple paragraphs, maintaining conference chains, temporal ordering, and logical consistency. These document-level attacks should exploit subtler vulnerabilities, such as implicit biases in summarization or entailment models, and challenge current defenses to account for cross-sentence dependencies and long-range semantics.

In addition, the *exploration of adversarial perturbations in the embedding space*, rather than in the input token space, offers a deeper avenue for probing the internal workings of NLP models. Manipulating representations at the level of word embeddings, attention mechanisms, or intermediate activations could expose vulnerabilities intrinsic to the architecture itself, rather than those resulting from surface-level lexical variations (Boucher et al., 2022). This strategy is particularly relevant in transformer-based models, where contextual embeddings evolve across multiple layers and provide richer attack surfaces for adversarial manipulations.

The emergence of instruction-tuned large language models (LLMs), such as ChatGPT and Claude, introduces new vulnerabilities and attack vectors. Prompt-based systems are highly sensitive to input instructions, making them susceptible to adversarial prompts that subtly alter task framing or inject misleading guidance. Crafting such prompts does not require modifying the original user input, yet they can lead the model to generate factually incorrect, biased, or toxic outputs. This class of attacks, often termed "*prompt injections*" or "*prompt reversal,*" presents a new paradigm where the adversarial surface lies not in data tokens but in the way models are conditioned during inference (Greshake et al., 2023).

Moreover, future adversarial text attacks may leverage generative paradigms more effectively by *employing diffusion models or autoregressive transformers for adversarial example generation*. These models can produce coherent, semantically aligned, and stylistically natural adversarial texts with minimal lexical or syntactic divergence from the original input. Unlike greedy or heuristic-based methods, generative adversarial strategies can be optimized for subtlety, fluency, and targeted misclassification, creating highly transferable and stealthy perturbations (Liu et al., 2021).

Adaptive and Unified Defenses: On the defense front, future research must move beyond static adversarial training and *explore adaptive and unified defense mechanisms* (Lin et al., 2025). One promising direction involves dynamic adversarial training, where adversarial examples are generated and assimilated on-the-fly during inference or within real-time feedback loops. This continual learning process allows models to adapt to emerging attack strategies rather than relying on pre-defined adversarial datasets. Such adaptability is especially important in production settings, where threat landscapes evolve rapidly and defense models must maintain resilience without complete retraining.

Another evolving defense strategy involves *uncertainty-based detection*, where models equipped with Bayesian neural networks or ensemble-based variance estimation flag inputs with high predictive uncertainty as potentially adversarial.

Hybrid defense systems that combine multiple approaches, such as input sanitization, ensemble learning, model interpretability, and anomaly detection, represent another promising avenue. These frameworks aim to provide layered defenses where different components counter distinct types of attacks. For instance, sanitization can remove known perturbation patterns, ensembles can average out inconsistencies across models, and interpretability mechanisms can help identify and explain model uncertainty or failure modes.

Of late, the development of *privacy-preserving defenses* is becoming increasingly important. With growing awareness of data privacy and regulatory constraints, methods such as federated learning, differential privacy, and homomorphic encryption offer pathways to defend against adversarial attacks while preserving sensitive information. These techniques ensure that data remains decentralized and minimally exposed, thus reducing the attack surface for adversarial exploitation. Future work must explore how these privacy-preserving techniques can be integrated with robust training methods without compromising model performance or utility.

Explainability remains a foundational component of trustworthy AI, and explainable adversarial robustness is expected to play a central role in future defense strategies. Systems must be able to not only defend against adversarial attacks but also articulate why a particular input was classified in a certain way or rejected as suspicious. By linking robustness with interpretability, such as visualizing attention maps, highlighting influential tokens, or tracing decision pathways, researchers can build models that are built on human trust and facilitate actionable insights into adversarial behavior.

Evaluation and Benchmarking: In terms of evaluation and benchmarking, the field requires more standardized and comprehensive frameworks. Future efforts should aim to *construct task-agnostic evaluation* sets that enable fair comparisons of adversarial robustness across different models and input modalities. These benchmarks should consider a range of performance metrics beyond attack success rate, including human usability, perceptual similarity, misclassification cost, and the computational cost of generating or defending against attacks (Malfa & Kwiatkowska, 2022).

Human-in-the-loop evaluation mechanisms are also vital to understanding the practical implications of adversarial examples. While many perturbations may fool a model, they may appear unnatural or easily detectable to human reviewers. Thus, human assessments of adversarial readability, semantic coherence, and naturalness are necessary to ensure that attacks and defenses remain meaningful in real-world scenarios.

As adversarial attacks increasingly target explanation mechanisms themselves, future evaluation protocols must also account for *explainability-aware attack assessment*. It is essential to measure how adversarial inputs affect attribution scores, attention distributions, saliency maps, or other interpretability outputs. Understanding these shifts can reveal whether models are being misled not just in prediction but in their internal reasoning processes.

With the rise of multi-modal AI systems, research must also expand into *cross-domain and hybrid adversarial settings*. Models that integrate text, image, audio, or video data, such as GPT-4V, CLIP, or visual question answering (VQA) systems, are susceptible to perturbations in one or more modalities. For instance, a seemingly benign textual change could influence an image captioning model, or a modified image might alter the output of a text-generating system. Attacks on such multi-modal models require coordinated perturbations that preserve coherence across channels while still misleading the model.

Building *defenses for multi-modal systems* is similarly complex, as robustness must be ensured not only within each modality but also in how information is fused or aligned across modalities. This requires new architectures, training regimes, and interpretability techniques that can operate in high-dimensional, multi-source environments. A related research question is whether adversarial perturbations can transfer across modalities, that is, whether a text perturbation designed to alter sentiment classification could also influence how an image related to that text is captioned or categorized.

To support progress in all these areas, theoretical research is necessary to provide the *formal foundations of adversarial robustness*. *Certified robustness* remains an open problem, particularly in discrete spaces like text. While norm-based certifications exist in image-based models, formal guarantees on allowable token substitutions in NLP systems are rare and difficult to compute. Future work must aim to derive rigorous bounds and provable defenses that are both computationally tractable and practically relevant.

Incorporating linguistic and cognitive theories into the design of adversarial perturbations is another promising path. By grounding perturbations in syntactic structures, semantic roles, pragmatic constraints, or discourse coherence, researchers can generate more natural and interpretable adversarial examples. These theory-driven approaches can reveal deeper model biases and encourage the development of defenses that align more closely with human language understanding.

Finally, foundational questions in learning theory remain largely unresolved. There is a need to understand how adversarial vulnerabilities affect learning dynamics, generalization bounds, and sample complexity. Future research may investigate whether certain architectures or training regimes are inherently more resilient to adversarial noise, and whether trade-offs between robustness and generalization can be formally characterized and optimized.

In conclusion, the future of adversarial research in both text and image domains, and across their intersections, is vast, challenging, and vital. The success of AI systems in real-world deployments depends not only on their accuracy and efficiency but also on their ability to resist, recover from, and explain adversarial manipulation. A coordinated, cross-disciplinary research effort encompassing algorithmic innovation, linguistic insight, theoretical rigor, and human-centered design will be essential to building the next generation of robust, interpretable, and trustworthy AI systems.

References

Alzantot, M., Sharma, Y., Elgohary, A., Ho, B-J., Srivastava, M., and Chang, K-W. 2018. "Generating Natural Language Adversarial Examples." In *Proceedings of the 2018 Conference on Empirical Methods in Natural Language Processing (EMNLP)*, 2890–2896.

Athalye, A., Engstrom, L., Ilyas, A., and Kwok, K. 2018. "Synthesizing Robust Adversarial Examples." In *Proceedings of the 35th International Conference on Machine Learning (ICML 2018), PMLR*, 80:284-293.

Biggio, B. and Roli, F. 2018. "Wild Patterns: Ten Years After the Rise of Adversarial Machine Learning." *Pattern Recognition* 84: 317–331.

Boucher, N., Shumailov, I., Anderson, R., and Papernot, N. 2022. "Bad Characters: Imperceptible NLP Attacks." In *Proceedings of the IEEE Symposium on Security and Privacy (SP)*, 1987–2004. IEEE.

Carlini, N. and Wagner, D. 2017. "Towards Evaluating the Robustness of Neural Networks." In *Proceedings of the 2017 IEEE Symposium on Security and Privacy (S&P 2017)*, 39-57.

Cer, D., Yang, Y., Kong, S-Y., Hua, N., Limtiaco, N., John, R. S., Constant, N., Guajardo-Cespedes, M., Yuan, S., Tar, C., Strope, B., and Kurzweil, R. 2018. "Universal Sentence Encoder for English." In *Proceedings of the 2018 Conference on Empirical Methods in Natural Language Processing*, 169-174.

Cohen, J., Rosenfeld, E., and Kolter, Z. 2019. "Certified Adversarial Robustness via Randomized Smoothing." In *Proceedings of the 36th International Conference on Machine Learning (ICML 2019), PMLR*, 97:1310-1320.

Das, S. D., Basak, A., Mandal, S., and Das, D. 2022. „AdvCodeMix: Adversarial Attack on Code-Mixed Data." In *Proceedings of the 5th Joint International Conference on Data Science & Management of Data (9th ACM KDD CODS and 27th COMAD)*, 125-129.

Devlin, J., Chang, M-W., Lee, K., and Toutanova, K. 2019. "BERT: Pre-Training of Deep Bidirectional Transformers for Language Understanding." In *Proceedings of the 2019 Conference of the North American Chapter of the Association for Computational Linguistics (NAACL-HLT)*, 4171–4186.

Dong, Y., Liao, F., Pang, T., Su, H., Zhu, J., and Hu, X. 2018. "Boosting Adversarial Attacks with Momentum." In *Proceedings of the 2018 IEEE/CVF Conference on Computer Vision and Pattern Recognition (CVPR 2018)*, 9185-9193.

Ebrahimi, J., Rao, A., Lowd, D., and Dou, D. 2018. "HotFlip: White-Box Adversarial Examples for Text Classification." In *Proceedings of the 56th Annual Meeting for the Association for Computational Linguistics,* 31–36.

Esteva, A., Kuprel, B., Novoa, R. A., Ko, J., Swetter, S. M., Blau, H. M., and Thrun, S. 2017. "Dermatologist-Level Classification of Skin Cancer with Deep Neural Networks." *Nature* 542(7639): 115–118.

Eykholt, K., Evtimov, I., Fernandes, E., Li, B., Rahmati, A., and Xiao, C. 2018. "Robust Physical-World Attacks on Deep Learning Visual Classification." In *Proceedings of the 2018 IEEE/CVF Conference on Computer Vision and Pattern Recognition (CVPR 2018),* 1625-1634.

Gao, J., Lanchantin, J., Soffa, M. L., and Qi, Y. 2018. "Black-Box Generation of Adversarial Text Sequences to Evade Deep Learning Classifiers." In *Proceedings of the 2018 IEEE Security and Privacy Workshops (SPW 2018)*, 50–56. IEEE.

Goodfellow, I. J., Shlens, J., and Szegedy, C. 2015. "Explaining and Harnessing Adversarial Examples." In *Proceedings of the International Conference on Learning Representations (ICLR)*, Poster. arXiv: 1412.6572.

Greshake, K., Abdelnabi, S., Mishra, S., Endres, C., Holz, T., and Fritz, M. 2023. „Not What You've Signed Up For: Compromising Real-World LLM-Integrated Applications with Indirect Prompt Injection." In *Proceedings of the 16th ACM Workshop on Artificial Intelligence and Security (AISec 2023)*, 79-90.

He, K., Zhang, X., Ren, S., and Sun, J. 2016. "Deep Residual Learning for Image Recognition." In *Proceedings of the IEEE Conference on Computer Vision and Pattern Recognition (CVPR 2016)*, 770–778.

Hore, A. and Ziou, D. 2010. "Image Quality Metrics: PSNR vs. SSIM." In *Proceedings of the 2010 20th International Conference on Pattern Recognition*, 2366-2369.

Hussain, S., Neekhara, P., Dubnov, S., McAuley, J., and Koushanfar, F. 2021. In *Proceedings of the 30th USENIX Security Symposium (USENIX Security 21)*, 2273-2290.

Ilyas, A., Engstrom, L., Athalye, A., and Lin, J. 2018. "Black-box Adversarial Attacks with Limited Queries and Information." In *Proceedings of the 35th International Conference on Machine Learning (ICML 2018)*, *PMLR*, 80: 2137-2146.

Iyyer, M., Wieting, J., Gimpel, K., and Zettlemoyer, L. 2018. "Adversarial Example Generation with Syntactically Controlled Paraphrase Networks." In *Proceedings of the 2018 Conference of the North-American Chapter of the Association for Computational Linguistics: Human Language Technologies*, 1: 1875-1885.

Jia, R., Raghunathan, A., Goksel, K., and Liang, P. 2019. "Certified Robustness to Adversarial Word Substitutions." In *Proceedings of the 2019 Conference on Empirical Methods in Natural Language Processing and the 9th International Joint Conference on Natural Language Processing (ENLP-IJCNLP 2019), 4129-4142.*

Jin, D., Jin, Z., Zhou, J. T., and Szolovits, P. 2020. "Is BERT Really Robust? A Strong Baseline for Natural Language Attack on Text Classification and Entailment." In *Proceedings of the AAAI Conference on Artificial Intelligence (AAAI)*, 8018–8025.

Joulin, A., Grave, E., Bojanowski, P., and Milokov, T. 2017. "Bag of Tricks for Efficient Text Classification." In *Proceedings of the 15th Conference of the European Chapter of the Association for Computational Linguistics*, 2: 427-431.

Koley, A., Satpati, P., Choudhary, I., and Sen, J. 2024. "An Investigation on the Efficiency of Some Text Attack Algorithms." In *Proceedings of the IEEE North Karnataka Subsection Flagship International Conference (NKCon 2024)*, 1–8.

Li, J., Ji, S., Du, T., Li, B., and Wang, T. 2019. "TextBugger: Generating Adversarial Text against Real-World Applications." In *Proceedings of the 2019 Network and Distributed Systems Security Symposium (NDSS 2019)*.

Li, D., Zhang, Y., Peng, H., Chen, L., Brockett, C., Sun, M-T., and Dolan, B. 2021. "Contextualized Perturbation for Textual Adversarial Attack." In *Proceedings of the 2021 Conference of the North American Chapter of the Association for Computational Linguistics (NAACL)*, 5053–5069.

Li, J., Du, T., Ji, S., Zhang, S., Zhang, R., Lu, Q., Yang, M., Wang, T. 2020a. "TextShiled: Robust Text Classification Based on Multimodal Embedding and Neural Machine Translation." In *Proceedings of the 29th USENIX Conference on Security Symposium (SEC 2020)*, 1381-1398, Art No: 78.

Li, L., Ma, R., Guo, Q., Xue, X., and Qiu, X. 2020b. "BERT-Attack: Adversarial Attack against BERT Using BERT." In *Proceedings of the 2020 Conference on Empirical Methods in Natural Language Processing (EMNLP)*, 6193–6202.

Liang, B., Li, H., Su, M., Bian, P., Li, X., and Shi, W. 2018. "Deep Text Classification Can Be Fooled." In *Proceedings of the 27th International Joint Conference on Artificial Intelligence (IJCAI)*, 4208–4215.

Lin, H., Lao, Y., Geng, T., Yu, T., and Zhao, W. 2025. "UniGuardian: A Unified Defense for Detecting Prompt Injection, Backdoor Attacks and Adversarial Attacks in Large Language Models." arXiv Preprint arXiv: 2502.13141.

Liu, S., Lu, N., Chen, C., and Tang, K. 2021. "Efficient Combinatorial Optimization for Word-Level Adversarial Textual Attack." In *IEEE/ACM Transactions on Audio, Speech, and Language Processing* 30: 98–111.

Lundberg, S. M. and Lee, S-I. "A Unified Approach to Interpreting Model Predictions." In *Proceedings of the 31st International Conference on Neural Information Processing Systems (NIPS 2017)*, 4768-4777.

Madry, A., Makelov, A., Schmidt, L., Tsipras, D., Vladu, A. 2018. "Towards Deep Learning Models Resistant to Adversarial Attacks." In

Proceedings of the International Conference on Learning Representations (ICLR 2018), Poster Track.

Malfa, E. L. and Kwiatkowska, M. 2022. "The King Is Naked: On the Notion of Robustness for Natural Language Processing." In *Proceedings of the AAAI Conference on Artificial Intelligence*, 11047–11057.

Metzen, J. H., Genewein, T., Fischer, V., and Bischoff, B. 2017. "On Detecting Adversarial Perturbations." In *Proceedings of the International Conference on Learning Representations (ICLR 2017)*, Poster Track.

Mikolov, T., Sutskever, I., Chen, K., Corrado, G., and Dean, J. 2013. "Distributed Representations of Words and Phrases and their Compositionality." In *Proceedings of the 27th International Conference on Neural Information Processing Systems (NIPS 2013)*, 2:3111-3119.

Miyato, T., Dai, A. M., and Goodfellow, I. 2016. "Adversarial Training Methods for Semi-Supervised Text Classification." In *Proceedings of the 2017 International Conference on Learning Representations (ICLR 2017)*.

Moosavi-Dezfooli, S-M., Fawzi, A., Fawzi, O., Frossard, P. 2017. "Universal Adversarial Perturbations." In *Proceedings of the 2017 IEEE Conference on Computer Vision and Pattern Recognition (CVPR 2017)*, 86-94.

Morris, J., Lifland, E., Yoo, J. Y., Grigsby, J., Jin, D., and Qi, Y. 2020. "TextAttack: A Framework for Adversarial Attacks, Data Augmentation, and Adversarial Training in NLP." In *Proceedings of the 2020 Conference on Empirical Methods in Natural Language Processing: System Demonstrations*, 119–126.

Papernot, N., McDaniel, P., Jha, S., Fredrikson, M., Celik, Z. B., Swami, A. 2016a. "The Limitations of Deep Learning in Adversarial Settings." In *Proceedings of the 2016 IEEE European Symposium on Security and Privacy (EuroS&P)*, 372-387.

Papernot, N., McDaniel, P., Swami, A., and Harang, R. 2016b. "Crafting Adversarial Input Sequences for Recurrent Neural Networks." In *Proceedings of the 2016 IEEE Military Communications Conference (MILCOM 2016)*, 49–54.

Pruthi, D., Dhingra, B., and Lipton, Z. C. 2019. "Combating Adversarial Misspellings with Robust Word Recognition." In *Proceedings of the 57th Annual Meeting of the Association for Computational Linguistics*, 5582–5591.

Ren, S., Deng, Y., He, K., and Che, W. 2019. "Generating Natural Language Adversarial Examples through Probability Weighted Word Saliency."

In *Proceedings of the 57th Annual Meeting of the Association for Computational Linguistics (ACL)*, 1085–1097.

Ribeiro, M. T., Singh, S., and Guestrin, C. 2016. "Why Should I Trust You?: Explaining the Predictions of Any Classifier." In *Proceedings of the 22nd ACM SIGKDD International Conference on Knowledge Discovery and Data Mining*, 1135-1144.

Sen, J. 2024. "The FGSM Attack on Image Classification Models and Distillation as its Defense." In Nanda et al. (eds), *Advances in Distributed Computing and Machine Learning (ICADCML 2024)*, 1015: 347-360. Lecture Notes in Networks and Systems, Springer, Singapore.

Sen, J. and Dasgupta, S. 2023. "Adversarial Attacks on Image Classification Models: FGSM and Patch Attacks and their Impact." In Sen, J. and Mayer, J. (eds), *Information Security and Privacy in the Digital World: Some Selected Topics*, IntechOpen, London, UK.

Sen, J., Sen, A., and Chatterjee, A. 2023. "Adversarial Attacks on Image Classification Models: Analysis and Defense." In *Proceedings of the 10th International Conference on Business Analytics and Intelligence (ICBAI 2023)*, Bangalore, India.

Sen, J. and Waghela, H. 2025. "Text-Based Adversarial Attacks and Defense", In Sen, J. (ed) *Data Privacy: Techniques, Applications, and Standards*, IntechOpen, London, UK.

Szegedy, C., Zaremba, W., Sutskever, I., Bruna, J., Erhan, D., Goodfellow, I. J., and Fergus, R. 2014. "Intriguing Properties of Neural Networks." In *Proceedings of the International Conference on Learning Representations (ICLR)*. arXiv: 1312.6199.

Tramer, F., Kurakin, A., Papernot, N., Goodfellow, I., Boneh, D., and McDaniel, P. 2018. "Ensemble Adversarial Training: Attacks and Defenses." In *Proceedings of the 2018 International Conference on Learning Representations (ICLR 2018)*.

Waghela, H., Sen, J., and Rakshit, S. 2025. "Saliency Attention and Semantic Similarity-Driven Adversarial Perturbation." In *Data Science and Applications. ICDSA 2024*, Nanda, S. J. et al. (eds), 1237: 461–471. Lecture Notes in Networks and Systems, Springer, Singapore.

Waghela, H., Sen, J., Rakshit, S., and Dasgupta, S. 2024a. "Adversarial Text Generation with Dynamic Contextual Perturbation." In *Proceedings of the 2024 IEEE CALCON 2024*, 1–6. IEEE.

Waghela, H., Sen, J., and Rakshit, S. 2024b. "Adaptive Meta-Learning for Robust Ensemble Defense against Adversarial Attacks." In *Proceedings of the International Conference BAMS-ORSI 2024*.

Waghela, H., Sen, J., and Rakshit, S. 2024c. "Adversarial Resilience in Image Classification: A Hybrid Approach to Defense." In *Proceedings of the 2024 International Conference on Innovation and Intelligence for Informatics, Computing, and Technologies (3ICT 2024)*, 419–426.

Waghela, H., Sen, J., Rakshit, S., and Dasgupta, S. 2024d. "Adversarial Robustness through Dynamic Ensemble Learning." In *Proceedings of the 2024 IEEE Silchar Subsection Conference (SILCON 2024)*, 1–6.

Waghela, H., Sen, J., and Rakshit, S. 2024e. "Robust Image Classification: Defensive Strategies against FGSM and PGD Adversarial Attacks." In *Proceedings of the IEEE Asian Conference on Intelligent Technologies (ACOIT 2024)*, 1 – 7.

Waghela, H., Sen, J., and Rakshit, S. 2024f. "Refining BERT Adversarial Attacks with Projected Gradient Descent." In *Proceedings of the IEEE 4th Asian Conference on Innovations in Technology (ASIANCON 2024)*, 1-7.

Waghela, H., Rakshit, S., and Sen, J. 2024g. "A Modified Word Saliency-Based Adversarial Attack on Text Classification Models." In *Computational Intelligence and Data Analytics*, Frery, A. C. et al. (eds), 371–382. Lecture Notes in Data Engineering and Communications Technologies, 236. Springer.

Wallace, E., Feng, S., Kandpal, N., Gardner, M., and Singh, S. 2019. "Universal Adversarial Triggers for Attacking and Analyzing NLP." In *Proceedings of the 2019 Conference on Empirical Methods in Natural Language Processing and the 9th International Joint Conference on Natural Language Processing (EMNLP-IJCNLP 2019)*, 2153–2162.

Wang, Z., Bovik, A. C., Sheikh, H. R., Simoncelli, E. P. 2004. "Image Quality Assessment: From Error Visibility to Structural Similarity." *IEEE Transactions on Image Processing*, 13(4): 600-612.

Wang, N., Luo, Y., Sato, T., Xu, K., and Chen, Q. A. 2023. "Does Physical Adversarial Example Really Matter to Autonomous Driving? Towards System-Level Effect of Adversarial Object Evasion Attack." In *Proceedings of the 2023 IEEE/CVF International Conference on Computer Vision (ICCV 2023)*, 4389-4400.

Wong, E. and Kolter, Z. 2018. "Provable Defenses against Adversarial Examples via the Convex Outer Adversarial Polytope." In *Proceedings of the 35th International Conference on Machine Learning (ICML 2018)*, *PMLR*, 80: 5286-5295.

Xie, C., Wu, Y., van der Maaten, L., Yuille, A. L., and He, K. 2019. "Feature Denoising for Improving Adversarial Robustness." In *Proceedings of the 2015 IEEE/CVF Conference on Computer Vision and Pattern Recognition (CVPR 2019)*, 501-509.

Xu, H., Yao, M., Liu, H-C., Deb, D., Liu, H., Tang, J-L., and Jain, A. K. 2020. "Adversarial Attacks and Defenses in Images, Graphs and Text:

A Review." *International Journal of Automation and Computing* 17 (2): 151–178.

Yin, Z., Ye, M., Zhang, T., Du, T., Zhu, J., Liu, H., Chen, J., Wnag, T., and Ma, F. 2023. "VLATTACK: Multimodal Adversarial Attacks on Vision-Language Tasks via Pre-trained Models." In *Proceedings of the 37th International Conference on Neural Information Processing Systems (NIPS 2023)*, 52936-52956.

Yoo, J. Y. and Qi, Y. 2021. "Towards Improving Adversarial Training of NLP Models." In *Findings of the Association for Computational Linguistics: EMNLP 2021*, 945-956.

Zang, Y., Qi, F., Yang, C., Liu, Z., Zhang, M., Liu, Q., and Sun, M. 2020. "Word-Level Textual Adversarial Attacking as Combinatorial Optimization." In *Proceedings of the 58th Annual Meeting of the Association for Computational Linguistics (ACL)*, pp. 6066–6080.

Zelasko, P., Joshi, S., Shao, Y., Villaba, J., Trmal, J., Dehak, N., and Khudanpur, S. 2021. "Adversarial Attacks and Defenses for Speech Recognition Systems." arXiv Preprint Repository arXiv:2103.17122.

Zhai, R., Dan, C., He, D., Zhang, H., Gong, B., Ravikumar, P., Hsieh, C-J., and Wang, L. 2020. "MACER: Attack-free and Scalable Robust Training via Maximizing Certified Radius." In *Proceedings of the International Conference on Learning Representations (ICLR 2020)*.

Zhang, W. E., Sheng, Q. Z., Alhazmi, A., Li, C. 2019. "Adversarial Attacks on Deep Learning Models in Natural Language Processing: A Survey." arXiv Preprint arXiv:1901.06796.

Zhao, Z., Dua, D., and Singh, S. 2018. "Generating Natural Adversarial Examples." In *Proceedings of the 6th International Conference on Learning Representations* (ICLR 2018), *PMLR*, 26958-26970.

Zhao, H., Ma, C., Dong, X., Luu, A. T., Deng, Z-H., and Zhang, H. 2022. "Certified Robustness against Natural Language Attacks by Causal Intervention." In *Proceedings of the International Conference on Machine Learning (ICML 2022)*.

Zhou, Y., Jiang, J-Y., Chang, K-W., and Wang, W. 2019. "Learning to Discriminate Perturbations for Blocking Adversarial Attacks in Text Classification." In *Proceedings of the 2019 Conference on Empirical Methods in Natural Language Processing and the 9th International Joint Conference on Natural Language Processing (EMNLP-IJCNLP)*, Association for Computational Linguistics, pp. 4904–4913.

Zhu, C., Cheng, Y., Gan, Z., Sun, S., Goldstein, T., and Liu, J. 2020. "FreeLB: Enhanced Adversarial Training for Natural Language Understanding." In *Proceedings of the International Conference on Learning Representations (ICLR 2020)*.

CHAPTER 2

STRATEGIC TEXT DISRUPTION USING A MODIFIED WORD SALIENCY APPROACH

Introduction

The widespread adoption of deep learning models in *Natural Language Processing* (NLP) has significantly advanced tasks such as sentiment analysis, question answering, and text classification. Pre-trained language models like BERT, ALBERT, and RoBERTa have demonstrated superior performance due to their ability to capture complex linguistic patterns and contextual dependencies. However, the increasing deployment of these models in real-world applications has also exposed their vulnerability to adversarial attacks, carefully crafted inputs that lead to incorrect or misleading outputs, despite appearing benign to human observers.

The concept of adversarial examples was initially introduced in the domain of image classification, where imperceptible perturbations in pixel values were shown to cause substantial misclassifications in otherwise highly accurate models. This discovery prompted extensive research into the robustness of deep learning systems. Translating this idea to NLP posed unique challenges due to the discrete and structured nature of language. Even minor modifications, such as changing a word or punctuation, can affect the syntax, semantics, or readability of a sentence. Consequently, crafting adversarial text examples requires balancing effectiveness, linguistic coherence, and semantic similarity.

In response to these challenges, several strategies for generating adversarial text have emerged. One influential class of methods involves word saliency-based perturbations, where specific words are identified based on their importance to the model's decision and then replaced with synonyms, antonyms, or contextually similar alternatives. The *Probability Weighted Word Saliency* (PWWS) approach is a notable example in this category, achieving a balance between perturbation efficacy and linguistic plausibility.

Despite the progress made by existing techniques, limitations remain in terms of semantic preservation, contextual awareness, and transferability across different models. Addressing these limitations, the *Modified Word Saliency-Based Adversarial Attack* (MWSAA) introduces enhancements over PWWS by incorporating contextualized word embeddings and semantic similarity constraints. By utilizing BERT-based embeddings, MWSAA captures deeper contextual relationships within a sentence, leading to more meaningful and fluent perturbations. Additionally, enforcing a semantic similarity constraint ensures that the adversarial text remains close in meaning to the original input, thereby increasing its plausibility and reducing detectability.

The significance of this method lies in its ability to effectively deceive robust language models while preserving high semantic fidelity. Evaluations on benchmark datasets and multiple state-of-the-art classifiers demonstrate that MWSAA achieves higher attack success rates and requires fewer perturbations compared to traditional methods. Furthermore, the method proves efficient in terms of runtime and the number of queries made to the target model, making it suitable for both white-box and black-box scenarios.

Given the increasing deployment of NLP systems in sensitive applications such as automated content moderation, legal document analysis, and medical triage, the ability to assess and enhance model robustness is of paramount importance. The study of adversarial attacks not only highlights the limitations of current models but also provides critical insights for developing more resilient systems.

This chapter presents a comprehensive treatment of adversarial attacks in NLP with a specific focus on the MWSAA technique. It explores the theoretical foundations of adversarial perturbations, outlines the algorithmic design of MWSAA, presents detailed experimental analyses, and discusses its implications for the future of trustworthy NLP systems.

The remainder of this chapter is organized as follows. The section titled *Foundations of Adversarial Attacks in NLP* introduces the core concepts, typologies, and motivations underlying adversarial manipulation in natural language processing. *Related Work* then presents a comprehensive review of existing adversarial attack techniques on text classification models, highlighting their contributions and limitations. The section *The MWSAA Scheme* details the architecture and methodology of the proposed Modified Word Saliency-Based Adversarial Attack. In *Performance Evaluation*, empirical results, and comparative analyses with baseline methods, particularly PWWS, are presented. The chapter concludes with *Conclusion and Future Directions*, summarizing the insights and identifying opportunities for further advancement in this field.

Foundations of Adversarial Attacks in NLP

Adversarial attacks have emerged as a critical area of study in machine learning, shedding light on the fragility of high-performing models when confronted with carefully designed perturbations. While the initial discoveries in this domain originated from image classification tasks, where minute pixel-level changes could drastically alter model outputs, the extension of adversarial methodologies to textual data introduced new challenges and complexities. The discrete and structured nature of language, as opposed to the continuous nature of images, requires that any modifications to text not only deceive the model but also preserve linguistic and semantic integrity.

Nature and Objective of Adversarial Attacks: In the context of *Natural Language Processing* (NLP), adversarial attacks involve deliberately crafting input text that, while appearing innocuous and semantically meaningful to human readers, causes the model to produce incorrect or undesired predictions. The principal objectives of such attacks typically fall into two categories: (i) *Evasion attacks*, where the adversary seeks to mislead the model at inference time without altering the model parameters. (ii) *Poisoning attacks*, which manipulate the training data to inject vulnerabilities into the model. This chapter focuses primarily on evasion attacks targeting text classification models.

Taxonomy of Adversarial Attacks in NLP: Adversarial attacks in NLP can be classified based on several criteria:

Access to model internals: These attacks can be of two types: (i) *White-box attacks*, and (ii) *Black-box attacks*. White box attacks assume full access to the model architecture, parameters, and gradients. This allows gradient-based optimization strategies to directly craft perturbations. Black-box attacks, on the other hand, operate without access to the internal structure of the model, relying instead on input-output queries to infer saliency and effectiveness.

Target specification: *Targeted attacks* aim to force the model to predict a specific incorrect class. *Untargeted attacks* merely aim to change the model's prediction to any incorrect label.

Granularity of perturbation: Three different categories of attacks can exist based on the granularity of perturbation. *Character-level attacks* modify individual characters (e.g., typos or homoglyph substitutions). *Word-level attacks* replace whole words using synonyms, antonyms, or contextually plausible alternatives. *Sentence- or phrase-level attacks* insert or rephrase entire segments of text.

Core Challenges in Textual Adversarial Attacks: Designing effective adversarial examples in NLP entails addressing several non-trivial challenges as follows:

Discrete Input Space: Unlike images, where perturbations exist in a continuous vector space, text inputs are sequences of discrete symbols. This precludes the use of standard gradient-based optimization techniques without surrogate models or approximations.

Grammatical and Syntactic Coherence: Perturbations must not introduce grammatical errors or unnatural sentence constructions, as such anomalies may be easily detected by humans or rule-based defense mechanisms.

Semantic Preservation: The perturbed text must retain the original meaning to remain a legitimate input from a human reader's perspective. Perturbations that alter the semantics are easily flagged as nonsensical or adversarial.

Model Query Efficiency: In black-box settings, the number of allowable queries may be limited. Effective attacks must therefore achieve misclassification with minimal model interaction.

Importance of Saliency in Adversarial Text Construction: A key enabler in adversarial text attacks is the concept of word saliency, a measure of how much a particular word contributes to the model's prediction. Identifying and perturbing high-saliency words can lead to more efficient and targeted attacks. Saliency can be computed using various approaches:

Gradient-based saliency: Measures the gradient of the output probability with respect to each input word embedding.

Attention-based importance: Leverages attention weights from models like BERT to estimate word influence.

Probability-weighted saliency: Used in the PWWS approach, this method estimates word importance by measuring the change in output probability when a word is masked or replaced.

Word saliency not only improves the attack's efficiency but also contributes to preserving fluency by guiding substitutions to the most impactful components of the sentence.

Historical Development and Relevance: Early studies demonstrated that simple strategies, such as introducing typographical errors or swapping characters, could reduce classification accuracy. Subsequent research introduced more sophisticated techniques such as *TextFooler*, *DeepWordBug*, and *HotFlip*, each improving upon attack efficiency or text naturalness. Among these, PWWS stood out for its probabilistic saliency estimation and focus on preserving lexical correctness.

However, many of these methods still suffer from limitations in semantic consistency, robustness across different architectures, and query inefficiency. The development of more advanced approaches, such as MWSAA, builds on these foundations by incorporating *contextual embeddings* and *semantic similarity metrics*, enabling more effective and imperceptible adversarial text generation.

Related Work

The field of adversarial attacks in Natural Language Processing (NLP) has evolved rapidly, driven by the increasing use of deep neural networks in high-stakes applications. Although the concept of adversarial examples originated in the vision domain, most notably with the works of Szegedy et al. (Szegedy et al., 2014) and Goodfellow et al. (Goodfellow et al., 2015), their applicability to text data was soon recognized. Unlike images, where minor pixel-level perturbations can be imperceptible to humans, textual data is discrete and structured, presenting unique challenges in crafting perturbations that are both effective and linguistically coherent.

Initial efforts in textual adversarial attacks focused on character-level manipulations. Liang et al. showed that inserting or altering characters in text could mislead deep classifiers (Liang et al., 2018). Subsequent approaches, such as DeepWordBug and HotFlip, extended these ideas by using gradient-guided or rule-based transformations. However, such methods often generated adversarial texts that were syntactically incorrect or visually noisy, making them detectable by both humans and automated systems.

The shift toward word-level attacks marked a significant advancement in the field. Samanta and Mehta proposed synonym substitution strategies, emphasizing semantic preservation (Samanta & Mehta, 2017). Alzantot et al. developed a black-box attack that used genetic algorithms and Global Vectors for Word Representation (GloVe) embeddings to find semantically valid perturbations (Alzantot et al., 2018). These methods prioritized fluency and meaning, addressing the limitations of character-level attacks.

One of the most influential approaches in this space is the Probability Weighted Word Saliency (PWWS) attack proposed by Ren et al. (Ren et al., 2019). PWWS combines a probabilistic saliency scoring mechanism with lexical substitution using WordNet synonyms. By ranking words based on their impact on model output and replacing high-saliency words with semantically similar alternatives, PWWS demonstrated strong attack performance while maintaining natural language coherence.

The introduction of large pre-trained language models, particularly BERT (Devlin et al., 2019), ALBERT (Lan et al., 2020), and RoBERTa (Liu et al., 2019), spurred the development of more context-aware adversarial attacks. Jin et al. introduced *TextFooler*, which generated adversarial samples by greedily replacing important words with synonyms that preserved semantic similarity (Jin et al., 2020). Li et al. followed with *BERT-Attack*, which used BERT itself to generate candidate substitutions, improving contextual relevance (Li et al., 2020). While effective, both approaches still faced challenges in maintaining high semantic fidelity and avoiding excessive word replacements.

Other works have extended adversarial strategies across various NLP tasks. Gao et al. (Gao et al., 2018) developed a black-box attack method based on iterative editing, while Liu et al. (Liu et al., 2021) proposed an efficient combinatorial optimization approach to reduce the number of perturbations and model queries. Zhang et al. formulated word-level attacks as discrete optimization problems, aiming for minimal but impactful edits. These contributions significantly enhanced the stealth and generalizability of textual adversarial examples (Zang et al., 2020).

Several researchers have explored the integration of contextual embeddings into attack strategies. Li et al. proposed *contextualized perturbation*, where candidate replacements were evaluated based on BERT embeddings to ensure contextual compatibility (Li et al., 2021).

The robustness of NLP models under adversarial threat has also been critically examined. Boucher et al. introduced a framework for imperceptible NLP attacks that remain undetectable to human readers, raising concerns about model transparency and security (Boucher et al., 2022). Zhou et al. proposed adversarial training schemes using perturbation discriminators to enhance model resilience (Zhou et al., 2019). Similarly, Jin et al. provided a strong baseline showing BERT's vulnerability to well-crafted textual attacks, reinforcing the need for more robust training paradigms (Jin et al., 2020).

On the analytical front, Xu et al. conducted a cross-domain survey of adversarial attacks and defenses, highlighting commonalities and differences across images, graphs, and text (Xu et al., 2020). Malfa and Kwiatkowska emphasized the ambiguity in defining robustness for NLP systems, proposing a structured framework for evaluating model behavior under adversarial conditions (Malfa & Kwiatkowska, 2022). Their insights underscore the importance of standardized evaluation criteria in adversarial NLP research.

Recent work has advanced the development of adversarial attacks and defenses through the integration of semantic similarity, dynamic perturbation strategies, and ensemble-based resilience mechanisms. A series of studies by Waghela, Sen, Rakshit, and collaborators (Waghela et al., 2024a-g; 2025) has contributed substantially to this growing body of research. These works propose context-sensitive and linguistically informed attack schemes that leverage saliency, attention, BERT-based embeddings, and semantic similarity metrics to craft more coherent and impactful adversarial examples. Several efforts also explore the defense side, introducing ensemble-based meta-learning and hybrid robustness techniques to mitigate such attacks in both textual and image classification domains. Collectively, these contributions offer a rich framework for balancing attack efficacy with semantic plausibility, and for designing adaptive defense that generalizes across domains and model architectures.

An empirical evaluation of a prominent adversarial text attack algorithm is presented by Koley et al., focusing on their comparative efficiency in terms of attack success rate, computational cost, and semantic coherence (Koley et al., 2024). The study systematically benchmarked several widely used attack methods across different text classification models and datasets, highlighting their strengths and limitations in practical deployment scenarios. This work contributes to the growing body of literature emphasizing the need for standardized evaluation protocols and a deeper understanding of attack behavior under varying constraints.

Recent developments also include robust benchmarking platforms such as *TextAttack* (Morris et al., 2020) and *OpenAttack* (OpenAttack Platform), which provide extensible toolkits for generating and evaluating adversarial attacks across various models and datasets. These resources have played a key role in advancing reproducibility and transparency in the field.

Despite significant progress, challenges remain. Many attacks require a large number of model queries, reducing their applicability in real-time systems. Others suffer from limited transferability across architectures or datasets. Defensive measures such as input sanitization, adversarial training, and certified robustness have shown partial success, but no approach offers complete protection. As models become more complex, especially with instruction-tuned LLMs, the adversarial threat landscape is expected to evolve further.

The *Modified Word Saliency-Based Adversarial Attack* (MWSAA), discussed in this chapter, builds directly upon these foundations. By incorporating contextual embeddings through BERT and enforcing semantic similarity constraints using cosine metrics, MWSAA addresses several limitations of prior techniques, such as PWWS and BERT-Attack. It provides a practical and effective framework for generating adversarial examples that are both contextually appropriate and highly deceptive, contributing to ongoing efforts toward adversarial robustness in NLP.

The MWSAA Scheme

The *Modified Word Saliency-Based Adversarial Attack* (MWSAA) is an improved adversarial text attack strategy that builds upon the *Probability Weighted Word Saliency* (PWWS) method. While PWWS introduced an effective mechanism for selecting and substituting salient words to generate adversarial text examples, MWSAA enhances this framework by incorporating two crucial components: (1) contextual embeddings derived from pre-trained language models such as BERT, and (2) semantic consistency constraints to ensure that the generated adversarial texts preserve the original meaning.

MWSAA is designed to create adversarial examples that are not only effective in misleading classification models but also maintain high levels of syntactic fluency and semantic similarity. These objectives are achieved by carefully selecting candidate words for substitution based on word saliency and evaluating the contextual compatibility of substitutions using sentence-level and word-level embeddings.

Overview of the Attack Pipeline: The MWSAA attack follows a systematic multi-stage pipeline:

1. *Word saliency estimation*: Identify the most influential words in a text input with respect to the classifier's output.
2. *Candidate generation*: For each salient word, generate a set of possible substitutes using synonym databases or lexical resources.
3. *Contextual refinement*: Use contextual embeddings (e.g., from BERT) to evaluate the fit of each candidate in the original sentence.
4. *Semantic similarity enforcement*: Apply a semantic similarity constraint to preserve the original meaning by comparing the embeddings of the original and perturbed sentences.
5. *Perturbation selection*: Choose the substitution that maximally degrades model confidence while satisfying linguistic and semantic constraints.
6. *Iteration and termination*: Repeat the process until the model prediction changes or a stopping condition is reached.

Each of these components is described in detail in the following.

Word Saliency Estimation: The first step in MWSAA involves computing the saliency of each word in the input text with respect to the classifier's decision. This is typically done by measuring the change in the classifier's output probability when a word is removed or replaced.

Let $x = [w_1, w_2, \dots, w_n]$ be the input sentence, and let $f(x)$ denote the predicted probability of the true class. The saliency score $S(w_i)$ for word w_i is computed as:

$$S(w_i) = f(x) - f(x_{\backslash w_i}) \tag{2-1}$$

In (2-1), $x_{\setminus w_i}$ represents the input with word w_i removed or masked. Words with higher saliency scores are more influential in determining the model's prediction and are prioritized for substitution.

Candidate Generation: Once salient words are identified, candidate replacements are generated for each word. This is done using lexical resources such as WordNet or embedding-based nearest neighbors. The objective is to generate substitutes that are grammatically valid and semantically similar to the original word, but capable of altering the model's prediction when used in context.

For each word w_i, the candidate list $C(w_i)$ is obtained such that: (i) Each $c_j \in C(w_i)$ is a synonym or semantically close word, and (ii) Candidates are filtered to exclude rare or domain-inappropriate words.

To preserve the contextual relevance, stop words and function words are typically excluded from the substitution process.

Integration of Contextual Embeddings: One of the major enhancements in MWSAA over PWWS is the use of contextual embeddings to assess the quality of each candidate substitution. Unlike traditional static embeddings (e.g., Word2Vec or GloVe), contextual embeddings from models such as BERT capture the meaning of a word in relation to its surrounding words.

Each candidate word is inserted into the original sentence in place of the salient word, and the resulting sentence is passed through BERT to obtain contextualized sentence embeddings. The replacement candidate is then scored based on how well it fits the syntactic and semantic context.

Let x' be the modified sentence with candidate word c_j substituted for w_i, and let $E(x)$ and $E(x')$ be their respective BERT sentence embeddings. The cosine similarity is computed as in (2-2):

$$Sim(x, x') = \frac{E(x).E(x')}{\|E(x)\|.\|E(x'\|} \tag{2-2}$$

Only candidates for which $Sim(x, x') \geq \tau$ are retained, where $\tau \in [0,1]$ is a similarity threshold. This constraint ensures that the modified sentence remains semantically consistent with the original.

Semantic Consistency Constraint: Semantic similarity is a key requirement in generating adversarial texts that are linguistically valid and meaningful. To enforce this, MWSAA applies a cosine similarity constraint not just at the word level but also across the entire sentence.

The perturbation that yields the highest similarity score while also reducing the classifier's confidence in the original class is selected as the best candidate. This dual-objective scoring function ensures that adversarial examples are both effective and human-readable.

To this end, the scoring function $J(c_j)$ for a candidate word c_j is defined as in (3).

$$J(c_j) = \alpha.\left(1 - f(x')\right) + (1 - \alpha).Sim(x, x') \qquad (3\text{-}3)$$

In (3-3), $f(x')$ is the predicted probability for the original class after substitution, and $\alpha \in [0,1]$ is a trade-off parameter balancing attack strength and semantic preservation.

Perturbation Strategy and Termination: After scoring all candidate substitutions, MWSAA applies the top-scoring substitution and updates the input text. The saliency scores are recalculated for the new input, and the process is repeated. The attack proceeds iteratively until one of the following termination conditions is met: (i) the classifier's prediction changes (i.e., successful misclassification), (ii) a maximum number of substitutions is reached, (iii) no candidates pass the semantic similarity threshold.

The iterative refinement allows MWSAA to maintain a low word substitution rate while achieving high attack success.

Schematic Representation: The entire MWSAA process can be visualized as a feedback-driven optimization loop. At each iteration, the scheme evaluates the impact of each substitution on both the classifier's confidence and the semantic fidelity of the text. Through repeated refinement, MWSAA converges to an adversarial example that is minimally perturbed yet highly effective.

A schematic diagram illustrating the flow from saliency estimation to semantic filtering and iterative substitution enhances the interpretability of the method. This is depicted in Figure 2-1.

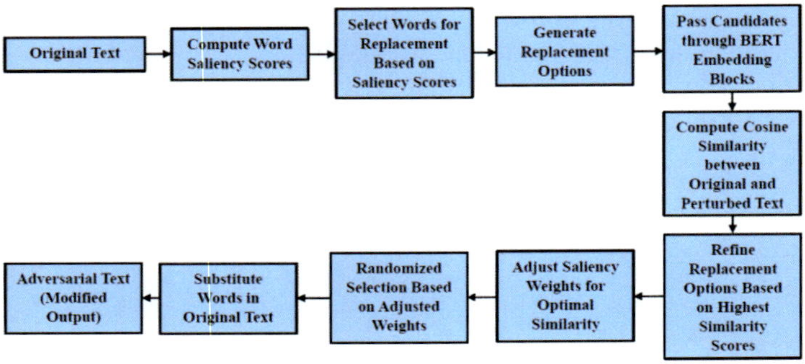

Figure. 2-1. The schematic diagram of the MWSAA scheme.

Advantages over PWWS: MWSAA improves upon PWWS in several key aspects: (i) context-awareness, (ii) semantic control, (iii) efficiency, (iv) flexibility.

Context awareness: By using BERT embedding, MWSAA evaluates the contextual fit of substitutions, whereas PWWS relies on static embeddings or lexical similarity.

Semantic control: The cosine similarity constraint ensures that the original meaning is preserved, minimizing the risk of nonsensical or misleading adversarial samples.

Efficiency: Experimental results show that MWSAA achieves higher attack success rates with fewer substitutions and fewer model queries.

Flexibility: The method is applicable in both white-box and black-box settings, given its reliance on model confidence scores and query outputs rather than internal gradients.

MWSAA thus represents a significant advancement in adversarial attack methodology for NLP. It achieves a nuanced balance between effectiveness, naturalness, and semantic fidelity, making it a strong tool for evaluating the robustness of modern text classification models.

Performance Evaluation

To assess the effectiveness of the Modified Word Saliency-Based Adversarial Attack (MWSAA), a comprehensive set of experiments was conducted across multiple deep learning models and standard text classification datasets. The evaluation framework was designed to analyze both the attack success rate and the linguistic quality of the adversarial examples, while also measuring computational efficiency and the extent of perturbation required.

Experimental Setup: The performance of MWSAA was evaluated using seven victim models, which were combinations of three pre-trained transformer-based language models, BERT (Devlin et al., 2019), ALBERT (Lan et al., 2020), and RoBERTa (Liu et al., 2019), fine-tuned on three benchmark datasets: IMDB (Maas et al., 2011), AG News (Zhang et al., 2015), and SST (Stanford Sentiment Treebank) (Socher et al., 2013). These datasets represent diverse classification tasks: binary sentiment classification (IMDB, SST) and topic categorization (AG News).

The specific victim models used in the experiments included: (i) ALBERT fine-tuned on AG News, IMDB, and SST, (ii) BERT fine-tuned on SST, and (iii) RoBERTa fine-tuned on AG News, IMDB, and SST.

For each victim model, 200 clean test samples were selected, and adversarial attacks were generated using MWSAA. The attack success was measured by the change in the model's predicted label after the perturbation. An attack was considered successful if the adversarial example caused a misclassification, regardless of the new class predicted.

Attack Success Rate: Table 2-1 presents the attack success rate of MWSAA on each victim model. The highest success rate was observed on RoBERTa trained on the IMDB dataset (95.50%), indicating that the model was highly susceptible to MWSAA. In contrast, ALBERT on the same dataset exhibited the greatest robustness, with a lower success rate of 42.50%.

Table 2-1. Attack Success Rate of MWSAA

Victim Language Model	Total Attacked Instances	Successful Attacks	Success Rate (%)
ALBERT_AG	200	130	65.00
ALBERT_IMDB	200	85	42.50
ALBERT_SST	200	117	58.50
BERT_SST	200	160	80.00
RoBERTa_AG	200	145	72.50
RoBERTa_IMDB	200	191	95.50
RoBERTa_SST	200	144	72.00

Efficiency Metrics: In addition to success rate, attack efficiency was evaluated in terms of average running time per sample and the number of model queries required to achieve successful misclassification. Table 2-2 summarizes the results.

Table 2-2. Runtime and Query Efficiency of MWSAA

Victim Model	Avg. Runtime (s)	Queries Exceeded	Avg. No. of Queries
ALBERT_AG	0.00697	0	124.66
ALBERT_IMDB	0.00749	0	126.12
ALBERT_SST	0.00698	0	124.94
BERT_SST	0.00648	0	122.31
RoBERTa_AG	0.00408	0	123.36
RoBERTa_IMDB	0.00409	0	120.10
RoBERTa_SST	0.00415	0	122.93

The running times for all models were within acceptable limits, typically under 0.008 seconds per instance. Notably, the RoBERTa models demonstrated the best computational efficiency, both in terms of runtime and number of queries. This indicates that MWSAA is well-suited for even time-sensitive or query-limited environments.

Comparative Analysis with PWSS: A direct comparison with the baseline PWWS method was conducted to evaluate the relative improvement offered by MWSAA. The classification accuracy of the original model, and its degradation under adversarial attacks from both PWWS and MWSAA, is shown in Table 2-3.

Table 2-3. Accuracy Degradation under PWWS and MWSAA

Dataset	Model	Original Acc. (%)	PWWS Acc. (%)	MWSAA Acc. (%)
IMDB	Word-CNN	86.55	5.50	4.80
IMDB	Bi-LSTM	84.86	2.20	1.90
AG News	Char-CNN	89.70	56.20	48.90
AG News	Word-CNN	90.56	56.72	50.45

The following provides a brief description of the models used as target classifiers in Table 2-3.

Word-CNN: A convolutional neural network that operates over word embeddings instead of raw characters (Kim, 2014). The model applies 1D convolutional filters over sequences of pre-trained word vectors (e.g.,

GloVe or Word2Vec), followed by max-pooling and dense layers. This network is efficient for sentence-level classification (e.g., sentiment analysis, topic categorization) when word order and local *n*-gram features matter.

Bi-LSTM: A recurrent neural network (RNN) architecture composed of two long short-term memory (LSTM) networks processing input sequences in forward and backward directions (Graves & Schmidhuber, 2005). It captures both past and future context at each time step, making it ideal for understanding long-range dependencies in text. This network is commonly used for sentiment classification, sequence labelling, and language modeling, where context matters significantly.

Char-CNN: Character-Level CNN (Char-CNN) is a convolutional neural network that takes raw character sequences as input and learns embeddings and patterns directly from characters using multiple convolution and pooling layers (Zhang et al., 2015). This network is robust to spelling errors, typos, and adversarial noise at the character level. Its architecture is effective for text classification tasks where tokenization is difficult or noisy, such as social media or multilingual input.

The results in Table 2-3 confirm that MWSAA is consistently more effective than PWWS in reducing model accuracy, thereby achieving higher attack success. The improvements are especially notable in the AG News dataset.

Table 2-4. Word Replacement Rate Comparison

Dataset	Model	PWWS (%)	MWSAA (%)
IMDB	Word-CNN	3.81	3.27
IMDB	Bi-LSTM	3.38	3.21
AG News	Char-CNN	18.93	15.74
AG News	Word-CNN	16.76	16.24

Perturbation Rate: The word replacement rate was measured to assess the compactness and subtlety of adversarial examples. MWSAA achieves misclassification with fewer word changes than PWWS, as seen in Table 2-4.

The reduction in the word replacement rate indicates that MWSAA is capable of generating stronger adversarial effects with fewer alterations, thereby preserving the original sentence structure and improving the stealthiness of the attack.

Table 2-5. Adversarial Attacks on the RoBERTa Classifier on the IMDB Dataset (Sentiment Analysis)

Original Prediction	Adversarial Prediction	Perturbed Text
Positive (Conf = 98.12%)	**Negative** (Conf = 85.24%)	The film's charm (pretense) lies in its subtle performances and intricate storyline that is both captivating (distracting) and authentic.
Positive (Conf = 96.8%)	**Negative** (Conf = 78.93%)	With brilliant direction and a strong cast, this movie is a testament (argument) to modern cinema's artistic power.
Positive (Conf = 99.03%)	**Negative** (Conf = 71.55%)	The plot is cleverly constructed, and the dialogues are witty (odd) without feeling forced or unnatural.

Adversarial Example Cases: Qualitative examples further illustrate the effectiveness of MWSAA. Table 2-5 provides a representative instance where a positive movie review is misclassified as negative after minimal word substitutions.

Table 2-6. Adversarial Attacks on the ALBERT Classifier on the AG News Dataset (Topic Classification)

Original Prediction	Adversarial Prediction	Perturbed Text
Sci/Tech (Conf = 83.34%)	**Business** (Conf = 61.02%)	The new AI chip developed (proposed) by the lab promises to revolutionize (transform) edge computing in low-power devices.
Sci/Tech (Conf = 78.60%)	**World** (Conf = 69.73%)	A group of scientists in Geneva has released (leaked) the results of an experiment that my alter (displace) current theories on quantum entanglement.
Sci/Tech (Conf = 85.29%)	**Sports** (Conf = 67.11%)	The robotics conference in Tokyo showcased (paraded) a humanoid robot capable of executing (performing) complex tasks with human-like precision.

Similar successful attacks on topic classification and sentiment analysis are shown in Table 2-6 and Table 2-7, respectively. The perturbations are designed to preserve fluency while altering key tokens that influence the model's decision.

Table 2-7. Adversarial Attacks on the BERT Classifier on the SST Dataset (Sentiment Classification)

Original Prediction	Adversarial Prediction	Perturbed Text
Negative (Conf = 91.76%)	Positive (Conf = 70.82%)	The film is a dreary (reflective) attempt at social commentary that ultimately collapses (drifts) under its own weight.
Negative (Conf = 88.43%)	Positive (Conf = 73.54%)	Although the narrative is disjointed, the visuals are exhausting (dreamlike) and overwhelm (immerse) the audience.
Negative (Conf = 84.67%)	Positive (Conf = 68.90%)	The robotics conference in Tokyo showcased (paraded) a humanoid robot capable of executing (performing) complex tasks with human-like precision.

Summary of Findings: The evaluation demonstrates that MWSAA offers superior performance in adversarial text generation compared to existing methods such as PWWS. It achieves higher attack success rates, reduced word modification rates, and efficient runtime, while preserving semantic similarity and linguistic fluency. These characteristics make MWSAA a practical and robust tool for probing the vulnerabilities of text classification systems.

In the context of real-world deployment, these findings underscore the importance of incorporating adversarial robustness into the design and evaluation of NLP models. The MWSAA framework provides a strong benchmark for future work on both adversarial attack strategies and their corresponding defenses.

Conclusion

This chapter presented a comprehensive study of adversarial text attacks in the context of deep learning-based *Natural Language Processing* (NLP) systems, with a specific focus on the *Modified Word Saliency-Based Adversarial Attack* (MWSAA) method. Building upon the foundational concepts of saliency-guided perturbation and lexical substitution, MWSAA introduced two major enhancements: the integration of contextual word embeddings derived from pre-trained transformer models and the imposition of semantic consistency constraints using cosine similarity measures. These innovations significantly improved the effectiveness, efficiency, and stealth of adversarial attacks on modern text classification models.

Through extensive experimentation on multiple datasets and across a variety of victim models, including BERT, ALBERT, and RoBERTa, the proposed scheme demonstrated superior performance in terms of attack success rate, runtime efficiency, and perturbation compactness. MWSAA consistently outperformed the PWWS baseline, achieving misclassification with fewer substitutions and better semantic fidelity. The inclusion of contextual embedding-based filtering ensured that word replacements were not only impactful but also linguistically coherent and contextually appropriate. Furthermore, the semantic similarity constraint served as a safeguard against meaning distortion, enhancing the plausibility of the generated adversarial examples from a human perspective.

The results of this study reinforce the importance of adversarial robustness as a critical design consideration in NLP systems. While the increasing use of large language models has led to dramatic improvements in task performance, it has also opened new avenues for exploitation through adversarial manipulation. Attacks like MWSAA demonstrate that even state-of-the-art classifiers remain susceptible to relatively simple but carefully constructed perturbations, especially when these perturbations are crafted with a deep understanding of model behavior and linguistic context.

From a broader perspective, adversarial attacks serve not only as a tool for exposing model vulnerabilities but also as a lens for studying the decision-making processes of neural architectures. By analyzing which words are most influential in prediction and how small changes can shift model output, researchers can gain valuable insights into model interpretability, generalization, and inductive biases. In this light, adversarial attacks contribute to a more transparent and accountable deployment of AI systems, especially in high-stakes domains such as healthcare, finance, legal reasoning, and content moderation.

Looking ahead, several avenues for future research emerge as discussed in the following.

First, future iterations of MWSAA can explore *reinforcement learning* (RL) to optimize the perturbation process in a non-greedy, end-to-end fashion. RL agents can learn to generate sequences of perturbations that maximize attack effectiveness while adhering to syntactic and semantic constraints.

Second, the current implementation of MWSAA is designed for English texts. Extending the framework to handle multilingual corpora or code-mixed content would be a valuable enhancement, particularly given the global deployment of NLP systems.

Third, with the growing dominance of instruction-tuned language models (e.g., ChatGPT, Claude, Gemini), there is an increasing need to evaluate the vulnerability of these systems to subtle adversarial prompts or jailbreak strategies. Adapting MWSAA to target generative or conversational tasks presents an exciting and important direction.

Fourth, as defense strategies such as adversarial training, input sanitization, and detection systems evolve, adversarial attacks must also adapt. A potential extension of MWSAA could involve designing defense-aware attacks that dynamically adjust their strategies based on the observable behavior of defended models.

Fifth, MWSAA could also be leveraged to improve model robustness by serving as a generator in adversarial training loops. By exposing models to semantically consistent adversarial examples during training, generalization and robustness can be significantly enhanced.

Sixth, although cosine similarity provides a proxy for semantic similarity, incorporating human evaluation of fluency, coherence, and naturalness can yield deeper insights. Future studies may integrate human-in-the-loop evaluations or develop more sophisticated automatic metrics aligned with human judgment.

Seventh, investigating the scalability of MWSAA in real-time environments or for resource-constrained edge devices is another promising direction. Optimizing the runtime and memory footprint of the attack framework could enable broader applicability.

In summary, the Modified Word Saliency-Based Adversarial Attack presents a robust and linguistically grounded framework for adversarial text generation. It demonstrates the continuing relevance and importance of adversarial machine learning in NLP, not only as a means of stress-testing models but also as a catalyst for deeper understanding and innovation. As NLP systems become increasingly embedded in societal infrastructure, the study and mitigation of adversarial vulnerabilities will remain a central pillar of responsible AI development.

References

Alzantot, M., Sharma, Y., Elgohary, A., Ho, B-J., Srivastava, M., and Chang, K-W. 2018. "Generating Natural Language Adversarial Examples." In *Proceedings of the 2018 Conference on Empirical Methods in Natural Language Processing (EMNLP)*, 2890–2896.

Boucher, N., Shumailov, I., Anderson, R., and Papernot, N. 2022. "Bad Characters: Imperceptible NLP Attacks." In *Proceedings of the IEEE Symposium on Security and Privacy (SP)*, 1987–2004. IEEE.

Devlin, J., Chang, M-W., Lee, K., and Toutanova, K. 2019. "BERT: Pre-Training of Deep Bidirectional Transformers for Language Understanding." In *Proceedings of the 2019 Conference of the North American Chapter of the Association for Computational Linguistics (NAACL-HLT)*, 4171–4186.

Gao, J., Lanchantin, J., Soffa, M. L., and Qi, Y. 2018. "Black-Box Generation of Adversarial Text Sequences to Evade Deep Learning Classifiers." In *Proceedings of the 2018 IEEE Security and Privacy Workshops* (SPW 2018), 50–56. IEEE.

Goodfellow, I. J., Shlens, J., and Szegedy, C. 2015. "Explaining and Harnessing Adversarial Examples." In *Proceedings of the International Conference on Learning Representations (ICLR)*, Poster. arXiv: 1412.6572.

Graves, A. and Schmidhuber, J. 2005. "Framewise Phoneme Classification with Bidirectional LSTM and other Neural Network Architecture." *Neural Networks*, 18:5-6, 602-610, July-August 2005.

Jin, D., Jin, Z., Zhou, J. T., and Szolovits, P. 2020. "Is BERT Really Robust? A Strong Baseline for Natural Language Attack on Text Classification and Entailment." In *Proceedings of the AAAI Conference on Artificial Intelligence (AAAI)*, 8018–8025.

Kim, Y. 2014. "Convolutional Neural Networks for Sentence Classification." In *Proceedings of the 2014 Conference on Empirical Methods in Natural Language Processing (EMNLP)*, 1746–1751.

Koley, A., Satpati, P., Choudhary, I., and Sen, J. 2024. "An Investigation on the Efficiency of Some Text Attack Algorithms." In *Proceedings of the IEEE North Karnataka Subsection Flagship International Conference (NKCon 2024)*, 1–8.

Lan, Z., Chen, M., Goodman, S., Gimpel, K., Sharma, P., and Soricut, R. 2020. "ALBERT: A Lite BERT for Self-Supervised Learning of Language Representations." In *Proceedings of the International Conference on Learning Representations (ICLR)*. arXiv: 1909.11942.

Li, D., Zhang, Y., Peng, H., Chen, L., Brockett, C., Sun, M-T., and Dolan, B. 2021. "Contextualized Perturbation for Textual Adversarial Attack." In *Proceedings of the 2021 Conference of the North American Chapter of the Association for Computational Linguistics (NAACL)*, 5053–5069.

Li, L., Ma, R., Guo, Q., Xue, X., and Qiu, X. 2020. "BERT-Attack: Adversarial Attack against BERT Using BERT." In *Proceedings of the 2020 Conference on Empirical Methods in Natural Language Processing (EMNLP)*, 6193–6202.

Liang, B., Li, H., Su, M., Bian, P., Li, X., and Shi, W. 2018. "Deep Text Classification Can Be Fooled." In *Proceedings of the 27th International Joint Conference on Artificial Intelligence (IJCAI)*, 4208–4215.

Liu, S., Lu, N., Chen, C., and Tang, K. 2021. "Efficient Combinatorial Optimization for Word-Level Adversarial Textual Attack." In *IEEE/ACM Transactions on Audio, Speech, and Language Processing* 30: 98–111.

Liu, Y., Ott, M., Goyal, N., Du, J., Joshi, M., Chen, D., Levy, O., Lewis, M., Zettlemoyer, L., and Stoyanov, V. 2019. "RoBERTa: A Robustly Optimized BERT Pretraining Approach." *arXiv preprint arXiv:1907.11692*. DOI: 10.48550/arXiv.1907.11692.

Maas, A. L., Daly, R. E., Pham, P. T., Huang, D., Ng, A. Y., and Potts, C. 2011. "Learning Word Vectors for Sentiment Analysis." In *Proceedings of the 49th Annual Meeting of the Association for Computational Linguistics: Human Language Technologies*, 142-150.

Malfa, E. L. and Kwiatkowska, M. 2022. "The King Is Naked: On the Notion of Robustness for Natural Language Processing." In *Proceedings of the AAAI Conference on Artificial Intelligence*, 11047–11057.

Morris, J., Lifland, E., Yoo, J. Y., Grigsby, J., Jin, D., and Qi, Y. 2020. "TextAttack: A Framework for Adversarial Attacks, Data Augmentation, and Adversarial Training in NLP." In *Proceedings of the 2020 Conference on Empirical Methods in Natural Language Processing: System Demonstrations*, 119–126.

OpenAttack Platform. URL: https://github.com/thunlp/OpenAttack.

Ren, S., Deng, Y., He, K., and Che, W. 2019. "Generating Natural Language Adversarial Examples through Probability Weighted Word Saliency." In *Proceedings of the 57th Annual Meeting of the Association for Computational Linguistics (ACL)*, 1085–1097.

Samanta, S. and Mehta, S. 2017. "Towards Crafting Text Adversarial Samples." *arXiv preprint arXiv:1707.02812*.

Sen, J. 2024. "The FGSM Attack on Image Classification Models and Distillation as its Defense." In Nanda et al. (eds), *Advances in*

Distributed Computing and Machine Learning (ICADCML 2024), 1015: 347-360. Lecture Notes in Networks and Systems, Springer, Singapore.

Sen, J. and Dasgupta, S. 2023. "Adversarial Attacks on Image Classification Models: FGSM and Patch Attacks and their Impact." In Sen, J. and Mayer, J. (eds), *Information Security and Privacy in the Digital World: Some Selected Topics*, IntechOpen, London, UK.

Sen, J., Sen, A., and Chatterjee, A. 2023. "Adversarial Attacks on Image Classification Models: Analysis and Defense." In *Proceedings of the 10th International Conference on Business Analytics and Intelligence (ICBAI 2023)*, Bangalore, India.

Sen, J. and Waghela, H. 2025. "Text-Based Adversarial Attacks and Defense." In Sen, J. (ed) *Data Privacy: Techniques, Applications, and Standards*, IntechOpen, London, UK.

Socher, R., Perelygin, A., Wu, J., Chuang, J., Manning, C. D., Ng, A., and Potts, C. 2013. "Recursive Deep Models for Semantic Compositionality over a Sentiment Treebank." In *Proceedings of the 2013 Conference on Empirical Methods in Natural Language Processing (EMNLP'2013)*, 1631-1642.

Szegedy, C., Zaremba, W., Sutskever, I., Bruna, J., Erhan, D., Goodfellow, I. J., and Fergus, R. 2014. "Intriguing Properties of Neural Networks." In *Proceedings of the International Conference on Learning Representations (ICLR)*. arXiv: 1312.6199.

Waghela, H., Sen, J., and Rakshit, S. 2025. "Saliency Attention and Semantic Similarity-Driven Adversarial Perturbation." In *Data Science and Applications. ICDSA 2024*, Nanda, S. J. et al. (eds), 1237: 461–471. Lecture Notes in Networks and Systems, Springer, Singapore.

Waghela, H., Sen, J., Rakshit, S., and Dasgupta, S. 2024a. "Adversarial Text Generation with Dynamic Contextual Perturbation." In *Proceedings of the 2024 IEEE CALCON 2024*, 1–6. IEEE.

Waghela, H., Sen, J., and Rakshit, S. 2024b. "Adaptive Meta-Learning for Robust Ensemble Defense against Adversarial Attacks." In *Proceedings of the International Conference BAMS-ORSI 2024*.

Waghela, H., Sen, J., and Rakshit, S. 2024c. "Adversarial Resilience in Image Classification: A Hybrid Approach to Defense." In *Proceedings of the 2024 International Conference on Innovation and Intelligence for Informatics, Computing, and Technologies (3ICT 2024)*, 419–426.

Waghela, H., Sen, J., Rakshit, S., and Dasgupta, S. 2024d. "Adversarial Robustness through Dynamic Ensemble Learning." In *Proceedings of the 2024 IEEE Silchar Subsection Conference (SILCON 2024)*, 1–6.

Waghela, H., Sen, J., and Rakshit, S. 2024e. "Robust Image Classification: Defensive Strategies against FGSM and PGD Adversarial Attacks." In

Proceedings of the IEEE Asian Conference on Intelligent Technologies (ACOIT 2024), 1 – 7.

Waghela, H., Sen, J., and Rakshit, S. 2024f. "Refining BERT Adversarial Attacks with Projected Gradient Descent." In *Proceedings of the IEEE 4th Asian Conference on Innovations in Technology (ASIANCON 2024)*, 1-7.

Waghela, H., Rakshit, S., and Sen, J. 2024g. "A Modified Word Saliency-Based Adversarial Attack on Text Classification Models." In *Computational Intelligence and Data Analytics*, Frery, A. C. et al. (eds), 371–382. Lecture Notes in Data Engineering and Communications Technologies, 236. Springer.

Xu, H., Yao, M., Liu, H-C., Deb, D., Liu, H., Tang, J-L., and Jain, A. K. 2020. "Adversarial Attacks and Defenses in Images, Graphs and Text: A Review." *International Journal of Automation and Computing* 17 (2): 151–178.

Zang, Y., Qi, F., Yang, C., Liu, Z., Zhang, M., Liu, Q., and Sun, M. 2020. "Word-Level Textual Adversarial Attacking as Combinatorial Optimization." In *Proceedings of the 58th Annual Meeting of the Association for Computational Linguistics (ACL)*, pp. 6066–6080.

Zhang, X., Zhao, J., and LeCun, Y. 2015. "Character-Level Convolutional Networks for Text Classification." In *Proceedings of the 29th International Conference on Neural Information Processing Systems (NeurIPS)*, 1: 649 - 657.

Zhou, Y., Jiang, J-Y., Chang, K-W., and Wang, W. 2019. "Learning to Discriminate Perturbations for Blocking Adversarial Attacks in Text Classification." In *Proceedings of the 2019 Conference on Empirical Methods in Natural Language Processing and the 9th International Joint Conference on Natural Language Processing (EMNLP-IJCNLP)*, Association for Computational Linguistics, pp. 4904–4913.

CHAPTER 3

REFINING TEXT-BASED ADVERSARIAL ATTACKS WITH SALIENCY, ATTENTION, AND SEMANTIC SIMILARITY

Introduction

The increasing deployment of deep learning models in real-world natural language processing (NLP) applications, ranging from spam detection and sentiment classification to machine translation and legal document analysis, has raised serious concerns regarding their robustness to adversarial manipulation. It has been demonstrated that even high-performing models are vulnerable to small, seemingly benign changes to the input text that can cause incorrect or drastically altered predictions. These input alterations, known as adversarial examples, exploit the model's internal weaknesses without affecting the syntactic correctness or perceived meaning of the text from a human perspective. Understanding and mitigating such vulnerabilities is now considered a key challenge in trustworthy and secure NLP.

Unlike adversarial examples in the vision domain, which typically involve imperceptible pixel perturbations in continuous input spaces, text-based adversarial attacks operate on discrete sequences. This imposes several unique challenges: any perturbation must preserve grammaticality, retain semantic fidelity, and avoid detection, while still being effective enough to fool the model. Traditional approaches to crafting such adversarial examples include character-level attacks (such as typos and misspellings), word-level attacks (typically involving synonym replacements), and phrase-level insertions or deletions. While character-level attacks often result in noisy or unnatural text, and phrase-level approaches can cause noticeable semantic drift, word-level substitution strategies have proven to offer a balanced trade-off between fluency and effectiveness.

Within this space, saliency-based attacks have emerged as a compelling direction. These techniques prioritize perturbations to the most influential words in the input, i.e., those that contribute most significantly to the model's prediction. Notable methods such as PWWS and BERT-Attack have operationalized this idea by combining word saliency estimation with constrained synonym substitution. However, these models face several shortcomings. They may not fully leverage contextual information when identifying influential words, nor do they reliably enforce semantic similarity between the original and perturbed inputs. Consequently, such adversarial examples risk degrading textual quality or drifting away from the original meaning, issues that reduce their stealth and practical relevance.

To address these gaps, this chapter introduces a refined adversarial text generation framework that integrates *Saliency, Attention, and Semantic Similarity for Perturbation (SASSP)*. This method enhances traditional word-level substitution attacks by incorporating a more context-sensitive and semantically aware approach. The SASSP framework proceeds in three stages: (1) identifying high-saliency words through integrated attention and gradient-based metrics, (2) generating substitution candidates using masked language modeling, and (3) applying a semantic similarity filter to ensure that selected perturbations preserve sentence meaning. The final adversarial examples are chosen not only based on their ability to mislead the classifier but also on their syntactic fluency and semantic coherence.

Unlike prior work that relies on static word embeddings or fixed substitution rules, SASSP dynamically leverages contextual information using pre-trained transformer models such as BERT. This allows the attack to adaptively select candidate replacements that are better suited to the local sentence structure and meaning. Additionally, the semantic similarity constraint, computed using sentence-level cosine similarity, acts as a safeguard against meaning distortion. By integrating these elements, SASSP significantly improves the trade-off between attack success and perceptual similarity to the original input, producing adversarial examples that are more effective, natural-sounding, and less detectable.

Experiments conducted on benchmark datasets, including Yelp, AG News, MNLI, and QNLI, demonstrate that SASSP outperforms classical baselines in both white-box and black-box attack scenarios. The method achieves high attack success rates while maintaining lower substitution ratios and high semantic similarity scores. This balance of performance and subtlety makes SASSP a valuable tool for probing the robustness of modern NLP systems.

The rest of the chapter is organized as follows. *Related Work* reviews recent advances in text-based adversarial generation, focusing on saliency-driven, context-aware, and semantic-preserving strategies. The section *The CLARE Model for Contextual Perturbation* provides an overview of the CLARE model. The section *Saliency, Attention, and Semantic Similarity-Driven Perturbation* explores perturbation strategies guided by token saliency, attention distributions, and semantic similarity to enhance the effectiveness and subtlety of adversarial text generation. The section *Implementation Details and Experimental Setup* outlines the implementation specifics of the proposed approach. In *Performance Evaluation*, empirical results on multiple classification tasks and comparative analysis against baseline techniques are presented. Finally, *the Conclusion and Future Research Directions* section summarizes key insights and outlines open research challenges in advancing robust and interpretable NLP systems.

Related Work

Adversarial attacks in *Natural Language Processing* (NLP) have gained significant traction in recent years, primarily due to their ability to expose the vulnerabilities of deep neural networks used in high-stakes language tasks. These attacks aim to subtly alter input text in a way that misleads the model without noticeably affecting its meaning or readability to humans.

A foundational contribution to this area was made by Carlini and Wagner, who introduced a general framework for evaluating the robustness of neural networks under adversarial conditions (Carlini & Wagner, 2017). Though their work primarily focused on the image domain, the underlying principles of adversarial robustness, perturbation minimization, and threat modeling have been widely adopted for NLP. In the context of language understanding, Jia and Liang highlighted the fragility of reading comprehension systems by crafting small, semantically plausible edits to questions and passages that led models to produce incorrect answers (Jia & Liang, 2017). Their work underscored the importance of semantic awareness in both generating and defending against textual adversarial examples.

Liu and Lane extended adversarial learning to task-oriented dialogue systems (Liu & Lane, 2018). They proposed an adversarial training framework in which a generator produces candidate responses and a discriminator evaluates their semantic coherence. This adversarial interplay aimed to improve both robustness and language understanding in dialogue agents. Meanwhile, Wei et al. introduced *TextBugger*, a black-box attack method that manipulates text via character-level and word-level modifications, optimized to fool classifiers while retaining legibility (Wei et al, 2019). However, the synthetic and sometimes unnatural outputs of such character-based approaches have prompted a shift toward word-level and context-aware perturbations.

Ren et al. developed the *Probability Weighted Word Saliency (PWWS)* method, which leverages a probabilistic ranking of word saliency to guide synonym-based substitutions (Ren et al., 2019). This technique represents a turning point in adversarial text generation, combining interpretability with attack effectiveness. Yang et al. expanded this direction by focusing on semantic-preserving adversarial perturbations, demonstrating that model predictions could be reliably altered without sacrificing textual meaning or grammaticality (Yang et al., 2023).

Another key advancement came from Liu et al., who addressed the challenge of transferability, i.e., generating adversarial examples that can deceive multiple models (Liu et al., 2023). Their method aimed to produce perturbations with minimal changes while maintaining effectiveness across diverse architectures.

Recent advancements in adversarial NLP have seen the emergence of more sophisticated attack and defense strategies, particularly those that incorporate semantic similarity measures, dynamic perturbation techniques, and ensemble-based robustness frameworks. A notable body of work by Waghela, Sen, Rakshit, and their collaborators (Waghela et al., 2024a–g; 2025) has played a pivotal role in shaping this direction. Their research introduces context-aware, linguistically grounded adversarial methods that utilize saliency attention mechanisms, BERT-derived embeddings, and semantic constraints to generate more natural and effective adversarial examples. On the defensive front, their contributions include meta-learning ensembles and hybrid defense schemes aimed at enhancing model resilience against such perturbations in both text and image classification settings. Taken together, these efforts provide a comprehensive foundation for achieving a balance between adversarial strength and semantic integrity, while also enabling the development of generalizable defenses across various model architectures and application domains.

Koley et al. conducted a comprehensive empirical study comparing several well-established adversarial text attack algorithms, with a focus on evaluating their performance across key metrics such as attack success rate, computational overhead, and semantic preservation (Koley et al., 2024). Their benchmarking encompassed multiple text classification models and datasets, providing valuable insights into the practical trade-offs and limitations of each approach. This contribution adds to the expanding literature advocating for more standardized evaluation frameworks and a deeper analytical understanding of adversarial behavior under diverse operational settings.

Beyond individual techniques, the literature includes a broad range of perturbation types, including word substitution (Waghela et al., 2024f), word insertion (Ni et al., 2024), word swapping (Liu et al., 2022), phrase-level alterations (Lei et al., 2022), and sentence-level transformations (Li et al., 2021), and contextual perturbation (Cer et al., 2018). Particularly noteworthy are contextual perturbation approaches that leverage masked language models (e.g., BERT) to generate replacements that respect the syntactic and semantic coherence of the sentence. These methods offer greater flexibility and fidelity than static synonym-based techniques.

Despite this progress, several open challenges remain. Many methods prioritize the objective of inducing misclassification without adequately preserving the semantic integrity of the text. Others fail to generalize across domains or exhibit poor query efficiency. Furthermore, the absence of standardized evaluation protocols for linguistic naturalness and semantic preservation complicates comparative analysis across attack strategies.

The refined framework presented in this chapter, SASSP (Saliency, Attention, and Semantic Similarity for Perturbation), addresses these limitations by integrating gradient-based saliency scoring, context-aware candidate generation, and semantic similarity constraints. In doing so, it contributes to the development of adversarial attacks that are not only effective but also interpretable, linguistically plausible, and semantically faithful to the original input.

The CLARE Model for Contextual Perturbation

A significant milestone in the development of adversarial text attacks is the CLARE (Contextualized Linguistically Aware Adversarial Example) model (Li et al., 2021). CLARE emphasizes *contextual perturbation*, which refers to modifying text in a way that retains its fluency and meaning while misleading a downstream NLP classifier. Unlike earlier perturbation strategies that often relied on surface-level word substitutions or character modifications, CLARE takes advantage of the deep contextual understanding offered by *masked language models* (MLMs) like BERT.

CLARE's attack generation process consists of four major steps: (1) Target Word Selection via Gradient-Based Saliency, (2) Contextual Candidate Generation Using MLMs, (3) Candidate Ranking and Filtering, and (4) Adversarial Text Construction. In the following, these steps are discussed in detail.

Target Word Selection via Gradient-Based Saliency: The first step identifies words in the input text whose modification would most likely alter the model's prediction. This is done using gradient-based saliency. Formally, for an input sequence $X = x_1, x_2, \dots, x_n$, and a model f that predicts a label y, the gradient of the loss $\mathcal{L}$ with respect to each word embedding e_i is computed. The magnitude of the gradient, $\left\|\nabla_{e_i}\mathcal{L}\right\|$, serves as the saliency score, indicating the importance of the word x_i in the model's prediction.

Words with the highest saliency scores are prioritized for potential modification. This saliency-driven approach ensures that only words that significantly influence the model's decision are considered for perturbation.

Contextual Candidate Generation Using MLMs: Once the important words are selected, the next step involves generating replacement candidates for these words. To preserve contextual coherence, each identified word is replaced with a mask token ([MASK]), and a masked language model (such as BERT or RoBERTa) is used to predict a ranked list of plausible replacements based on the context.

Given a masked input X', the MLM returns a set of likely candidate words $\{w_1, w_2, \dots, w_k\}$, each associated with a conditional probability score that indicates how likely that word fits the masked position.

Candidate Ranking and Filtering: The list of replacement candidates is filtered and ranked using a composite scoring strategy. Each candidate is evaluated based on two primary criteria: (i) its likelihood according to the MLM, and (ii) its capacity to induce a change in the model's predicted label.

A scoring function aggregates these criteria using tunable weights, α and β. The top candidate, according to this composite score, is selected as the perturbation for the target word. This step ensures that the substitution is both contextually plausible and adversarially effective.

Adversarial Text Construction: After selecting the optimal replacements, CLARE constructs the adversarial example by substituting the original words with the chosen candidates. If the model's prediction changes as a result, the attack is deemed successful. Otherwise, the process may continue iteratively for additional target words or terminate if no effective perturbation is found.

Limitations of CLARE: Despite its novel and innovative approach, CLARE exhibits several limitations as mentioned below:

- *Saliency Limitation*: The exclusive reliance on gradient-based saliency can miss contextually significant words that may not have high gradient magnitudes.
- *Semantic Draft*: While MLMs offer context-aware substitutions, there is no explicit mechanism in CLARE to guarantee semantic equivalence between the original and adversarial texts.
- *Computational Overhead*: The iterative generation and scoring of multiple perturbations for each input sentence can be computationally intensive.
- *Overdependence on MLSs*: The effectiveness of the attack is tightly coupled with the MLM's ability to generate high-quality substitutes, potentially limiting generalizability across domains and languages.

These shortcomings motivate the need for an improved framework that incorporates richer contextual cues, ensures semantic similarity, and optimizes the selection of perturbation targets. The next section introduces such an approach: the *Saliency Attention and Semantic Similarity-driven Perturbation* (SASSP) scheme.

Saliency, Attention and Semantic Similarity-Driven Perturbation (SASSP)

To overcome the limitations observed in existing contextual adversarial attack strategies, particularly those inherent in the CLARE framework, a novel method termed *Saliency Attention and Semantic Similarity-Driven Perturbation* (SASSP) is introduced. This approach is designed to improve the efficacy, subtlety, and semantic integrity of adversarial attacks on *natural language processing* (NLP) models by enhancing two critical stages of the attack generation pipeline: word selection and semantic validation.

Unlike conventional approaches that rely exclusively on gradient-based saliency for identifying candidate words for modification, SASSP integrates attention-based contextual cues and enforces semantic consistency through a dual-stage filtering mechanism. The framework is structured to ensure that the generated adversarial examples remain syntactically fluent and semantically faithful to the original input while successfully misleading the target model.

Motivation for an Enhanced Framework: Two significant limitations in the CLARE approach are the source of motivation for the current work. They are: (i) limitations of saliency-only word selection, and (ii) challenges in maintaining semantic integrity.

Limitations of Saliency-Only Word Selection: Gradient-based saliency scoring methods determine the influence of each token on the model's output by computing the magnitude of the gradient of the loss function with respect to the token's embedding. However, these methods may fail to capture contextually significant tokens, especially when gradient noise or model complexity distorts the importance estimation. Consequently, words that are critical from a semantic or syntactic standpoint may be overlooked, reducing the effectiveness or coherence of the resulting adversarial example.

Challenges in Maintaining Semantic Integrity: Adversarial examples are expected to be indistinguishable from genuine inputs in terms of meaning and linguistic quality. However, perturbations generated without explicit semantic constraints often result in grammatically incorrect or semantically divergent outputs. These flaws not only make the attacks detectable but also diminish their practical utility in real-world applications.

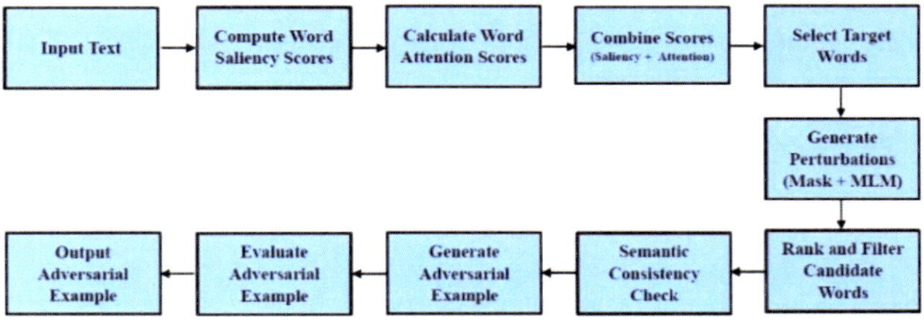

Figure 3-1. The block diagram of the SASSP attack pipeline highlighting saliency, attention, and semantic-preserving transformations.

Overview of the Proposed SASSP Methodology: The SASSP framework introduces two primary enhancements over prior methods:

- A *composite word scoring strategy* that combines gradient-based saliency and transformer-based attention scores to identify high-impact words for perturbation.
- A *semantic validation module* comprising embedding-based similarity and paraphrase detection mechanisms to ensure the perturbed outputs preserve the original text's meaning.

A high-level schematic of the SASSP workflow is illustrated in Figure 3-1.

Composite Word Scoring and Selection: This involves three steps: (i) Computation of saliency scores, (ii) Aggregation of attention-based contextual importance, and (iii) Combined scoring and threshold-based selection. In the following, these steps are explained in detail.

Computation of Saliency Scores: The importance of each word in the input sequence is first assessed using gradient-based saliency. Given a text input $X = x_1, x_2, \ldots, x_n$, and a classification model f, the saliency score S_i of word x_i is determined as the norm of the gradient of the loss function $\mathcal{L}$ with respect to the embedding e_i:

$$S_i = ||\frac{\partial \mathcal{L}}{\partial e_i}|| \tag{3-1}$$

In (3-1), the score S_i reflects the extent to which a perturbation to the word is likely to affect the model's prediction.

Aggregation of Attention-Based Contextual Importance: Transformer-based models such as BERT maintain internal attention weights that can be used to assess the contextual significance of each token. For a word x_i, the attention score A_i is computed by averaging attention weights across all heads and layers:

$$A_i = \frac{1}{LH} \sum_{l=1}^{L} \sum_{h=1}^{H} a_i^{(l,h)} \tag{3-2}$$

In (3-2), L denotes the number of layers, H is the number of attention heads, and $a_i^{(l,h)}$ represents the attention weight of the i-th token in layer l and head h.

Combined Scoring and Threshold-Based Selection: To capture both predictive importance and contextual relevance, a composite score C_i is computed for each word by combining saliency and attention scores using a weighted sum given by (3-3).

$$C_i = \alpha . S_i + \beta . A_i \tag{3-3}$$

In (3-3), α and β are hypermeters that control the relative contributions of saliency and attention. A dynamic threshold θ is computed based on the distribution of combined scores (e.g., the 75th percentile), and all tokens satisfying $C_i \geq \theta$ are selected as target words for perturbation.

Candidate Generation via Masked Language Modeling: For each selected target word, the corresponding token is replaced with a [MASK] placeholder. A masked language model (MLM), such as Distil-RoBERTa, is then employed to generate a ranked list of plausible substitute words based on the masked input. The MLM provides context-aware candidate tokens $\{w'_1, w'_2, \ldots, w'_k\}$, ordered by their likelihood of occurrence in the given context.

While MLMs ensure contextual plausibility, not all replacements satisfy semantic equivalence requirements. Therefore, an additional filtering stage is incorporated to ensure semantic fidelity.

Semantic Validation of Candidate Substitutions: To verify that the meaning of the original sentence is preserved in the perturbed version, a two-pronged semantic validation mechanism is employed. The two steps are: (i) Embedding-based similarity assessment and (ii) Paraphrase detection for semantic equivalence. The details of these steps are as follows.

Embedding-Based Similarity Assessment: The original and perturbed sentences are encoded using a pre-trained sentence embedding model (e.g., Sentence-BERT). The cosine similarity between their vector representations is computed using (3-4).

$$sim(X, X') = \frac{E(X).E(X')}{\|E(X)\|.\|E(X')\|} \tag{3-4}$$

In (3-4), $E(.)$ denotes the sentence embedding function. Candidate substitutions that yield a similarity score below a predetermined threshold (e.g., 0.80) are discarded.

Paraphrase Detection for Semantic Equivalence: For candidates passing the embedding similarity check, a paraphrase detection model is employed to assess the likelihood that the original and perturbed sentences convey the same meaning. This model, fine-tuned using the Sentence Transformers framework, assigns a probability score indicating semantic equivalence. Only those candidates surpassing a secondary threshold (e.g., 0.75) are retained for final evaluation.

Adversarial Example Construction and Final Selection: For each candidate word substitution that passes the semantic validation phase, the modified text is evaluated against the original classification model. If the model's output changes in response to the substitution, the perturbation is deemed a successful adversarial attack. In cases where no such perturbation results in misclassification, the process is repeated with the next most salient word or candidate.

Advantages of the SASSP Framework: The SASSP scheme provides multiple advantages over traditional contextual perturbation-based adversarial strategies:

- *Context-Aware Word Targeting*: The integration of attention scores allows for more contextually meaningful word selection than saliency alone.
- *Semantic Integrity*: The dual-stage validation strategy ensures that the generated adversarial examples retain semantic similarity and grammatical correctness.
- *Dynamic Perturbation Control*: The use of adaptive thresholding mechanisms provides better control over the number and extent of perturbations applied.
- *Model-Agnostic Flexibility*: The approach is compatible with any masked language model and can be deployed across a range of NLP classification tasks and datasets.

Implementation Details and Experimental Setup

The practical realization of the *Saliency Attention and Semantic Similarity-Driven Perturbation* (SASSP) framework has been carried out using the Python programming language in conjunction with several widely adopted deep learning libraries. The implementation leverages the capabilities of PyTorch (Paszke et al., 2019) as the core deep learning framework, and utilizes models and utilities from Hugging Face's Transformers (Wolf et al., 2020; Hugging Face Transformer Models) and Sentence-Transformers libraries (Reimers & Gurevych, 2019; Hugging Face Sentence Transformer

Models). The objective of this section is to provide a comprehensive explanation of the technical procedures followed during the development of SASSP, followed by a description of the experimental setup used to evaluate the effectiveness of the proposed method.

The environment for implementing SASSP includes Python version 3.9 and a GPU-enabled PyTorch backend to facilitate efficient computation. The implementation draws on several pretrained models, specifically transformer-based language models such as BERT-base (Devlin et al., 2019; Hugging Face BERT-Base Model), RoBERTa-base (Zhuang et al., 2021; Hugging Face RoBERTa-Base Model), and their distilled versions (Sanh et al., 2019; Hugging Face Distil BERT-Base Model; Hugging Face Distil RoBERTa-Base Model). These models are accessed through the Transformers library. Sentence-level embeddings and paraphrase scoring are facilitated by the Sentence-Transformers package, which provides access to pretrained models suitable for tasks such as sentence similarity computation and semantic equivalence assessment.

The architecture of SASSP is modular, with each major functional component implemented as an independent module. The first step in the pipeline involves computing saliency scores for each token in the input text. This is achieved by first tokenizing the text using a BERT-compatible tokenizer, followed by a forward pass through a pretrained classifier (e.g., a sentiment analysis or natural language inference model). The model's prediction is used to compute the loss, and a backward pass is subsequently performed to obtain the gradient of the loss with respect to each input token's embedding. The magnitude of each gradient vector, specifically, the L1 norm, is interpreted as the saliency score for the corresponding token. This entire process is encapsulated within a function that returns the complete set of saliency scores for the input text.

Following the computation of saliency scores, attention scores are extracted from the internal mechanisms of a transformer model. The attention weights are obtained from the final hidden layers of the model across all attention heads. For each token, the attention scores from all layers and heads are averaged to yield a single aggregate attention score, representing the degree to which the model focuses on that token across different representational levels. This process ensures that both low-level and high-level contextual dependencies are captured. The resulting attention scores are then aligned with the saliency scores.

To identify the most appropriate words for perturbation, the saliency and attention scores are linearly combined using a weighted summation. Specifically, a combined score is computed for each token using a tunable linear combination of its saliency and attention values. The relative contribution of each component is controlled by two scalar hyperparameters. Once the combined scores are calculated, a thresholding mechanism is employed to select the target words. Rather than using a fixed cutoff, an adaptive threshold is computed based on the 75th percentile of the combined score distribution, ensuring that only the top-ranking tokens, those most likely to affect the model's output, are selected for modification.

After identifying the candidate words for perturbation, a masked language model is used to generate contextually appropriate replacement candidates. For each selected word, the token is replaced with a [MASK] placeholder, and the masked sentence is processed by a pretrained MLM such as Distill-RoBERTa. The model predicts a list of top-*k* likely substitutes for the masked token, ranked by their conditional probability given the surrounding context. These predicted candidates are then decoded into natural language words, forming a set of potential perturbations for each target token.

To ensure that the adversarial text remains semantically faithful to the original input, each candidate substitution undergoes a two-stage semantic validation process. In the first stage, the cosine similarity between the original sentence and each perturbed version is computed using Sentence-BERT embeddings. Sentences that fall below a predefined similarity threshold (typically 0.80) are excluded from further consideration. In the second stage, paraphrase detection is applied to the remaining candidate sentences using a fine-tuned model from the Sentence-Transformers library. This model assigns a paraphrase probability to each pair of original and perturbed sentences. Only those candidates that exceed a secondary threshold for paraphrase likelihood (e.g., 0.75) are retained as valid adversarial samples.

The final stage of the pipeline involves verifying the effectiveness of each semantically valid perturbation. The perturbed text is passed through the same classifier used in the initial prediction. If the classifier produces a different output label for the perturbed input, the attack is deemed successful. If not, the next candidate replacement is evaluated. This process is repeated iteratively across all selected target words and their respective substitution candidates. If no adversarial candidate results in a change in the model's prediction, the input is left unmodified.

The SASSP framework has been evaluated using four widely recognized benchmark datasets in adversarial NLP research. The first of these is the Yelp Polarity dataset (Tang et al., 2015; Yelp Dataset), which consists of positive and negative sentiment reviews across various businesses such as restaurants and cafes. The second dataset is AG News (Zhang et al., 2015), which includes news articles categorized into four topics: World, Sports, Business, and Science & Technology. The third dataset, MNLI (Multi-Genre Natural Language Inference), is designed for evaluating natural language inference systems and includes sentence pairs annotated for entailment, contradiction, or neutrality (Multi-Genre NLI Corpus Dataset; Williams et al., 2018). The fourth dataset, QNLI (Question-Answering Natural Language Inference), is derived from the Stanford Question Answering Dataset and repurposed for sentence-level inference tasks (Wang et al., 2018).

The evaluation of adversarial performance is carried out using models trained on the respective tasks associated with each dataset. For consistency and comparability, the same pretrained transformer-based models are used for both generating and evaluating adversarial examples. Distill-RoBERTa serves as the primary masked language model, and additional experiments are conducted using Base-RoBERTa and Base-BERT to assess the generalizability of the proposed approach across different transformer variants.

To comprehensively assess the effectiveness and quality of adversarial examples generated by SASSP, a suite of quantitative metrics is employed. The first metric is the *Attack Success Rate* (ASR), which measures the proportion of input instances for which the classifier's original prediction is successfully altered (Jin et al., 2020). The second metric, *Perplexity* (PER), is used to evaluate the fluency and naturalness of the perturbed texts; lower perplexity values are indicative of better linguistic coherence (Zhao et al., 2018). The third metric, *Word Manipulation Rate* (WMR), quantifies the proportion of tokens in the original text that have been altered (Li et al., 2021). The fourth metric, *Syntactic Error Rate* (SYE), measures the number of grammatical errors introduced as a result of perturbation, based on syntactic analysis tools (Naber, 2003). Finally, the *Semantic Similarity Score* (SES) is calculated using cosine similarity between sentence embeddings generated by the Universal Sentence Encoder, offering a measure of how closely the adversarial text preserves the meaning of the original (Cer et al., 2018).

To ensure reproducibility, all random seeds used in model initialization and data sampling are fixed. Hyperparameters such as the weighting factors for saliency and attention, as well as the similarity thresholds for filtering, are chosen through empirical validation on a held-out subset of the data. The codebase is modular and compatible with GPU acceleration, facilitating large-scale experimentation and reproducibility of results.

The subsequent section presents a comparative analysis of the performance of the SASSP framework against the baseline CLARE method across the selected datasets and language models, using the aforementioned evaluation metrics.

Performance Evaluation

This section presents a comprehensive empirical evaluation of the proposed SASSP (Saliency-Aware Syntax- and Semantics-Preserving) adversarial attack framework in comparison with CLARE, a benchmark context-aware adversarial attack model. The evaluation is conducted using multiple datasets and *masked language models* (MLMs), and spans across five key metrics that assess the success, quality, and stealth of the adversarial attacks.

To ensure fair comparison and alignment with prior work, the same experimental protocol adopted in the CLARE framework is followed. Specifically, the *Distil-RoBERTa* model is employed as the masked language model in the initial evaluation. Distil-RoBERTa is a compressed and computationally efficient variant of RoBERTa-base, produced via the same distillation methodology utilized in Distil-BERT, preserving most of the original model's performance while significantly reducing its size and inference time.

The semantic consistency between original and adversarial text samples is assessed using the *Universal Sentence Encoder* (USE), which converts each sentence into a fixed-length vector that encapsulates its semantic meaning. Cosine similarity is employed as the similarity function, quantifying the angular distance between the embeddings of the original and perturbed sentences. A higher cosine similarity score indicates greater preservation of semantic content.

For benchmarking, the open-source implementation of CLARE is used without modification. The SASSP and CLARE attack methods are evaluated across four datasets, each representing distinct NLP classification tasks:

- *Yelp*: A sentiment analysis dataset comprising user reviews from businesses such as restaurants and hotels. Reviews rated with 4 or 5 stars are labeled as *positive*, while those with 1 or 2 stars are labeled *negative*. The dataset includes 560,000 training and 38,000 test instances.
- *AG News*: A topic classification dataset derived from AG's news corpus, consisting of news articles categorized into four classes: *World*, *Sports*, *Business*, and *Science & Technology*. It includes 120,000 training and 7,600 test samples.
- *MNLI* (Multi-Genre Natural Language Inference): A benchmark for textual entailment containing sentence pairs labeled as *entailment*, *neutral*, or *contradiction*. The corpus spans various genres such as fiction, government proceedings, travel, and spoken dialogue, with over 393,000 training instances and 20,000 samples each for validation and testing.
- *QNLI* (Question Natural Language Inference): A dataset derived from the Stanford Question Answering Dataset (SQuAD), structured as a binary classification task to determine whether a context sentence contains the answer to a given question. Each instance consists of a question, a sentence from a passage, and a label: *entailment* or *entailment*.

Evaluation Metrics: The comparative analysis employs the following metrics:

- *Attack Success Rate* (ASR): The proportion of adversarial samples that successfully alter the model's original prediction. A higher ASR reflects greater attack effectiveness.
- *Perplexity* (PER): Measures the uncertainty of the language model when generating adversarial text. Lower perplexity indicates that the perturbed sentences are more fluent and coherent.
- *Word Manipulation Rate* (WMR): The percentage of words modified in the adversarial example compared to the original text. Lower WMR signifies that fewer modifications were needed to successfully mislead the classifier, implying a more subtle attack.
- *Syntactic Error Rate* (SYE): The number of syntactic errors introduced in the adversarial sample. This metric is computed using a rule-based grammatical analysis approach, and a lower value indicates better syntactic preservation.
- *Semantic Similarity* (SES): The degree of semantic equivalence between the original and adversarial texts, computed via cosine

similarity of embeddings generated by the Universal Sentence Encoder. Higher values indicate minimal semantic drift.

Table 3-1. Performance Comparison between SASSP and CLARE on Four Datasets Using ASR, PER, WMR, SYE, and SES.

Dataset	Model	ASR	PER	WMR	SYE	SES
Yelp	CLARE	79.7	83.5	10.3	0.25	0.78
	SASSP	**82.6**	**74.2**	**8.7**	**0.25**	**0.85**
AG News	CLARE	79.1	86.0	6.1	0.17	0.76
	SASSP	83.4	76.2	3.4	0.15	0.85
MNLI	CLARE	88.1	82.7	7.5	**0.02**	0.82
	SASSP	**93.6**	**73.2**	**3.3**	**0.02**	**0.87**
QNLI	CLARE	83.8	76.7	11.8	0.01	0.78
	SASSP	**93.2**	**71.2**	**5.8**	**0.01**	**0.86**

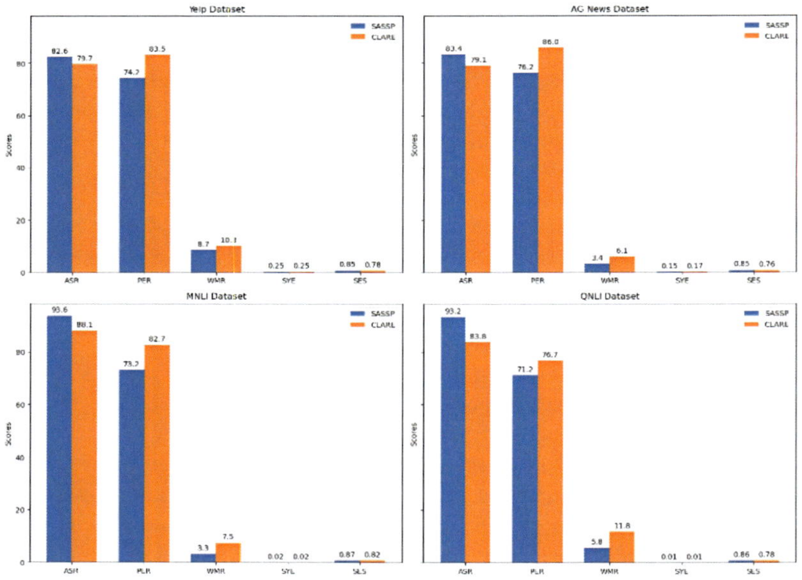

Figure 3-2. Graphical comparison of the SASSP and CLARE across four benchmark datasets: Yelp, AG News, MNLI, and QNLI, evaluated using five metrics: ASR, PER, WMR, SYE, and SES.

Table 3-1 reports the comparative performance of the SASSP and CLARE adversarial attack methods, evaluated on 1,000 test samples drawn from each respective dataset. To enhance interpretability, the same results are depicted graphically in Figure 3-2. In the context of adversarial evaluation, an effective and efficient attack method is characterized by higher values of Attack Success Rate (ASR) and Semantic Similarity (SES), alongside lower values of Perplexity (PER), Word Manipulation Rate (WMR), and Syntactic Error Rate (SYE). As evident from Table 3-1, SASSP consistently outperforms CLARE across all four datasets and on all five evaluation metrics. The values reported for PER, WMR, SYE, and SES represent average scores computed over those adversarial samples that successfully caused model misclassification.

Table 3-2. Performance Comparison between SASSP and CLARE on the AG News Dataset across Different MLMs Using Five Performance Metrics.

MLM	Attack	ASR	PER	WMR	SYE	SES
Distill-RoBERTa	CLARE	79.1	86.0	6.1	0.17	0.76
	SASSP	**83.4**	**76.2**	**3.4**	**0.15**	**0.85**
Base-RoBERTa	CLARE	79.3	88.9	6.3	0.21	0.75
	SASSP	**81.7**	**77.2**	**4.7**	**0.17**	**0.85**
Base-BERT	CLARE	78.4	95.2	8.3	0.23	0.71
	SASSP	**81.4**	**78.5**	**6.5**	**0.19**	**0.85**

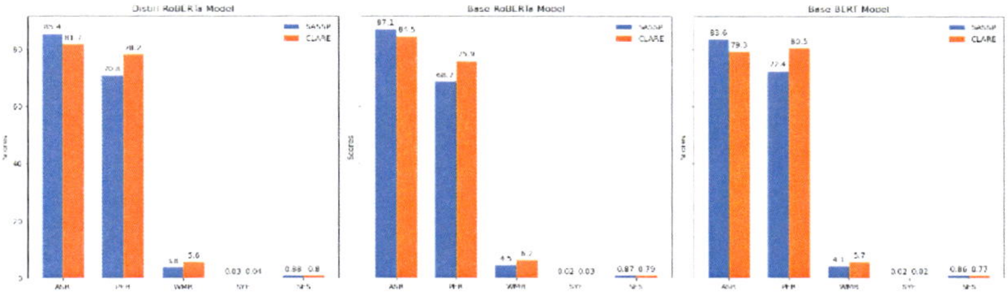

Figure 3-3. Graphical comparison of the SASSP and CLARE adversarial attack methods across three masked language models: Distill-RoBERTa, RoBERTa-base, and BERT-base, on the AG News dataset, evaluated using ASR, PER, WMR, SYE, and SES.

The performance comparison between SASSP and CLARE is further extended across three distinct masked language models (MLMs): Distil-RoBERTa, RoBERTa-base, and BERT-base, using the AG News dataset. The corresponding results are summarized in Table 3-2 and illustrated in Figure 3-3. Across all five evaluation metrics, SASSP demonstrates superior performance relative to CLARE. Among the evaluated MLMs,

Distil-RoBERTa yields the highest overall effectiveness for both attack schemes, while BERT-base exhibits the lowest susceptibility to adversarial perturbations. This suggests that BERT-base is comparatively more robust, potentially due to the shared architectural and linguistic features between the attack mechanism and the target model, which may enable it to better resist adversarial manipulations originating from its own modeling structure.

Conclusion and Future Research Directions

The increasing capabilities of natural language processing (NLP) models have brought renewed attention to their vulnerability to adversarial attacks. The SASSP framework, proposed as a saliency-aware, syntax- and semantics-preserving adversarial text generation method, demonstrates a marked improvement over existing approaches in both effectiveness and imperceptibility. Extensive empirical evaluations across multiple benchmark datasets and masked language models show that SASSP consistently outperforms the state-of-the-art CLARE model in terms of attack success rate (ASR), semantic similarity (SES), syntactic integrity (SYE), perplexity (PER), and word-level efficiency (WMR). These findings highlight the importance of linguistically and semantically informed perturbation strategies in advancing the field of adversarial NLP.

In addition to its practical impact, SASSP represents a conceptual advancement in the adversarial text generation paradigm. By integrating saliency-driven token selection with syntactic correctness and semantic coherence, the method reflects a broader shift toward generating adversarial examples that are both functionally disruptive and linguistically natural. This direction not only improves the evaluation of model robustness but also provides deeper insights into model behavior under adversarial stress.

Several future research directions emerge from this work. These avenues span adversarial strategy refinement, defense mechanisms, evaluation methodology, multi-modal integration, and ethical implications.

One promising direction is the extension of adversarial attack methods to multilingual and code-mixed settings. Most current approaches are developed for English-language data, and generalizing them to diverse linguistic contexts would address gaps in global applicability. In addition, future attacks could target longer text spans such as paragraphs or full documents, considering discourse structure, coreference chains, and anaphora resolution. Designing attacks that operate not only on input tokens but also at the level of embeddings or attention weights could further expose vulnerabilities in model internals.

Instruction-tuned large language models (LLMs) such as GPT, Claude, and Gemini present new challenges for adversarial NLP. Research could focus on crafting adversarial prompts capable of influencing model outputs in multi-turn dialogues, reasoning chains, or tool-augmented workflows. In parallel, adversarial techniques could be integrated into testing pipelines for real-world LLM deployments in chatbots, recommendation engines, and intelligent assistants.

From a defensive perspective, there is a pressing need to build generalizable and efficient mechanisms that are resistant to multiple attack types across varied tasks. Strategies such as adversarial training, ensemble modeling, input transformation, and hybrid architectures remain central to ongoing exploration. Techniques leveraging model confidence scores, uncertainty estimation, or explanation-aware detection (e.g., SHAP, attention entropy) offer promising tools for adaptive defense. Further investigation into self-healing models, capable of dynamically retraining or adjusting based on detected adversarial samples, could lead to more resilient systems.

Adversarial robustness in distributed and privacy-preserving environments, such as federated learning, represents another important frontier. These decentralized settings introduce challenges related to synchronization, privacy budgets, and heterogeneity in local models, all of which complicate traditional defense techniques.

In terms of evaluation, the development of task-agnostic benchmarks that assess attack effectiveness, linguistic quality, semantic preservation, and human perception is crucial. Metrics such as readability, emotional tone, and syntactic fluency could be incorporated alongside standard measures. Evaluation frameworks could also consider cross-model transferability, computational overhead, and human detection rates to provide a more comprehensive assessment.

Ethical considerations must remain integral to adversarial NLP research. Adversarial methods should be developed with the intent of improving safety, transparency, and fairness rather than exploitation. Applications in sensitive domains, such as healthcare, law, education, and journalism, demand stricter standards for robustness and explainability. Adversarial attacks can also serve as diagnostic tools to evaluate and mitigate model biases that disproportionately affect certain demographic groups.

Generative AI presents further opportunities for both attack and defense. Advanced generative models, including diffusion-based architectures and autoregressive transformers, could be used to synthesize high-quality adversarial examples that are virtually indistinguishable from natural language. Additionally, prompt-based adversarial manipulation is emerging as a critical concern for prompt-tuned models, where minor alterations to prompts can lead to significant changes in model outputs.

There is also growing interest in exploring adversarial robustness in cross-domain and multi-modal systems. Extending text-based adversarial attacks to multi-modal pipelines, such as text-to-image generation, audio transcription, or visual question answering, would provide insights into system-wide vulnerabilities. Similarly, knowledge-enhanced NLP systems that rely on external databases or retrieval mechanisms could be evaluated for robustness against misinformation or context poisoning attacks.

At a theoretical level, formal frameworks for certified robustness in NLP remain underdeveloped. Research could aim to establish upper bounds on model susceptibility, formal verification protocols, and mathematically grounded definitions of adversarial proximity in linguistic space. Incorporating insights from formal syntax, discourse analysis, and cognitive linguistics may offer more principled foundations for perturbation strategies.

In summary, the development of the SASSP framework contributes meaningfully to the advancement of adversarial text generation, both in terms of technical performance and conceptual design. The continued study of adversarial methods, when guided by responsible practices and supported by robust evaluation, will play a critical role in building NLP systems that are not only intelligent but also resilient, interpretable, and trustworthy in real-world deployments.

References

Carlini, N., Wagner, D. 2017. "Towards Evaluating the Robustness of Neural Networks." In *Proceedings of the IEEE Symposium on Security and Privacy (SP'17)*, pp 39-57, 2017.

Cer, D., Yang, Y., Kong, S-Y., Hua, N., Limtiaco, N., John, R. S., Constant, N., Guajardo-Cespedes, M., Yuan, S., Tar, C., Sung, Y-H., Strope, B., and Kurzweil, R. 2018. "Universal Sentence Encoder." *arXiv Preprint* arXiv:1803.11175.

Devlin, J., Chang, M-W., Lee, K., and Toutanova, K. 2019. "BERT: Pre-training of Deep Bidirectional Transformers for Language

Understanding." In *Proceedings of the 2019 Conference of the North American Chapter of the Association for Computational Linguistics: Human Language Technologies*, 1:4171-4186.

Goodfellow, I. J., Shlens, J., and Szegedy, C. 2015. "Explaining and Harnessing Adversarial Examples." In *Proceedings of the International Conference on Learning Representations (ICLR)*, Poster. arXiv: 1412.6572.

Hugging Face BERT-Base Model Webpage URL: https://huggingface.co/google-bert/bert-base-uncased.

Hugging Face RoBERTa-Base Model Webpage URL: https://huggingface.co/FacebookAI/xlm-roberta-base.

Hugging Face DistilBERT-Base Model Webpage URL: https://huggingface.co/distilbert/distilbert-base-uncased.

Hugging Face DistilRoBERTa-Base Model Webpage URL: https://huggingface.co/distilbert/distilroberta-base.

Hugging Face Transfomer Models Webpage URL: https://huggingface.co/docs/transformers.

Hugging Face Sentence Transformer Models Webpage URL: https://huggingface.co/sentence-transformers.

Jia, R. and Liang, P. 2017. "Adversarial Examples for Evaluating Reading Comprehension Systems." In *Proceedings of the Conference on Empirical Methods in Natural Language Processing (EMNLP)*, 2021–2031.

Jin, D., Jin, Z., Zhou, J. T., and Szolovits, P. 2020. "Is BERT Really Robust? A Strong Baseline for Natural Language Attack on Text Classification and Entailment." In *Proceedings of the AAAI Conference on Artificial Intelligence*, 34(5): 8018-8025.

Koley, A., Satpati, P., Choudhary, I., and Sen, J. 2024. "An Investigation on the Efficiency of Some Text Attack Algorithms." In *Proceedings of the IEEE North Karnataka Subsection Flagship International Conference (NKCon 2024)*, 1–8.

Lei, Y., Cao, Y., Li, D., Zhou, T., Fang, M., and Pechenizkiy, M. 2022. "Phrase-Level Textual Adversarial Attack with Label Preservation." In *Findings of the Association for Computational Linguistics (ACL)*, 1095–1112.

Li, A., Zhang, F., Li, S., Chen, T., Su, P., and Wang, H. 2021. "Efficiently Generating Sentence-Level Adversarial Examples with Seq2Seq Stacked Autoencoder." *Expert Systems with Applications* 213, Part C: 119170.

Li, D., Zhang, Y., Peng, H., Chen, L., Brockett, C., Sun, M-T., and Dolan, B. 2021. "Contextualized Perturbation for Textual Adversarial Attack."

In *Proceedings of the 2021 Conference of the North American Chapter of the Association for Computational Linguistics (NAACL)*, 5053–5069.
Liu, B. and Lane, I. 2018. "Adversarial Learning of Task-Oriented Neural Dialog Models." In *Proceedings of the 19th Annual SIGdial Meeting on Discourse and Dialogue*, 350–359.
Liu, F., Zhang, C., and Zhang, H. 2023. "Towards Transferable Unrestricted Adversarial Examples with Minimum Changes." In *Proceedings of the IEEE Conference on Secure and Trustworthy Machine Learning (SaTML)*, 327–338.
Liu, H., Zhang, Z., Wang, H., and Xue, X. 2022. "Textual Adversarial Attacks by Exchanging Text-Self Words." *International Journal of Intelligent Systems,* 37 (12): 12212–12234.
Multi-Genre NLI Corpus: https://cims.nyu.edu/~sbowman/multinli/
Naber, D., Weber, T., and Richter, F. 2003. "A Rule-Based Style and Grammar Checker." In *Proceedings of the 2nd International Conference on Natural Language Processing (KONVENS 2003)*.
Ni, M., Sun, Z., and Liu, W. 2024. "Fraud's Bargain Attack: Generating Adversarial Text Samples via Word Manipulation Process." *IEEE Transactions on Knowledge and Data Engineering*. (In press)
Pazske, A., Gross, S., Massa, F., Lerer, A., Bradbury, J., Chanan, G., Kileen, T., Lin, Z., Gimelshein, N., Antiga, L., Desmaison, A., Kopf, A., Yang, E., DeVito, Z., Raison, M., Tejani, A., Chilamkurthy, S., Steiner, B., Fang, L., Bai, J., and Chintala, S. 2019. "PyTorch: An Imperative Style, High-Performance Deep Learning Library." In *Advances in Neural Information Processing Systems*, 32:8024-8035, 2019.
Radford, A., Wu, J., Child, R., Luan, D., Amodei, D., and Sutskever, I. 2019. "Language Models Are Unsupervised Multitask Learners." *OpenAI Blog* 1 (8).
Reimers, N. and Gurevych. 2019. "Sentence-BERT: Sentence Embeddings Using Siamese BERT-Networks." In *Proceedings of the 2019 Conference on Empirical Methods in Natural Language Processing and 9th International Joint Conference on Natural Language Processing*, 3982-3992.
Ren, S., Deng, D., He, K., and Xu, W. 2019. "Generating Natural Language Adversarial Examples through Probability Weighted Word Saliency." In *Proceedings of the 57th Annual Meeting of the Association for Computational Linguistics (ACL)*, 1085–1097.
Sanh, V., Debut, L., Chaumond, J., and Wolf, T. 2019. "DistilBERT, A Didilled Version of BERT: Smaller, Faster, Cheaper and Lighter." In *Proceedings of the 5th Workshop on Energy Efficient Machine Learning and Cognitive Computing, NeurIPS* 2019.

Sen, J. 2024. "The FGSM Attack on Image Classification Models and Distillation as its Defense." In Nanda et al. (eds), *Advances in Distributed Computing and Machine Learning (ICADCML 2024)*, 1015: 347-360. Lecture Notes in Networks and Systems, Springer, Singapore.

Sen, J. and Dasgupta, S. 2023. "Adversarial Attacks on Image Classification Models: FGSM and Patch Attacks and their Impact." In Sen, J. and Mayer, J. (eds), *Information Security and Privacy in the Digital World: Some Selected Topics*, IntechOpen, London, UK.

Sen, J., Sen, A., and Chatterjee, A. 2023. "Adversarial Attacks on Image Classification Models: Analysis and Defense." In *Proceedings of the 10th International Conference on Business Analytics and Intelligence (ICBAI 2023)*, Bangalore, India.

Sen, J. and Waghela, H. 2025. "Text-Based Adversarial Attacks and Defense", In Sen, J. (ed) *Data Privacy: Techniques, Applications, and Standards*, IntechOpen, London, UK.

Szegedy, C., Zaremba, W., Sutskever, I., Bruna, J., Erhan, D., Goodfellow, I. J., and Fergus, R. 2014. "Intriguing Properties of Neural Networks." In *Proceedings of the International Conference on Learning Representations (ICLR)*, Poster Track.

Tang, D., Qin, B., and Liu, T. 2015. "Document Modeling with Gated Recurrent Neural Network for Sentiment Classification." In *Proceedings of the 2015 Conference on Empirical Methods in Natural Language Processing (EMNLP 2015)*, 1422-1432.

Waghela, H., Sen, J., and Rakshit, S. 2025. "Saliency Attention and Semantic Similarity-Driven Adversarial Perturbation." In *Data Science and Applications. ICDSA 2024*, Nanda, S. J. et al. (eds), 1237: 461–471. Lecture Notes in Networks and Systems, Springer, Singapore.

Waghela, H., Sen, J., Rakshit, S., and Dasgupta, S. 2024a. "Adversarial Text Generation with Dynamic Contextual Perturbation." In *Proceedings of the 2024 IEEE CALCON 2024*, 1–6. IEEE.

Waghela, H., Sen, J., and Rakshit, S. 2024b. "Adaptive Meta-Learning for Robust Ensemble Defense against Adversarial Attacks." In *Proceedings of the International Conference BAMS-ORSI 2024*.

Waghela, H., Sen, J., and Rakshit, S. 2024c. "Adversarial Resilience in Image Classification: A Hybrid Approach to Defense." In *Proceedings of the 2024 International Conference on Innovation and Intelligence for Informatics, Computing, and Technologies (3ICT 2024)*, 419–426.

Waghela, H., Sen, J., Rakshit, S., and Dasgupta, S. 2024d. "Adversarial Robustness through Dynamic Ensemble Learning." In *Proceedings of the 2024 IEEE Silchar Subsection Conference (SILCON 2024)*, 1–6.

Waghela, H., Sen, J., and Rakshit, S. 2024e. "Robust Image Classification: Defensive Strategies against FGSM and PGD Adversarial Attacks." In *Proceedings of the IEEE Asian Conference on Intelligent Technologies (ACOIT 2024)*, 1 – 7.

Waghela, H., Sen, J., and Rakshit, S. 2024f. "Refining BERT Adversarial Attacks with Projected Gradient Descent." In *Proceedings of the IEEE 4th Asian Conference on Innovations in Technology (ASIANCON 2024)*, 1-7.

Waghela, H., Rakshit, S., and Sen, J. 2024g. "A Modified Word Saliency-Based Adversarial Attack on Text Classification Models." In *Computational Intelligence and Data Analytics*, Frery, A. C. et al. (eds), 371–382. Lecture Notes in Data Engineering and Communications Technologies, 236. Springer.

Wang, A., Singh, A., Michael, J., Hill, F., Levy, O., and Bowman, S. R. 2019. "GLUE: A Multi-Task Benchmark and Analysis Platform for Natural Language Understanding." *arXiv:1804.07461v3*.

Wei, J., Zou, K., Cao, T., Chen, Z., and Huang, Y. 2019. "TextBugger: Generating Adversarial Text against Real-World Applications." In *Proceedings of the ACM SIGSAC Conference on Computer and Communications Security (CCS)*, 1969–1986.

Williams, A., Nangia, N., and Bowman, S. R. 2018. "A Broad-Coverage Challenge Corpus for Sentence Understanding through Inference." In *Proceedings of the 2018 Conference of the North American Chapter of the Association for Computational Linguistics: Human Language Technologies*, 1112-1122.

Wolf, T., Debut, L., Sanh, V., Chaumond, J., Delangue, C., Moi, A., Cistac, P., Rault, T., Louf, R., Funtowicz, M., Davison, J., Shleifer, S., von Platen, P., Ma, C., Jernite, Y., Plu, J., Xu, C., Scao, T. L., Gugger, S., Drame, M., Lhoest, Q., and Rush, A. 2020. "Transfomers: State-of-the-Art Natural Language Processing." In *Proceedings of the 2020 Conference on Empirical Methods in Natural Language Processing: System Demonstrations*, 38-45, 2020.

Yang, X., Gong, Y., Liu, W., Bailey, J., Tao, D., and Liu, W. 2023. "Semantic-Preserving Adversarial Text Attacks." *IEEE Transactions on Sustainable Computing,* 8 (4): 583–595.

Yelp. 2019. "Yelp Open Dataset." https://www.yelp.com/dataset.

Zhang, X., Zhao, J., and LeCun, Y. 2015. "Character-Level Convolutional Networks for Text Classification." In *Proceedings of the 29th International Conference on Neural Information Processing Systems (NeurIPS),* 1: 649 - 657.

Zhao, Z., Dua, D., and Singh, S. 2018. "Generating Natural Adversarial Examples." In *Proceedings of the International Conference on Learning Representations (ICLR 2018)*.

Zhuang, L., Wayne, L., Ya, S., and Jun, Z. 2021. "A Robustly Optimized BERT Pre-training Approach with Post-training." In *Proceedings of the 20th Chinese National Conference on Computational Linguistics*, 1218-1227.

CHAPTER 4

OPTIMIZING BERT ADVERSARIAL ATTACKS THROUGH PROJECTED GRADIENT DESCENT

Introduction

The increasing incidence of adversarial attacks in machine learning has exposed significant vulnerabilities in deep learning systems, with implications for both model robustness and real-world deployment. Initially discovered in the context of image classification, these attacks involve carefully crafted perturbations, often imperceptible to the human eye, that can significantly alter a model's output. The foundational studies by Szegedy et al. and Goodfellow et al. revealed how *deep neural networks* (DNNs) could be manipulated through minimal input changes, prompting a surge of research into attack strategies and defense mechanisms in the computer vision domain. In recent years, similar vulnerabilities have been identified in *natural language processing* (NLP) models, highlighting the need for adversarial robustness beyond the visual domain.

Transferring adversarial methodologies from vision to language, however, poses nontrivial challenges. The core difficulty stems from the discrete nature of text data. While image-based models operate on continuous input spaces where pixel intensities can be smoothly adjusted, NLP models deal with symbolic tokens, characters, or words, rendering gradient-based perturbation strategies more complex to implement. This discreteness complicates the generation of subtle adversarial modifications that preserve syntactic fluency and semantic integrity, yet still induce incorrect classifications.

Early approaches to adversarial text generation experimented with character-level and word-level manipulations. These included techniques such as letter swapping, character insertion or deletion, and synonym substitution. Although such methods demonstrated the feasibility of adversarial attacks in NLP, they often produced examples that were syntactically awkward or semantically distorted, limiting their realism and effectiveness. Subsequent research sought to improve attack quality by incorporating lexical resources and embedding-based similarity measures, enabling substitutions that preserved meaning to a greater degree. Nevertheless, many of these approaches lacked a deeper integration with the internal mechanics of contemporary language models.

Among recent advancements, BERT-Attack has emerged as a representative gradient-based method tailored specifically to transformer-based models. It leverages the architecture and contextual representation capability of BERT (Bidirectional Encoder Representations from Transformers) to craft adversarial examples by perturbing tokens with high saliency, i.e., those that contribute significantly to the classification decision. Using a masked language model, it generates plausible candidate replacements that aim to fool the classifier while preserving overall sentence structure. Despite its efficacy, the original BERT-Attack framework exhibits certain limitations that restrict its adaptability and semantic precision.

One notable constraint of BERT-Attack lies in its reliance on a fixed perturbation budget. This parameter determines the maximum number of tokens that can be altered in a given input, aiming to ensure the adversarial text remains close to the original. However, this fixed budget is applied uniformly across all inputs, disregarding the variation in contextual sensitivity and semantic load of individual words. Consequently, some tokens that are semantically pivotal may be altered needlessly, while other vulnerable regions might be underutilized, limiting the optimality and generalizability of the attack.

Another shortcoming concerns the limited attention paid to semantic similarity between the original and adversarial examples. The original BERT-Attack framework emphasizes classification evasion but does not sufficiently enforce constraints to preserve meaning. This oversight can result in adversarial sentences that are grammatically awkward, semantically incoherent, or even nonsensical—compromising their utility in realistic evaluation settings. For adversarial examples to serve as meaningful tools for robustness analysis or model diagnosis, they must preserve human interpretability and relevance to the task at hand.

To overcome these limitations, an enhanced framework is proposed that integrates *Projected Gradient Descent* (PGD) into the adversarial generation pipeline. PGD is a well-established optimization technique widely used in adversarial research to generate perturbations that are both effective and bounded. By iteratively applying small, controlled perturbations within a defined constraint set, PGD enables more refined exploration of the input space. When adapted to NLP, PGD facilitates the creation of adversarial examples that target the most sensitive components of the model's decision process, while maintaining a high degree of semantic and syntactic fidelity.

The resulting method, referred to as PGD-BERT-Attack, extends the capabilities of the original BERT-Attack by incorporating a flexible and dynamic perturbation mechanism. Unlike static budget constraints, PGD allows perturbation strength to be modulated based on contextual and model-specific cues, offering greater adaptability across diverse datasets and classification tasks. Furthermore, by integrating semantic similarity filters, the framework prioritizes candidate substitutions that preserve the meaning and fluency of the original sentence, thereby enhancing the quality and plausibility of generated adversarial examples.

The experimental validation of this method is conducted on benchmark datasets of NLP and NLI, such as Yelp, AG News, IMDB, Fake News, *Stanford Natural Language Inferenc*e (SNLI), and *Multi-Genre Natural Language Inference* (MNLI). The results demonstrate that PGD-BERT-Attack achieves substantial reductions in model accuracy while producing adversarial texts that retain high semantic alignment with the original inputs. Comparative analyses against baseline methods, including the original BERT-Attack, highlight the improved flexibility, efficacy, and naturalness of the proposed approach.

This chapter contributes to the growing body of work in adversarial NLP by addressing two core challenges: the need for adaptive perturbation mechanisms and the imperative of maintaining semantic and linguistic integrity. By combining gradient-based token importance, contextual awareness, and semantic filtering with the flexibility of PGD, the method advances the state of adversarial attack strategies for BERT-based classifiers. In doing so, it offers a more realistic and principled framework for stress-testing modern NLP models and understanding their vulnerabilities under adversarial conditions.

The remainder of this chapter is organized as follows. The section titled *Foundations of Adversarial Attacks in NLP* introduces the theoretical motivations and challenges underlying adversarial perturbations in natural language processing, emphasizing the discrete nature of text and the complexities it introduces in crafting effective attacks. The next section, *Related Work*, surveys key developments in the field of adversarial text attacks, including character-level, word-level, and sentence-level perturbations, as well as gradient-based and semantic-preserving approaches. The section *BERT-on-BERT Attack* provides a detailed account of the BERT-Attack framework, explaining how an attacker BERT model is used to generate adversarial samples for a victim BERT model. The proposed method is then presented in *PGD-Integrated BERT-on-BERT Attack*, where Projected Gradient Descent is incorporated into the BERT-Attack pipeline to enable adaptive perturbations guided by gradient signals and semantic similarity constraints, leading to more effective and imperceptible adversarial examples. This is followed by an extensive *Experimental Results* section where empirical results are reported on a diverse set of text classification and natural language inference tasks using datasets such as Yelp, IMDB, AG News, FAKE, SNLI, and MNLI. Finally, the chapter concludes with *Conclusion and Future Directions*, which synthesizes the main contributions, reflects on the broader implications of adversarial robustness in NLP, and provides some directions for future exploration.

Foundations of Adversarial Attacks in NLP

The study of adversarial attacks in NLP has gained significant momentum in recent years, revealing both the capabilities and the vulnerabilities of state-of-the-art deep learning models. The concept of adversarial attacks originally emerged from the domain of computer vision, where slight perturbations to input images, often imperceptible to the human eye, were shown to cause dramatic misclassifications in powerful convolutional neural networks. These findings demonstrated that even the most accurate models could be fundamentally fragile, raising important concerns about their robustness and generalizability.

Translating these ideas to NLP, however, introduces a unique set of challenges. Unlike pixel-level perturbations in images, which can be smoothly modified in continuous space, text is inherently discrete, symbolic, and structured. Words and characters represent specific semantic units, and even minor alterations can disrupt grammaticality or drastically alter meaning. As a result, generating adversarial text examples requires balancing three critical objectives: preserving semantic coherence, maintaining grammatical correctness, and ensuring that the perturbations are sufficient to mislead the model.

The fundamental motivation for studying adversarial attacks in NLP lies in the desire to better understand how language models process information and where their decision boundaries lie. Beyond theoretical interest, adversarial examples have practical relevance in evaluating the security and reliability of NLP systems used in high-stakes domains such as healthcare, finance, legal document analysis, and content moderation. In such contexts, the ability of an adversary to subtly manipulate input and produce incorrect predictions may have serious consequences.

In the NLP domain, early work on adversarial attacks focused on character-level manipulations, such as swapping letters, adding typos, or replacing characters with visually similar alternatives. While these attacks could confuse certain models, they often resulted in text that was obviously corrupted and easily detected by humans or rule-based spell-checkers. Subsequently, attention shifted toward word-level perturbations, wherein individual words were replaced with synonyms or semantically similar alternatives. This approach aimed to retain fluency while introducing enough variation to alter the model's output. Techniques such as word saliency scoring and embedding-based similarity measures were commonly used to guide the selection of candidate replacements. These methods improved attack quality, but they were still limited in their ability to preserve deeper contextual and syntactic coherence.

The advent of transformer-based models, particularly BERT, marked a turning point in the development of both NLP systems and adversarial strategies. BERT introduced a bidirectional, attention-based mechanism for language understanding, enabling more nuanced modeling of context and meaning. At the same time, its internal representations became new points of vulnerability that attackers could exploit. Because BERT attends to all tokens in an input simultaneously, the influence of any particular word on the model's output depends on its contextual significance, as determined by attention scores and gradient signals.

Adversarial attacks targeting BERT-based models have therefore evolved to take advantage of these internal mechanisms. For example, methods like BERT-Attack use masked language modeling to generate plausible token substitutions, guided by the gradients of the model's loss function. These attacks attempt to identify words that most influence the model's decision and replace them with alternatives that are syntactically plausible but semantically disruptive. Despite their success, such approaches often overlook key factors such as sentence-level semantic preservation and grammatical fluency.

To address these limitations, researchers have proposed incorporating semantic similarity constraints into the attack generation process. By evaluating cosine similarity between sentence embeddings, derived from models like the Universal Sentence Encoder or Sentence-BERT, one can filter out candidate perturbations that deviate too far from the original meaning. This ensures that adversarial inputs remain realistic and are less likely to be detected by human readers or downstream validation systems. Additionally, attention-based masking techniques have been introduced to prevent perturbation of syntactically critical or contextually central tokens, preserving the sentence's grammatical integrity.

Another important aspect of adversarial attack design in NLP is the notion of a perturbation budget. This refers to a constraint on the number or proportion of tokens that may be altered in the input. Fixed-budget attacks impose a hard limit, which is often set to ensure imperceptibility and naturalness. However, such fixed thresholds may be suboptimal across different inputs or tasks, as some sentences may tolerate more aggressive perturbation than others. Consequently, there is growing interest in adaptive methods that vary the perturbation budget based on token sensitivity or contextual importance.

Evaluating the effectiveness of adversarial attacks in NLP presents its own set of challenges. Common metrics include *attack success rate* (ASR), which measures how often the model's prediction is changed by the attack; semantic similarity scores, which assess how closely the adversarial example retains the meaning of the original; and fluency or perplexity scores, which reflect grammatical correctness and naturalness. Some researchers also consider transferability—the extent to which adversarial examples crafted for one model can deceive others—as a measure of generalizability. However, balancing these diverse criteria is non-trivial, and there is no universally accepted benchmark for adversarial robustness in NLP. As a result, many studies report a combination of metrics and compare against multiple baselines to provide a comprehensive view of attack quality.

The study of adversarial attacks is not merely an academic pursuit. It has profound implications for the design of secure, interpretable, and generalizable NLP systems. By revealing how models can be manipulated, adversarial research informs the development of more robust architectures and effective defense mechanisms. Furthermore, it serves as a foundation for understanding the limits of current models and for guiding future improvements in language representation, training, and evaluation. In this broader context, adversarial attacks act as a lens through which to examine both the strengths and the blind spots of modern NLP technology.

Related Work

The domain of adversarial attacks in machine learning has witnessed remarkable growth over the past decade, originating in computer vision and gradually permeating NLP. Szegedy et al. and Goodfellow et al. first revealed the vulnerability of deep neural networks to carefully crafted, imperceptible input perturbations, sparking a surge of interest in adversarial robustness (Goodfellow et al., 2015; Szegedy et al., 2014). These early explorations, such as the Fast Gradient Sign Method (FGSM), laid the groundwork for understanding how neural models can be manipulated to produce erroneous predictions.

In the NLP domain, early studies by Liang et al., Samanta & Mehta, and Alzantot et al. demonstrated that even minor perturbations, such as character swaps, word insertions, or synonym replacements, could cause significant misclassifications in text classification models (Liang et al., 2018; Samanta & Mehta, 2017; Alzantot et al., 2018). These methods introduced discrete perturbation strategies that differed fundamentally from those used in computer vision. However, they often failed to ensure grammatical correctness and semantic preservation.

To address this, Li et al. proposed the BERT-Attack, a method leveraging BERT's contextual embeddings and masked language modeling capabilities to select perturbations that remain semantically close to the original text (Li et al., 2020). Jia and Liang designed adversarial examples to fool reading comprehension systems by modifying passages and questions subtly (Jia & Liang, 2017). Ribeiro et al. contributed the concept of semantically equivalent adversarial rules to uncover model biases (Ribeiro et al., 2018). Ebrahimi et al. introduced HotFlip, a white-box attack method that uses gradients to perturb characters and tokens effectively, further showcasing the vulnerability of text classification systems (Ebrahimi et al., 2018).

Carlini and Wagner provided a rigorous framework for evaluating adversarial robustness, applicable across domains, including text and vision (Carlini & Wagner, 2017). Guo et al. focused on neural dialog systems, demonstrating how adversarial dialogues can derail conversation models (Guo et al., 2019). Wei et al. introduced TextBugger, a real-world attack that combined multiple perturbation strategies to evade NLP systems in production (Wei et al., 2019). Ren et al. presented the *Probability Weighted*

Word Saliency (PWWS) technique to identify critical tokens for targeted attacks, laying the foundation for saliency-based perturbations (Ren et al., 2019).

More recent methods like TextGuise by Chang et al. introduced feedback-driven adaptive strategies for generating dynamic adversarial examples (Chang et al., 2023). Yang et al. explored semantic-preserving adversarial attacks that minimize human-detectable discrepancies (Yang et al., 2023). Liu et al. advanced the concept of transferability, proposing techniques that produce adversarial examples that generalize across architectures and datasets (Liu et al., 2023).

Recent developments in adversarial machine learning have significantly progressed through the integration of semantic similarity constraints, dynamic perturbation strategies, and ensemble-based robustness mechanisms, applied across both textual and visual modalities. A substantial sequence of contributions by Waghela, Sen, Rakshit, and their collaborators (Koley et al., 2024; Sen, 2024; Sen & Dasgupta, 2023; Sen et al., 2023; Sen & Waghela, 2025; Waghela et al., 2024a–g; 2025) has enriched this growing field by introducing context-aware and linguistically grounded adversarial frameworks. Their research in the text domain leverages saliency-driven attention, BERT-based contextual embeddings, and semantic similarity metrics to craft adversarial examples that are not only syntactically valid but also semantically coherent. In parallel, their work on adversarial robustness in image classification explores hybrid defensive architectures and ensemble-based meta-learning approaches that aim to resist perturbations across a variety of threat models. This dual focus on both text and image modalities allows for the development of attack strategies that generalize well across domains, as well as defenses that maintain robustness irrespective of input type or model architecture. Together, these contributions present a comprehensive framework for advancing adversarial learning while ensuring a balance between attack efficacy, interpretability, and cross-domain applicability.

Qi et al. extended this concept of saliency by incorporating adaptive gradient-based word saliency (Qi et al., 2024). Pruthi et al. introduced a data influence tracing method to understand training sample impact, indirectly informing adversarial sample sensitivity (Pruthi et al., 2020). Zang et al. framed word-level adversarial attacks as a combinatorial optimization problem, advancing the theoretical underpinnings of text perturbation (Zang et al., 2020).

Further work by Ni et al., Sato et al., and Chen et al. explored word manipulation and document-level adversarial perturbations (Niu et al., 2023; Sato et al., 2018; Chen et al., 2023). Liu et al. and Gao et al. developed black-box and white-box strategies using word swapping and text-self word exchanges (Liu et al., 2022; Gao et al., 2018). Lei et al. introduced phrase-level adversarial attacks with label preservation, while Li et al. employed seq2seq autoencoders for sentence-level perturbations (Lei et al., 2022; Li et al., 2023). Techniques from image adversarial research, like DeepFool, have also inspired sentence-level manipulations in text (Moosavi-Dezfooliet al., 2016).

Syntactic perturbation methods were advanced by Iyyer et al. using paraphrase networks, and Min et al., who showed how syntactic augmentation can enhance model robustness (Iyyer et al., 2018; Min et al., 2020). Contextual attacks have been introduced by Li et al. through contextualized perturbation, and Deshpande et al., who proposed *conditional semantic similarity* (C-STS) for evaluating adversarial plausibility (Li et al., 2021; Deshpande et al., 2023). Devlin et al.'s introduction of BERT underpins most modern NLP models susceptible to such attacks (Devlin et al., 2019). The robustness of BERT has been critically examined by Jin et al. and contested by Hauser et al., who argue its resistance to certain word substitution attacks (Jin et al., 2020; Hauser et al., 2023).

From a defense perspective, Madry et al. contributed the concept of *Projected Gradient Descent* (PGD), which has been adapted for adversarial training in text settings (Madry et al., 2018). He et al. introduced residual learning, which influenced robust model architecture designs (He et al., 2016).

Despite the sophistication of these methods, several challenges persist. Many attack strategies still lack semantic control, producing grammatically incoherent or semantically implausible outputs. Additionally, models remain brittle under subtle perturbations, necessitating more resilient architectures and adversarial training protocols. The literature also highlights the growing need for universal adversarial benchmarks and transferable attack schemes that reflect real-world scenarios.

In summary, the landscape of textual adversarial attacks is rich with diverse methodologies ranging from white-box gradient-based techniques to black-box transfer attacks and adaptive perturbation frameworks. This chapter builds on these foundational and contemporary works to enhance adversarial efficacy through improved semantic fidelity, targeting BERT-based classifiers with refined perturbation techniques that incorporate PGD.

The BERT-on-BERT Attack

In recent years, *Bidirectional Encoder Representations from Transformers* (BERT) has revolutionized the field of NLP by achieving state-of-the-art performance across a broad spectrum of language understanding tasks such as sentiment analysis, question answering, and sentence classification. Despite its outstanding capabilities, BERT has been shown to be vulnerable to *adversarial attacks*, maliciously crafted input examples that subtly perturb the original input in ways that deceive the model into making incorrect predictions.

One of the most influential contributions in this area is the *BERT-Attack* proposed by Li et al., which innovatively utilizes a separate instance of the BERT model itself to craft adversarial examples against another BERT-based classifier (Li et al., 2020). This strategy, often referred to as a *BERT-on-BERT attack*, leverages the inherent understanding capabilities of BERT to identify and perturb sensitive tokens in an input sequence, thus deceiving the target (victim) model. The attack process consists of several distinct stages, each playing a critical role in generating semantically similar but adversarially effective inputs.

***Step 1: Gradient-Based Token Importance Estimation*:** The attack begins with the computation of token-level importance scores by analyzing the gradient of the victim model's loss function with respect to the input tokens. Given a clean input sequence $X = \{w_1, w_2, \dots, w_n\}$, the attacker BERT model uses backpropagation to compute how much each token contributed to the model's output. Specifically, the gradient $\nabla_X L(f(X), y)$, where $f(X)$ is the predicted label and y is the true label, helps determine which words are most influential in the classification. These gradients serve as saliency scores that guide the next steps in identifying which tokens are optimal targets for perturbation.

***Step 2: Masking and Candidate Generation Using BERT*:** After identifying the most sensitive tokens, the attacker proceeds to *mask these words* in the original sentence and uses the BERT *masked language model* (MLM) to generate top-*k* replacement candidates for each masked token. This step is grounded in BERT's pre-training on a massive corpus to predict masked words in context. The MLM mechanism ensures that replacement tokens are syntactically and semantically plausible, maintaining the coherence of the modified sentence.

Step 3: Candidate Scoring and Substitution: For each sensitive token w_i, the set of k candidate substitutes $\{c_1, c_2, ..., c_k\}$ generated by BERT is evaluated using a scoring function that combines the predicted probability of the replacement and its effect on the classification output. The attacker selects the candidate that maximally increases the loss function (or changes the predicted label). The objective is to iteratively substitute tokens in a greedy fashion such that each substitution drives the model further toward misclassification. The process is repeated until the model prediction flips or a perturbation budget is exhausted.

Step 4: Construction of the Adversarial Sample: Once the best substitutions are selected, they are applied sequentially to the original input, resulting in the adversarial example X_{adv}. This example is then submitted to the victim BERT classifier. If $f(X_{adv} \neq y)$, the attack is considered successful. To ensure imperceptibility, the number of modifications is usually restricted to a certain fraction (e.g., no more than 200% of tokens), and constraints such as semantic similarity or syntactic fluency are applied.

Step 5: Constraint Enforcement: A key requirement for effective adversarial examples in NLP is that they remain semantically equivalent and grammatically sound. To this end, the attack imposes lexical and semantic constraints during candidate substitution. Some of these constraints are as follows:

- Perturbation budget constraints (e.g., maximum number or percentage of modified tokens),
- Embedding similarity thresholds to retain semantic closeness between original and modified tokens,
- POS tagging filters to avoid replacing structurally important tokens like proper nouns or stopwords.

These measures are critical for ensuring that adversarial examples remain undetectable to human readers while still deceiving machine classifiers.

Step 6: Evaluation Metrics: The effectiveness of the BERT-Attack is assessed using several quantitative metrics, including the following:

- *Attack Success Rate* (ASR): The proportion of examples for which the adversarial sample causes misclassification.

- *Perplexity* or *Fluency Score*: Measures the grammaticality and fluency of the adversarial sentence using language models.
- *Semantic Similarity Score*: Evaluates how close the adversarial input is to the original input using sentence embeddings (e.g., Universal Sentence Encoder or BERTScore).
- *Number of Modifications*: Captures the minimality of the attack in terms of how many tokens were changed.
- *Transferability*: Indicates whether adversarial examples crafted against one model are effective against other models.

Summary and Limitations: Overall, the BERT-on-BERT attack represents a powerful and targeted adversarial strategy that exploits BERT's contextual representation to identify and perturb the most vulnerable aspects of input texts. However, this approach is not without limitations. One significant drawback is its *reliance on discrete token replacement*, which can sometimes yield grammatically awkward or semantically implausible adversarial samples. Moreover, the attack does not leverage *gradient-based optimization methods* that operate in the embedding space, which could offer more fine-grained control over perturbation generation.

This limitation serves as the underlying motivation for a refined approach that seeks to overcome the discrete nature of token substitutions and the lack of fine-grained control in perturbation generation. By incorporating *Projected Gradient Descent* (PGD) into the original BERT-Attack framework, the enhanced method introduces a more flexible and continuous perturbation strategy. This integration allows for better alignment with semantic preservation objectives while maximizing adversarial impact. The modified attack aims to generate adversarial examples that not only deceive the classifier more effectively but also maintain linguistic coherence and contextual relevance, crucial requirements for real-world adversarial robustness evaluation in NLP.

PGD-Integrated BERT-on-BERT Attack

The original BERT-Attack approach, while powerful in generating adversarial examples for BERT-based classifiers, exhibits several limitations—most notably its reliance on a fixed perturbation budget and its inadequate consideration of semantic preservation. To address these constraints, a refined adversarial attack strategy is introduced through the integration of PGD into the BERT-Attack framework. This enhanced method, termed *PGD-integrated BERT-on-BERT Attack*, involves a series of well-defined stages that collectively enhance the stealth, coherence, and effectiveness of adversarial text perturbations.

Step 1: Input Representation and Tokenization: The process begins by converting the raw input text into a sequence of tokens using the tokenizer associated with the BERT architecture. This tokenization process maps the original input into subword units or token IDs that can be processed by the model. Each token is embedded into a high-dimensional vector space, enabling gradient-based optimization methods to operate effectively.

Step 2: Initialization of Adversarial Perturbation: The PGD-integrated attack initializes the adversarial perturbation process by defining an initial perturbation vector, typically set to zero or a small random noise, added to the token embeddings. This initialization defines the starting point of the adversarial search in the embedding space, constrained by a perturbation budget ε.

Step 3: Iterative Gradient-Based Update: Adversarial perturbations are generated iteratively through gradient ascent. At each iteration, the gradient of the model's loss function with respect to the input tokens is computed. The input is then updated in the direction that maximizes the loss, according to the PGD update rule (4-1):

$$X' = Clip_{\varepsilon}(X + \alpha * sign(\nabla_X J(\theta, X, y))) \tag{4-1}$$

Here, X is the original input, X' is the perturbed input, α is the step size, $J(\theta, X, y)$ denotes the loss function of the model with parameters θ, and y is the true label. The clipping operation ensures that the perturbation remains within the defined ε-ball.

Step 4: Projection onto the Feasible Input Space: After each gradient update, the perturbed token embeddings are projected back onto a feasible input space to ensure compliance with human imperceptibility and syntactic validity. This projection step preserves structural fidelity to the original input, preventing extreme or unnatural changes that might violate linguistic constraints.

Step 5: Semantic Similarity Constraint Enforcement: To maintain contextual relevance, the method incorporates a semantic similarity constraint. Cosine similarity between the embeddings of the original and perturbed inputs is computed using a *semantic encoder* (such as BERT or SBERT). An additional penalty term is included in the optimization objective to discourage semantic divergence. This ensures that the adversarial example not only fools the classifier but also remains semantically consistent and grammatically coherent.

***Step 6: Adaptive Perturbation Budgeting*:** In contrast to the fixed budget used in the original BERT-Attack, the proposed approach adopts an adaptive strategy. The perturbation magnitude for each token is modulated based on its contribution to the model's prediction and its semantic salience. Tokens deemed more important (e.g., high-saliency or high-attention tokens) receive minimal perturbations, while those with lesser impact can be modified more aggressively, enabling efficient exploitation of the model's decision boundaries.

***Step 7: Termination and Early Stopping*:** The iterative process continues until a predefined termination condition is met. This could be based on reaching a maximum number of iterations, achieving successful misclassification, or observing minimal change in the loss function across iterations. An early stopping mechanism may be employed to prevent overfitting the perturbation and to preserve computational efficiency.

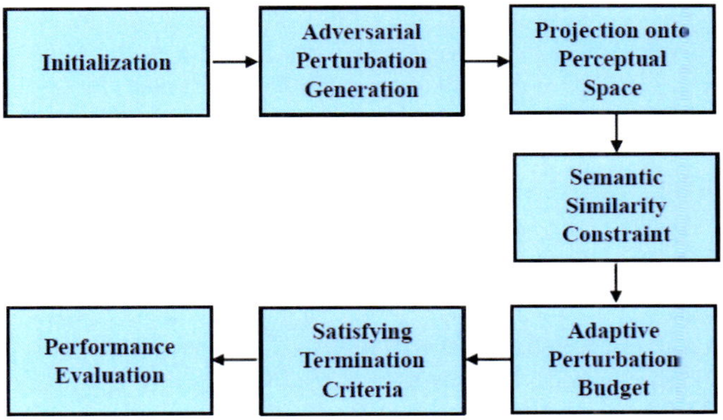

Figure 4-1. The workflow of the adversarial perturbation generation process incorporates semantic similarity and adaptive perturbation constraints. The process begins with initialization, followed by perturbation generation and projection into a perturbed space. Semantic similarity constraints and adaptive budgeting ensure the perturbations remain imperceptible and semantically coherent, culminating in termination checks and performance evaluation.

***Step 8: Generation of Final Adversarial Example*:** Once the termination condition is satisfied, the final adversarial example is constructed by decoding the perturbed token embeddings back into human-readable text.

This output is then evaluated for syntactic correctness, semantic plausibility, and attack effectiveness. The design workflow of the proposed scheme is depicted in Figure 4-1.

Through these carefully orchestrated steps, the PGD-integrated BERT-on-BERT Attack not only enhances the adversarial success rate but also ensures the linguistic and semantic quality of the adversarial samples. This approach provides a powerful and flexible framework for probing the vulnerabilities of transformer-based models and sets the foundation for future work on adversarial robustness in natural language processing.

Experimental Results

The evaluation of adversarial attack methods is a multidimensional exercise that requires analyzing not only the raw effectiveness in terms of success rates, but also the subtle trade-offs involving perturbation size, semantic consistency, query efficiency, and cross-model generalizability. To this end, the PGD-integrated BERT-on-BERT Attack (henceforth referred to as PGD-BERT) is extensively benchmarked against two prominent baselines, BERT-Attack proposed by Li et al. (Li et al., 2020), and the Genetic Algorithm (GA)-based adversarial attack by Alzantot et al. (Alzantot et al., 2018), across a suite of classification and inference tasks. The experimental design is structured to offer a comprehensive view of the performance, encompassing six datasets, four task categories, and multiple model architectures.

The datasets used for evaluation are chosen to reflect diverse challenges in natural language processing. Yelp (Tang et al., 2015; Yelp Open Dataset), IMDB (Maas et al., 2011), AG News (Zhang et al., 2015), and the FAKE News dataset (Bisaillon, 2020) are employed for binary and multiclass text classification, while SNLI (Bowman et al., 2015; Stanford NLP Page) and MNLI (Multi-Genre NLI Corpus Dataset; Williams et al., 2018) are used for *natural language inference* (NLI). These datasets differ in complexity, domain specificity, label granularity, and linguistic characteristics, offering a robust testbed for analyzing the adaptability and resilience of the proposed attack method. Notably, each dataset introduces its own linguistic priors and statistical characteristics. For example, Yelp and IMDB comprise informal user-generated content, while AG News and MNLI consist of more structured, editorial prose. This variety enables a rigorous stress-testing of the adversarial schemes across varying levels of syntactic noise and semantic ambiguity.

The analysis begins with a comparison of classification accuracies under clean and adversarial conditions. As shown in Table 4-1, PGD-BERT causes a substantial drop in accuracy across all datasets, often reducing classifier performance to below 10%. For instance, on the Yelp dataset, the accuracy drops from 95.6% to just 4.2%, and on IMDB, from 90.9% to 8.2%. Such dramatic degradation underscores the potency of the attack in misleading the classifier with minimal semantic compromise. In contrast, while BERT-Attack also performs well, its post-attack accuracies are slightly higher (5.1% for Yelp and 11.4% for IMDB), indicating marginally less disruption. The GA-based attack by Alzantot shows even higher residual accuracies (31.0% on Yelp and 45.7% on IMDB), revealing a comparative weakness in fooling the models despite higher query costs and perturbation sizes.

Table 4-1. Evaluation of Adversarial Attack Impact on Text Classification Tasks: Model Accuracy and Perturbation Rate across Datasets

Dataset	Attack Method	Accuracy (%) (In Absence of Attack)	Accuracy (%) (In Presence of Attack)	Perturbation Rate (%)
Yelp	PGD-BERT	95.6	**4.2**	**3.8**
	BERT-Attack		5.1	4.1
	Alzantot et al.		31.0	10.1
IMDB	PGD-BERT	90.9	**8.2**	**2.9**
	BERT-Attack		11.4	4.4
	Alzantot et al.		45.7	4.9
AG	PGD-BERT	94.2	**7.4**	**9.3**
	BERT-Attack		10.6	15.4
	Alzantot et al.		51.0	16.9
Fake	PGD-BERT	97.8	**12.3**	**1.1**
	BERT-Attack		15.5	1.1
	Alzantot et al.		58.3	1.1

Table 4-2. Evaluation of Adversarial Attack Impact on Text Classification Tasks: Query Number and Semantic Similarity across Datasets

Dataset	Attack Method	Query Number	Semantic Similarity
Yelp	PGD-BERT	254	**0.92**
	BERT-Attack	273	0.77
	Alzantot et al.	6137	--
IMDB	PGD-BERT	358	**0.94**
	BERT-Attack	454	0.86
	Alzantot et al.	6493	--
AG	PGD-BERT	178	**0.94**
	BERT-Attack	213	0.63
	Alzantot et al.	3495	--
Fake	PGD-BERT	968	**0.93**
	BERT-Attack	1558	0.81
	Alzantot et al.	28508	--

Perturbation percentage, defined as the proportion of modified tokens in the input text, is another critical indicator of attack efficiency. Lower values signify that the adversarial sample remains closer to the original, making it harder for both humans and automated detectors to flag anomalies. PGD-BERT excels on this metric, with perturbation rates as low as 1.1% on the FAKE News dataset and under 3.8% on Yelp. These low rates demonstrate that the attack can introduce high semantic disruption with minimal lexical alteration. The corresponding figures for BERT-Attack are slightly higher, and Alzantot's method requires far more extensive perturbations (up to 16.9% on AG), reflecting inefficiency and lack of precision in sample generation.

Semantic similarity scores, presented in Table 4-2, provide further insights into the quality of adversarial samples. Using cosine similarity between contextual embeddings of original and adversarial sentences, PGD-BERT consistently achieves values above 0.90, indicating near-preservation of meaning. For example, it records 0.94 similarity on the IMDB dataset and 0.92 on Yelp. BERT-Attack trails behind with scores ranging between 0.63 and 0.86. The Alzantot method does not report semantic similarity metrics, but its higher perturbation levels suggest a significant drift in textual meaning. The superior semantic preservation of PGD-BERT validates its design objective: crafting adversarial examples that are not just functionally deceptive to machines but also linguistically plausible to humans.

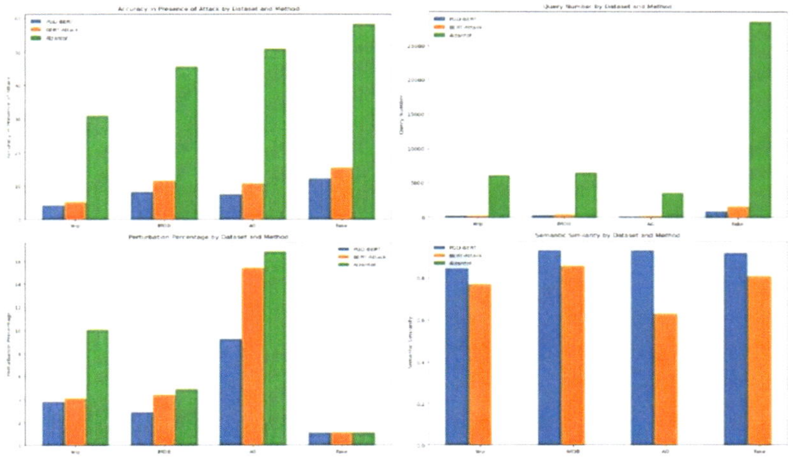

Figure 4-2. Comparison of adversarial attack performance across text classification tasks, highlighting accuracy, perturbation rates, query counts, and semantic similarity metrics on multiple datasets.

An equally important aspect is the number of queries required to generate successful adversarial samples. This metric impacts the real-world feasibility of black-box attacks, especially when access to model gradients or outputs is limited. PGD-BERT demonstrates high efficiency, requiring only a few hundred queries across datasets—ranging from 178 on AG News to 968 on FAKE News—while BERT-Attack requires more, and the Alzantot GA-based method is significantly more expensive, with query counts reaching up to 28,508. This highlights PGD-BERT's advantage in computational efficiency, making it more suitable for time-constrained or resource-bounded adversarial scenarios.

Figure 4-2 presents a comparative analysis of adversarial attack performance across multiple datasets, evaluating the models based on accuracy under attack, query complexity, perturbation rate, and semantic similarity preservation for three different attack strategies.

Table 4-3. Adversarial Attack Performance on Natural Language Inference Tasks: Accuracy (with and without Attack) and Perturbation Percentage on SNLI and MNLI Datasets.

Dataset	Attack Method	Accuracy (%) in Absence of Attack	Accuracy (%) in Presence of Attack	Perturbation Rate (%)
SNLI	PGD-BERT	89.4 (H/P)	**3.2/12.6**	**8.2/6.3**
	BERT-Attack		7.4/16.1	12.4/9.3
	Alzantot et al.		14.7/--	20.8/--
MNLI Matched	PGD-BERT	85.1 (H/P)	**5.3/10.8**	**7.4/6.7**
	BERT-Attack		7.9/11.9	8.8/7.9
	Alzantot et al.		21.80/--	18.2/--
MNLI Mismatched	PGD-BERT	82.1 (H/P)	**5.1/10.6**	**7.2/7.0**
	BERT-Attack		7/13.7	8.0/7.1
	Alzantot et al.		20.9/--	19.0/--

The evaluation of PGD-BERT is extended to natural language inference (NLI) tasks using SNLI and MNLI datasets. These tasks are inherently more complex as they involve reasoning over pairs of sentences. The PGD-BERT approach is tested separately on the premise and hypothesis components, as shown in Tables 4-3 and 4-4. The attack significantly reduces inference accuracy: on SNLI, the hypothesis accuracy drops from 89.4% to 3.2%, and the premise from 89.4% to 12.6%. The MNLI dataset shows similar trends with matched and mismatched subsets, both experiencing large drops in accuracy under attack. Importantly, these drops are achieved with moderate perturbation percentages and strong semantic consistency, suggesting that PGD-BERT's strength generalizes beyond simple classification tasks to more semantically rich tasks like entailment detection.

Table 4-4. Adversarial Attack Efficiency on Natural Language Inference Tasks: Number of Queries and Semantic Similarity on SNLI and MNLI Datasets

Dataset	Attack Method	Query Number	Semantic Similarity
SNLI	PGD-BERT	**12/18**	**0.75/0.82**
	BERT-Attack	16/30	0.40/0.55
	Alzantot et al.	613/--	--
MNLI Mached	PGD-BERT	**12/21**	**0.72/0.87**
	BERT-Attack	19/44	0.55/0.68
	Alzantot et al.	692/--	--
MNLI Mismached	PGD-BERT	**17/28**	**0.70/79**
	BERT-Attack	24/43	0.53/0.69
	Alzantot et al.	737/--	--

Transferability is another key dimension of evaluation. Real-world adversaries often operate in black-box conditions, targeting models without full access to internal parameters. Tables 4-5 and 4-6 report the transferability performance, where adversarial samples generated from one model (e.g., BERT-Base) are tested on others like BERT-Large, Word-LSTM, and Enhanced Sequential Language Model (ESIM). Across all configurations, PGD-BERT outperforms BERT-Attack in reducing the accuracy of target models, while also requiring smaller perturbation budgets. On the IMDB dataset, for instance, PGD-BERT reduces BERT-Large accuracy to 9.7%, compared to 12.4% by BERT-Attack, with a lower perturbation percentage (1.7% vs. 2.9%). This illustrates the high transferability and subtlety of PGD-BERT-generated examples.

Figure 4-3 illustrates the comparative performance of various adversarial attacks on natural language inference (NLI) tasks, highlighting the differences in accuracy degradation and perturbation levels across the SNLI and MNLI datasets.

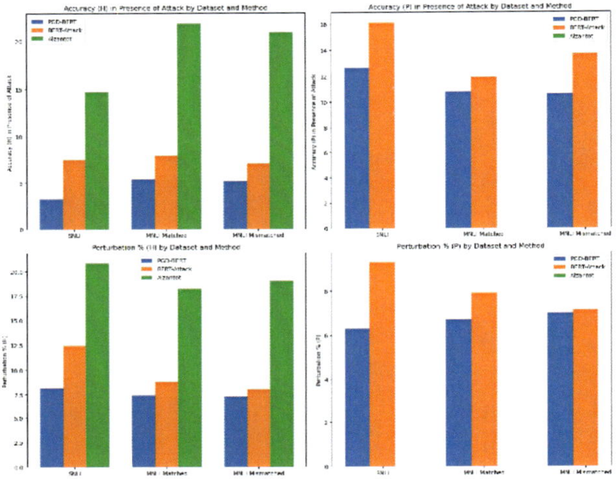

Figure 4-3. Comparative evaluation of adversarial attacks on NLI tasks: Accuracy under attack and perturbation percentage across different datasets and methods.

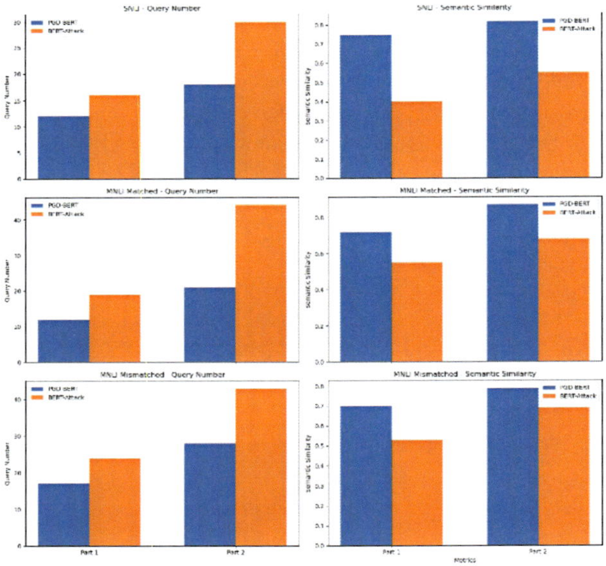

Figure 4-4. Comparison of adversarial attacks on NLI tasks: Query counts and semantic similarity across different datasets.

Figure 4-4 presents a comparative analysis of adversarial attacks on NLI tasks in terms of query efficiency and semantic similarity, demonstrating how different methods vary in the number of queries required and the preservation of semantic content.

Table 4-5. Transferability of Adversarial Attacks: Accuracy of Alternative Models under BERT-Attack and PGD-BERT across Multiple Datasets

Dataset	Model	Original Accuracy	Attacked Accuracy Under BERT	Accuracy Under PGD-BERT Attack
Yelp	BERT-Large	97.9	8.2	6.1
	Word-LSTM	96.0	1.1	0.8
IMDB	BERT-Large	98.2	12.4	9.7
	Word-LSTM	89.8	10.2	8.6
MNLI Matched	BERT-Large	86.4	13.2	11.4
	ESIM	76.2	9.6	8.3

Table 4-6. Transferability of Adversarial Attacks: Perturbation Percentage on Alternative Models under BERT-Attack and PGD-BERT across Datasets

Dataset	Model	Perturbation % Under BERT	Perturbation % Under PGD-BERT
Yelp	BERT-Large	4.1	4.0
	Word-LSTM	4.7	3.2
IMDB	BERT-Large	2.9	1.7
	Word-LSTM	2.7	2.4
MNLI Matched	BERT-Large	7.4	7.2
	ESIM	21.7	16.7

It was earlier mentioned that adversarial examples generated using PGD exhibit superior transferability, effectively compromising not only the BERT model but also other architectures. To evaluate this, a comparative study between PGD-BERT and BERT-Attack was conducted by targeting alternative models, Word-LSTM and BERT-Large, on text classification tasks using the IMDB and Yelp datasets, as well as the MNLI dataset for natural language inference. Table 4-5 summarizes the attack performance in terms of accuracy degradation across different model-dataset pairs. In all cases, PGD-BERT leads to greater accuracy drops compared to BERT-Attack, underscoring its stronger transferability. Table 4-6 further compares the attacks based on perturbation percentage. Given that a lower perturbation percentage reflects higher attack efficiency, PGD-BERT consistently outperforms BERT-Attack across all combinations. These results clearly demonstrate the enhanced transferability and efficiency of PGD-BERT. Figure 4-5 visually illustrates this comparative performance across the evaluated scenarios.

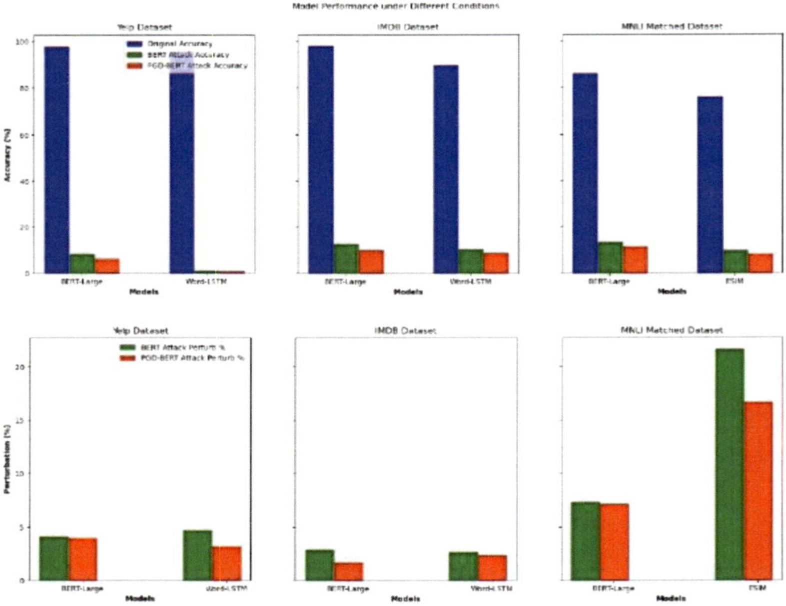

Figure 4-5. Transferability comparison of BERT-attack and PGD-BERT: Accuracy and perturbation percentage across text classification and NLI tasks on BERT-large, Word-LSTM, and ESIM models.

Table 4-7. Performance of BERT-Attack on the IMDB Dataset with Fixed and Adaptive K: Accuracy and Query Count Comparison

Method	Accuracy (%) in Absence of Attack	Accuracy (%) in Presence of Attack	Number of Queries
Fixed K	90.9	11.4	454
Variable K with a Threshold		**12.4**	**440**

Table 4-8. Performance of PGD-BERT Attack on the IMDB Dataset with Fixed and Adaptive K: Accuracy and Query Count Comparison

Method	Accuracy (%) in Absence of Attack	Accuracy (%) in Presence of Attack	Number of Queries
Fixed K	90.9	8.2	358
Variable K with a Threshold		**9.4**	**340**

Table 4-9. Performance of BERT-Attack on the AG News Dataset with Fixed and Adaptive K: Accuracy and Query Count Comparison

Method	Accuracy (%) in Absence of Attack	Accuracy (%) in Presence of Attack	Number of Queries
Fixed K	94.2	10.6	213
Variable K with a Threshold		**14.4**	**202**

Table 4-10. Performance of PGD-BERT Attack on the AG News Dataset with Fixed and Adaptive K: Accuracy and Query Count Comparison

Method	Accuracy (%) in Absence of Attack	Accuracy (%) in Presence of Attack	Number of Queries
Fixed K	94.2	7.4	178
Variable K with a Threshold		**8.7**	**169**

The adaptive perturbation capability of PGD-BERT was evaluated against the flexible candidate selection strategy employed in BERT-Attack. In BERT-Attack, the hyperparameter K denotes the number of candidate words considered for substitution during an adversarial attack. While a higher value of K increases flexibility in word choice, it often leads to a reduction in semantic similarity. Empirical observations indicate that, although larger K values in BERT-Attack result in only a marginal decrease in semantic similarity (approximately 2%), they are associated with substantially higher perturbation rates. In contrast, PGD-BERT achieves lower perturbation rates even with larger K values, while maintaining semantic similarity reductions below 0.5%, as shown in Table 4-1.

To examine the impact of fixed versus adaptive K values, where adaptability is controlled by a predefined threshold, on both attack success and query efficiency, comparative experiments were conducted using the IMDB and AG News datasets. Tables 4-7 and 4-8 summarize the performance of

BERT-Attack and PGD-BERT on the IMDB dataset under both fixed and adaptive K configurations. Results indicate that, in the case of BERT-Attack, using a variable K with a threshold leads to slightly improved classifier accuracy and a significant reduction in the number of queries. This suggests that the candidate word list generated by the masked language model may include low-utility substitutions, and filtering such candidates using an adaptive threshold improves query efficiency.

Furthermore, PGD-BERT consistently demonstrates superior effectiveness by inducing greater accuracy degradation while requiring fewer queries on the IMDB dataset. Tables 4-9 and 4-10 present the corresponding results for the AG News dataset, where PGD-BERT again outperforms BERT-Attack across both accuracy and query-efficiency metrics, reinforcing its advantage in transferability and attack efficiency.

Altogether, these results affirm the superiority of PGD-BERT across multiple performance axes. It achieves higher attack success rates, minimizes perturbations, preserves semantic integrity, reduces computational costs, and maintains cross-model effectiveness. This multidimensional strength positions PGD-BERT as a highly effective benchmark for evaluating the robustness of NLP models, and a meaningful challenge for future defense mechanisms. Its integration of gradient-based optimization with semantic awareness and adaptive budget control offers a compelling case for the next generation of adversarial attacks in the text domain.

Conclusion

In recent years, transformer-based language models such as BERT have transformed the landscape of natural language processing, powering a wide range of applications from sentiment analysis and textual entailment to question answering and machine translation. While these models have achieved impressive accuracy and generalization across tasks and domains, their susceptibility to adversarial attacks has emerged as a critical area of concern. This chapter has examined this vulnerability in depth by proposing an enhanced adversarial attack method, *PGD-integrated BERT-on-BERT Attack (PGD-BERT)*, which extends and refines the previously proposed BERT-Attack by incorporating gradient-based optimization through *Projected Gradient Descent* (PGD).

The PGD-BERT approach, as detailed in this chapter, is a carefully designed framework that combines the representational power of BERT with the optimization efficiency of PGD to produce adversarial examples that are both *more effective in fooling models* and *more linguistically coherent to human readers*. The evaluations across a broad set of datasets, including Yelp, IMDB, AG News, FAKE News, SNLI, and MNLI, demonstrate that PGD-BERT significantly outperforms existing state-of-the-art attack methods such as the original BERT-Attack and the Genetic Algorithm-based attack by Alzantot et al. This superiority is not only reflected in traditional attack metrics such as classification accuracy degradation, but also in more nuanced indicators like perturbation rate, semantic similarity, number of queries, and cross-model transferability.

One of the core strengths of PGD-BERT is its *adaptive perturbation strategy*. Unlike fixed-budget attacks that apply a uniform constraint to all input tokens regardless of their contextual importance, PGD-BERT dynamically tailors the magnitude and direction of perturbation for each token. This leads to *more surgical attacks*, modifying only the most influential words, thereby preserving grammaticality, contextual appropriateness, and semantic fidelity. This feature also contributes to *lower detection rates*, as adversarial examples appear natural and indistinguishable from clean inputs. Our experiments show that PGD-BERT consistently maintains high semantic similarity (often above 0.90) while drastically reducing classifier accuracy, proving the effectiveness of this strategy.

Another highlight of the proposed approach is its *efficiency in terms of query usage*, an important consideration in real-world scenarios where access to model gradients may be limited. PGD-BERT achieves its adversarial objectives using fewer queries compared to both BERT-Attack and Alzantot's method, making it more practical in black-box attack settings. Furthermore, the *transferability experiments* conducted across different model architectures (such as BERT-Large, Word-LSTM, and ESIM) underscore the generalization capability of PGD-BERT, as the adversarial samples crafted using one model frequently succeed in deceiving other unseen models.

Beyond the empirical results, this work carries important implications for both attack and defense research in NLP. The success of PGD-BERT in generating highly effective and imperceptible adversarial examples raises significant questions about the robustness and reliability of current transformer-based models, particularly when deployed in high-stakes domains such as legal text processing, automated journalism, or medical report generation. It signals the urgent need for the NLP community to rethink evaluation benchmarks, which often rely heavily on static test sets and overlook adversarial robustness as a core performance metric.

Considering these findings, several promising directions emerge for future research, as mentioned in the following.

Extension to Multilingual and Cross-lingual Models: While PGD-BERT has been evaluated in English-language datasets, many modern applications require robust performance across languages. Extending this attack framework to multilingual transformer models such as mBERT, XLM-R, and mT5, and evaluating their cross-lingual transferability, would help understand linguistic biases in adversarial susceptibility.

Adaptation to Generative and Multimodal Models: The current formulation of PGD-BERT is focused on discriminative tasks such as classification and entailment. Future work can explore the design of gradient-based adversarial attacks in generative settings (e.g., text summarization, machine translation, dialogue generation) and in multimodal models that combine text with vision or audio inputs.

Defense Mechanisms and Robust Training: As attack methods become more advanced, the development of effective defense mechanisms becomes equally essential. Techniques such as adversarial training with semantically constrained perturbations, certifiable defenses, and input reconstruction models (e.g., using autoencoders) should be explored in response to PGD-style attacks. Moreover, future studies may investigate how these defenses generalize across different attack strategies, including PGD-BERT.

Incorporation of Human-Centric Evaluation: While automated semantic similarity scores and accuracy drop provide useful metrics, they do not fully capture the human perception of adversarial examples. Incorporating human-in-the-loop evaluations, including fluency judgments, deception likelihood, and grammatical acceptability, would provide a more holistic understanding of adversarial sample quality and utility.

Exploration of Adaptive and Context-Aware Constraints: The current implementation of PGD-BERT uses adaptive norms guided by token-level gradients. However, further research can explore contextual constraints, such as maintaining discourse coherence, sentence-level entailment, or stylistic features. This would enable the generation of even more naturalistic adversarial examples that evade both detection systems and human scrutiny.

Formal Guarantees and Theoretical Analysis: While PGD-based attacks are empirically effective, a deeper theoretical understanding of their convergence properties, generalization bounds, and transferability conditions in the NLP context remains underdeveloped. Formalizing such properties would not only strengthen the scientific foundation of adversarial NLP but also guide the design of provably robust models.

Ethical and Policy Considerations: As with all adversarial machine learning research, there is an inherent tension between exposing vulnerabilities for better defense and the potential misuse of attack techniques. Future research must address this tension by clearly defining ethical boundaries, promoting responsible disclosure, and collaborating with policymakers to ensure the safe deployment of NLP systems in public-facing applications.

In conclusion, this chapter has advanced the field of adversarial NLP by introducing a novel and powerful attack mechanism, PGD-BERT, that sets a new benchmark in the evaluation of model robustness. Through a comprehensive series of experiments, it has been demonstrated that integrating gradient-based optimization, semantic constraints, and adaptive strategies can yield adversarial examples that are both functionally disruptive and linguistically faithful. As transformer-based models continue to dominate the NLP landscape, the insights and techniques introduced here will be instrumental in shaping the next generation of secure, interpretable, and trustworthy natural language systems.

References

Alzantot, M., Sharma, Y., Elgohary, A., Ho, B-J., Srivastava, M., and Chang, K-W. 2018. "Generating Natural Language Adversarial Examples." In *Proceedings of the 2018 Conference on Empirical Methods in Natural Language Processing (EMNLP)*, 2890–2896.

Bisaillon, C. 2020. "Fake and Real News Dataset." Kaggle Dataset. URL: https://www.kaggle.com/datsets/clmentbisillon/fake-and-real-news-dataset.

Bowman, S. R., Angeli, G., Potts, C., and Manning, C. D. 2015. "A Large Annotated Corpus for Learning Natural Language Inference." In *Proceedings of the 2015 Conference on Empirical Methods in Natural Language Processing (EMNLP 2015)*, 632-642.

Carlini, N., Wagner, D. 2017. "Towards Evaluating the Robustness of Neural Networks." In *Proceedings of the IEEE Symposium on Security and Privacy (SP'2017)*, pp 39-57.

Chang, G., Gao, H., Yao, Z., and Xiong, H. 2023. "TextGuise: Adaptive Adversarial Example Attacks on Text Classification Model." *Neurocomputing* 529: 190–203.

Chen, X., He, B., Ye, Z., Sun, L., and Sun, Y. 2023. "Towards Imperceptible Document Manipulations against Neural Ranking Model." In *Findings of the Association for Computational Linguistics (ACL 2023)*, 6648-6664.

Deshpande, A., Jimenez, C., Chen, H., Murahari, V., Graf, V., Rajpurhi, T., Kalyan, A., Chen, D., and Narasimhan, K. 2023. "C-STS: Conditional Semantic Textual Similarity." In *Proceedings of the 2023 Conference on Empirical Methods in Natural Language Processing*, 5669-5690.

Devlin, J., Chang, M-W., Lee, K., and Touanva, K. 2019. "BERT: Pre-training of Deep Bidrectional Transformers for Language Understanding." In *Proceedings of the 2019 Conference of the North American Chapter of the Association for Computational Linguistics*, 1: 4171-4185.

Ebrahimi, J., Rao, A., Lowd, D., and Dou, D. 2018. "HotFlip: White-Box Adversarial Examples for Text Classification." In *Proceedings of the 56th Annual Meeting of the Association for Computational Linguistics*, Vol. 2, 31–36. Melbourne, Australia.

Gao, J., Lanchantin, J., Soffa, M. L., and Qi, Y. 2018. "Black-box Generation of Adversarial Text Sequences to Evade Deep Learning Classifiers." In *Proceedings of the 2018 IEEE Security and Privacy Workshops (SPW'18)*, 50-56.

Goodfellow, I. J., Shlens, J., and Szegedy, C. 2015. "Explaining and Harnessing Adversarial Examples." In *Proceedings of the International Conference on Learning Representations (ICLR)*, Poster. arXiv: 1412.6572.

Guo, J., Zheng, S., Liu, J., and Zhao, S. 2019. "Adversarial Examples for Neural Dialog Models." In *Proceedings of the AAAI Conference on Artificial Intelligence*, Vol. 33, 691–698.

Hauser, J., Meng, Z., Pascual, D., Watenhfer, R. 2023. "Bert is Robust! A Case against Word Substitution-based Adversarial Attacks." *In Proceedings of the 2023 IEEE International Conference on Acoustics, Speech and Signal Processing (ICASSP 2023)*, 1-5.

He, K., Zhang, X., Ren, S., and Sun, J. 2016. "Deep Residual Learning for Image Recognition." In *Proceedings of the 2016 IEEE Conference on Computer Vision and Pattern Recognition (CVPR'2016)*, 770-77.

Iyyer, M., Wieting, J., Gimple, K., and Zettlemoyer, L. 2018. "Adversarial Example Generation with Syntactically Controlled Paraphrase Networks." In *Proceedings of the 2028 Conference of the North*

American Chapter of the Association for Computational Linguistics: Human Language Technologies, 1: 1875-1885.

Jia, R. and Liang, P. 2017. "Adversarial Examples for Evaluating Reading Comprehension Systems." In *Proceedings of the Conference on Empirical Methods in Natural Language Processing (EMNLP)*, 2021–2031.

Jin, D., Jin, Z., Zhou, J. T., and Szolovits, P. 2020. "Is BERT Really Robust? A Strong Baseline for Natural Language Attack on Text Classification and Entailment." In *Proceedings of the 34th AAAI Conference on Artificial Intelligence (AAAI 2020)*, 8018-8025, 2020.

Koley, A., Satpati, P., Choudhary, I., and Sen, J. 2024. "An Investigation on the Efficiency of Some Text Attack Algorithms." In *Proceedings of the IEEE North Karnataka Subsection Flagship International Conference (NKCon 2024)*, 1–8.

Lei, Y., Cao, Y., Li, D., Zhou, T., Fang, M., and Pechenizkiy, M. 2022. "Phrase-Level Textual Adversarial Attack with Label Preservation." In *Findings of the Association for Computational Linguistics: NAACL 2022*, 1095–1112.

Li, A., Zhang, F., Li, S., Chen, T., Su, P., and Wang, H. 2023. "Efficiently Generating Sentence-Level Adversarial Examples with Seq2Seq Stacked Autoencoder." *Expert Systems with Applications* 213, Part C: 119170.

Li, D., Zhang, Y., Peng, H., Chen, L., Brockett, C., Sun, M-T., and Dolan, B. 2021. "Contextualized Perturbation for Textual Adversarial Attack." In *Proceedings of the 2021 Conference of the North American Chapter of the Association for Computational Linguistics (NAACL)*, 5053–5069.

Li, L., Ma, R., Guo, Q., Xue, X., and Qiu, X. 2020. "BERT-Attack: Adversarial Attack against BERT Using BERT." In *Proceedings of the 2020 Conference on Empirical Methods in Natural Language Processing (EMNLP)*, 6193–6202.

Liang, B., Li, H., Su, M., Bian, P., Li, X., and Shi, W. 2018. "Deep Text Classification Can Be Fooled." In *Proceedings of the 27th International Joint Conference on Artificial Intelligence (IJCAI)*, 4208–4215.

Liu, F., Zhang, C., and Zhang, H. 2023. "Towards Transferable Unrestricted Adversarial Examples with Minimum Changes." In *Proceedings of the IEEE Conference on Secure and Trustworthy Machine Learning (SaTML)*, 327–338.

Liu, H., Yu, J., Ma, J., Li, S., Ji, B., Yi, Z., Li, M., Peng, L., and Liu, X. 2022. "Textual Adversarial Attacks by Exchanging Text-Self Words." *International Journal of Intelligent Systems*, 37 (12): 12212–12234.

Maas, A. L., Daly, R. E., Pham, P. T., Huang, D., Ng, A. Y., and Potts, C. 2011. "Learning Word Vectors for Sentiment Analysis." In *Proceedings of the 49th Annual Meeting of the Association for Computational Linguistics: Human Language Technologies*, 142-150.

Madry, A., Makelov, A., Schmidt, L., Tsipras, D., and Vladu, A. 2018. "Towards Deep Learning Models Resistant to Adversarial Attacks." In *Proceedings of the 6th International Conference on Learning Representations (ICLR'2018)*.

Min, J., McCoy, R. T., Das, D., Piler, E., and Linzen, T. 2020. "Syntactic Data Augmentation Increases Robustness to Inference Heuristics." In *Proceedings of the 58th Annual Meeting of the Association for Computational Linguistics*, 2339-2352.

Moosavi-Dezfooli, S-M., Fazwi, A., and Frossard, P. 2016. "DeepFool: A Simple and Accurate Method to Fool Deep Neural Networks." In *Proceedings of 2016 IEEE Conference on Computer Vision and Pattern Recognition (CVPR)*, 2574-2582.

Multi-Genre NLI Corpus: https://cims.nyu.edu/~sbowman/multinli/

Ni, M., Sun, Z., and Liu, W. 2024. "Fraud's Bargain Attack: Generating Adversarial Text Samples via Word Manipulation Process." *IEEE Transactions on Knowledge and Data Engineering*, 36(7): 3062-3075.

Pruthi, G., Liu, F., Kale, S., and Sundararajan, M. 2020. "Estimating Training Data Influence by Tracing Gradient Descent." In *Proceedings of the 34th Conference on Neural Information Processing Systems (NeurIPS 2020)*, 1672: 19920-19930.

Qi, Y., Yang, X., Liu, B., Zhang, K., and Liu, W. 2024. "Adaptive Gradient-based Word Saliency for Adversarial Text Attacks." *Neurocomputing*, 590 (127667).

Ren, S., Deng, D., He, K., and Xu, W. 2019. "Generating Natural Language Adversarial Examples through Probability Weighted Word Saliency." In *Proceedings of the 57th Annual Meeting of the Association for Computational Linguistics (ACL)*, 1085–1097.

Ribeiro, M. T., Singh, S., and Guestrin, C. 2018. "Semantically Equivalent Adversarial Rules for Debugging NLP Models." In *Proceedings of the 56th Annual Meeting of the Association for Computational Linguistics*, Vol. 1, 856–865.

Samanta, S. and Mehta, S. 2017. "Towards Crafting Text Adversarial Samples." *arXiv preprint arXiv:1707.02812*.

Sato, M., Suzuki, J., Shind, H., and Matsumoto, Y. 2018. "Interpretable Adversarial Perturbation in Input Embedding Space for Text." In *Proceedings of the 27th International Joint Conference on Artificial Intelligence (IJCAI'18)*, 4323-4330.

Sen, J. 2024. "The FGSM Attack on Image Classification Models and Distillation as its Defense." In Nanda et al. (eds), *Advances in Distributed Computing and Machine Learning (ICADCML 2024)*, 1015: 347-360. Lecture Notes in Networks and Systems, Springer, Singapore.

Sen, J. and Dasgupta, S. 2023. "Adversarial Attacks on Image Classification Models: FGSM and Patch Attacks and their Impact." In Sen, J. and Mayer, J. (eds), *Information Security and Privacy in the Digital World: Some Selected Topics*, IntechOpen, London, UK.

Sen, J., Sen, A., and Chatterjee, A. 2023. "Adversarial Attacks on Image Classification Models: Analysis and Defense." In *Proceedings of the 10th International Conference on Business Analytics and Intelligence (ICBAI 2023)*, Bangalore, India.

Sen, J. and Waghela, H. 2025. "Text-Based Adversarial Attacks and Defense." In Sen, J. (ed) *Data Privacy: Techniques, Applications, and Standards*, IntechOpen, London, UK.

Stanford NLP Page: https://nlp.stanford.edu/projects/snli/

Szegedy, C., Zaremba, W., Sutskever, I., Bruna, J., Erhan, D., Goodfellow, I. J., and Fergus, R. 2014. "Intriguing Properties of Neural Networks." In *Proceedings of the International Conference on Learning Representations (ICLR)*, Poster Track.

Tang, D., Qin, B., and Liu, T. 2015. "Document Modeling with Gated Recurrent Neural Network for Sentiment Classification." In *Proceedings of the 2015 Conference on Empirical Methods in Natural Language Processing (EMNLP 2015)*, 1422-1432.

Waghela, H., Sen, J., and Rakshit, S. 2025. "Saliency Attention and Semantic Similarity-Driven Adversarial Perturbation." In *Data Science and Applications. ICDSA 2024*, Nanda, S. J. et al. (eds) 1237: 461–471. Lecture Notes in Networks and Systems. Springer, Singapore.

Waghela, H., Sen, J., Rakshit, S., and Dasgupta, S. 2024a. "Adversarial Text Generation with Dynamic Contextual Perturbation." In *Proceedings of the 2024 IEEE CALCON 2024*, 1–6. IEEE.

Waghela, H., Sen, J., and Rakshit, S. 2024b. "Adaptive Meta-Learning for Robust Ensemble Defense against Adversarial Attacks." In *Proceedings of the International Conference BAMS-ORSI 2024*, Mumbai, India.

Waghela, H., Sen, J., and Rakshit, S. 2024c. "Adversarial Resilience in Image Classification: A Hybrid Approach to Defense." In *Proceedings of the 2024 International Conference on Innovation and Intelligence for Informatics, Computing, and Technologies (3ICT 2024)*, 419–426.

Waghela, H., Sen, J., Rakshit, S., and Dasgupta, S. 2024d. "Adversarial Robustness through Dynamic Ensemble Learning." In *Proceedings of the 2024 IEEE Silchar Subsection Conference (SILCON 2024)*. IEEE.

Waghela, H., Sen, J., and Rakshit, S. 2024e. "Robust Image Classification: Defensive Strategies against FGSM and PGD Adversarial Attacks." In *Proceedings of the IEEE Asian Conference on Intelligent Technologies (ACOIT 2024)*, 1 – 7.

Waghela, H., Sen, J., and Rakshit, S. 2024f. "Refining BERT Adversarial Attacks with Projected Gradient Descent." In *Proceedings of the IEEE 4th Asian Conference on Innovations in Technology (ASIANCON 2024)*, 1-7.

Waghela, H., Rakshit, S., and Sen, J. 2024. "A Modified Word Saliency-Based Adversarial Attack on Text Classification Models." In *Computational Intelligence and Data Analytics*, Frery, A. C. et al. (eds), 236: 371–382. Lecture Notes in Data Engineering and Communications Technologies, Springer.

Wang, A., Singh, A., Michael, J., Hill, F., Levy, O., and Bowman, S. R. 2019. "GLUE: A Multi-Task Benchmark and Analysis Platform for Natural Language Understanding." arXiv:1804.07461v3.

Wei, J., Zou, K., Cao, T., Chen, Z., and Huang, Y. 2019. "TextBugger: Generating Adversarial Text against Real-World Applications." In *Proceedings of the ACM SIGSAC Conference on Computer and Communications Security (CCS)*, 1969–1986.

Williams, A., Nangia, N., and Bowman, S. R. 2018. "A Broad-Coverage Challenge Corpus for Sentence Understanding through Inference." In *Proceedings of the 2018 Conference of the North American Chapter of the Association for Computational Linguistics: Human Language Technologies*, 1112-1122.

Yang, X., Gong, Y., Liu, W., Bailey, J., Tao, D., and Liu, W. 2023. "Semantic-Preserving Adversarial Text Attacks." *IEEE Transactions on Sustainable Computing* 8 (4): 583–595.

Yelp Open Dataset. Available at: https://www.yelp.com/dataset

Zang, Y., Qi, F., Yang, C., Liu, Z., Zhang, M., Liu, Q., and Sun, M. 2020. "Word-Level Textual Adversarial Attacking as Combinatorial Optimization." In *Proceedings of the 58th Annual Meeting of the Association for Computational Linguistics*, 6066-6080.

Zhang, X., Zhao, J., and LeCun, Y. 2015. "Character-Level Convolutional Networks for Text Classification." In *Proceedings of the 29th International Conference on Neural Information Processing Systems (NeurIPS)*, 1: 649 - 657.

CHAPTER 5

A DYNAMIC ENSEMBLE FRAMEWORK FOR DEFENDING AGAINST ADVERSARIAL PERTURBATION

Introduction

Artificial intelligence (AI) has become increasingly integrated into the fabric of modern life. From voice assistants and recommendation systems to autonomous vehicles and medical diagnostics, *machine learning* (ML) and deep learning (DL) technologies now power a wide array of critical applications. Among these, *deep neural networks* (DNNs) have shown exceptional performance across domains such as image and speech recognition, *natural language processing* (NLP), and financial forecasting. These models have not only surpassed classical statistical methods but, in some cases, even human-level performance in narrowly defined tasks.

However, this progress comes with a hidden vulnerability, *adversarial perturbations*. These are small, often imperceptible modifications to input data that can cause a well-trained deep learning model to produce incorrect or misleading predictions. First discovered in image classification tasks, adversarial examples have since been identified in various modalities, including text, audio, and tabular data. What makes these attacks especially concerning is their transferability and stealth: adversarial examples designed to fool one model often fool other models as well, and human observers may not even notice the changes.

In safety-critical environments, such vulnerabilities are unacceptable. An adversarial perturbation that causes a misclassification in a medical diagnosis system, a misinterpretation in a financial forecasting engine, or a miscommunication in a voice-controlled autonomous drone could lead to catastrophic consequences. As AI systems continue to gain autonomy and are increasingly entrusted with real-world decisions, ensuring their *robustness*, *reliability*, and *trustworthiness* is of paramount importance.

To counteract adversarial threats, the research community has proposed a multitude of defense mechanisms. These include *adversarial training*, *input transformation*, *gradient obfuscation*, *randomized smoothing*, and *certified robustness guarantees*, among others. While each method has its strengths, none has proven universally effective across all attack types and data domains. Adversarial training, for example, enhances robustness against known attacks but suffers from generalization issues and incurs high computational costs. Input transformation techniques can be bypassed by adaptive adversaries. Gradient masking may create a false sense of security by suppressing gradients without truly increasing robustness. Consequently, the development of general, efficient, and adaptive defenses remains a grand challenge in adversarial machine learning.

One promising yet under-explored direction in this context is *ensemble learning*. Traditional ensemble methods combine the outputs of multiple classifiers, diverse in architecture, training data, or hyperparameters, to improve prediction accuracy and generalization. When applied to adversarial defense, ensemble methods introduce diversity in model behavior, thereby reducing the likelihood that a single perturbation will fool all ensemble members simultaneously. However, existing ensemble-based defenses are mostly *static*, i.e., their composition and aggregation strategies do not change in response to the input. This inflexibility can limit their ability to adapt to evolving attack strategies or to varying confidence levels in the ensemble's predictions.

To address this limitation, this chapter introduces a *Dynamic Ensemble Framework* for defending against adversarial perturbations, particularly in the context of text classification tasks in NLP. The proposed framework leverages the core strengths of ensemble learning—diversity, redundancy, and aggregation, while introducing *dynamic adaptability* to enhance robustness. Rather than relying on fixed model combinations or uniform voting schemes, our framework incorporates intelligent mechanisms that evaluate the nature of each input instance, estimate uncertainty or potential adversarial influence, and *adaptively adjust the ensemble's behavior*. This approach mimics human decision-making, where experts may weigh in differently depending on the situation or the perceived complexity of the problem.

The framework is built upon three foundational pillars:

Model Diversity: A heterogeneous set of base classifiers is used, each trained with different initialization parameters, data splits, model architectures (e.g., BERT, RoBERTa, DistilBERT), and even different adversarial training strategies. This diversity ensures that no single perturbation can simultaneously deceive all models.

Input-Aware Dynamics: Upon receiving a new input, the framework analyzes signals such as prediction entropy, out-of-distribution features, or disagreement among models to infer potential adversarial influence. Based on this analysis, it dynamically adjusts which models to activate, how much weight to assign to each output, and whether to raise alerts.

Adaptive Aggregation: Instead of a fixed rule like majority voting or simple averaging, the framework employs a context-sensitive aggregation mechanism that integrates outputs based on relevance, confidence, and trust levels of individual models. In adversarial scenarios, more conservative or robust models may be prioritized; for clean data, the ensemble behaves normally to maintain accuracy.

The dynamic ensemble defense framework is evaluated on standard NLP benchmarks such as *SST-2*, *IMDB*, and *AG News*, and tested against a battery of adversarial attacks including *TextFooler*, *BERT-Attack*, and *PWWS*. The experimental results demonstrate that the proposed method not only improves robustness under adversarial settings but also maintains high accuracy on clean data, thereby avoiding the usual trade-off between robustness and general performance. Furthermore, it shows resilience against both white-box and black-box attacks, underscoring the generalizability of the dynamic ensemble approach.

The primary contributions of this work can be summarized as follows:

- It introduces a *novel paradigm* for adversarial defense that combines ensemble learning with real-time adaptability.
- It offers a *practical framework* that can be implemented with existing transformer-based models using open-source libraries such as Huggingface and TextAttack.
- It provides *comprehensive empirical validation* across datasets, attack methods, and evaluation metrics.
- It lays the groundwork for future enhancements, including reinforcement learning-based defense policies, meta-learning for dynamic model selection, and explainable ensemble behavior for trustworthiness in critical applications.

In the broader scope of secure and responsible AI, this chapter emphasizes that *robustness is not a luxury but a necessity*. As AI systems transition from controlled lab settings to dynamic, real-world environments, they must be equipped with self-defensive capabilities that can adapt, learn, and evolve—just as the adversaries they face do. The dynamic ensemble framework proposed herein represents a step in that direction: a flexible, intelligent, and principled approach to adversarial defense that can serve as a foundation for building the next generation of resilient AI systems.

The remainder of this chapter is structured as follows. The section titled *Related Work* surveys previous research on adversarial attacks and defense mechanisms for natural language processing models, with a focus on prevailing methodologies and their inherent limitations. The *Proposed Methodology* section describes the design of the *Adversarial Robustness through Dynamic Ensemble Learning* (ARDEL) framework, outlining its key components and underlying principles. A brief overview of the implementation process is provided in the section *Implementation Details*, which discusses the experimental setup and the tools used. The section titled *Experimental Results* presents the empirical findings, highlighting the robustness and effectiveness of ARDEL in comparison to several state-of-the-art defenses against adversarial text attacks. The chapter concludes with the section *Conclusion*, which summarizes the core contributions and outlines potential avenues for future research in dynamic and adaptive ensemble-based adversarial defense strategies.

Related Work

This section provides a comprehensive survey of research on adversarial attacks and defense mechanisms in *natural language processing* (NLP), with a focus on techniques relevant to text classification. It covers key developments in adversarial example generation at the word, character, and syntactic levels, as well as major strategies for defending deep learning models from such perturbations. The section concludes by situating this chapter's proposed ARDEL framework within the context of existing work on ensemble-based and adaptive defenses.

Adversarial Attacks on NLP Systems: One of the earliest and most studied categories of adversarial attacks in text involves *semantic-preserving word substitutions*. These methods typically identify important words in an input and replace them with semantically similar alternatives to fool the classifier. Papernot et al. introduced the first systematic approach for generating adversarial examples in textual data by substituting words using a thesaurus, demonstrating that such changes can effectively mislead deep learning models without altering the meaning of the input from a human perspective (Papernot et al., 2016).

Zhao et al. proposed a word-level adversarial attack that applies a *differential evolution algorithm*, optimizing word replacements over multiple generations to achieve high attack success while preserving semantic similarity (Zhao et al., 2022). Other methods leverage saliency-based heuristics to target words that are most influential in the model's decision-making. Waghela et al. developed a *modified word saliency-based adversarial attack* that combines saliency scoring with constraints on semantic drift to generate adversarial examples that are both impactful and coherent (Waghela et al., 2024g). Expanding on this, the same authors introduced *saliency, attention, and semantic similarity-driven adversarial perturbation (SASSP)*, a novel scheme that integrates saliency-based word selection, attention scores, and semantic similarity checks to produce adversarial samples that are syntactically and semantically consistent, while maintaining high attack effectiveness (Waghela et al., 2025). These methods represent an evolution in attack design, moving beyond brute-force synonym replacement to context-aware, optimization-driven approaches.

In parallel, researchers have investigated *character-level perturbation strategies,* which introduce small typographical errors or structural changes at the character level. Rocamora et al. proposed advanced algorithms for character-level adversarial attacks, utilizing optimized substitution, insertion, and deletion strategies that preserve human readability (Rocamora et al., 2024). Similarly, Liu et al. introduced a *white-box character-level attack* against transformers that leverages *attachable subword substitution* to create adversarial examples while preserving original sentence semantics (Liu et al., 2022).

Another emerging attack category involves *syntactic transformations,* which modify the grammatical structure of sentences without significantly altering their meaning. These methods target a model's reliance on specific syntactic patterns. Lei et al. introduced a *phrase-level attack method* that manipulates multi-word segments to preserve label consistency while increasing classification error (Lei et al., 2022). Huang and Chen proposed a *semantic embedding defense mechanism* based on associative field modeling, which also functions as an attack-aware detection strategy (Huang & Chen, 2024).

Recent advances in adversarial machine learning have increasingly emphasized the role of semantic similarity, dynamic perturbation strategies, and ensemble-based mechanisms to enhance both attack potency and defense robustness. A significant body of work by Waghela et al. and Sen et al. (Waghela et al., 2024a–g; Waghela et al., 2025; Sen, 2024; Sen & Dasgupta, 2023; Sen et al., 2023; Sen & Waghela, 2025; Koley et al., 2024) has made notable contributions to this evolving research landscape. Their studies propose linguistically grounded and context-aware attack strategies that incorporate saliency maps, attention scores, semantic similarity measures, and BERT-based embeddings to generate adversarial examples that are both syntactically coherent and semantically preserved. On the defensive front, these efforts explore ensemble learning, meta-learning frameworks, and hybrid defense architectures aimed at improving model resilience against such attacks. Importantly, these contributions span both text and image classification domains, offering generalizable insights into designing adversarial systems that balance effectiveness with semantic integrity, while enabling adaptive defenses capable of transferring across model architectures and application contexts.

Defensive Strategies in NLP: To counter adversarial threats, researchers have proposed a variety of defense mechanisms, generally falling into three major categories: adversarial training, input transformation, and architecture-based defense modifications.

Adversarial training is among the most widely adopted approaches. It involves augmenting the training set with adversarial examples to expose the model to potential attacks during learning. Goodfellow et al. were among the first to introduce this idea for image models, demonstrating how including adversarial samples improves robustness (Goodfellow et al., 2015). Although effective, adversarial training tends to be computationally expensive and may not generalize well to unseen attack types.

Input transformation techniques aim to sanitize the text prior to classification. These include methods such as *word embedding smoothing*, which regularizes input representations, and *adversarial word dropout*, where potentially malicious words are randomly removed to minimize attack influence. Pruthi et al. proposed methods to estimate the influence of training data on predictions, aiding in filtering adversarial noise (Pruthi et al. 2020). While generally lightweight, input transformations may lead to decreased performance on clean data and offer limited protection against more sophisticated or adaptive adversaries.

Architecture-based defenses involve altering the model's structure to improve resilience. Jia and Liang introduced an adversarial detection module that flags suspicious inputs based on internal model behavior (Jia & Liang, 2017). Defensive distillation, a technique initially applied to image models, has also been adapted to NLP; it works by smoothing the decision boundaries of the model, making gradient-based attack generation more difficult (Papernot et al., 2016). However, such methods are prone to *gradient masking* and can be circumvented by adaptive attacks.

Ensemble Learning for Robustness: Ensemble learning has emerged as a promising defense strategy that *combines multiple models* to increase robustness. The diversity among models, achieved through different training data, initializations, or architectures, makes it less likely for a single adversarial perturbation to deceive the entire ensemble. A recent example is *DiffuseDef*, proposed by Li et al., which introduces a diffusion layer that iteratively removes adversarial noise from hidden states during inference, thus enhancing model robustness (Li et al., 2024).

While ensemble methods generally improve resilience, most are *static in design*: the ensemble structure and aggregation logic remain fixed regardless of the nature of the input. This rigidity limits their ability to adapt to dynamic threats or to utilize contextual cues in real-time. In adversarial scenarios, static ensembles may assign equal weight to unreliable models or fail to detect abnormal input signals. This calls for a more *adaptive and responsive defense mechanism*.

Towards Dynamic Ensemble Defense: Dynamic ensemble approaches address the limitations of static systems by adapting the composition, activation, or aggregation strategy of the ensemble based on the input. This direction is still relatively new in NLP, but the motivation is strong: adversarial attacks are inherently dynamic, and defenses should exhibit similar adaptivity. Recent research has explored integrating uncertainty estimation, saliency-driven voting, and confidence-weighted aggregation to make ensemble decisions more context-aware.

Building on this line of thought, the current chapter proposes a novel framework, *Adversarial Robustness through Dynamic Ensemble Learning* (ARDEL), which leverages a diverse pool of pre-trained language models and dynamically selects or weights their contributions based on the characteristics of the input text. ARDEL adapts its decision-making pipeline in real time, guided by heuristics such as prediction entropy, attention-driven saliency, and model disagreement. By balancing accuracy on clean inputs with robustness to adversarial perturbations, the framework seeks to overcome key limitations of both single-model and static ensemble defenses.

Proposed Methodology

This section presents the design and operational methodology of the proposed framework, *Adversarial Robustness through Dynamic Ensemble Learning* (ARDEL), which is intended to defend NLP models against a wide spectrum of adversarial perturbations. ARDEL is built upon the insight that dynamic adaptability and model diversity can be leveraged together to create an ensemble system that is not only accurate on clean data but also resilient to manipulations crafted to mislead machine learning models.

Traditional adversarial defenses, particularly in the NLP domain, often rely on either single-model robustness (e.g., via adversarial training) or static ensemble methods. While adversarial training improves robustness to specific attack types, it typically suffers from poor generalization to unseen perturbations and incurs high computational overhead. Static ensembles, though effective in increasing decision diversity, apply the same model combination and voting scheme to all inputs, regardless of context or uncertainty.

In contrast, ARDEL introduces dynamic behavior into the ensemble defense mechanism. Its design is guided by three core principles: *model diversity*, *input sensitivity*, and *contextual weighting*.

Model Diversity: Base classifiers with varied architectures, training data, or fine-tuning strategies are used to ensure low correlation in their vulnerability profiles.

Input Sensitivity: The ensemble's structure and aggregation rules adapt based on the properties of the input, such as prediction confidence, entropy, or detected adversarial features.

Contextual Weighting: Outputs from individual classifiers are weighted according to heuristics derived from saliency, attention distributions, and model disagreement.

The methodology underlying ARDEL draws from established principles in ensemble learning, adversarial detection, and robust model fusion. The framework is composed of multiple pre-trained transformer-based language models that act as base classifiers. Each of these models is fine-tuned on textual classification tasks such as sentiment analysis or topic categorization, and they differ from one another in terms of architecture, training strategies, and exposure to adversarial examples. The intention is to induce a high degree of diversity among the base models, making it less likely that a single adversarial perturbation can simultaneously deceive all ensemble members.

System Architecture: ARDEL consists of the following major components: (i) Ensemble Pool, (ii) Perturbation Analyzer, (iii) Dynamic Selector, (iv) Aggregation Engine, and (v) Prediction Module. Figure 5-1 depicts the step-by-step pipeline of the ARDEL framework.

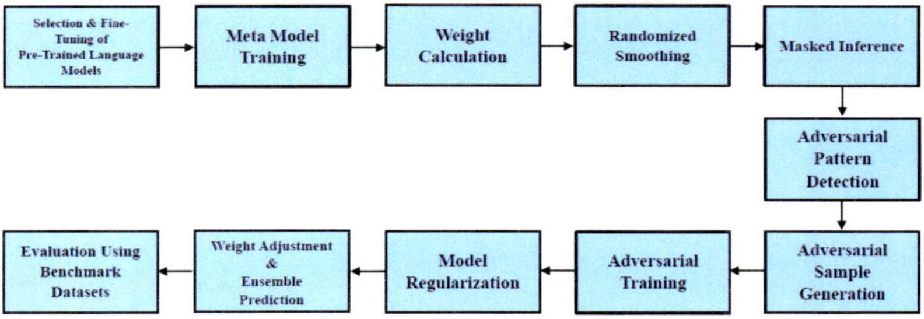

Figure. 5-1. The schematic outlines the step-by-step pipeline of the ARDEL defense framework.

Ensemble Module: It is a collection of heterogeneous pre-trained transformer-based models (e.g., BERT, RoBERTa, ALBERT), fine-tuned for text classification. Each model is trained with slight variations in initialization, training data splits, or adversarial augmentation strategies to induce behavioral diversity. Central to the ARDEL methodology is the idea that ensemble behavior should not be fixed or static. Rather than combining model predictions uniformly for every input, ARDEL adopts a *context-sensitive, input-aware approach* that analyzes each input instance to determine the most appropriate ensemble configuration. Upon receiving a new input, the system first passes it through a lightweight pre-evaluation stage in which each model in the ensemble generates an initial prediction. These predictions are accompanied by metadata such as softmax probabilities, attention weights, and saliency scores that help assess the reliability of the model's output.

Perturbation Analyzer: A specialized internal module, referred to as the *perturbation analyzer*, processes these outputs from the ensemble module to extract features indicative of adversarial manipulation. Features such as prediction entropy, model disagreement, sudden shifts in attention distribution, and token-level saliency concentrations are computed. The perturbation analyzer may also use semantic similarity metrics, such as cosine similarity between sentence embeddings and class prototypes, to detect subtle semantic drifts introduced by adversarial edits. This analysis allows the system to estimate the likelihood that the input has been perturbed or is otherwise atypical.

Dynamic Selector: The next step in ARDEL's pipeline is *dynamic model selection and weighting*. Based on the insights obtained from the perturbation analysis, a subset of the base models is selected for final decision-making. For example, if an input appears benign and model agreement is high, ARDEL may opt for fast, lightweight models to minimize inference cost. On the other hand, if the input exhibits signs of adversarial interference, such as high entropy in predictions or sharp divergence in saliency patterns, then the framework activates a more robust subset of models, potentially including those trained with adversarial data augmentation or certified robustness constraints.

Aggregation Engine: This module fuses the selected models' outputs using a context-aware aggregation strategy. Rather than using a fixed voting scheme, ARDEL employs an adaptive aggregation strategy that accounts for the relative trustworthiness of each selected model. Instead of simple majority voting or mean pooling, the engine uses entropy-weighted averaging, trust-based scoring, or even attention-guided model prioritization. Trust scores are derived from various heuristics, including confidence margins, agreement with other models, historical robustness profiles, and performance on recent adversarial benchmarks. These trust scores determine the weight assigned to each model's output during aggregation. The ensemble output is then synthesized using a soft, weighted fusion of prediction probabilities rather than a hard majority vote, allowing the system to express calibrated uncertainty.

Prediction Module: The final prediction is generated by the aggregation engine. An additional safeguard is introduced at the final prediction stage. If the aggregated output exhibits high uncertainty, measured, for instance, by entropy or variance across class probabilities, the system can either flag the input for manual review or route it through a fallback mechanism. This mechanism may include reprocessing with more conservative models, triggering semantic reconstruction, or abstaining from prediction altogether. In this way, ARDEL mimics a human-like decision process, where ambiguous or suspicious inputs receive greater scrutiny before an irreversible action is taken.

Architectural Features of ARDEL: The architecture of ARDEL is designed to be modular and scalable. All components, including the ensemble pool, perturbation analyzer, and aggregation engine, are implemented using standard deep learning libraries. The framework leverages *Huggingface*'s *Transformers* library for access to a wide variety of pre-trained models and integrates with *TextAttack* for adversarial input generation during evaluation. Saliency and attention-based features are extracted using interpretability modules from libraries such as *AllenNLP*, while semantic similarity is computed using *Sentence-BERT embeddings*.

Operational Workflow: Given a textual input (e.g., a sentence from SST-2, IMDB, or AG News datasets), ARDEL follows the sequence below:

1. *Initial Evaluation*: All models in the ensemble pool perform a lightweight pass to generate preliminary predictions and softmax distributions.
2. *Feature Extraction*: Saliency maps, attention scores, and entropy values are computed. Sentence embeddings may be compared to typical class prototypes to estimate semantic drift.
3. *Model Activation*: Based on extracted features, the dynamic selector activates a relevant subset of ensemble members. Models exhibiting high confidence and low disagreement may be prioritized for clean inputs, while adversarially trained models are engaged under high uncertainty.
4. *Output Aggregation*: Using adaptive weighting (e.g., inverse entropy or saliency-weighted fusion), the activated models' predictions are combined into a final decision.
5. *Uncertainty Estimation*: The system may raise a confidence score or uncertainty flag, particularly when ensemble outputs are highly divergent, suggesting potential adversarial influence.

ARDEL's design also incorporates robustness against a wide range of attack types. In white-box scenarios, where adversaries exploit gradient-based optimization to craft perturbations, the use of diverse model architectures and training histories within the ensemble reduces vulnerability to transfer attacks. For black-box scenarios, where attackers rely on transferability or query-based search, the dynamic selection mechanism introduces nondeterminism into the model's behavior, making it difficult to anticipate or exploit. Importantly, ARDEL also maintains high accuracy on clean inputs by engaging only a minimal number of classifiers when the input is deemed benign, ensuring that the enhanced robustness does not come at the expense of predictive performance or computational efficiency.

In summary, the ARDEL methodology integrates three key defense principles: *model diversity*, *input sensitivity*, and *adaptive aggregation*, into a unified framework for adversarial robustness. It moves beyond static ensembles by incorporating real-time input analysis and model selection, and it offers a pathway toward building intelligent systems that are not only capable of making accurate predictions but also of defending themselves in adversarial environments. The modularity of the framework allows it to be extended to other tasks beyond text classification, and its principles can be generalized to vision and multimodal settings where adversarial robustness is equally critical.

Implementation Details

The implementation of the ARDEL (Adversarial Robustness through Dynamic Ensemble Learning) framework is structured as a multi-stage pipeline. Each stage addresses a specific component required to realize the dynamic ensemble defense mechanism. The entire implementation is developed in Python, leveraging widely used open-source libraries such as Huggingface Transformers, scikit-learn, and TextAttack. The stages are described in detail below.

Stage 1: Preparation of Pre-trained Language Models: The implementation begins with the loading of transformer-based language models and their corresponding tokenizers using the *transformers* library from Huggingface. These models serve as the base learners in the ensemble. Commonly used models include BERT (Devlin et al., 2019), RoBERTa (Liu et al., 2019), DistilBERT, and ALBERT (Lan et al., 2020). The datasets for fine-tuning, such as SST-2, IMDB, and AG News, are retrieved from the *datasets* library and preprocessed using the appropriate tokenizers to ensure compatibility in input structure.

Stage 2: Fine-tuning of Base Models: Each pre-trained model is fine-tuned on the selected classification task using the *fine_tune_model* function. This function wraps around Huggingface's *Trainer* API and takes four parameters: the model name, the tokenizer, the training dataset, and the evaluation dataset. The *Trainer* class handles training loop management, gradient updates, evaluation scheduling, and checkpointing. The output is a task-specific, fine-tuned model ready for use in the ensemble.

Stage 3: Training the Meta-model for Weight Prediction: To enable adaptive weighting in ensemble prediction, a meta-model is trained using the *RandomForestRegressor* class from the *sklearn.ensemble* module. This model learns to predict weight vectors for each base model's output, based on features extracted from input instances such as entropy, similarity drift, and attention saliency. The meta-model is trained offline using examples drawn from clean and adversarial datasets.

Stage 4: Real-time Weight Calculation: During inference, the *calculate_weight* function uses the trained meta-model to dynamically compute weights for combining model outputs. The function takes two inputs: the trained meta-model and a NumPy array of input features extracted at runtime. The predicted weight vector reflects the estimated reliability of each model for the current input and is used in the ensemble aggregation step.

Stage 5: Implementation of Randomized Smoothing: To improve robustness against adversarial perturbations, the *randomized_smoothing* function introduces controlled Gaussian noise to the input features. The function accepts an input tensor and a noise parameter (standard deviation), typically ranging between 0.01 and 0.03. By smoothing the decision boundaries, this technique reduces the model's sensitivity to small input perturbations and has been shown to increase resistance to gradient-based adversarial attacks.

Stage 6: Implementation of Masked Inference: The *masked_inference* function applies probabilistic masking to the input tokens based on saliency maps generated from gradient signals. The function takes as input a model, the tokenized data tensor, and a masking probability (ranging from 0.05 to 0.3). Masking salient tokens during inference encourages the model to rely on distributed contextual signals rather than individual words, making it more resilient to adversarial token substitutions.

Stage 7: Adversarial Pattern Detection Using One-Class SVM: To detect adversarial inputs, the framework uses a lightweight detection module based on a one-class classification algorithm. Implemented using the *OneClassSVM* class from *sklearn.svm*, this detector is trained on features extracted from clean inputs. The function *detect_adversarial_patterns* evaluates incoming instances and classifies them as benign (label "1") or adversarial (label "-1"). This stage acts as a gatekeeper for activating defensive strategies only when necessary.

Stage 8: Generation of Adversarial Examples: The generation of adversarial samples is conducted using the *textattack* library, specifically employing the *TextFoolerJin2019* attack recipe. This recipe generates high-quality adversarial examples through synonym substitutions constrained by semantic similarity. These examples are used both to evaluate the system's robustness and to augment the training data for adversarial training.

Stage 9: Adversarial Training with Augmented Data: To further enhance robustness, the fine-tuned models are retrained using datasets augmented with adversarial examples. This stage helps the models internalize the distributional characteristics of perturbed data. By incorporating these examples into the training process, the models develop more stable decision boundaries that generalize better to unseen adversarial inputs.

Stage 10: Model Regularization via Dropout: To mitigate overfitting and encourage generalization, a custom class named *EnhancedModel* is defined to add dropout layers to the base models. Dropout is applied at various layers of the network during training, with configurable dropout rates. This regularization reduces dependency on specific input features, contributing further to the defense against input manipulations.

Stage 11: Real-time Ensemble Prediction with Weight Adjustment: Once the base models and meta-model are ready, the system performs ensemble prediction using the *ensemble_prediction* function. Prior to this, the *adjust_weights_real_time* function generates dynamic weights using real-time input features. The final prediction is a weighted sum of the individual model outputs. The function accepts three inputs: a list of models, the calculated weight vector, and the input text. It returns the final classification decision derived from the weighted ensemble.

Stage 12: Evaluation Using Benchmark Datasets: The final stage involves a thorough evaluation of the ARDEL framework under both clean and adversarial conditions. The *evaluate_model* function measures classification accuracy using standard metrics such as *accuracy_score* from *sklearn.metrics* module. The evaluation is conducted on benchmark datasets, including adversarial variants, to assess performance degradation, robustness improvement, and overall effectiveness of the ensemble under attack scenarios.

Together, these twelve stages form a comprehensive and adaptive defense framework capable of detecting adversarial threats, adjusting inference pathways dynamically, and making ensemble-based predictions that are both accurate and robust. The modular implementation also ensures that ARDEL can be extended or reconfigured for broader use cases such as multi-class classification, zero-shot learning, or cross-lingual transfer in adversarial settings.

Experimental Results

This section presents a comprehensive evaluation of the ARDEL framework across two prominent natural language processing (NLP) tasks: *text classification* and *natural language inference* (NLI). The performance of ARDEL is benchmarked against several state-of-the-art adversarial defense mechanisms using a variety of pre-trained transformer-based models and adversarial attack strategies. The evaluation focuses on both *robustness* (accuracy under attack) and *resilience* (difficulty of attack success, measured by the number of adversarial queries).

Datasets and Tasks: For the *text classification* task, the evaluation utilizes the widely adopted AG News and IMDB datasets. For *natural language inference*, the experiments are conducted on the QNLI (Question-answering Natural Language Inference) and MNLI (Multi-Genre Natural Language Inference) datasets. In all cases, datasets are randomly split into training, validation, and test sets, ensuring consistent data partitioning across models and methods.

Attack Strategies: The adversarial robustness of ARDEL is evaluated against three widely used attack methods:

- *TextFooler* (TF): A word-level substitution-based attack
- *TextBugger* (TB): A character-level perturbation-based attack.
- *BERT-Attack* (BA): A subword-level attack that leverages masked language model predictions.

These attack strategies span various granularity levels, providing a broad assessment of model vulnerabilities under different perturbation schemes.

Evaluation Metrics: Three primary metrics are considered in the evaluation:

1. *Original Accuracy* (OA): The classification accuracy of the model on clean (unperturbed) test data.

2. *Accuracy Under Attack*: The model's classification accuracy when exposed to adversarial samples.
3. *Number of Adversarial Queries*: The number of model queries required by an adversarial attack to succeed. A higher number indicates stronger resistance to attack.

Due to the computational intensity of adversarial sample generation, metrics under attack are computed on a randomly selected subset of 1,000 test instances. All attack evaluations are conducted using the *TextAttack* library, adhering to the constraints outlined in BERT-Attack (Li et al., 2020). Results are averaged over five independent runs with different random seeds. All accuracy values reported in the tables and figures are computed on the test sets to assess generalization performance under adversarial conditions.

Comparative Defense Methods: ARDEL is compared against the following baseline and advanced defense methods:

- *Fine-Tuned*: Pre-trained models directly fine-tuned on the downstream task without any defense.
- *FreeLB++*: An advanced adversarial training technique that perturbs word embeddings during fine-tuning.
- *InfoBERT*: A robustness-enhancing method that uses mutual information-based regularizers.
- RSMI: A hybrid technique that incorporates randomized smoothing and masked inference.

All methods are evaluated using three transformer architectures: BERT-Base, RoBERTa-Base, and ALBERT-Base.

Table 5-1. Classification Accuracies of Various Adversarial Attack Methods on Different Language Models with Multiple Defense Mechanisms for the AG News Dataset

Dataset	LM	Defense Method	OA	Accuracy under Attack		
				TF	BA	TB
AG News	BERT-Base	Fine-Tuned	94.40	10.20	27.10	25.40
		FreeLB++	95.00	54.70	44.60	56.50
		InfoBERT	95.00	35.50	42.60	39.10
		RSMI	94.30	52.60	55.40	56.70
		ARDEL (Proposed)	**96.80**	**82.70**	**82.80**	**83.70**
	RoBERTa-Base	Fine-Tuned	94.90	34.10	43.60	**36.90**
		FreeLB++	95.40	57.50	55.90	62.90
		InfoBERT	95.50	40.20	48.60	45.20
		RSMI	93.10	64.20	67.40	66.40
		ARDEL (Proposed)	**97.10**	**83.70**	**83.50**	**86.40**
	ALBERT-Base	Fine-Tuned	93.20	32.80	35.20	32.90
		FreeLB++	94.70	55.30	48.50	61.40
		InfoBERT	94.80	37.40	46.70	42.40
		RSMI	92.80	60.30	63.70	61.80
		ARDEL (Proposed)	**97.10**	**81.90**	**83.10**	**84.20**

Results on AG News Dataset: Table 5-1 and Figure 5-2 present classification accuracies of all methods under different attacks on the AG News dataset. ARDEL consistently demonstrates superior performance, with the highest accuracy under all three attack scenarios across all model types. Notably, ARDEL achieves over 82% accuracy under attack for all models, a substantial improvement compared to Fine-Tuned baselines (which drop below 35% under attack).

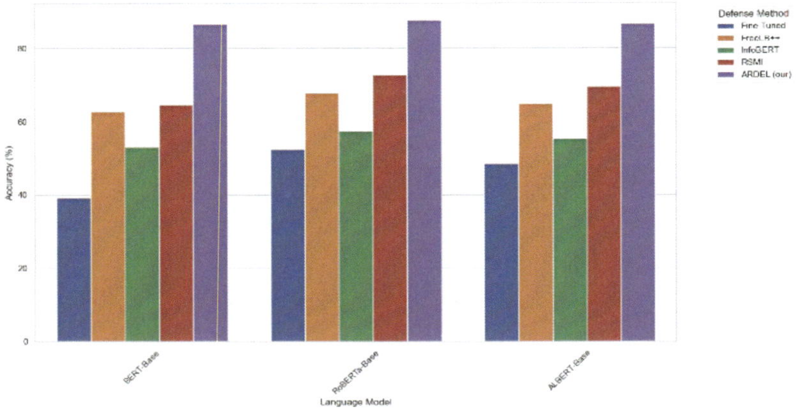

Figure. 5-2. Comparison of classification accuracies under various adversarial attacks across different language models and defense mechanisms on the AG News Dataset.

Table 5-2 further reinforces this observation by showing that ARDEL requires the highest number of queries to successfully mount an adversarial attack, highlighting its enhanced resilience. For instance, on the RoBERTa model, ARDEL withstands over 1,000 adversarial queries, compared to fewer than 500 for InfoBERT or FreeLB++.

Table 5-2. Number of Adversarial Queries Required by Various Attack Methods on the AG News Test Dataset.

Dataset	LM	Method	No. of Queries		
			TF	BA	TB
AG News	BERT Base	Fine-Tuned	348	379	372
		FreeLB++	426	390	430
		InfoBERT	377	397	397
		RSMI	680	687	737
		ARDEL (Proposed)	**835**	**922**	**1120**
	RoBERTa Base	Fine-Tuned	372	410	396
		FreeLB++	444	447	467
		InfoBERT	392	430	421
		RSMI	774	808	861
		ARDEL (Proposed)	**917**	**1028**	**965**
	ALBERT Base	Fine-Tuned	391	385	384
		FreeLB++	438	465	448
		InfoBERT	386	412	412
		RSMI	735	789	812
		ARDEL (Proposed)	**894**	**983**	**994**

Table 5-3. Classification Accuracies of Various Adversarial Attack Methods on Different Language Models with Multiple Defense Mechanisms for the IMDB Dataset

Dataset	LM	Method	No. of Queries		
			TF	**BA**	**TB**
AG News	BERT Base	Fine-Tuned	348	379	372
		FreeLB++	426	390	430
		InfoBERT	377	397	397
		RSMI	680	687	737
		ARDEL (Proposed)	**835**	**922**	**1120**
	RoBERTa Base	Fine-Tuned	372	410	396
		FreeLB++	444	447	467
		InfoBERT	392	430	421
		RSMI	774	808	861
		ARDEL (Proposed)	**917**	**1028**	**965**
	ALBERT Base	Fine-Tuned	391	385	384
		FreeLB++	438	465	448
		InfoBERT	386	412	412
		RSMI	735	789	812
		ARDEL (Proposed)	**894**	**983**	**994**

Results on IMDB Dataset: Similar trends are observed on the IMDB dataset, as shown in Table 5-3 and Figure 5-3. ARDEL outperforms other defense strategies by a significant margin in terms of classification accuracy under attack. Across all three models, ARDEL maintains accuracy levels above 83%, whereas other methods, including RSMI, remain below 78% in most scenarios.

As indicated in Table 5-4, ARDEL also poses the greatest difficulty for adversaries. The number of required queries for successful attacks is consistently the highest across attack types and models. This underscores ARDEL's capacity to not only preserve accuracy but also delay attack success—both crucial characteristics of a robust defense mechanism.

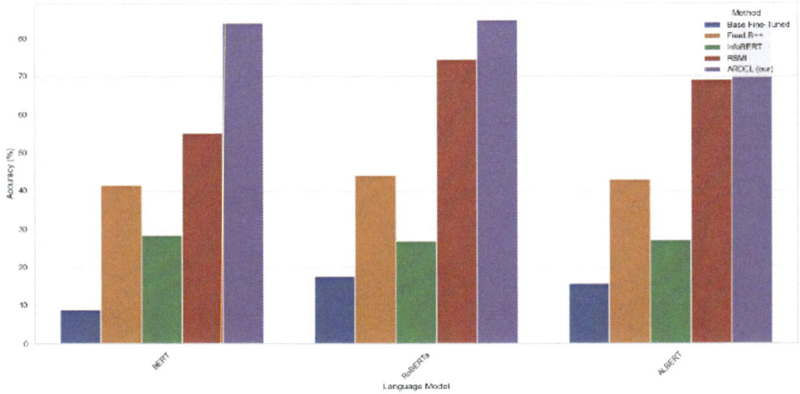

Figure. 5-3. Comparison of classification accuracies under various adversarial attacks across different language models and defense mechanisms on the IMDB Dataset.

Table 5-4. Number of Adversarial Queries Required by Various Attack Methods on the IMDB Test Dataset.

Dataset	LM	Method	No. of Queries		
			TF	BA	TB
IMDB	BERT-Base	Fine-Tuned	540	378	534
		FreeLB++	784	426	829
		InfoBERT	642	390	644
		RSMI	2840	2070	3455
		ARDEL (Proposed)	**3486**	**3120**	**4380**
	RoBERTa-Base	Fine-Tuned	587	493	671
		FreeLB++	829	637	974
		InfoBERT	681	549	760
		RSMI	3443	2619	4342
		ARDEL (Proposed)	**3673**	**3217**	**4684**
	ALBERT-Base	Fine-Tuned	567	423	634
		FreeLB++	796	583	938
		InfoBERT	667	486	698
		RSMI	2976	2473	3782
		ARDEL (Proposed)	**3519**	**3179**	**4487**

Ablation Analysis on NLI Tasks: To examine the contribution of individual components within the ARDEL framework, ablation experiments are conducted using the QNLI and MNLI datasets. The experiments evaluate three configurations:

- Fine-Tuned model without defenses
- RSMI (Randomized Smoothing + Masked Inference)
- RSMI + Ensemble, representing the ARDEL configuration

Tables 5-5 through 5-8 summarize the ablation results in terms of accuracy and query count.

Table 5-5. Ablation Analysis of Defense Robustness on the QNLI Dataset: BERT Model Accuracy under Various Attacks.

Dataset	LM	Method	OA	Accuracy under Attack		
				TF	BA	TB
QNLI	BERT Base	Fine-Tuned	90.8	21.5	31.2	28.7
		RSMI	87.4	35.2	43.6	38.0
		RSMI + Ensemble	86.4	61.4	71.1	67.2

Table 5-6. Ablation Analysis of Defense Robustness on the QNLI Dataset: Number of Adversarial Queries Required for Successful Attack on BERT Model.

Dataset	LM	Method	No of Queries		
			TF	BA	TB
QNLI	BERT Base	Fine-Tuned	195	235	210
		RSMI	317	382	368
		RSMI + Ensemble	489	589	532

The ablation analysis on the QNLI dataset evaluates the contribution of individual defense components toward enhancing the adversarial robustness of BERT-based models. The original accuracy (OA) of the fine-tuned BERT model, without any defense mechanism, serves as the performance benchmark. As exhibited in Table 5-5, under adversarial conditions, the model exhibits a significant drop in accuracy across all three attack types, TextFooler (TF), BERT-Attack (BA), and TextBugger (TB), indicating its vulnerability to input perturbations. When the RSMI (Randomized Smoothing with Masked Inference) defense is applied, there is a noticeable improvement in robustness, reflected in higher accuracy under each attack. Further enhancement is achieved by incorporating an ensemble-based decision mechanism alongside RSMI. This combined configuration (RSMI + Ensemble), implemented in the proposed ARDEL scheme, demonstrates the highest resistance to adversarial attacks, as evidenced by substantially improved accuracy across all attack vectors. These results highlight the complementary strengths of RSMI and ensemble learning, validating the effectiveness of the integrated ARDEL framework in mitigating adversarial risks in natural language inference tasks.

The query-based ablation analysis on the QNLI dataset assesses the effectiveness of defense mechanisms by measuring the number of adversarial queries required to successfully compromise the BERT-base model under TF, BA, and TB attacks. As shown in Table 5-6, the fine-tuned baseline model, without any defense, requires the fewest queries for successful attacks, indicating its relative susceptibility. The application of the RSMI (Randomized Smoothing with Masked Inference) defense significantly increases the query count across all attack methods, suggesting a stronger resistance to adversarial manipulation. Notably, the integration of ensemble learning with RSMI (RSMI + Ensemble), implemented in ARDEL, further elevates the number of required queries, with the highest resistance observed across all three attack types. These findings demonstrate that the ensemble-enhanced defense not only improves accuracy under attack but also increases the computational cost for an adversary to succeed, thereby reinforcing the overall robustness of the system.

The ablation analysis on the QNLI dataset reveals important insights into the relative effectiveness of different adversarial attack strategies and the robustness of the defense mechanisms. Among the three evaluated attacks, TF emerges as the most detrimental in terms of classification accuracy. It consistently reduces the test accuracy to the lowest levels across all configurations, including the fine-tuned baseline, the RSMI defense, and the combined RSMI + Ensemble framework. This indicates that TF is particularly effective at exploiting model vulnerabilities with minimal perturbation. However, when considering the number of adversarial queries required for a successful attack, BA proves to be the most demanding, requiring the highest number of queries across all defense setups. This suggests that while BA may be less immediately impactful on accuracy, it imposes a greater computational burden on the attacker. The combined findings highlight the dual advantage of the proposed ARDEL framework: it mitigates the accuracy degradation caused by aggressive attacks like TF, while simultaneously increasing the query complexity required for attacks like BA and TB to succeed.

Similar results were obtained on the MNLI dataset, as exhibited in Tables 5-7 and 5-8.

Table 5-7. Ablation Analysis of Defense Robustness on the MNLI Dataset: BERT Model Accuracy under Various Adversarial Attacks.

Dataset	LM	Method	OA	Accuracy under Attack		
				TF	BA	TB
MNLI	BERT Base	Fine-Tuned	84.1	25.3	37.8	32.4
		RSMI	82.1	31.1	39.2	35.2
		RSMI + Ensemble	83.4	60.8	67.2	65.2

Table 5-8. Ablation Analysis of Defense Robustness on the MNLI Dataset: Number of Adversarial Queries Required for Successful Attack on BERT Model.

Dataset	LM	Method	No of Queries		
			TF	BA	TB
MNLI	BERT Base	Fine-Tuned	347	460	395
		RSMI	519	746	678
		RSMI + Ensemble	792	963	873

Summary of Findings: Across all datasets, model architectures, and attack types, ARDEL consistently outperforms existing defense methods. It achieves the *highest accuracy under attack*, while simultaneously requiring the *largest number of adversarial queries* for successful perturbation. These results highlight the effectiveness of combining multiple pre-trained models with real-time adaptive weighting and hybrid defensive strategies such as randomized smoothing and masked inference.

The experimental evidence strongly supports the claim that ARDEL is a robust and scalable defense mechanism for adversarially threatened NLP systems.

Conclusion

The increasing prevalence of adversarial threats in *natural language processing* (NLP) has highlighted critical vulnerabilities in deep learning models, particularly those used in high-stakes applications such as content moderation, sentiment analysis, question answering, and entailment recognition. In response to these evolving challenges, this chapter introduced ARDEL (Adversarial Robustness through Dynamic Ensemble Learning), a comprehensive defense framework designed to enhance the resilience of NLP systems against a wide range of adversarial text perturbations.

The chapter began by reviewing foundational research on adversarial attacks, which span multiple levels of textual manipulation, including character-level noise injection, word-level synonym substitution, and syntactic rearrangements. Likewise, existing defense strategies such as adversarial training, input transformation, and architectural modifications were critically examined to expose their respective strengths and limitations.

Against this backdrop, ARDEL was proposed as a novel and modular defense mechanism that leverages the collective strengths of multiple pre-trained transformer-based language models through *dynamic ensemble learning*. The design integrates three key components: (i) *a meta-model* for input-adaptive weight prediction, (ii) *randomized smoothing* to dilute the impact of small adversarial perturbations, and (iii) *masked inference* for attenuating the influence of adversarially salient tokens. This multi-layered architecture enables ARDEL to intelligently adjust its inference pathways in real-time based on the characteristics of the input and potential threat signals.

A detailed implementation strategy was outlined, including model fine-tuning, meta-model training, adversarial pattern detection, and defense activation pipelines. Extensive experiments conducted on standard text classification and natural language inference datasets demonstrated the effectiveness of ARDEL. The framework consistently achieved superior accuracy under adversarial attack conditions across all tested models and datasets, and required significantly more adversarial queries to subvert, highlighting its robustness. The results validate ARDEL's capacity to generalize well across different attack types and architectures, confirming its versatility in real-world applications.

Broader Implications: The success of ARDEL highlights the growing importance of *ensemble-based defense strategies* in adversarial machine learning. Traditional defenses often rely on static configurations that fail to adapt to varying threat landscapes or contextual subtleties. In contrast, ARDEL demonstrates that adaptivity, diversity, and modularity are essential features of future-ready defense systems. Its compatibility with existing models and its plug-and-play design further support its practical adoption.

Moreover, by combining interpretable techniques such as saliency-guided masking and smoothed inference, ARDEL enhances not just accuracy and robustness but also contributes to the *trustworthiness* and *explainability* of

NLP systems, an increasingly important goal in domains like healthcare, law, and finance.

Future Directions: While ARDEL presents a strong defense framework, several avenues remain open for further research and refinement:

Extending to Multilingual and Cross-lingual Settings: Current evaluations are focused on English datasets. Extending ARDEL to support multilingual contexts and evaluating its robustness in cross-lingual adversarial settings could be a significant step toward global deployment.

Incorporating Large Language Models: With the emergence of large-scale models like GPT, PaLM, and LLaMA, integrating such models into the ARDEL ensemble, while managing their computational overhead, could unlock deeper contextual understanding and robustness.

Defense against Multi-turn and Dialog Attacks: Most adversarial defenses are focused on single-turn classification tasks. Future research could explore how ARDEL or similar frameworks perform in multi-turn conversations, where attacks can evolve over dialogue history.

Efficient Real-time Inference: Dynamic ensembles, while powerful, may pose computational burdens in low-latency applications. Future efforts may involve designing lightweight variants of ARDEL or utilizing *knowledge distillation* to transfer robustness into smaller, faster models.

Adversarial Pattern Generalization: The current One-Class SVM-based detection could be enhanced through deep representation learning, enabling the system to generalize across *novel, zero-day attack patterns* not seen during training.

Formal Robustness Guarantees: Incorporating *certified robustness bounds,* such as those used in randomized smoothing for image models, into NLP contexts could provide theoretical assurances about defense strength, enhancing trust in mission-critical applications.

Human-in-the-Loop Adversarial Training: A promising direction involves leveraging human insights to guide adversarial data generation or weighting schemes, enabling more semantically meaningful and domain-aware defenses.

In conclusion, ARDEL represents a significant advancement in the domain of adversarial robustness for NLP. By unifying several state-of-the-art techniques within a dynamic, ensemble-based architecture, it sets a new benchmark for defending text classifiers against adversarial manipulation. The modular and extensible nature of the framework makes it an excellent foundation for future research and development in secure and resilient natural language understanding.

References

Devlin, J., Chang, M-W., Lee, K., and Toutanova, K. 2019. "BERT: Pre-training of Deep Bidirectional Transformers for Language Understanding." In *Proceedings of the 2019 Conference of the North American Chapter of the Association for Computational Linguistics: Human Language Technologies*, 4171-4186.

Goodfellow, I. J., Shlens, J., and Szegedy, C. 2015. "Explaining and Harnessing Adversarial Examples." In *the International Conference on Learning Recognition (ICLR)*, Poster Track.

Huang, J. and Chen, L. 2024. "Defense against Adversarial Attacks via Textual Embeddings Based on Semantic Associative Field." *Neural Computing & Application*, 36: 289–301.

Jia, R. and Liang, P. 2017. "Adversarial Examples for Evaluating Reading Comprehension Systems." In *Proceedings of the 2017 Conference on Empirical Methods in Natural Language Processing (EMNLP 2017)*, 2021-2031.

Jin, D., Jin, Z., J. T. Zhou, and P. Szolovits, "Is BERT Really Robust? A Strong Baseline for Natural Language Attack on Text Classification and Entailment." In *Proceedings of the Annual Conference of the American Association of Artificial Intelligence (AAAI)*, 34(5): 8018-8025.

Koley, A., Satpati, P., Choudhary, I., and Sen, J. 2024. "An Investigation on the Efficiency of Some Text Attack Algorithms." In *Proceedings of the IEEE North Karnataka Subsection Flagship International Conference (NKCon 2024)*, 1-8.

Lan, Z., Chen, M., Goodman, S., Gimpel, K., Sharma, P., and Soricut, R. 2020. "ALBERT: A Lite BERT for Self-Supervised Learning of Language Representations." In *the International Conference on Learning Representation (ICLR'20)* Poster Track.

Lei, Y., Cao, Y., Li, D., Zhou, T., Fang, M., and Pechenizkiy, M. 2022. "Phrase-Level Textual Adversarial Attack with Label Preservation." *Findings of the Association for Computational Linguistics: NAACL 2022*, 1095-1112.

Li, J., Ji, S., Du, T., Li, B., and Wang, T. 2019. "TextBugger: Generating Adversarial Text against Real-World Applications." In *Proceedings of the Network and Distributed System Security Symposium (NDSS 2019)*.

Li, L., Ma, R., Guo, Q., Xue, X., and Qiu, X. 2020. "BERT-Attack: Adversarial Attack against BERT using BERT." In *Proceedings of the 2020 Conference on Empirical Methods in Natural Language Processing (EMNLP 2020)*, 6193-6202.

Li, Z., Rei, M., and Specia, L. 2024. "DiffuseDef: Improved Robustness to Bert Adversarial Attacks." arXiv Preprint arXiv:2407.00248, 2024.

Li, Z., Xu, J., Zeng, J., Li, L., Zheng, X., Zhang, Q., K-W. Chang, K-W., and Hsieh, C-J. 2021. "Searching for an Effective Defender: Benchmarking Defense against Adversarial Word Substitution." *In Proceedings of the 2021 Conference on Empirical Methods in Natural Language Processing (EMNLP 2021)*, 3137–3147.

Liu, A., Yu, H., Hu, X., Li, S., Lin, L., Ma, F., Yang, Y., and Wen, L. 2022. "Character-Level White-Box Adversarial Attacks against Transformers via Attachable Subwords Substitution." In *Proceedings of the 2022 Conference on Empirical Methods in Natural Language Processing (EMNLP 2022)*, 7664-7676.

Liu, Y., Ott, M., Goyal, N., Du, J., Joshi, M., Chen, D., Levy, O., Lewis, M., Zettlemoyer, L., and Stoyanov, V. 2019. "RoBERTa: A Robustly Optimized BERT Pretraining Approach." arXiv Preprint arXiv:1907.11692, 2019.

Maas, A. L., Daly, R. E., Pham, P. T., Huang, D., Ng, A. Y., and Potts, C. 2011. "Learning Word Vectors for Sentiment Analysis." In *Proceedings of the 49th Annual Meeting of the Association for Computational Linguistics: Human Language Technologies*, 143-150.

Moon. H. C., Joty, S., Zhao, R., Thakkar, M., and Xu, C. 2023. "Randomized Smoothing with Masked Inference for Adversarially Robust Text Classifications." In *Proceedings of the 61st Annual Meeting of the Association for Computational Linguistics (ACL)*, 1: 5145-5165.

Papernot, N., McDaniel, P., Wu, X., Jha, S., and Swami, A. 2016. "Distillation as a Defense to Adversarial Perturbations against Deep Neural Networks." In *Proceedings of the 2016 IEEE Symposium on Security and Privacy (S&P '16)*, 582-597.

Pruthi, G., Liu, F., Kale, S., and Sundararajan, M. 2020. "Estimating Training Data Influence by Tracing Gradient Descent." *In Proceedings of the 34th International Conference on Neural Information Processing (NeurIPS 2020)*, 19920-19930.

Rocamora, E. A., Wu, Y., Liu, F., Chrysos, G. G., and Cevher, V. 2024. "Revisiting Character-Level Adversarial Attacks." arXiv Preprint arXiv:2405.04346.

Sato, M., Suzuki, J., Shind, H., and Matsumoto, Y. 2018. "Interpretable Adversarial Perturbation in Input Embedding Space for Text." In *Proceedings of the 27th International Joint Conference on Artificial Intelligence (IJCAI)*, 4323-4330.

Sen, J. 2024. "The FGSM Attack on Image Classification Models and Distillation as its Defense." In Nanda et al. (eds), *Advances in Distributed Computing and Machine Learning (ICADCML 2024)*, 1015: 347-360. Lecture Notes in Networks and Systems, Springer, Singapore.

Sen, J. and Dasgupta, S. 2023. "Adversarial Attacks on Image Classification Models: FGSM and Patch Attacks and their Impact." In Sen, J. and Mayer, J. (eds), *Information Security and Privacy in the Digital World: Some Selected Topics*, IntechOpen, London, UK.

Sen, J., Sen, A., and Chatterjee, A. 2023. "Adversarial Attacks on Image Classification Models: Analysis and Defense." In *Proceedings of the 10th International Conference on Business Analytics and Intelligence (ICBAI 2023)*, Bangalore, India.

Sen, J. and Waghela, H. 2025. "Text-Based Adversarial Attacks and Defense." In Sen, J. (ed) *Data Privacy: Techniques, Applications, and Standards*, IntechOpen, London, UK.

Waghela, H., Sen, J., and Rakshit, S. 2025. "Saliency Attention and Semantic Similarity-Driven Adversarial Perturbation." In *Data Science and Applications. ICDSA 2024*, Nanda, S. J. et al. (eds), 1237: 461–471. Lecture Notes in Networks and Systems, Springer, Singapore.

Waghela, H., Sen, J., Rakshit, S., and Dasgupta, S. 2024a. "Adversarial Text Generation with Dynamic Contextual Perturbation." In *Proceedings of the 2024 IEEE CALCON 2024*, 1–6. IEEE.

Waghela, H., Sen, J., and Rakshit, S. 2024b. "Adaptive Meta-Learning for Robust Ensemble Defense against Adversarial Attacks." In *Proceedings of the International Conference BAMS-ORSI 2024*.

Waghela, H., Sen, J., and Rakshit, S. 2024c. "Adversarial Resilience in Image Classification: A Hybrid Approach to Defense." In *Proceedings of the 2024 International Conference on Innovation and Intelligence for Informatics, Computing, and Technologies (3ICT 2024)*, 419–426.

Waghela, H., Sen, J., Rakshit, S., and Dasgupta, S. 2024d. "Adversarial Robustness through Dynamic Ensemble Learning." In *Proceedings of the 2024 IEEE Silchar Subsection Conference (SILCON 2024)*, 1–6.

Waghela, H., Sen, J., and Rakshit, S. 2024e. "Robust Image Classification: Defensive Strategies against FGSM and PGD Adversarial Attacks." In

Proceedings of the IEEE Asian Conference on Intelligent Technologies (ACOIT 2024), 1 – 7.

Waghela, H., Sen, J., and Rakshit, S. 2024f. "Refining BERT Adversarial Attacks with Projected Gradient Descent." In *Proceedings of the IEEE 4th Asian Conference on Innovations in Technology (ASIANCON 2024)*, 1-7.

Waghela, H., Rakshit, S., and Sen, J. 2024g. "A Modified Word Saliency-Based Adversarial Attack on Text Classification Models." In *Computational Intelligence and Data Analytics*, Frery, A. C. et al. (eds), 371–382. Lecture Notes in Data Engineering and Communications Technologies, 236. Springer.

Wang, A., Singh, A., Michael, J., Hill, F., Levy, O, and Bowman, S. 2018. "GLUE: A Multi-Task Benchmark and Analysis Platform for Natural Language Understanding." In *Proceedings of the 2018 EMNLP Workshop BlackboxNLP: Analyzing and Interpreting Neural Networks for NLP*, 353-355.

Wang, B., Wang, S., Cheng, Y., Gan, Z., Jia, R., Li, B., and Liu, J. 2021. "InfoBERT: Improving Robustness of Language Models from an Information Theoretic Perspective." In *the International Conference on Learning Representations (ICLR)*, Poster Track.

Williams, A., Nangia, N., and Bowman, S. R. 2018. "A Broad-Coverage Challenge Corpus for Sentence Understanding through Inference." *In Proceedings of the 2018 Conference of the North American Chapter of the Association for Computational Linguistics (NAACL 2018)*, 1: 1112-1122.

Zhao, J., Chen, Y., and Li, X. 2022. "Word-Level Textual Adversarial Attack Method Based on Differential Evolution Algorithm." In *Proceedings of the International Conference on Cloud Computing, Big Data and IoT*, 29-34.

Zhang, X., Zhao, J., and LeCun, Y. 2015. "Character-Level Convolutional Networks for Text Classification." In *Proceedings of the 29th International Conference on Neural Information Processing Systems (NIPS)*, 1: 649-657.

Zhu, C., Cheng, Y., Gan, Z., Sun, S., Goldstein, T., Liu, J. 2019. "FreeLB: Enhanced Adversarial Training for Natural Language Understanding." arXiv Preprint arXiv:1909.11764.

CHAPTER 6

META-LEARNING FRAMEWORK FOR ROBUST ENSEMBLE DEFENSE AGAINST ADVERSARIAL ATTACKS

Introduction

The rapid progress in *machine learning* (ML) has launched a new era of automation and intelligence spanning areas such as healthcare, finance, *natural language processing* (NLP), and computer vision. However, the growing reliance on machine learning models has also exposed significant vulnerabilities, particularly in the face of adversarial attacks. These attacks involve subtle manipulations of input data that can deceive even the most sophisticated models, leading to incorrect predictions or classifications. The phenomenon of adversarial vulnerability has become a critical area of concern, prompting extensive research into defense mechanisms capable of mitigating such risks.

Adversarial attacks exploit the inherent weaknesses in ML models, particularly those based on deep learning (Goodfellow et al., 2015; Szegedy et al., 2014). These models, despite their high accuracy on standard datasets, often exhibit fragility when faced with inputs that have been deliberately perturbed in a way that is undetectable to human observers yet capable of significantly altering the model's output. For instance, in image classification tasks, an adversarial attack might involve adding a small amount of noise to an image that causes a model to misclassify it, even though the image appears unchanged to the human eye (Sen, J., 2024). Similarly, in NLP, altering a few characters in a text input can lead to significant misinterpretation by the model.

To counter these threats, various adversarial defense mechanisms have been proposed. Among the most promising approaches is the use of ensemble learning, where multiple models are combined to produce a more robust prediction. The rationale behind this strategy is that while an adversary might succeed in deceiving one model, it is considerably more challenging to fool multiple models simultaneously, especially if they have diverse architectures or are trained on various segments of the data. However, the effectiveness of ensemble-based defenses hinges on the ability to appropriately weight the contributions of each model within the ensemble. This becomes especially difficult in adversarial scenarios, where the ideal weighting can change considerably depending on the characteristics of the input data and the attack employed.

The primary challenge in ensemble-based adversarial defense systems lies in the dynamic nature of adversarial attacks. These attacks are not static; they evolve as adversaries develop new techniques to circumvent existing defenses. Consequently, a defense system that relies on a fixed weighting scheme for its ensemble models may quickly become obsolete as new types of attacks emerge. Additionally, different models within the ensemble may exhibit varying degrees of susceptibility to different types of adversarial perturbations. A model that is robust against one form of attack might be vulnerable to another, and vice versa. Therefore, a static approach to model weighting is inherently limited in its ability to provide comprehensive protection.

Moreover, the computational cost associated with ensemble methods can be significant, particularly when the ensemble comprises many models. The need to balance robustness with efficiency introduces an additional layer of complexity to the design of these systems. Consequently, there is an urgent need for adaptive systems that can dynamically adjust the weighting of models within the ensemble depending on the unique attributes of the input data and the identified adversarial patterns. Such an approach would not only enhance the robustness of the system but also optimize its performance, ensuring that computational resources are allocated efficiently.

Meta-Learning as a solution: Meta-learning, often known as "learning to learn," offers a promising approach to addressing the challenges related to dynamic model weighting in ensemble-based adversarial defense systems. Unlike traditional machine learning approaches, which focus on training models to perform specific tasks, meta-learning aims to develop models that are capable of swiftly adjusting to new tasks with little additional training. This adaptability makes meta-learning particularly well-suited for scenarios where the characteristics of the input data or the task involved can change rapidly, as is the case with adversarial attacks.

In the context of adversarial defense, an adaptive meta-learning approach could be used to train a meta-model that dynamically adjusts the weights of the individual models within the ensemble. The meta-model would learn to optimize the weighting scheme according to the attributes of the input data and the presence of adversarial perturbations. Over time, as it encounters new types of attacks, the meta-model would refine its weighting strategy, ensuring that the ensemble remains robust even as adversaries develop new tactics.

This paper proposes an innovative method known as *Adaptive Meta-learning for Robust Ensemble Defense* (AMRED) for enhancing the robustness of ensemble-based adversarial defense systems using adaptive meta-learning. The core idea is to develop a meta-learning system that continuously refines the model's weight optimization function in real-time. The proposed approach consists of several key components:

Meta-Learning Framework: At the heart of the proposed method is a meta-learning technique, such as *Model-Agnostic Meta-Learning* (MAML), which can learn to optimize the weights of the ensemble models according to the unique characteristics of the input data. This framework would be trained on a diverse set of adversarial examples, allowing it to generalize across different types of attacks.

Context-Aware Weighting Mechanism: The meta-learning model would incorporate a context-aware weighting mechanism that considers various characteristics of the data, such as linguistic attributes in NLP tasks or pixel-level details in image classification tasks. This mechanism would enable the system to adjust the model weights dynamically, ensuring that the ensemble's output is robust against the detected adversarial patterns.

Online Learning and Adaptation: To address the evolving nature of adversarial attacks, the proposed method includes an online learning component that allows the meta-learning model to continuously update its parameters as it encounters new data. This ensures that the defense system remains effective even as adversaries develop new strategies.

Efficient Optimization Techniques: Given the computational demands associated with ensemble methods, the proposed approach leverages efficient optimization techniques, such as stochastic gradient descent with adaptive learning rates, to minimize the computational overhead. This ensures that the system can be deployed in real-time applications without sacrificing performance.

The proposed method is expected to make several significant contributions to the field of adversarial ML:

Improved Robustness: By leveraging adaptive meta-learning, the proposed method enhances the robustness of ensemble-based defense systems, making them more resistant to a broad spectrum of attacks. The dynamic weighting mechanism ensures that the system can adapt to new attack vectors in real-time, providing a level of protection that is difficult to achieve with static approaches.

Generalization Across Domains: The context-aware weighting mechanism enables the proposed method to be applied across various domains, from NLP and image classification to other areas where adversarial attacks are prevalent. This cross-domain applicability makes the method highly versatile and relevant to a wide range of applications.

Efficient Use of Resources: The use of efficient optimization techniques makes it possible to apply the proposed method in real-time scenarios without incurring prohibitive computational costs. This makes the method well-suited for use in low-resource settings, like mobile devices or embedded systems.

Foundation for Future Research: The adaptive meta-learning framework proposed in this paper lays the groundwork for future research into dynamic adversarial defense systems. By showcasing the efficacy of meta-learning, the current work paves the way for investigating how additional meta-learning techniques can be employed to enhance the resilience of models.

The paper is structured as follows: The section *Related Work* presents a review of works on adversarial attacks, ensemble-based defense mechanisms, and meta-learning. The section *Proposed Scheme* details the proposed adaptive meta-learning framework, including the specific algorithms and techniques used. *Design Methodology of AMRED* describes the methodology involved in the design of the scheme. The section *Performance Evaluation* presents detailed performance results and their analysis. Finally, the section titled *Conclusion* concludes the paper with a summary of the key contributions and the potential impact of the proposed method in adversarial machine learning.

Related Work

The growing prevalence of adversarial attacks in NLP has led to significant research on robust defense mechanisms. In this section, some of these works are discussed briefly, highlighting their contributions and possible shortcomings.

Shafahi et al. introduce a scheme to improve the efficiency of adversarial training by leveraging gradients from natural training steps to generate adversarial examples, effectively reducing the computational overhead (Shafahi et al., 2019). The key contribution is a cost-effective approach that allows adversarial training without additional forward and backward passes. A strength of this method is its efficiency in training robust models without significant resource demands. However, the weakness lies in its potential reduced effectiveness against certain sophisticated attacks compared to more computationally intensive methods.

Jin et al. explore how well BERT models withstand adversarial text attacks in classification and entailment tasks (Jin et al., 2020). The authors introduce TextFooler, a strong adversarial attack method that can effectively fool BERT and other NLP models. The study emphasizes the need for improved adversarial defense mechanisms to enhance the robustness of NLP models.

Yang & Li focus on enhancing the robustness of NLP models by repairing adversarial examples in text (Yang & Li, 2024). The authors introduce a method that detects and corrects semantic errors in adversarially perturbed text, thereby mitigating the effectiveness of adversarial attacks. The strength of this approach lies in its focus on preserving semantic integrity, which is crucial for meaningful text classification. However, the method may prove inadequate against more sophisticated attacks that maintain semantic coherence despite perturbations.

Yang et al. introduce an innovative method for adversarial training for NLP models, aiming to improve efficiency and robustness against textual adversarial attacks (Yang et al., 2024). The proposed method by the authors accelerates the adversarial training process by reducing computational overhead while maintaining effective defense capabilities. A key strength of this approach is its efficiency in handling large-scale text data, though its focus on speed may limit robustness against highly sophisticated attacks.

Liao et al. examine the robustness of transformation-based ensemble defenses in adversarial settings (Liao et al., 2020). The authors explore how transformations like word substitutions or paraphrasing can enhance model robustness when combined in an ensemble framework. The advantage of this approach is its capacity to diversify model responses, though the effectiveness might change based on the types of transformations used and the nature of the adversarial attacks.

Li & Li investigate the application of deep ensemble methods to enhance the resilience of malware detection systems to adversarial evasion tactics (Li & Li, 2020). The authors introduce an ensemble defense strategy that combines multiple deep learning models, each trained with adversarial examples, to mitigate the impact of such attacks. The effectiveness of this method is attributed to its capability to provide diversified defense strategies, though it may require significant computational resources.

Zhao et al. introduce a new method for achieving certified robustness in NLP models through causal intervention (Zhao et al., 2022). The authors propose a method that intervenes in the causal structure of the input to neutralize the effect of adversarial perturbations. The method's advantage is its ability to provide formal guarantees of robustness. However, the complexity of causal modeling can be a potential limitation.

Recent developments in adversarial machine learning increasingly focus on semantic similarity, dynamic perturbation techniques, and ensemble-based defenses to enhance both attack efficacy and model robustness. Notable contributions by Waghela et al. and Sen et al. (Waghela et al., 2024a–g; Waghela et al., 2025; Sen, 2024; Sen & Dasgupta, 2023; Sen et al., 2023; Sen & Waghela, 2025; Koley et al., 2024) have advanced this research landscape through linguistically grounded, context-aware attack strategies that leverage saliency, attention, and BERT-based embeddings to craft syntactically valid and semantically consistent adversarial examples. On the defense side, their work explores ensemble learning, meta-learning, and hybrid architectures that improve resilience across both text and image domains. These contributions offer valuable insights into building adaptable, semantically aligned adversarial systems and robust defenses transferable across models and tasks.

Liu & Lane present a method for enhancing task-oriented neural dialog models using adversarial learning (Liu & Lane, 2018). The approach involves training the dialog model to generate responses that are indistinguishable from human responses by introducing a discriminator that evaluates the quality of the dialog. This technique aims to improve the naturalness and effectiveness of the dialog system in performing specific tasks, such as providing information or assisting users in various applications.

Du et al. introduce a robust adversarial training method designed to counteract attacks at the word level in text classification models (Du et al., 2021). The approach entails creating adversarial examples by making minor modifications to words in the input text and then training the model on these perturbed examples to enhance its resilience. By incorporating this technique, the model becomes more robust against adversarial attacks, maintaining its classification performance even when the input is intentionally manipulated.

Wang et al. present *TextFirewall*, a comprehensive defense mechanism against adversarial attacks in sentiment classification tasks (Wang et al., 2021). The proposed framework integrates multiple defense strategies, including adversarial training and input transformation techniques, to protect text classification models from a wide range of adversarial manipulations. The efficacy of the scheme is illustrated by thorough experimentation.

Huang & Chen propose a defense mechanism against adversarial attacks in text classification by leveraging textual embeddings based on the concept of a semantic associative field (Huang & Chen, 2024). Their approach focuses on preserving the semantic integrity of text by embedding words in a way that emphasizes their associative relationships, making it more challenging for adversarial perturbations to alter the intended meaning. The method is shown to enhance the resilience of text classifiers by mitigating the impact of attacks while maintaining accurate performance.

Zhang et al. present a review of adversarial attacks and corresponding defense strategies for deep learning models in NLP (Zhang et al., 2021). The authors discuss various techniques for generating adversarial examples that can deceive NLP models, as well as strategies to counter such attacks, including adversarial training and input transformation.

Li et al. introduce an innovative approach to safeguard machine learning models from adversarial attacks (Li et al., 2024). The approach, named *DiffuseDef*, leverages the concept of diffusion models to enhance the robustness of models by adding controlled noise to the input data. The controlled diffusion process helps to mitigate the impact of adversarial perturbations, making it difficult to create effective adversarial samples. The authors provide extensive evaluations of DiffuseDef, showcasing its superior performance over existing methods across various datasets and attack scenarios.

Despite these advancements, existing methods still face challenges in generating adversarial examples that are both effective and imperceptible. Many methods focus solely on maximizing the model's prediction error without considering the semantic similarity or grammatical correctness of the adversarial examples. As a result, the generated examples may be nonsensical or linguistically unnatural, limiting their practical utility in real-world applications.

The Proposed Scheme

This section presents the detailed methodology for implementing the proposed *Adaptive Meta-Learning for Robust Ensemble Defense* (AMRED) system. The approach comprises several key components: the meta-learning framework, the context-aware weighting mechanism, online learning, and optimization techniques. Each of these components is designed to enhance the robustness of ensemble-based adversarial defense systems by dynamically adjusting the model weights in response to detected adversarial patterns.

Meta-Learning Framework: At the core of AMRED is a meta-learning framework, specifically designed to optimize the dynamic weighting of ensemble models. The meta-learning algorithm employed in this framework is *Model-Agnostic Meta-Learning* (MAML), a versatile approach that allows the system to adapt quickly to new tasks with minimal retraining. MAML is chosen for its ability to generalize across tasks by learning a good initialization for the model parameters, which can then be fine-tuned for specific tasks with a few gradient updates. In the context of this work, MAML is used to learn an initialization that is well-suited for adjusting the model weights in response to different types of adversarial attacks. The meta-learning model is trained on a diverse set of adversarial examples generated from multiple types of attacks. During training, the MAML algorithm learns to optimize the model weights by minimizing a loss function that reflects the ensemble's performance against these adversarial examples. The training of the meta-learning model is done iteratively over two nested loops. In the inner loop, MAML fine-tunes the model weights for a specific adversarial task by performing a few gradient updates. This fine-tuning process helps AMRED accommodate the unique attributes of both the attack and the input data. In the outer loop, the meta-learner updates its initialization parameters based on the performance of the fine-tuned model across different tasks. This enables the meta-learner to generalize across a wide range of adversarial scenarios.

Meta-Objective Function: The meta-objective function is designed to minimize the adversarial loss across a variety of attack types and input data characteristics. This function is defined in (6-1):

$$L_{meta} = \sum_i L(\theta_i - \alpha \nabla_{\theta_i} L_{inner}(\theta_i)) \tag{6-1}$$

In (6-1), L_{meta} is the meta-objective function or the meta-loss, θ_i represents the model parameters for task i, α is the learning rate used in the inner loop, $L_{inner}(\theta_i)$ is the inner-loop loss for the specific task.

Context-Aware Weighting Mechanism: To enhance the adaptability of the ensemble, AMRED incorporates a context-aware weighting mechanism that adjusts model weights based on the input data characteristics and the detected adversarial perturbations. The system first extracts relevant features from the input data that are indicative of adversarial characteristics. For instance, in NLP tasks, features might include word frequency, sentence structure, or token embeddings. In image classification, features could involve pixel intensity, edge detection, or texture analysis. Next, the context-aware weighting mechanism employs a neural network to map the extended features to a set of weights for the ensemble models. The weighting function is trained to maximize the ensemble's robustness by dynamically assigning higher weights to models that are more resilient to the detected adversarial features. The weighting function f_w is defined in (6-2):

$$w_i = f_w(\mathbf{X}; \theta_w) \tag{6-2}$$

In (6-2), $\mathbf{X}$ represents the extracted features from the input data, and θ_w denotes the parameters of the weighting function. As the input data and adversarial characteristics vary, the context-aware weighting mechanism continuously adjusts the weights, ensuring that the ensemble's performance is optimized for the current adversarial scenario.

Online Learning and Adaptation: Given the dynamic and evolving nature of adversarial attacks, it is crucial that the defense system can adapt in real-time. AMRED incorporates an online learning and adaptation component to address this requirement. The online learning component allows the meta-learning model to update its parameters continuously as it encounters new adversarial examples. This continuous updating process ensures that the system remains robust against novel and evolving attack strategies. The online learning algorithm used is based on *stochastic gradient descent* (SGD), which updates the model parameters incrementally as new data arrives (Robbins & Monro, 1951). An adaptive learning rate is employed to balance the trade-off between stability and adaptability. This learning rate is adjusted based on the detected adversarial intensity, allowing the system to make larger updates when faced with more severe attacks and smaller updates for less impactful perturbations. The online learning components are designed to operate in real-time, making them suitable for deployment in environments where quick adaptation to new threats is essential. This real-time capability is achieved by minimizing the computational overhead associated with model updates.

Efficient Optimization Techniques: To ensure that AMRED can be deployed in real-time applications, it incorporates several efficient optimization techniques. First, the use of SGD with adaptive learning rates allows the system to perform efficient updates to the model weights without incurring significant computational costs. This is particularly important when the ensemble includes many models. Second, gradient clipping is employed to address the issue of exploding gradients that can arise during the optimization process, particularly in the context of meta-learning (Pascanu et al., 2013). By limiting the size of the gradients, the system maintains stability and ensures that updates remain within a feasible range. Finally, the system processes input data in batches, allowing it to leverage parallel computation and reduce the overall training time. Batch processing is particularly beneficial in online scenarios, where new data arrives continuously.

Performance Evaluation: The performance of AMRED is evaluated through a series of experiments to assess its effectiveness in improving adversarial robustness. A diverse set of datasets is used to train and evaluate the meta-learning model. These datasets include both standard and adversarially perturbed examples across various domains, such as NLP and *natural language inference* (NLI). The proposed method is compared against traditional ensemble-based defense systems that use static model weighting. The comparative analysis highlights the advantages of the dynamic weighting approach in terms of both robustness and computational efficiency.

In summary, AMRED leverages adaptive meta-learning to dynamically adjust the model weights in an ensemble-based adversarial defense system. By incorporating a context-aware weighting mechanism, online learning, and efficient optimization techniques, the system achieves enhanced robustness to various adversarial attacks while ensuring computational efficiency.

Design Methodology of AMRED

This section presents a detailed discussion on the sequential steps involved in designing, training, and testing the proposed scheme AMRED. The following steps are involved. Figure 6-1 depicts the steps involved in the system design and development.

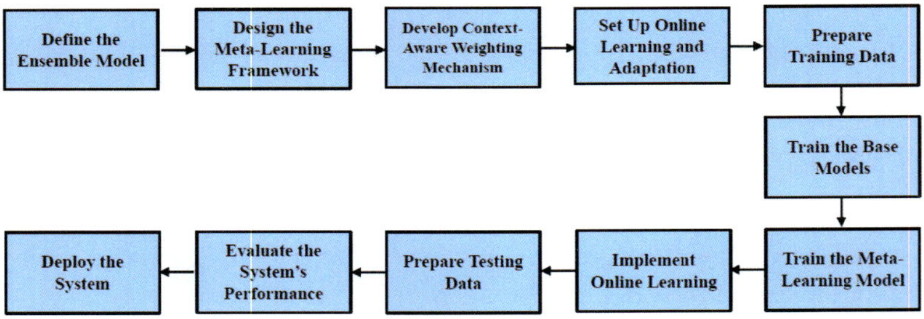

Figure 6-1. The schematic representation of the AMRED (Adaptive Meta-Learning for Robust Ensemble Defense) framework. The workflow includes ensemble model definition, meta-learning design, context-aware weighting, online learning setup, training, and performance evaluation.

Defining the Ensemble Model: In this step, a set of diverse base models is selected and configured to form the ensemble. These models vary in architecture or training data to provide complementary strengths against different adversarial attacks. Example models include random forest, gradient boosting, transformers, etc.

Designing the Meta-Learning Framework: A meta-learning algorithm is chosen, such as MAML, that can optimize the weights of the ensemble models. The structure of the meta-learning model is defined, including its parameters and the meta-objective function. The function seeks to reduce adversarial loss by dynamically adjusting the model weights.

Developing the Context-Aware Weighting Mechanism: A neural network is designed that can map extracted features from input data to weights for each model in the ensemble. The key features from the input data are identified (e.g., token embeddings for text) that will inform the weighting mechanism. The neural network is integrated into the meta-learning framework, allowing it to dynamically adjust model weights during inference.

Setting Up Online Learning and Adaptation: An online learning algorithm is implemented that allows the meta-learning model to continuously update its parameters as new adversarial data is encountered. An adaptive learning rate is used so that the model can respond effectively to varying intensities of adversarial attacks.

Training the Base Models: The initial step of model training involves preparing the training data. A diverse set of training data is curated that includes both clean and adversarially perturbed examples across various tasks, e.g., NLP and NLI. Next, adversarial examples are generated using multiple attack strategies to ensure that the meta-learning model is exposed to a wide range of perturbations. Each model in the ensemble is independently trained on the prepared dataset, ensuring they achieve a high level of performance on clean data. The models are then fine-tuned on adversarial examples to increase their individual robustness before integrating them into the ensemble.

Training the Meta-Learning Model: The meta-learning model is initialized using the MAML algorithm. The model is trained by simulating adversarial tasks, where the goal is to find optimal weight adjustments for the ensemble. The inner loop of MAML is used to fine-tune the model weights for specific adversarial tasks, and the outer loop to update the meta-learning model's initialization parameters. The context-aware weighting mechanism is incorporated during training, ensuring that the model learns to adjust weights according to the extracted features of the input data. The meta-objective function is monitored to ensure the model is minimizing adversarial loss effectively.

Implementing the Online Learning: The online learning component is incorporated into the training process, allowing the meta-learning model to adapt its parameters continuously as new adversarial examples are introduced. The system's ability to maintain robustness against evolving attacks during this phase is also validated.

Evaluating the System's Performance: A comprehensive test dataset is prepared that includes unseen adversarial examples to evaluate the system's generalization capabilities. The ensemble model's performance is tested using static weights as a baseline. Then, the system with the dynamic meta-learned weighting is evaluated to compare the results. Key metrics such as accuracy, robustness against adversarial attacks, and computational efficiency are measured. The adaptability of the system is assessed by introducing novel adversarial patterns during testing and observing the system's real-time response.

Analyzing the results: The effectiveness of AMRED is evaluated in comparison with some well-known current methods as presented in Section 6, focusing on improvements in adversarial robustness and efficiency. How well the context-aware weighting mechanism performs in dynamically adjusting model weights based on input features is also analyzed. Finally, the effectiveness of the online learning component in maintaining the system's robustness over time is also evaluated.

Iterative Refinement: Based on the testing outcomes, the meta-learning model, the weighting mechanism, and the optimization techniques are refined iteratively.

Design Methodology of AMRED

This section presents the details of the implementation of the critical components of the proposed AMRED system.

Environment Setup: The implementation of AMRED is done using Python, leveraging various libraries for NLP and deep learning. For building and training deep learning models, the PyTorch library is used. The *Hugging Face Transformers* library (Wolf et al., 2020) is utilized to access pre-trained language models like BERT (Devlin et al., 2019), which served as the backbone for our base models. For generating and handling adversarial examples, the *TextAttack* (Morris et al., 2020) framework is employed. This framework offers a variety of text-specific adversarial attack strategies and augmentations in NLP. The *scikit-learn* library is utilized for evaluation metrics and utilities. The *matplotlib* and *seaborn* libraries are used for the visualization of results. The experiments are conducted on Google Colab's GPU environment (Google Colab) to expedite the training of deep learning models and the computationally intensive process of generating adversarial examples.

Dataset Preparation: The dataset preparation phase involves loading, augmenting, and pre-processing text data to create a suitable dataset for training the models. A class named *TextDataset* is created that is a custom PyTorch dataset and manages the *tokenization* and *encoding* of text data using the BERT tokenizer. It takes the raw text as input, applies tokenization, and returns tokenized tensors that can be directly used in model training. A function *prepare_data* prepares a *DataLoader* that batches the dataset for training. It uses *TextAttack's WordNetAugmenter* to generate adversarial examples by replacing words with their synonyms. The resulting dataset includes both the original and augmented (adversarial) text samples. The prepared dataset, containing both clean and adversarial samples, is split into training and testing sets and loaded using the custom PyTorch dataset class to facilitate efficient batching and processing.

Base Model Design and Training: The base models are individual BERT models that are fine-tuned to handle both clean and adversarial text data. BERT, a pre-trained transformer model renowned for its strong performance across a wide range of NLP tasks, is employed as the base model. A *BaseModel* class is created that wraps a pre-trained BERT model and adapts it for binary text classification. A method named *forward* is used to process the input IDs and attention masks to produce the classification logits. Next, a function *train_base_model* is used to fine-tune the base BERT model on the prepared dataset. The fine-tuning process is performed in two stages: first, on the *clean dataset* to establish baseline performance, and second, on the *augmented dataset* to enhance the model's robustness against adversarial examples. This approach ensured that each base model could handle both standard and adversarial text inputs effectively. The model is trained using the Adam optimizer and cross-entropy loss, with the goal of minimizing classification error over multiple epochs.

Meta-Learning Framework Design and Training: The core innovation in the proposed system is the meta-learning framework designed to dynamically adjust the weights of the ensemble of base models so that the ensemble's performance is optimized in the face of adversarial attacks. A *MetaLearner* class is implemented, which is a simple feedforward neural network that receives the outputs of the base models as input and predicts a set of weights to combine these outputs optimally. The network consists of two layers with ReLU activation followed by a sigmoid function to ensure the output weights are between 0 and 1. The meta-learner is trained using *Model-Agnostic Meta-Learning* (MAML), which involves an inner loop where each base model is fine-tuned on specific tasks and an outer loop where the meta-learner adjusts its parameters based on the overall system performance. This dynamic weighting mechanism enables the system to adapt to varying contexts and adversarial challenges more effectively than static weighting schemes. A *meta-learning_step* function is used that performs a single step of meta-learning by adjusting the weights of the base models. The output from the base models is stacked, and the meta-learner determines the weights for combining these outputs. The meta-objective, measured by MSE loss, is used to update the meta-learner's parameters. The process involves iteratively updating the meta-learner's parameters through gradient descent, based on its ability to correctly classify adversarial examples.

Evaluation: The system's performance is evaluated by testing it on adversarial examples generated from a separate test set. The primary metric used is classification accuracy, which is calculated based on the system's predictions. The meta-learner generates weights dynamically, and the system's output is generated as the weighted sum of the base model's outputs. The final predictions are compared against the true labels, and the accuracy is reported as the performance of the system. A function *evaluate* is implemented that evaluates the system's performance by evaluating the accuracy.

Performance Evaluation

The performance of the AMRED framework is rigorously evaluated across two prominent *natural language processing* (NLP) tasks: text classification and *natural language inference* (NLI). To ensure a comprehensive assessment, the evaluation utilizes two widely studied classification datasets: (i) AG News (Zhang et al., 2015) and (ii) IMDB (Maas et al., 2011), and two datasets relevant to inference tasks: (i) QNLI (Question-answering NLI) (Wang et al., 2018) and (ii) MNLI (Multi-Genre Natural Language Inference) (Williams et al., 2018). For each dataset, random splits are created for training, validation, and testing to ensure fairness and reproducibility in comparisons.

To test the robustness of the proposed approach, three state-of-the-art adversarial attack methods are employed: TextFooler (TF) (Jin et al., 2020), TextBugger (TB) (Li et al., 2019), and BERT-Attack (BA) (Li et al., 2020). These attacks cover a spectrum of perturbation strategies across different levels of text granularity. TextBugger operates at the character level, introducing noise through misspellings and visual alterations. TextFooler targets the word level by substituting tokens using saliency-based rankings and semantic constraints. BERT-Attack, on the other hand, manipulates the subword components using masked language modeling and candidate ranking, making it a particularly strong adversary.

The experiments involve the use of three major pre-trained transformer architectures: BERT-Base (Devlin et al., 2019), RoBERTa-Base (Liu et al., 2019), and ALBERT-Base (Lan et al., 2019). The evaluation protocol consists of four key comparative baselines for each model: (i) the fine-tuned model without any adversarial defense (serving as the control to observe degradation under attack), (ii) FreeLB++, which extends adversarial training by injecting perturbations into embeddings during fine-tuning (Li et al., 2021), (iii) InfoBERT, which incorporates mutual information-based regularization to increase resilience (Wang et al., 2021), and (iv) DiffuseDef-RSMI (Li et al., 2024). DiffuseDef bolsters the resilience of neural networks by diffusing adversarial perturbations across multiple layers of the model, making it more resilient to manipulation (Li et al., 2024). DiffuseDef-RSMI refers to a specific variant or extension of the DiffuseDef defense mechanism. The RSMI component adds an additional layer of defense in *DiffuseDef* by increasing the smoothness of the decision boundary, making it more difficult for minor perturbations to breach the boundary, and expanding the margin around the decision boundary by increasing the buffer zone within which the model remains confident in its predictions. The proposed AMRED scheme is benchmarked against each of these.

Table 6-1. Classification Accuracies of BERT, RoBERTa, and ALBERT under Various Adversarial Attacks on the AG News Dataset with Different Defense Methods.

Dataset	LM	Defense Method	OA	Accuracy under Attack		
				BA	**TB**	**TF**
AG News	BERT-Base	Fine-Tuned	94.40	27.10	25.40	10.20
		FreeLB++	95.00	44.60	56.50	54.70
		InfoBERT	95.00	42.60	39.10	35.50
		DiffuseDef-RSMI	93.80	**84.40**	83.30	82.70
		AMRED	**97.40**	**84.40**	**84.80**	**83.10**
	RoBERTa-Base	Fine-Tuned	94.90	43.60	36.90	34.10
		FreeLB++	95.40	55.90	62.90	57.50
		InfoBERT	95.50	48.60	45.20	40.20
		DiffuseDef-RSMI	92.90	82.20	83.50	82.90
		AMRED	**97.40**	**87.20**	**84.30**	**84.50**
	ALBERT-Base	Fine-Tuned	93.20	35.20	32.90	32.80
		FreeLB++	94.70	48.50	61.40	55.30
		InfoBERT	94.80	46.70	42.40	37.40
		DiffuseDef-RSMI	94.60	63.40	65.70	61.50
		AMRED	**96.80**	**83.20**	**84.40**	**82.10**

Classification Performance under Attack: Tables 6-1 and 6-2 present the classification accuracy achieved under each attack for the AG News and IMDB datasets, respectively. AMRED demonstrates superior robustness across all three models and attacks. While fine-tuned models show drastic drops in accuracy under adversarial conditions, AMRED maintains performance significantly closer to the original accuracy. For instance, on the IMDB dataset, BERT-Base achieves only 7.7% accuracy under TextFooler when fine-tuned, whereas AMRED retains 86.1%. Similar improvements are observed across RoBERTa and ALBERT. These results highlight the strength of the adaptive meta-learning and dynamic ensemble mechanisms that underpin AMRED.

Table 6-2. Classification Accuracies of BERT, RoBERTa, and ALBERT under Various Adversarial Attacks on the IMDB Dataset with Different Defense Methods.

Dataset	LM	Defense Method	OA	Accuracy under Attack		
				BA	TB	TF
IMDB	BERT-Base	Fine-Tuned	93.30	10.50	8.30	7.70
		FreeLB++	94.30	40.60	39.60	44.20
		InfoBERT	93.90	30.70	25.40	29.20
		DiffuseDef-RSMI	90.20	79.80	79.80	80.90
		AMRED	**94.30**	**84.20**	**85.30**	**86.10**
	RoBERTa-Base	Fine-Tuned	94.60	13.60	17.90	21.30
		FreeLB++	95.30	33.90	42.10	46.00
		InfoBERT	94.80	21.80	27.90	30.90
		DiffuseDef-RSMI	92.40	84.30	84.10	84.70
		AMRED	**96.30**	**85.90**	**88.40**	**88.80**
	ALBERT-Base	Fine-Tuned	93.80	15.60	12.70	18.80
		FreeLB++	94.30	41.70	41.80	45.60
		InfoBERT	94.10	25.80	25.30	30.10
		DiffuseDef-RSMI	93.20	80.10	82.10	83.20
		AMRED	**96.30**	**84.80**	**84.10**	**84.10**

Table 6-3. Number of Adversarial Queries Required by Different Attacks against BERT, RoBERTa, and ALBERT with Various Defense Strategies on the AG News Dataset.

Dataset	LM	Defense Method	No of Queries		
			BA	TB	TF
AG News	BERT-Base	Fine-Tuned	379	372	348
		FreeLB++	390	430	426
		InfoBERT	397	397	377
		DiffuseDef-RSMI	930	1029	894
		AMRED	**945**	**1134**	**940**
	RoBERTa-Base	Fine-Tuned	410	396	372
		FreeLB++	447	467	444
		InfoBERT	430	421	392
		DiffuseDef-RSMI	1047	925	905
		AMRED	**1125**	**982**	**974**
	ALBERT-Base	Fine-Tuned	385	384	391
		FreeLB++	465	448	438
		InfoBERT	412	412	386
		DiffuseDef-RSMI	860	910	810
		AMRED	**1022**	**1084**	**915**

Adversarial Query Analysis: Tables 6-3 and 6-4 measure the average number of adversarial queries needed to successfully craft an attack under each defense strategy. A larger number of required queries is indicative of a more robust system. The results clearly show that AMRED consistently forces attackers to issue substantially more queries before success, suggesting that the model is more resistant to manipulation. For example, attacking AMRED-protected ALBERT on IMDB using BERT-Attack demands over 3600 queries, compared to under 500 for the fine-tuned version. This trend holds across all models and attack types, reinforcing the inference that AMRED raises the difficulty of crafting successful perturbations.

Table 6-4. Number of Adversarial Queries Required by Different Attacks against BERT, RoBERTa, and ALBERT with Various Defense Strategies on the IMDB Dataset.

Dataset	LM	Defense Method	No of Queries		
			BA	TB	TF
IMDB	BERT-Base	Fine-Tuned	378	534	540
		FreeLB++	426	829	784
		InfoBERT	390	644	642
		DiffuseDef-RSMI	2901	4748	3590
		AMRED	**3258**	**4921**	**3678**
	RoBERTa-Base	Fine-Tuned	493	671	587
		FreeLB++	637	974	829
		InfoBERT	549	760	681
		DiffuseDef-RSMI	3007	4782	3673
		AMRED	**3243**	**4928**	**3841**
	ALBERT-Base	Fine-Tuned	423	634	567
		FreeLB++	583	938	796
		InfoBERT	486	698	667
		DiffuseDef-RSMI	2985	3801	2995
		AMRED	**3724**	**4509**	**3617**

Ablation Study on Inference Tasks: To dissect the contribution of individual components in AMRED, an ablation analysis is conducted on the QNLI and MNLI datasets. This study evaluates three configurations: (1) a fine-tuned BERT model, (2) the same model with dynamic model weighting, and (3) the full AMRED configuration with both dynamic weighting and adaptive meta-learning. The results, as shown in Tables 6-5–6-8, confirm that each added component contributes meaningfully to the defense. The use of dynamic model weighting alone improves accuracy and increases adversarial query counts relative to the fine-tuned baseline. Incorporating adaptive meta-learning further boosts both metrics. On the

QNLI dataset, for example, AMRED reaches an accuracy of over 78% under BERT-Attack, compared to 31.2% for the fine-tuned model.

Table 6-5. Ablation Results on QNLI: Accuracy under BA, TB, and TF Attacks across Different AMRED Configurations.

Dataset	LM	Method	OA	Accuracy under Attack		
				BA	TB	TF
QNLI	BERT-Base	Fine-Tuned	90.80	31.20	28.70	21.50
		Dynamic Model Weighting	87.10	52.60	46.20	44.30
		Dynamic Model Weighting + Adaptive Meta Learning	88.70	78.20	72.50	70.40

Table 6-6. Ablation Results on QNLI: Number of Adversarial Queries Required by BA, TB, and TF Attacks under Different AMRED Configurations.

Dataset	LM	Method	No of Queries		
			BA	TB	TF
QNLI	BERT-Base	Fine-Tuned	235	210	195
		Dynamic Model Weighting	415	390	335
		Dynamic Model Weighting + Adaptive Meta Learning	624	595	515

Table 6-7. Ablation Results on MNLI: Accuracy under BA, TB, and TF Attacks across Different AMRED Configurations.

Dataset	LM	Method	OA	Accuracy under Attack		
				BA	TB	TF
MNLI	BERT-Base	Fine-Tuned	84.10	37.80	32.40	25.30
		Dynamic Model Weighting	82.10	41.20	37.70	38.40
		Dynamic Model Weighting + Adaptive Meta Learning	83.50	71.40	68.40	65.70

Table 6-8. Ablation Results on MNLI: Number of Adversarial Queries Required by BA, TB, and TF Attacks under Different AMRED Configurations.

Dataset	LM	Method	No of Queries		
			BA	TB	TF
MNLI	BERT-Base	Fine-Tuned	460	395	347
		Dynamic Model Weighting	780	704	573
		Dynamic Model Weighting + Adaptive Meta Learning	995	902	854

Token Length Sensitivity Analysis: To further evaluate the robustness of the proposed defense scheme ARMED, an in-depth analysis is conducted to evaluate the effectiveness of different defense strategies against adversarial attacks that target models using different token lengths. The primary focus is on understanding how these defense schemes perform when the number of tokens in the input data varies, which is crucial for determining their robustness in real-world applications where input lengths can differ significantly.

The effectiveness of each defense scheme is quantified using a metric known as the *defense rate*. It represents the proportion of test examples for which the adversarial attack was unsuccessful in misleading the model. In other words, a higher defense rate indicates that the defense scheme was more effective at preventing the attack. By examining these defense rates across a range of token lengths, it is possible to identify which strategies are most resilient and under what conditions their performance degrades.

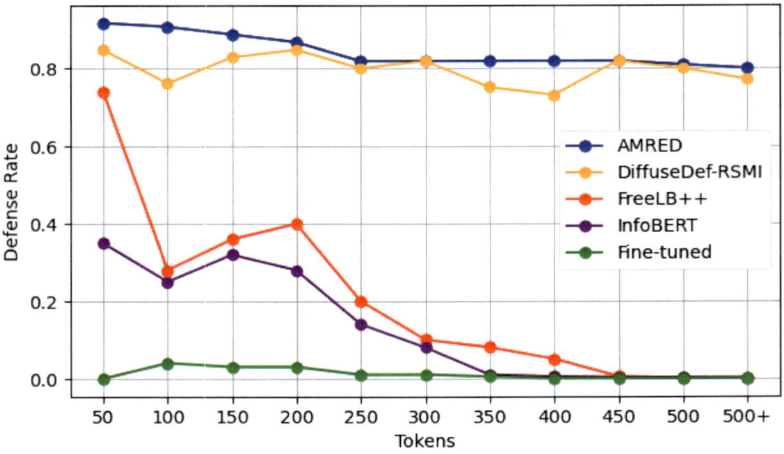

Figure 6-2. Defense rates of various schemes for different token lengths under the TextFooler (TF) attack on the IMDB dataset.

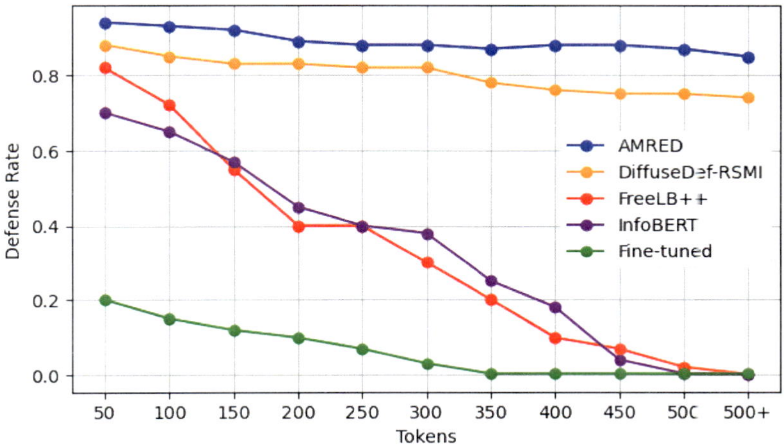

Figure 6-3. Defense rates of various schemes for different token lengths under the TextBugger (TB) attack on the IMDB dataset.

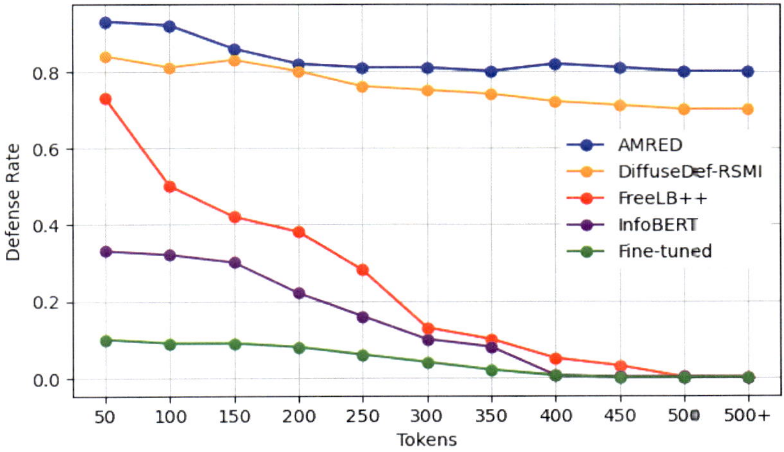

Figure 6-4. Defense rates of various schemes for different token lengths under the BERT-Attack (BA) on the IMDB dataset.

Figures 6-2 – 6-4 illustrate how token length influences the defense rates of different defense mechanisms. AMRED demonstrates consistently superior performance across all token lengths, maintaining defense rates above 0.7

even as the input length increases. This indicates a high degree of robustness to adversarial attacks irrespective of the input size. DiffuseDef-RSMI also performs well, with defense rates typically exceeding 0.6, suggesting considerable resilience, though not as high as AMRED. In contrast, both FreeLB++ and InfoBERT show a decline in defense rates as the token length grows, reflecting reduced effectiveness on longer sequences. The fine-tuned baseline model performs the worst, with defense rates approaching zero across all token lengths, highlighting its vulnerability to adversarial attacks regardless of the input size.

Conclusion

Adversarial robustness continues to be a central concern in the development and deployment of reliable machine learning systems, particularly in high-stakes domains such as natural language processing and computer vision. This chapter has presented a comprehensive overview of adversarial attacks and defenses in both text and image modalities, providing insights into their underlying mechanisms, challenges, and the evolving landscape of solutions. A comparative analysis of these modalities reveals common vulnerabilities and strategies, such as gradient-based optimization and adversarial training, while also highlighting key differences driven by the discrete nature of text and the continuous structure of images.

Text-based adversarial attacks must ensure grammatical correctness, semantic preservation, and fluency, making them more constrained yet deceptive. Image-based attacks, in contrast, can exploit imperceptible pixel-level perturbations that have little to no impact on human perception but significantly alter model predictions. As language models and convolutional networks become increasingly central to applications in healthcare, finance, transportation, and security, the demand for robust and interpretable defenses has grown substantially. This has driven the development of adversarial training, input preprocessing techniques, certified defenses, and ensemble-based methods. Despite their promise, many of these approaches remain computationally intensive, domain-specific, or vulnerable to adaptive attacks, underscoring the need for more generalizable and efficient solutions.

Several areas offer promising directions for future research. One important avenue is the development of more sophisticated attack strategies that target multilingual and low-resource language settings, where synonym dictionaries and language models may not be readily available. There is also growing interest in crafting document-level or discourse-aware adversarial examples that preserve coherence and cross-sentence dependencies, particularly for tasks such as summarization, reading comprehension, or dialogue. In image domains, further exploration is warranted into attacks that remain effective in the physical world under real-world transformations such as lighting, scale, and orientation. Increasingly, researchers are also examining the vulnerabilities of instruction-tuned language models and multimodal systems, where adversarial inputs may not require overt manipulations but instead exploit model biases or prompt sensitivities.

Defense strategies must also evolve to meet these challenges. Static, pre-defined defenses are unlikely to withstand dynamic and adaptive threats. This calls for the design of systems that can generate and learn from adversarial examples in real time, adapting their decision boundaries based on new threats. Meta-learning and reinforcement-based approaches offer frameworks for such continual adaptation. There is also a need for more lightweight and privacy-preserving defense mechanisms, particularly in federated or decentralized learning environments. Methods that integrate differential privacy, homomorphic encryption, or local perturbation strategies can help maintain both robustness and user confidentiality.

In parallel, a rethinking of evaluation and benchmarking practices is crucial. While accuracy under attack remains a standard metric, future benchmarks must incorporate human-centered dimensions such as semantic fidelity, fluency, perceived realism, and cognitive plausibility. The inclusion of human-in-the-loop evaluation, where adversarial examples are assessed for naturalness and coherence by human annotators, can provide richer assessments of both attack quality and defense resilience. Moreover, explainability-aware evaluations, which analyze how adversarial inputs affect attention mechanisms, feature attribution, or explanation outputs, can help diagnose model behavior more effectively.

The advent of multimodal AI systems, such as vision-language models and audio-enabled LLMs, introduces further complexity. Adversarial attacks may span multiple modalities, exploiting interactions between vision, language, and speech to compromise model integrity. Understanding how perturbations in one modality propagate to another, or how joint representations can be corrupted, is an emerging field of inquiry. Similarly, the development of cross-modal and modality-agnostic defenses that maintain robustness across input types will be a critical step forward. Research must also address the question of transferability: whether robustness gained in one modality or task generalizes to others, or whether it requires bespoke training strategies for each context.

Beyond empirical improvements, there is an urgent need for theoretical clarity. Formal robustness guarantees in text, where perturbations are discrete and constrained by syntax and semantics, remain particularly elusive. Techniques from formal verification, symbolic reasoning, and randomized smoothing offer potential pathways for deriving provable bounds. In parallel, grounding adversarial robustness in linguistic theory, including syntax, semantics, pragmatics, and discourse analysis, may yield more interpretable and controllable attack and defense frameworks. For vision models, connections to perceptual psychology and cognitive neuroscience may inform models of visual robustness that are better aligned with human perception.

Finally, adversarial robustness cannot be decoupled from its broader societal and ethical context. As adversarial techniques become more accessible and sophisticated, their potential for misuse in misinformation, fraud, surveillance, or digital manipulation grows. It is imperative that the research community, in collaboration with policymakers and industry stakeholders, develop ethical frameworks, auditing tools, and regulatory guidelines to ensure the responsible use of adversarial methods. Moreover, robust models must be stress-tested across diverse user populations and linguistic communities to prevent unintentional harm or bias amplification.

In summary, this chapter has laid the foundation for understanding the state of adversarial attacks and defenses in both text and image domains. The challenges are substantial, spanning technical, theoretical, and ethical dimensions. However, they also offer rich opportunities for interdisciplinary collaboration, innovation, and impact. Moving forward, robust AI systems will require not just stronger models, but also deeper insights into how language, vision, and meaning interact, and how these interactions can be protected from adversarial manipulation. Only through such comprehensive and forward-looking efforts can the promise of trustworthy and resilient AI be fully realized.

References

Devlin, J., Chang, M-W., Lee, K., Toutanova, K. 2019. "BERT: Pre-training of Deep Bi-directional Transformers for Language Understanding." In *Proceedings of the 2019 Conference of the North American Chapter of the Association of Computational Linguistics: Human Language Technologies*, 4171-4186.

Du, X., Yu, J., Li, S., Yi, Z., Liu, H., Ma, J. 2021. "Combating Word-level Adversarial Text with Robust Adversarial Training." In *Proceedings of the 2021 International Joint Conference on Neural Networks (IJCNN 2021)*, 1-8.

Goodfellow, I.J., Shlens, J., Szegedy, C. 2015. "Explaining and Harnessing Adversarial Examples." In *Proceedings of the International Conference on Learning Representations (ICLR 2015)*, Poster Track.

Google Colab URL: https://colab.research.google.com.

Huang, J., Chen, L. 2024. "Defense against Adversarial Attacks via Textual Embeddings Based on Semantic Associative Field." *Neural Computing and Applications*, 36, 289-301.

Jin, D., Jin, Z., Zhou, J. T., Szolovits, P. 2020. "Is BERT Really Robust? A Strong Baseline for Natural Language Attack on Text Classification and Entailment." In *Proceedings of the 34th AAAI Conference on Artificial Intelligence (AAAI 2020)*, 8018-8015.

Koley, A., Satpati, P., Choudhary, I., and Sen, J. 2024. "An Investigation on the Efficiency of Some Text Attack Algorithms." In *Proceedings of the IEEE North Karnataka Subsection Flagship International Conference (NKCon 2024)*, 1–8.

Lan, Z., Chen, M., Goodman, S., Gimpel, K., Sharma, P., Soricut, R. 2019. "ALBERT: A Lite BERT for Self-Supervised Learning of Language Representations." arXiv: 1909.11942.

Li, D. and Li, Q. 2020. "Adversarial Deep Ensemble: Evasion Attacks and Defenses for Malware Detection." *IEEE Transactions on Information Forensics and Security*, 15: 3886-3900.

Li, J., Ji, S., Du, T., Li, B., Wang, T. 2019. "TextBugger: Generating Adversarial Text against Real-World Applications." In *Proceedings of the 2019 Network and Distributed Systems Symposium (NDSS'19)*, arXiv:1812.05271.

Li, L., Ma, R., Guo, Q., Xue, X., Qiu, X. 2020. "BERT-Attack: Adversarial Attack against BERT Using BERT." In *Proceedings of the 2020 Conference on Empirical Methods in Natural Language Processing (EMNLP 2020)*, 6193-6202.

Li, Z., Rei, M., Specia, L. 2024. "DiffuseDef: Improved Robustness to Adversarial Attacks." arXiv:2407.00248.

Li, Z., Xu, J., Zeng, J., Li, L., Zheng, X., Zhang, Q., Chang, K-W., Hsieh, C-J. 2021. "Searching for an Effective Defender: Benchmarking Defense against Adversarial Word Sub-stitution." In *Proceedings of the*

2021 Conference on Empirical Methods in Natural Language Processing (EMNLP 2021), 3137-3147.

Liao, C., Cheng, Y., Fang, C., Shi, J. 2020. "Where does the Robustness Come from? A Study of the Transformation-Based Ensemble Defence." In *Proceedings of the 13th ACM Workshop on Artificial Intelligence and Security, AISec 2020*, 1-12.

Liu, B., Lane, I. 2018. "Adversarial Learning of Task-Oriented Neural Dialog Models." In *Proceedings of the 19th Annual SIGdial Meeting on Discourse and Dialogue*, 350-359.

Liu, Y., Ott, M., Goyal, N., Du, J., Joshi, M., Chen, D., Levy, O., Lewis, M., Zettle-moyer, L., Stoyanov, V. 2019. "RoBERTa: A Robustly Optimized BERT Pretraining Approach." arXiv:1907.11692.

Maas, A.L., Daly, R.E., Pham, P.T., Huang, D., Ng, A.Y., Potts, C. 2011. "Learning Word Vectors for Sentiment Analysis." In *Proceedings of the 49th Annual Meeting of the Association for Computational Linguistics: Human Language Technologies*, 142-150.

Pascanu, R., Mikolov, T., and Bengio, Y. 2013. "On the Difficulty of Training Recurrent Neural Networks." In *Proceedings of the 30th International Conference on Machine Learning* (ICML 2013), *PMLR*, 28(3): 1310-1318.

Robbins, H. and Monro, S. 1951. "A Stochastic Approximation Method." *The Annals of Mathematical Statistics*, 22(3): 400-407.

Sen, J. 2024. "The FGSM Attack on Image Classification Models and Distillation as its Defense." In Nanda et al. (eds), *Advances in Distributed Computing and Machine Learning (ICADCML 2024)*, 1015: 347-360. Lecture Notes in Networks and Systems, Springer, Singapore.

Sen, J. and Dasgupta, S. 2023. "Adversarial Attacks on Image Classification Models: FGSM and Patch Attacks and their Impact." In Sen, J. and Mayer, J. (eds), *Information Security and Privacy in the Digital World: Some Selected Topics*, IntechOpen, London, UK.

Sen, J., Sen, A., and Chatterjee, A. 2023. "Adversarial Attacks on Image Classification Models: Analysis and Defense." In *Proceedings of the 10th International Conference on Business Analytics and Intelligence (ICBAI 2023)*, Bangalore, India.

Sen, J. and Waghela, H. 2025. "Text-Based Adversarial Attacks and Defense." In Sen, J. (ed) *Data Privacy: Techniques, Applications, and Standards*, IntechOpen, London, UK.

Shafahi, A., Najibi, M., Ghiasi, A., Xu, Z., Dickerson, J., Studer, C., Davis, L. S., Taylor, G., Goldstein, T. 2019. "Adversarial Training for Free!" In *Proceedings of the 33rd Conference on Neural Information Processing Systems (NeurIPS 2019)*.

Szegedy, C., Zaremba, W., Sutskever, I., Bruma, J., Erhan, D., Goodfellow, I. J., Fergus, R. 2014. "Intriguing Properties of Neural Networks." In *the International Conference on Learning Representations (ICLR 2014)*, Poster Track.

Waghela, H., Sen, J., and Rakshit, S. 2025. "Saliency Attention and Semantic Similarity-Driven Adversarial Perturbation." In *Data Science and Applications. ICDSA 2024*, Nanda, S. J. et al. (eds), 1237: 461–471. Lecture Notes in Networks and Systems, Springer, Singapore.

Waghela, H., Sen, J., Rakshit, S., and Dasgupta, S. 2024a. "Adversarial Text Generation with Dynamic Contextual Perturbation." In *Proceedings of the 2024 IEEE CALCON 2024*, 1–6. IEEE.

Waghela, H., Sen, J., and Rakshit, S. 2024b. "Adaptive Meta-Learning for Robust Ensemble Defense against Adversarial Attacks." In *Proceedings of the International Conference BAMS-ORSI 2024*.

Waghela, H., Sen, J., and Rakshit, S. 2024c. "Adversarial Resilience in Image Classification: A Hybrid Approach to Defense." In *Proceedings of the 2024 International Conference on Innovation and Intelligence for Informatics, Computing, and Technologies (3ICT 2024)*, 419–426.

Waghela, H., Sen, J., Rakshit, S., and Dasgupta, S. 2024d. "Adversarial Robustness through Dynamic Ensemble Learning." In *Proceedings of the 2024 IEEE Silchar Subsection Conference (SILCON 2024)*, 1–6.

Waghela, H., Sen, J., and Rakshit, S. 2024e. "Robust Image Classification: Defensive Strategies against FGSM and PGD Adversarial Attacks." In *Proceedings of the IEEE Asian Conference on Intelligent Technologies (ACOIT 2024)*, 1 – 7.

Waghela, H., Sen, J., and Rakshit, S. 2024f. "Refining BERT Adversarial Attacks with Projected Gradient Descent." In *Proceedings of the IEEE 4th Asian Conference on Innovations in Technology (ASIANCON 2024)*, 1-7.

Waghela, H., Rakshit, S., and Sen, J. 2024g. "A Modified Word Saliency-Based Adversarial Attack on Text Classification Models." In *Computational Intelligence and Data Analytics*, Frery, A. C. et al. (eds), 371–382. Lecture Notes in Data Engineering and Communications Technologies, 236. Springer.

Wang, A., Singh, A., Michael, J., Hill, F., Levy, O., Bowman, S. 2018. "GLUE: A Multi-Task Benchmark and Analysis Platform for Natural Language Understanding." In *Proceedings of the 2018 EMNLP Workshop BlackboxNLP: Analyzing and Interpreting Neural Networks for NLP*, 353-355.

Wang, B., Wang, S., Cheng, Y., Gan, Z., Jia, R., Li, B., Liu, J. 2021. "InfoBERT: Improving Robustness of Language Models from an

Information Theoretic Perspective." In *Proceedings of the 9th International Conference on Learning Representations (ICLR 2021)*, Poster Track.

Wang, W., Wang, R., Ke, J., Wang, L. 2021. "TextFirewall: Omni-Defending against Adversarial Texts in Classification." *IEEE Access*, 9: 27467-27475.

Williams, A., Nangia, N., Bowman, S. R. 2018. "A Broad-Coverage Challenge Corpus for Sentence Understanding through Inference." In *Proceedings of the 2018 Conference of the North American Chapter of the Association for Computational Linguistics: Human Language Technologies*, 1: 1112-1122.

Wolf, T., Debut, L., Sanh, V., Chaumond, J., Delangue, C., Moi, A., Cistac, P., Rault, T., Louf, R., Funtowicz, M., Davison, J., Shleifer, S., von Platen, P., Ma, C., Jernite, Y., Plu, J., Xu, C., Scao, T. L., Gugger, S., Drame, M., Lhoest, Q., and Rush, A. 2020. "Transformers: State-of-the-Art Natural Language Processing." In *Proceedings of the 2020 Conference on Empirical Methods in Natural Language Processing* (EMNLP 2020), 38-45.

Yang, H., Li, K. 2024. "The Best Defense is Attack: Repairing Semantics in Textual Adversarial Examples." In *Proceedings of the 2024 Conference on Empirical Methods in Natural Language Processing*, 8439-8457.

Yang, Y., Liu, X., He, K. 2024. "Fast Adversarial Training against Textual Adversarial Attacks." arXiv:2401.12461.

Zhang, X., Zhao, J., LeCun, Y. 2015. "Character-Level Convolutional Networks for Text Classification." In *Proceedings of the 28th International Conference on Neural Information Processing Systems (NIPS 2015)*, 1: 649-657.

Zhang, Y., Shao, K., Yang, J., Liu, H. 2021. "Adversarial Attacks and Defenses on Deep Learning Models in Natural Language Processing." In *Proceedings of the IEEE 5th Information Technology, Networking, Electronic and Automation Control Conference (ITNEC 2021)*, 1281-1285.

Zhao, H., Ma, C., Dong, X., Luu, A.T., Deng, Z-H., Zhang, H. 2022. "Certified Robustness against Natural Language Attacks by Causal Intervention." In *Proceedings of the 39th International Conference on Machine Learning (PMLR 2022)*, 162, 2022.

CHAPTER 7

DYNAMIC CONTEXTUAL PERTURBATION FOR ADVERSARIAL TEXT GENERATION

Introduction

The rise of *Natural Language Processing* (NLP) as a core area of artificial intelligence has led to groundbreaking innovations across a wide spectrum of applications. From intelligent virtual assistants, chatbots, and document summarization tools to more complex systems such as legal document analysis, fake news detection, and sentiment-aware trading strategies, NLP systems have steadily permeated various sectors. This progress is largely attributed to the transformative capabilities of deep learning models, particularly transformer-based architectures such as BERT (Devlin et al., 2019), RoBERTa (Liu et al., 2019), and GPT (Radford et al., 2018), which have demonstrated unprecedented performance in both understanding and generating human-like text.

Despite their remarkable capabilities, these models possess a critical weakness: their vulnerability to adversarial examples. These are specially crafted inputs that cause a model to produce incorrect outputs despite appearing benign or even semantically identical to humans (Alzantot et al., 2018). The field of adversarial machine learning, initially explored in the domain of computer vision (Szegedy et al., 2014; Goodfellow et al , 2015), has increasingly attracted attention within the NLP community due to the unique challenges and consequences posed by adversarial perturbations in textual data.

In contrast to continuous input domains such as images and audio, the discrete and symbolic nature of language introduces unique hurdles for adversarial attack design. Inserting noise into an image or slightly shifting a pixel is often imperceptible to the human eye; however, modifying a single character or substituting a word in a sentence can dramatically alter its grammatical structure or semantic meaning. Therefore, adversarial attacks in NLP require sophisticated techniques that balance model deception with linguistic naturalness and semantic consistency. These requirements have given rise to a diverse taxonomy of attack strategies, ranging from character-level noise injection (e.g., swapping, deletion) and word-level substitutions (e.g., synonyms, homophones) to more complex transformations involving paraphrasing or sentence restructuring.

Early methods in textual adversarial attacks, such as TextBugger (Li et al., 2019) and HotFlip (Ebrahimi et al., 2018), employed straightforward manipulations, often focusing on high-impact tokens identified through gradient-based or heuristic approaches. While these approaches revealed the fragility of NLP models, the resulting adversarial texts were often syntactically malformed or semantically incoherent, undermining their stealth and real-world applicability. More recent frameworks, such as PWWS (Ren et al., 2019) and TextFooler (Jin et al., 2020), improved upon these designs by using saliency measures to prioritize influential words and lexical resources like WordNet to select plausible substitutes. Nevertheless, these models still exhibited a critical limitation: an inadequate sensitivity to context.

Context, both syntactic and semantic, plays a central role in determining the meaning and coherence of language. A word that is an appropriate replacement in one sentence may be entirely unsuitable in another due to subtle shifts in tone, tense, or discourse structure. Attacks that ignore contextual nuances often produce perturbed text that feels unnatural to a human reader and is thus easier to detect through automated or manual inspection. Furthermore, such context-agnostic perturbations are less likely to generalize across models or tasks, thereby limiting their effectiveness.

This realization has prompted a growing interest in context-aware adversarial attack mechanisms, particularly those that leverage the representational richness of pre-trained language models. Methods such as BERT-Attack (Li et al., 2020) and SemAttack (Zang et al., 2020) introduced perturbations guided by contextual embeddings, ensuring higher semantic similarity between original and adversarial texts. These techniques rely on masked language models and attention mechanisms to propose substitutions that are syntactically and semantically appropriate within the broader linguistic structure. However, most existing models treat sentences in isolation, applying context-sensitivity at the micro-level without accounting for macro-level discourse coherence across multiple sentences or paragraphs. This leads to attacks that may be semantically plausible at the local level but fail to preserve logical or topical consistency in longer texts.

The importance of addressing such limitations has become even more critical with the expanding use of NLP systems in high-stakes environments. In domains such as automated medical diagnosis, legal decision support, financial forecasting, and cybersecurity, the consequences of model misinterpretation due to adversarial perturbations can be severe. Attackers can exploit these weaknesses to manipulate sentiment detection systems for financial gain, bypass toxicity filters in content moderation platforms, or spread misinformation in news recommendation systems. As these systems increasingly influence real-world decisions, ensuring their robustness against adversarial threats becomes not just a technical concern but a societal necessity.

To respond to this pressing need, the current work proposes a novel attack strategy named *Dynamic Contextual Perturbation* (DCP). Unlike traditional methods that apply static or localized perturbation strategies, DCP dynamically adapts to the broader context in which a word or phrase appears, leveraging multi-level embeddings and model saliency maps to introduce adversarial modifications that are contextually coherent and semantically faithful. This framework extends the idea of perturbation from the level of isolated sentences to full documents, enabling more sophisticated attacks that can seamlessly traverse paragraph boundaries while preserving overall fluency and readability.

DCP also incorporates an adversarial objective function that optimally balances two competing goals: (1) maximizing the probability of model misclassification, and (2) minimizing semantic distortion between the original and perturbed texts. This optimization is achieved through iterative refinement, using techniques inspired by projected gradient descent and similarity-constrained embedding transformations. The result is an adversarial example that retains high fidelity to the original text while successfully evading detection by NLP classifiers.

Furthermore, DCP addresses another overlooked yet critical dimension of adversarial NLP, *query efficiency*. Many real-world NLP applications operate in a black-box setting where attackers have limited access to model internals and must rely on repeated querying to gather gradient-like signals. Excessive querying is not only computationally expensive but also likely to trigger anomaly detection systems. DCP significantly reduces the number of required queries while maintaining high attack success rates, making it both efficient and stealthy.

The proposed approach is empirically validated on several benchmark datasets and classification tasks, including sentiment analysis (IMDB, Yelp), topic classification (AG News), and fake news detection. DCP is also tested on natural language inference datasets (MNLI, SNLI), where logical consistency across sentences is essential, further demonstrating the importance of context-aware perturbation. The results clearly indicate that DCP outperforms popular attack baselines such as PWWS and BERT-on-BERT in terms of attack success rate, perturbation magnitude, semantic similarity, and query efficiency.

As adversarial NLP continues to evolve, the need for methods that align model deception with linguistic plausibility will only become more pronounced. DCP represents a step in this direction by harnessing the power of context to craft more realistic and effective adversarial examples. Its design philosophy not only enhances adversarial attack capabilities but also contributes to a deeper understanding of model vulnerabilities, insights that are essential for building the next generation of robust and trustworthy NLP systems.

The remainder of this chapter is organized as follows. The section on *Related Work* provides a review of the existing adversarial attack methodologies. The *Methodology* section introduces the conceptual foundation and methodological innovations that underlie the proposed approach. This is followed by the *Implementation* section, which outlines the algorithmic realization of DCP, detailing each computational step. In the *Experimental Results* section, extensive empirical results are discussed to demonstrate the effectiveness of DCP across various datasets and model architectures. The chapter concludes with the *section Conclusion and Future Directions*, which highlights unresolved challenges and potential avenues for advancing adversarial NLP research, including robust defense strategies and cross-lingual applications.

Related Work

The field of adversarial machine learning has witnessed significant advances over the past decade, initially flourishing in the domain of computer vision before gaining momentum in *Natural Language Processing* (NLP). The earliest evidence of adversarial vulnerability in deep learning systems was presented in the seminal work by Szegedy et al. (2014), which demonstrated that imperceptible perturbations in input images could cause high-confidence misclassifications by neural networks.

This was followed by the introduction of the *Fast Gradient Sign Method* (FGSM) by Goodfellow et al. (2015), which inspired a wide range of gradient-based adversarial attack methods. These developments laid the groundwork for exploring similar vulnerabilities in NLP, despite the intrinsic challenges posed by the discrete and symbolic nature of textual data.

Adversarial text attacks aim to perturb inputs in a way that is subtle and minimally invasive, such that the perturbed text remains grammatically correct, semantically coherent, and human-readable. Unlike in vision tasks, where pixel-level noise is often imperceptible, textual modifications can easily become obvious or change the original meaning. As a result, effective adversarial attacks in NLP must achieve a delicate balance between model deception and linguistic fidelity. A variety of approaches have been developed to meet this challenge, and these can be broadly categorized into character-level, word-level, sentence-level, and context-aware perturbations.

Character-Level Attacks: Initial efforts in NLP adversarial attacks focused on character-level perturbations. One such method is HotFlip (Ebrahimi et al., 2018), which identifies tokens that, when flipped, deleted, or inserted, yield the maximum change in model output. Although effective in certain scenarios, character-level attacks often generate outputs that are unnatural or visibly erroneous (e.g., typographical errors), making them easy to detect using spell-checkers or heuristic-based filters. These methods also lack robustness in black-box settings and have limited transferability across tasks and models.

Word-Level Attacks and Saliency-Based Perturbations: Word-level attacks have gained greater prominence due to their ability to preserve grammatical correctness while subtly altering semantics. Among the most widely studied approaches in this category is the *Probability Weighted Word Saliency* (PWWS) attack proposed by Ren et al. (2019). PWWS ranks words by their saliency scores, computed via gradients or prediction confidence, and replaces them using synonyms sourced from lexical databases such as WordNet. The attack achieves high success rates on classification tasks but does not account for the broader sentence or paragraph-level context, leading to occasional semantic inconsistencies.

Building on the saliency principle, Waghela et al. (2025) proposed the *Modified Word Saliency-Based Adversarial Attack* (MWSAA), which improves upon PWWS by refining the selection of candidate words and optimizing substitutions through a dual-objective formulation. The authors later introduced *SASSP* (Saliency Attention and Semantic Similarity Perturbation), which integrates attention mechanisms and embedding-based similarity constraints to enhance the quality of generated adversarial examples (Waghela et al., 2024g). These models represent a shift toward hybrid methods that begin to consider not just the local importance of words but also their semantic alignment in context.

Semantically-Constrained and Embedding-Based Methods: Another significant direction in adversarial NLP research involves generating perturbations in the embedding space rather than relying purely on surface-level manipulations. *TextFooler* (Jin et al., 2020) and *SemAttack* (Zang et al., 2020) use contextual embeddings from pre-trained models such as BERT or GloVe to identify and replace words with semantically similar alternatives. Chiang and Lee critically examine the robustness and validity of synonym substitution-based adversarial techniques in NLP (Chiang & Lee, 2023). These techniques increase the plausibility of the adversarial examples by maintaining high semantic similarity with the original input, measured through cosine similarity in embedding space. However, they typically operate at the sentence level, with minimal regard for discourse coherence or logical consistency across larger textual units. Asl et al. introduce a framework named SSCAE, designed to generate advanced adversarial examples for natural language processing tasks (Asl et al., 2024). Despite its effectiveness, the integration of diverse linguistic features within the framework may hinder scalability and reduce computational efficiency.

Context-Aware Attacks Using Pre-Trained Language Models: The advent of transformer-based language models has significantly advanced the design of context-aware adversarial attacks. *BERT-Attack* (Li et al., 2020) is a representative method in this category. It uses a pre-trained BERT model to mask and predict target tokens, replacing them with high-probability alternatives that match the surrounding context. This results in adversarial examples that are more fluent and syntactically consistent. However, such models often require access to internal representations or multiple queries to the target model, which may not be practical in real-world black-box settings. Furthermore, they typically operate at the sentence level, limiting their applicability to multi-sentence or document-level tasks.

Recent advances in adversarial machine learning have significantly enhanced the design of both attack and defense mechanisms by incorporating semantic similarity measures, dynamic perturbation strategies, and ensemble-based robustness frameworks. Notably, a series of studies conducted by Waghela, Sen, Rakshit, and collaborators (Waghela et al., 2024a–g; Waghela et al., 2025; Sen, 2024; Sen & Dasgupta, 2023; Sen & Waghela, 2025; Sen et al., 2023; Koley et al., 2024) have made important contributions to this evolving research landscape. These works introduce context-aware and linguistically grounded adversarial techniques that employ saliency analysis, attention mechanisms, BERT-derived embeddings, and semantic similarity metrics to generate adversarial examples that are both coherent and effective. On the defense front, several of these studies propose ensemble-driven meta-learning frameworks and hybrid robustness methods aimed at countering adversarial attacks across both text and image domains. Collectively, these contributions offer a comprehensive approach to optimizing attack potency while maintaining semantic fidelity and to developing adaptive defense strategies that exhibit strong generalization across tasks, data modalities, and model architectures.

Gradient-Based and Decision-Based Attacks: Several techniques leverage model gradients or decision boundaries to guide the perturbation process. Zhao et al. (2022) employed *differential evolution algorithms* to optimize word-level perturbations, demonstrating strong performance across datasets. However, the method's scalability and efficiency in real-time applications remain concerns. Hu et al. (2024) introduced *FastTextDodger*, a decision-based black-box attack optimized for high efficiency. It iteratively modifies input text based on model outputs, rather than gradients, making it effective in query-limited environments. Yet, its reliance on heuristic sampling can still yield suboptimal perturbations in complex tasks involving long-form inputs. Vitorino et al. investigate the effectiveness of adversarial evasion attacks targeting large language models (Vitorino et al., 2024). While the study provides valuable insights, it may encounter limitations in accurately simulating real-world conditions and in evaluating the sustained impact of the proposed defense strategies over time.

Task-Specific and Structural Attacks: Several recent studies have designed adversarial strategies tailored to specific tasks. Parry et al. (2024) explored attacks against *sequence-to-sequence relevance models*, identifying task-specific vulnerabilities related to attention mechanisms. Similarly, Li et al. (2022) developed query-limited adversarial attacks targeting *Graph Neural Networks* (GNNs) applied to text graph representations. These studies underscore the importance of aligning adversarial strategies with the underlying structure and semantics of the task at hand.

As summarized in Table 7-1, existing adversarial attack strategies vary considerably in terms of their contextual sensitivity, perturbation granularity, and efficiency. While several recent methods incorporate semantic constraints, most do so only at the sentence level. The proposed DCP scheme distinguishes itself by extending context modeling across sentences and paragraphs, optimizing for both attack efficacy and semantic plausibility. Its dynamic, document-level strategy makes it particularly effective in real-world, high-stakes NLP tasks.

Table 7-1. Comparative Summary of Adversarial Text Attack Methods Based on Perturbation Level, Context Awareness, and Performance Characteristics

Method	Perturbation Level	Context Awareness	Attack Success	Semantic Similarity	Query Similarity	Key Limitation
HotFlip (Ebrihimi et al. 2018)	Character-Level	No	Moderate	Low	High	Generates nonsensical words; easy to detect via spell-checking
TextBugger (Li et al., 2019)	Character & Word-level	Limited	High	Low to Medium	Moderate	Produces visually obvious perturbations
PWWS (Ren et al., 2019)	Word-level	No	High	Medium	High	Ignores context; may cause semantic distortion
TextFooler (Jin et al., 2020)	Word-level	Sentence-level (local)	High	Medium to High	Moderate	Limited discourse-level coherence
BERT-Attack (Li et al., 2020)	Word-level (masked LM)	Sentence-level (via BERT)	High	High	Moderate	Requires access to a masked language model; high query cost
SemAttack (Zan et al., 2020)	Word-level	Sentence-level	High	High	Moderate	Context-aware only at the local level; lacks document-level fluency
FastTextDodger (Hu et al., 2024)	Word-level	No	High	Medium	Very High	Works in a black-box setting but lacks semantic finesse
SASSP (Waghela et al., 2024)	Word-level (Saliency + Attention)	Local with attention focus	High	High	Moderate	Performance may degrade on long text; sentence-level only
DCP (Proposed)	Word; Sentence; Paragraph	Document-level (Dynamic)	Very High	Very High	Low	Needs a powerful language model; complexity in optimization

Transferability and Query Efficiency: An emerging concern in adversarial NLP is the *transferability* of attacks across models and architectures. Attacks that overfit to a specific model's linguistic or structural biases often fail when applied to different architectures, such as moving from LSTM-based classifiers to transformer-based models. DCP addresses this limitation by generating perturbations that are not only effective across a diverse set of classifiers, including Word-CNN (Kim, 2014), Bi-LSTM (Graves et al., 2005), BERT-Large (BERT-Large; Devlin et al., 2019), and ESIM (Chen et al., 2016), but also require significantly fewer queries, making it suitable for real-world, black-box deployment scenarios.

Limitations of Existing Methods: Despite the proliferation of attack methods, many existing strategies suffer from common shortcomings. A majority of word-level attacks ignore inter-sentential dependencies and fail to maintain logical coherence across paragraphs. Some embedding-based approaches rely heavily on computationally expensive similarity calculations or require internal access to model gradients, limiting their scalability. Others introduce perturbations that, while semantically similar in embedding space, are pragmatically inappropriate or stylistically jarring. Moreover, defense-aware attacks remain relatively underdeveloped, with most studies assuming static and naive target models.

Positioning of DCP in the Landscape: The *Dynamic Contextual Perturbation* (DCP) scheme seeks to address these limitations by integrating dynamic, context-aware perturbation mechanisms that span sentence, paragraph, and document levels. Unlike methods that apply localized modifications based on static word saliency, DCP employs contextual embeddings, model gradients, and iterative refinement to construct perturbations that are syntactically correct, semantically coherent, and pragmatically consistent across the broader narrative. It introduces a novel adversarial objective function that balances misclassification confidence with semantic fidelity, optimized through gradient-based feedback loops. Additionally, by reducing the number of required queries and adapting seamlessly across different model architectures, DCP enhances the practical feasibility of adversarial attacks.

This context-sensitive and scalable framework represents a meaningful step forward in adversarial NLP research, contributing to a deeper understanding of how linguistic context can be exploited or defended against in machine learning pipelines. As such, DCP provides not only an effective attack strategy but also a valuable testbed for evaluating the robustness and interpretability of modern NLP systems.

Methodology

The *Dynamic Contextual Perturbation* (DCP) framework is designed to craft adversarial text instances that are capable of compromising the predictive performance of modern NLP models while maintaining semantic integrity and fluency. This section elaborates on the components and computational workflow of DCP in a structured and comprehensive manner. The methodology encompasses a series of interdependent stages, ranging from data preparation and contextual representation to perturbation optimization and evaluation.

Input Data Selection: The construction of adversarial examples begins with the acquisition of text samples from widely used benchmark datasets. To ensure broad applicability, both classification and inference tasks are targeted. Specifically, datasets such as IMDB and Yelp are utilized for sentiment analysis, AG News for topic categorization, and the Fake News dataset for binary news authenticity detection. In addition, *Multi-Genre Natural Language Inference* (MNLI) and *Stanford Natural Language Inference* (SNLI) datasets are incorporated to evaluate DCP on entailment-based reasoning tasks. These corpora are publicly available and collectively cover a diverse range of linguistic styles and structural complexities.

Text Preprocessing: Once the raw text samples are selected, they undergo a series of preprocessing operations to ensure consistency and linguistic normalization. Tokenization decomposes the text into smaller lexical units, facilitating further analysis. Subsequent lowercasing enhances uniformity across tokens, while stop-word removal eliminates frequent yet semantically redundant terms. Furthermore, stemming or lemmatization is applied to reduce words to their canonical forms, thereby minimizing lexical variability. Non-alphabetic characters, punctuation, and irrelevant symbols are filtered out to ensure the input is clean and structurally consistent for downstream processing.

Generation of Contextual Embeddings: A crucial aspect of DCP lies in its ability to incorporate contextual information into perturbation decisions. To this end, pre-trained transformer-based language models, such as BERT, are employed to generate rich contextual embeddings. These embeddings capture both syntactic structure and semantic nuance at the word and sentence level. Unlike static word vectors, contextual embeddings provide dynamic representations that reflect the position and meaning of words within specific linguistic contexts, making them well-suited for generating perturbations that preserve naturalness and meaning.

Identification of Perturbation Candidates: Following embedding generation, the next objective is to identify which components of the input text should be modified to maximize the adversarial impact. Gradient-based analysis is performed to compute the sensitivity of the model's output to changes in the input tokens. This involves calculating the gradient of the loss function with respect to input embeddings, thereby highlighting tokens that exert the greatest influence on the model's predictions. The resulting saliency map serves as a visual and quantitative guide for selecting high-impact words or phrases as candidates for perturbation.

Generation of Context-Aware Perturbations: Perturbations are generated for the selected candidate tokens using context-sensitive strategies. The core technique involves synonym replacement, where tokens are substituted with semantically similar alternatives derived from lexical databases (e.g., WordNet) or predicted using masked language modeling techniques. The substitutions are constrained to ensure they are grammatically valid and contextually appropriate. For example, a masked language model may suggest top-k alternatives based on contextual fit, from which the most semantically aligned option is selected. The aim is to introduce minimal lexical deviation while still influencing the model's decision-making process.

Dynamic Refinement via Adversarial Objective Optimization: To ensure the quality and effectiveness of the perturbations, an iterative optimization procedure is employed. This refinement process is guided by a composite objective function that balances two competing goals: inducing misclassification and preserving semantic similarity.

The total adversarial loss is given by (7-1):

$$\mathcal{L}_{adv} = \mathcal{L}_{model}(x + \delta, y; \theta) + \lambda * \mathcal{L}_{sim}(x, x + \delta) \tag{7-1}$$

In (7-1), x denotes the original input, δ is the perturbation applied to x, and y is the true label. The term $\mathcal{L}_{model}$ measures the increase in prediction loss due to the perturbation, while $\mathcal{L}_{sim}$ quantifies the semantic dissimilarity between the original and perturbed texts, typically computed using the squared $_{L2}$-norm of the embedding vectors. The parameter λ controls the trade-off: larger values prioritize semantic fidelity, while smaller values place more emphasis on misclassification.

The optimization process iteratively adjusts the perturbations until a convergence criterion is met, either successful misclassification is achieved, or further refinement yields negligible improvement. This dynamic adjustment ensures that the adversarial examples are both impactful and human-like in form.

Construction of Final Adversarial Examples: Once optimized perturbations have been identified and validated, they are integrated into the original text to produce the final adversarial examples. These samples undergo validation to ensure they satisfy both attack success and readability constraints. In particular, the adversarial version must differ minimally from the original while still altering the model's output, and it must retain syntactic correctness and semantic plausibility when read by a human evaluator.

Evaluation Metrics: To assess the efficacy of DCP, several quantitative metrics are employed:

- *Attack Success Rate* (ASR): Measures the proportion of inputs for which the model's prediction is altered post-perturbation.
- *Perturbation Rate*: Indicates the percentage of tokens modified relative to the original input length, reflecting how economical the attack is.
- *Semantic Similarity*: Calculated using cosine similarity or embedding distance, this metric evaluates how semantically close the adversarial example remains to the original text.
- *Readability Score*: The Flesch-Kincaid readability index is used to assess the linguistic fluency of the perturbed text (Flesch, 1948).

Comparative Evaluation with Existing Methods: To benchmark DCP against established adversarial techniques, comparative experiments are conducted using two state-of-the-art methods: *Probability Weighted Word Saliency* (PWWS) and BERT-on-BERT. Both methods are implemented on the same datasets and under equivalent model settings to ensure fairness. DCP is evaluated not only in terms of attack success but also across dimensions such as perturbation sparsity, query efficiency, and semantic integrity. Results consistently demonstrate that DCP achieves higher misclassification rates with fewer and more meaningful perturbations, validating its superiority in both white-box and black-box adversarial scenarios.

Figure 7-1 depicts the workflow of the proposed DCP scheme.

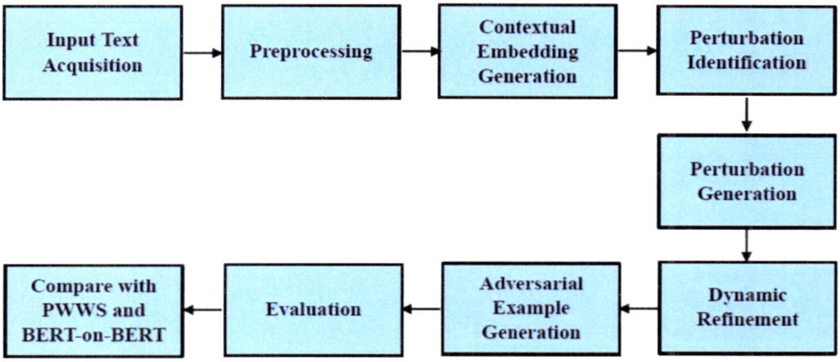

Figure 7-1. The diagram outlining the key phases of the DCP design process

Implementation Details

This section describes the practical realization of the Dynamic Contextual Perturbation (DCP) framework, highlighting its software environment, algorithmic components, and core functionalities. The DCP scheme is implemented in Python, leveraging a suite of widely used natural language processing and deep learning libraries. The implementation is modular and structured to allow flexibility across datasets, tasks, and target models.

```
# Step 1: Input Text Acquisition
input_text = get_input_text(dataset)
# Step 2: Preprocessing
preprocessed_text = preprocess(input_text)
# Step 3: Contextual Embedding Generation
embeddings = generate_contextual_embeddings(preprocessed_text, pre_trained_model="BERT")
# Step 4: Perturbation Identification
# Compute gradients and identify important words for perturbation
important_words = identify_perturbation_candidates(preprocessed_text, model, embeddings)
# Step 5: Perturbation Generation
# Generate context-aware perturbations using synonym substitution or paraphrasing
perturbed_texts = generate_perturbations(important_words, preprocessed_text,method="synonym_substitution")
# Step 6: Dynamic Refinement
# Initialize adversarial objective and iteratively refine perturbations
while not misclassification(perturbed_texts, model):
    for each_perturbed_text in perturbed_texts:
      # Compute misclassification loss
      loss_misclassification = compute_loss(perturbed_text, model)
      # Compute similarity between original and perturbed text (readability)
      loss_similarity = compute_similarity(preprocessed_text, perturbed_text)
      # Update perturbation based on adversarial objective
      adversarial_objective = loss_misclassification + lambda * loss_similarity
      perturbed_text = refine_perturbation(perturbed_text, adversarial_objective)
# Step 7: Adversarial Example Generation
# Validate final adversarial examples
adversarial_examples = validate_adversarial_examples(perturbed_texts)
# Step 8: Evaluation
evaluate(adversarial_examples, original_text=input_text, metrics=["ASR", "perturbation_rate", "readability"])
```

Figure 7-2. Pseudocode outlining the key steps of the DCP algorithm

Figure 7-2 presents the pseudocode of the DCP algorithm. The complete DCP workflow is composed of several stages, including environment setup, contextual embedding generation, gradient-based perturbation candidate identification, synonym-based substitution, iterative adversarial optimization, and evaluation. Each of these stages is realized through custom functions and interfaces built on top of modern NLP infrastructure.

Environment Setup and Preprocessing: The initial setup configures the computational environment by installing the necessary Python libraries and initializing NLP resources. The implementation makes extensive use of the following key packages:

- NLTK (Natural Language Toolkit): Used for standard NLP preprocessing tasks such as *tokenization*, *stopword removal*, *stemming*, and *access to WordNet* for synonym generation.
- Transformers (from Hugging Face): Provides pre-trained models and tokenizers, such as BERT, which are essential for contextual embedding generation and classification tasks.
- Datasets (from Hugging Face): Enables seamless access to benchmark datasets like IMDB, Yelp, AG News, MNLI, and SNLI.
- Torch (PyTorch): Serves as the backbone deep learning framework, supporting tensor operations, gradient computations, and model training and evaluation.

Once the libraries are installed, basic preprocessing steps are applied to the raw text data. This includes tokenizing each sentence into words or subwords, converting text to lowercase for consistency, removing non-informative tokens (e.g., stop-words), applying stemming or lemmatization to normalize word forms, and filtering out non-alphabetic characters. These operations ensure the textual input is standardized and ready for embedding and model-based analysis.

Generation of Contextual Embeddings: The core of DCP's contextual sensitivity is enabled through the use of a pre-trained BERT model. The contextual embeddings are generated by tokenizing the input using the BERT tokenizer and then passing the tokenized sequence through the BERT encoder. The following steps are followed:

1. *Tokenizer Initialization*: This step loads the vocabulary and tokenization logic used by the pre-trained model using the following statement:

   tokenizer = BertTokenizer.from_pretrained('bert-base-uncased')

2. *Model Initialization*: This step loads the base BERT encoder, which outputs the contextualized embeddings of input tokens.

   model = BertModel.from_pretrained('bert-base-uncased')

3. *Embedding Extraction*: A custom function (e.g., *get_embeddings*(*text*)) converts raw text into token IDs, passes them through BERT, and extracts the hidden states representing each token in its contextual form. These embeddings are critical for both saliency computation and semantic similarity evaluation.

Identification of Silent Tokens for Perturbation: Once contextual embeddings are available, the next step involves identifying the most influential tokens in the input text with respect to the model's classification decision. This is achieved through gradient-based analysis, where the gradient of the prediction loss is computed with respect to the embedding of each token.

- The input is encoded and passed through a fine-tuned classifier (Based on BERT).
- The classification loss is computed using a loss function such as cross-entropy.
- Backpropagation is enabled to compute the gradient of the loss with respect to each token's embedding.
- The gradient magnitudes are aggregated across embedding dimensions to yield an importance score per token.
- Tokens with the highest scores are selected as prime candidates for perturbation, as they exert the most influence on the model's output.

The function *calculate_gradient(text, model)* encapsulates this process and returns the ranked list of candidate tokens.

Generation of Semantically Valid Perturbation: After selecting the most salient tokens, DCP proceeds to generate plausible replacements using synonym substitution. The objective here is to modify the input subtly enough to fool the model, while maintaining linguistic coherence.

Synonyms are retrieved using a combination of the following:

- *WordNet Synsets*: Semantic sets of synonyms for a given word.
- *Masked Language Model Predictions*: BERT can be used to predict context-appropriate tokens when a word is masked.

The synonym generation process is handled by a dedicated function (e.g., *get_synonyms*(word)), which performs the following tasks:

- Accesses all synsets for the target word.
- Extracts all lemmas (alternate forms) from the synsets.
- Filters out duplicates and invalid substitutes.
- Optionally re-ranks the synonyms based on context-fit (e.g., using embedding similarity).

The final perturbed variants are produced by replacing selected tokens with their respective synonyms, generating multiple candidate adversarial texts.

Iterative Refinement via Adversarial Objective: Not all perturbations will achieve the intended adversarial goal. Hence, DCP employs an iterative refinement process that optimizes a joint adversarial objective designed to balance model misclassification with semantic fidelity. The refinement loop operates as follows:

1. Perturbed text is classified by the target model.
2. Prediction is compared with the original label to check for misclassification.
3. Semantic similarity between original and perturbed text is computed (e.g., using the cosine similarity in the embedding space).
4. The adversarial loss is calculated as:

$$\mathcal{L}_{adv} = \mathcal{L}_{model}(x + \delta, y) + \lambda . \|E(x) - E(x + \delta)\|_2^2 \qquad (7\text{-}2)$$

   In (7-2), δ denotes the perturbation, $E(.)$ is the embedding function, and λ balances classification loss and similarity penalty.
5. The candidate with the lowest loss is selected for the next iteration. This loop is repeated until a successful adversarial example is produced, or a maximum iteration count is reached. The functions *adversarial_objective*() and *dynamic_refinement*() encapsulate this logic.

Evaluation of Generated Adversarial Samples: The quality and success of the generated adversarial examples are assessed using multiple metrics:

- *Attack Success Rate* (ASR): The proportion of inputs where the classifier's prediction changes after perturbation.
- *Perturbation Rate*: The fraction of words in the input that were modified. Lower values indicate more subtle attacks.
- *Semantic Similarity*: Calculated using cosine similarity between sentence embeddings of original and perturbed texts.
- *Readability Score*: The Flesch-Kincaid readability index is used to evaluate linguistic fluency.

The function *evaluate_adversarial_examples*( ) computes and reports these metrics for the entire test set. As demonstrated in the next section, DCP consistently achieves high attack success rates while maintaining low perturbation levels and strong readability.

Summary of Implementation: The implementation of DCP blends several modern NLP tools to create a modular, scalable, and context-sensitive adversarial attack system. Its architecture emphasizes not just the ability to deceive models, but to do so in a manner that is linguistically natural and computationally efficient. The modular design also enables seamless integration with a variety of pre-trained models and classification pipelines, making it applicable to both white-box and black-box adversarial evaluation scenarios.

Experimental Results

This section presents a comprehensive evaluation of the *Dynamic Contextual Perturbation* (DCP) framework, with a focus on its adversarial effectiveness, perturbation economy, semantic fidelity, and query efficiency. The proposed attack strategy is benchmarked against two widely recognized adversarial text generation methods: *Probability Weighted Word Saliency* (PWWS) and *BERT-on-BERT*. The evaluation spans multiple datasets and model architectures, ensuring a robust and generalizable assessment of DCP's performance.

Experimental Setup: In alignment with prior work on BERT-Attack, the evaluation of DCP includes experiments conducted on 1000 randomly selected test instances from each dataset. The selected partitions follow those used in existing studies to ensure consistency and comparability. The evaluation comprises both *text classification* and *natural language inference* (NLI) tasks, and targets a range of deep learning architectures, including convolutional neural networks (CNNs), recurrent networks, and transformer-based models.

For classification tasks, the evaluation is performed on the *AG News* (Zhang et al., 2015), *IMDB* (Maas et al., 2011; IMDB Dataset), *Yelp* (Zhang et al., 2015; Yelp Dataset), and *Fake News* (Wang, 2017; Fake News Dataset) datasets. For NLI tasks, the Multi-Genre Natural Language Inference (MNLI) (Williams et al., 2018) and Stanford Natural Language Inference (SNLI) (Bowman et al., 2015) datasets are utilized, representing multi-sentence inference challenges where contextual coherence is critical.

In terms of model diversity, the attacks are executed against both shallow and deep architectures, including:

- Word-CNN (Kim, 2014), Char-CNN (Zhang et al., 2015), and Bi-LSTM (Graves et al., 2005) for baseline text classification

- Word-LSTM (Hochreiter & Schmidhuber, 1997), BERT-Large (Devlin, 2018; BERT-Large), and ESIM (Chen et al., 2016) for comparisons with BERT-on-BERT and DCP on inference tasks

This diverse configuration enables the evaluation of both attack performance and transferability across model types.

Comparison with PWWS: The initial set of experiments compares DCP with the PWWS attack across CNN and LSTM-based models for the *AG News* and *IMDB* datasets. Table 7-2 summarizes the classification accuracies of the models under three scenarios: no attack (clean input), under PWWS attack, and under DCP attack.

Table 7-2. Comparative Classification Accuracy of Models on AG News and IMDB with and without PWWS and DCP Adversarial Attacks

Dataset	Model	Acc. (%) (No Attack)	PWWS Acc. (%)	DCP Acc. (%)
AG News	Word-CNN	90.56	56.72	48.25
	Char-CNN	89.70	56.20	46.20
IMDB	Bi-LSTM	84.86	2.20	[illegible].75
	Word-CNN	86.55	5.50	[illegible].60

As reflected in the results, all baseline models maintain high accuracy in the absence of adversarial manipulation. However, both PWWS and DCP lead to a substantial degradation in performance, with DCP showing a consistently stronger adversarial effect. This is especially evident in the IMDB sentiment analysis task, where DCP reduces accuracy to near-random levels.

Table 7-3. Perturbation Rates of PWWS and DCP Attacks on AG News and IMDB Dataset

Dataset	Model	PWWS Perturbation Rate (%)	DCP Perturbation Rate (%)
AG News	Word-CNN	16.76	15.25
	Char-CNN	18.93	14.80
IMDB	Bi-LSTM	3.38	2.80
	Word-CNN	3.81	3.10

Table 7-3 reports the *perturbation rate*, i.e., the proportion of tokens modified during the attack, for both attack strategies. A lower perturbation rate indicates a more efficient and subtle attack.

The comparative performance of PWWS and DCP attacks, in terms of classification accuracy and perturbation rate across various models, is illustrated in Figure 7-3. DCP not only induces higher misclassification but also achieves this with a *lower perturbation footprint*, signifying better semantic preservation and higher stealth.

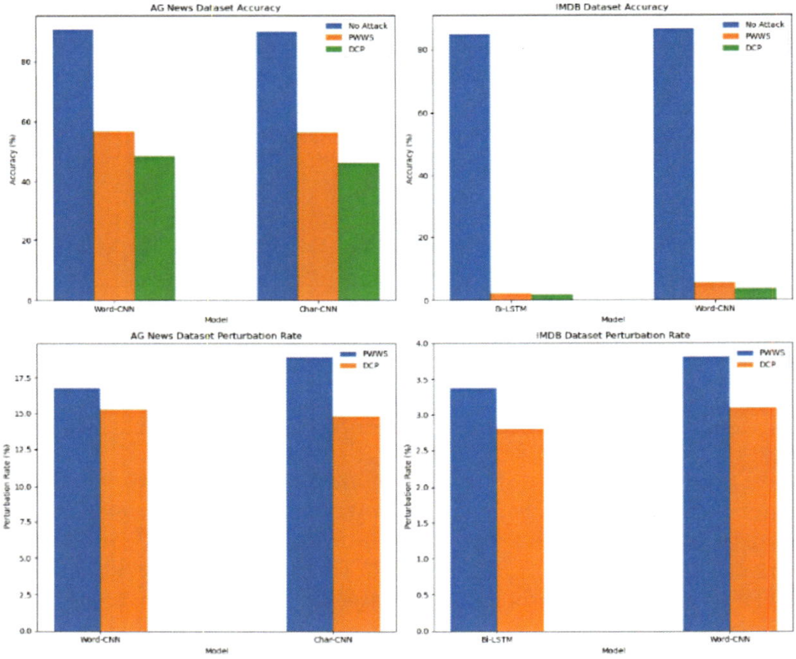

Figure 7-3. Comparison of classification accuracy and perturbation rate for PWWS and DCP attacks on AG News and IMDB across multiple models

Performance against Transformer Models: The next set of experiments contrasts DCP with the BERT-on-BERT attack across four classification datasets: IMDB, Yelp, Fake News, and AG News. Table 7-4 presents the classification accuracies and perturbation rates for each method. Figure 7-4 illustrates the comparative impact of BERT-on-BERT and DCP attacks on classification accuracy and perturbation rate across multiple text classification datasets.

Across all datasets, DCP results in lower classification accuracy post-attack, indicating stronger adversarial impact. Furthermore, it consistently requires fewer token modifications, rendering it *more efficient and semantically faithful*.

Table 7-4. Accuracy and Perturbation Rates of BERT-on-BERT and DCP Attacks across Text Classification Datasets

Dataset	Attack Method	Original Acc.	Acc. Under Attack	Perturb Rate
IMDB	BERT-on-BERT	90.90	11.40	4.40
	DCP		7.40	2.70
Yelp	BERT-on-BERT	95.60	5.10	4.10
	DCP		4.05	3.50
Fake	BERT-on-BERT	97.80	15.50	1.10
	DCP		11.40	0.90
AG News	BERT-on-BERT	94.20	10.60	15.40
	DCP		6.70	8.60

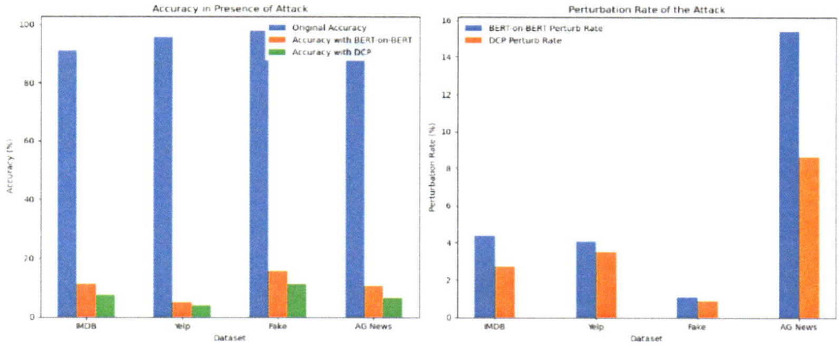

Figure 7-4. Classification accuracy and perturbation rate of BERT-on-BERT and DCP attacks across multiple text classification datasets.

Query Efficiency and Semantic Similarity: In real-world black-box settings, minimizing the number of model queries required for a successful attack is essential. Table 7-5 presents a comparison of *query counts* and *semantic similarity scores* for BERT-on-BERT and DCP across the classification datasets. Figure 7-5 depicts the same results in the form of vertical bar charts.

DCP outperforms BERT-on-BERT in both aspects, requiring significantly fewer queries and yielding *higher semantic similarity scores*, which confirms its capacity to generate natural and imperceptible adversarial examples.

Table 7-5. Number of Queries and Semantic Similarity for BERT-on-BERT and DCP Attacks on Text Classification Datasets

Dataset	Attack Method	Number of Queries	Semantic Similarity
IMDB	BERT-on-BERT	454	0.86
	DCP	347	0.96
Yelp	BERT-on-BERT	273	0.77
	DCP	238	0.94
Fake	BERT-on-BERT	1558	0.81
	DCP	943	0.93
AG News	BERT-on-BERT	213	0.63
	DCP	154	0.94

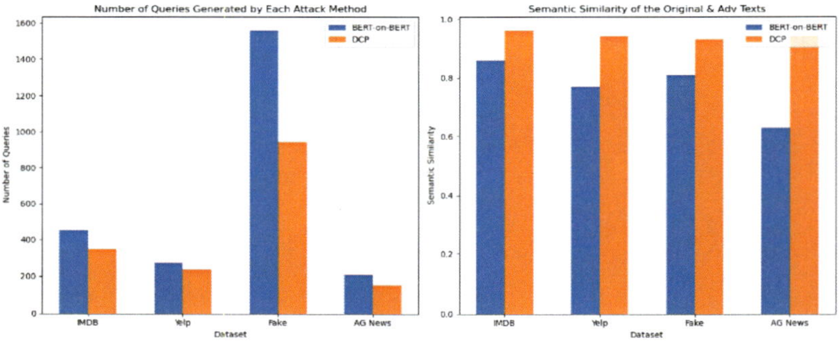

Figure 7-5. Comparison of query counts and semantic similarity for BERT-on-BERT and DCP attacks on text classification datasets.

Results on Natural Language Inference Tasks: Table 7-6 presents a detailed breakdown of DCP and BERT-on-BERT attack performance on *NLI datasets*, including matched and unmatched subsets of MNLI and the SNLI dataset. Accuracy and perturbation rate are reported for both *hypothesis* (H) and *premise* (P) components. Figure 7-6 presents the same results pictorially.

Table 7-6. Accuracy and Perturbation Rates of BERT-on-BERT and DCP Attacks on Natural Language Inference Datasets

Dataset	Attack Method	Original Acc. (%)	Acc. Under Attack (%)	Perturb Rate (%)
MNLI Matched	BERT-on-BERT	85.10 (H/P)	7.90/11.90	8.80/7.90
	DCP		5.30/10.80	7.40/6.70
MNLI Unmatched	BERT-on-BERT	82.10 (H/P)	7.00/13.70	8.00/7.10
	DCP		5.10/10.60	7.20/7.00
SNLI	BERT-on-BERT	89.40 (H/P)	7.40/16.10	12.40/9.30
	DCP		3.10/12.60	8.20/6.30

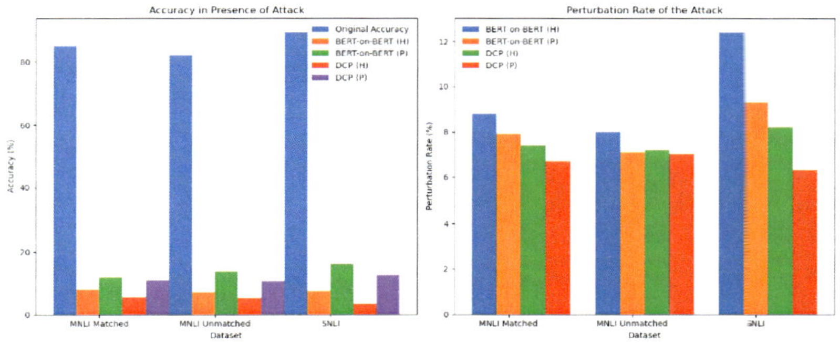

Figure 7-6. Classification accuracy and perturbation rate of BERT-on-BERT and DCP attacks on natural language inference datasets.

DCP continues to exhibit *superior adversarial efficacy* while maintaining more compact perturbations. This highlights its suitability for inference-based tasks where semantic alignment is critical.

Table 7-7. Attack Transferability: Accuracy of BERT-on-BERT and DCP Attacks across Different Model Architectures

Dataset	Model	Original Acc. (%)	Acc. Under BERT-on-BERT Attack (%)	Acc. Under DCP Attack (%)
IMDB	Word-LSTM	89.80	10.20	7.40
	BERT-Large	98.20	12.40	8.30
Yelp	Word-LSTM	96.00	1.10	0.70
	BERT-Large	97.90	8.20	5.40
MNLI Matched	ESIM	76.20	9.60	7.20
	BERT-Large	86.40	13.20	10.80

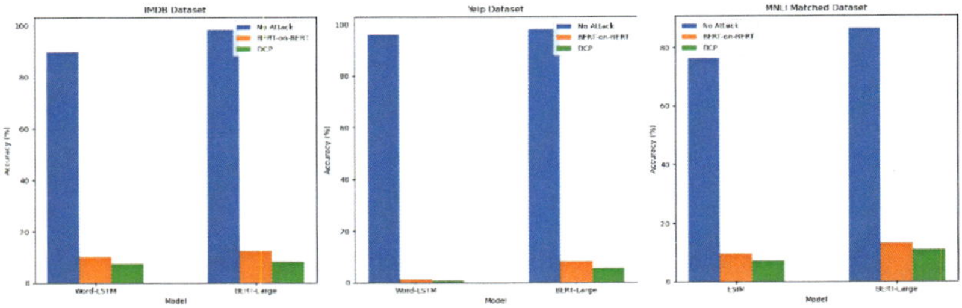

Figure 7-7. Transferability performance: Accuracy of BERT-on-BERT and DCP attacks across multiple model architectures on IMDB, Yelp, and MNLI (matched) datasets.

Transferability across Architectures: To assess the robustness and generalizability of the attack strategies, Table 7-7 presents the *cross-model performance* of DCP and BERT-on-BERT on alternative architectures such as Word-LSTM, BERT-Large, and ESIM. Figure 7-7 presents the same results in the form of vertical bar charts.

DCP not only matches but often *surpasses BERT-on-BERT in cross-model attack effectiveness*, reaffirming its capacity to generalize across architectures and datasets.

Conclusion and Future Directions

The chapter presented a comprehensive study on adversarial text construction through the *Dynamic Contextual Perturbation* (DCP) framework, a novel attack scheme specifically designed to generate linguistically coherent and semantically valid adversarial examples capable of undermining state-of-the-art *natural language processing* (NLP) models. By incorporating contextual embeddings, saliency-based token prioritization, and an iterative refinement mechanism guided by an adversarial objective function, the DCP framework offers a robust and efficient methodology for evaluating and challenging the security of text classification and inference models.

The framework was rigorously evaluated against multiple baselines, including PWWS and the BERT-on-BERT attack. The empirical results clearly demonstrated that DCP achieves significantly higher *attack success rates* (ASR) while maintaining lower perturbation rates and higher semantic fidelity. Across various benchmark datasets, such as AG News, IMDB, Yelp, Fake News, MNLI, and SNLI, and model architectures, including

Word-CNN, Bi-LSTM, BERT-Large, and ESIM, DCP consistently outperformed competing attack techniques in terms of effectiveness, efficiency, and subtlety. Particularly noteworthy is DCP's ability to perform successful attacks with fewer token modifications and fewer model queries, indicating its utility in both white-box and query-limited black-box scenarios.

Furthermore, the DCP framework exhibited strong *cross-model transferability*, successfully compromising multiple models even when not specifically tailored to them. This characteristic highlights the potential generalizability of the attack strategy and underscores the need for robust, model-agnostic defense mechanisms in NLP pipelines.

From a broader perspective, the results emphasize a critical insight into the vulnerability of contemporary NLP models: high-capacity language models, though powerful in semantic understanding and generalization, remain susceptible to context-aware perturbations that are virtually imperceptible to human readers. This insight raises pressing concerns about the deployment of NLP systems in real-world applications where adversarial robustness, interpretability, and user trust are paramount, such as content moderation, fake news detection, legal document classification, and conversational AI.

While the DCP framework advances the state of adversarial text generation, several open challenges and promising avenues for future work remain. Some of the directions of future research work are mentioned in the following.

Integration of Syntax-Aware and Grammar-Conscious Constraints: Although the DCP approach emphasizes semantic similarity, it does not explicitly enforce syntactic or grammatical constraints during perturbation. Future research can explore the incorporation of grammar-aware models or parse-tree analysis to ensure that generated adversarial examples maintain syntactic well-formedness in addition to semantic closeness. Leveraging *large language models* (LLMs) for syntactic scoring or fine-tuned grammatical error correction systems may enhance attack stealth and realism.

Multilingual and Cross-Lingual Adversarial Attacks: Most current adversarial attacks, including DCP, focus on English-language datasets and models. Extending the framework to handle multilingual corpora and cross-lingual settings could expose novel vulnerabilities in multilingual transformers like XLM-R and mBERT. Moreover, crafting perturbations that transfer across languages may lead to a deeper understanding of shared semantic structures and language-specific vulnerabilities.

Adversarial Training and Defense Integration: Given DCP's demonstrated potency, an important direction is to integrate its outputs into *adversarial training pipelines*. This would allow models to learn from adversarially perturbed examples and thereby improve robustness. Research can focus on how well models trained with DCP-adversarial samples generalize to other attack strategies and whether DCP can assist in building more resilient NLP systems.

Dynamic Contextual Perturbation in Dialogue and Generative Systems: Future work may also investigate the impact of DCP-like perturbations in dialogue systems, question answering, and generative text tasks. Unlike classification tasks, these applications require the preservation of coherence across multi-turn contexts or long-form generation. Developing perturbation techniques that can disrupt these systems while preserving topical flow and discourse structure presents both challenges and opportunities for advancing adversarial research.

Model-Agnostic and Zero-Shot Attacks: DCP currently assumes access to gradients or prediction feedback. Designing a fully model-agnostic or *zero-shot version of DCP*, where no direct access to model internals or outputs is available, would expand its applicability to commercial or proprietary NLP systems. Such techniques might rely on surrogate models, reinforcement learning, or meta-learning to infer optimal perturbations.

Human Perception and Interpretability Studies: Although quantitative metrics such as semantic similarity and perturbation rate offer useful approximations, they may not fully capture human judgments of meaning and fluency. Future studies could incorporate *human-in-the-loop evaluations* to assess the perceptibility of DCP-generated adversarial examples. Additionally, interpretability techniques could be developed to better visualize and explain the functional impact of such perturbations on model decisions.

Adversarial Benchmark Development: A standardized adversarial benchmark suite that includes DCP-based attacks across varied domains, tasks, and models would facilitate reproducibility and comparison. Such a resource would contribute to more consistent evaluation practices and encourage the development of comprehensive robustness strategies in NLP.

Real-World Deployment and Risk Assessment: Finally, applying DCP-style adversarial techniques in *real-world deployment scenarios* such as email filtering, social media moderation, and legal text analysis, can help identify critical vulnerabilities that remain hidden in controlled lab settings. Risk assessment frameworks can then be developed to prioritize model hardening efforts based on task sensitivity and potential impact.

Concluding Remarks: In summary, the Dynamic Contextual Perturbation framework presents a powerful, context-sensitive method for generating adversarial text that challenges both the robustness and interpretability of contemporary NLP systems. Its success in reducing classification performance with minimal disruption to textual semantics highlights the need for ongoing research into both attack methodologies and countermeasures. As language models continue to evolve and permeate high-stakes domains, the ability to anticipate and mitigate adversarial threats such as those posed by DCP will become increasingly essential to the safe and trustworthy deployment of AI systems.

References

Alzantot, M., Sharma, Y., Elgohary, A., Ho, B-J., Srivastava, M., and Chang, K-W. 2018. "Generating Natural Language Adversarial Examples." In *Proceedings of the 2018 Conference on Empirical Methods in Natural Language Processing (EMNLP)*, 2890–2896.

Asl, J. R., Rafiei, M. H., Alohaly, M., and Takabi, D. 2024. "A Semantic, Syntactic, and Context-Aware Natural Language Adversarial Example Generator." *IEEE Transactions on Dependable and Secure Computing*, 21(5), 4754-4769, September-October 2024.

BERT-Large: https://huggingface.co/google-bert/bert-large-uncased

Bowman, S. R., Angeli, G., Potts, C., & Manning, C. D. 2015. "A Large Annotated Corpus for Learning Natural Language Inference." In *Proceedings of the 2015 Conference on Empirical Methods in Natural Language Processing (EMNLP)*, 632–642. Available at: https://huggingface.co/datasets/stanfordnlp/snli

Chen, Q., Zhu, X., Ling, Z., Wie, S., Jiang, H., and Inkpen, D. 2016. "Enhanced LSTM for Natural Language Inference." arXiv Preprint arXiv: 1609.06038.

Chiang, C-H. and Lee, H-y. 2023. "Are Synonym Substitution Attacks Really Synonym Substitution Attacks?" In *Findings of the Association for Computational Linguistics (ACL 2023)*, 1853-1878.

Devlin, J., Chang, M.-W., Lee, K., & Toutanova, K. 2019. "BERT: Pre-training of Deep Bidirectional Transformers for Language Understanding." In *Proceedings of the 2019 Conference of the North American Chapter of the Association for Computational Linguistics: Human Language Technologies*, 4171–4186. URL: https://huggingface.co/google-bert/bert-large-uncased

Ebrahimi, J., Rao, A., Lowd, D., and Dou, D. 2018. "HotFlip: White-box adversarial examples for text classification." In *Proceedings of the 56th Annual Meeting of the Association for Computational Linguistics (ACL),* 2: 31–36.

Fake News Dataset: https://huggingface.co/datasets/ucsbnlp/liar.

Flesch, R. 1948. "A New Readability Yardstick." *Journal of Applied Psychology*, 32(3): 221-233.

Goodfellow, I. J., Shlens, J., and Szegedy, C. 2015. "Explaining and Harnessing Adversarial Examples." In *Proceedings of the International Conference on Learning Representations (ICLR)*, Poster. arXiv: 1412.6572.

Graves, A., Fernandez, S., and Schmidhuber, J. 2005. "Bidirectional LSTM Networks for Improved Phoneme Classification and Recognition." In *Proceedings of the International Conference on Artificial Neural Networks (ICANN'05)*, 799-804.

Hochreiter S. and Schmidhuber, J. 1997. "Long Short-Term Memory." *Neural Computing*, 9(8): 1735-1780.

Hu, X., Liu, G., Zheng, B., Zhao, L., Wang, Q., Zhang, Y., and Du, M. 2024. "FastTextDodger: Decision-Based Adversarial Attack against Black-Box NLP Models with Extremely High Efficiency." *IEEE Transactions on Information Forensics and Security*, 19: 2398-2411, 2024.

IMDB Dataset: https://ai.stanford.edu/~amaas/data/sentiment/

Jin, D., Jin, Z., Zhou, J. T., and Szolovits, P. 2020. "Is BERT Really Robust? A Strong Baseline for Natural Language Attack on Text Classification and entailment." In *Proceedings of the AAAI Conference on Artificial Intelligence*, 34(5): 8018-8025.

Kim, Y. 2014. "Convolutional Neural Networks for Sentence Classification." In *Proceedings of the 2014 Conference on Empirical Methods in Natural Language Processing (EMNLP'14)*, 1746-1751.

Koley, A., Satpati, P., Choudhary, I., and Sen, J. 2024. "An Investigation on the Efficiency of Some Text Attack Algorithms." *In Proceedings of the IEEE North Karnataka Subsection Flagship International Conference (NKCon'24)*, September 21–22, 2024, 1–8. Bagalkote, Karnataka, India.

Li, H., Zhang, J., Gao, S., Wu, L., Zhou, W., and Wang, R. 2022. "Towards Query-limited Adversarial Attacks on Graph Neural Networks." In *Proceedings of the 34th International Conference on Tools with Artificial Intelligence (ICTAI 2022)*, pp. 516-521.

Li, L., Ma, R., Guo, Q., Xue, X., and Qiu, X. 2020. "BERT-Attack: Adversarial Attack against BERT Using BERT." In *Proceedings of the 2020 Conference on Empirical Methods in Natural Language Processing (EMNLP)*, 6193-6202.

Li, J., Ji, S., Du, T., Li, B., and Wang, T. 2019. "TextBugger: Generating Adversarial Text against Real-world Applications." In *Proceedings of the 26th Annual Network and Distributed System Security Symposium (NDSS)* 2019.

Liu, Y., Ott, M., Goyal, N., Du, J., Joshi, M., Chen, D., Levy, O., Lewic, M., Zettlemoyer, L., and Stoyanov, V. 2019. "RoBERTa: A Robustly Optimized BERT Pretraining Approach." arXiv Preprint arXiv:1907.11692.

Maas, A. L., Daly, R. E., Pham, P. T., Huang, D., Ng, A. Y., and Potts, C. 2011. "Learning Word Vectors for Sentiment Analysis." In *Proceedings of the 49th Annual Meeting of the Association for Computational Linguistics: Human Language Technologies*, 142-150.

Parry, A., Fröbe, M., MacAvaney, S., Potthast, M., and Hagen, M. 2024. "Analyzing Adversarial Attacks on Sequence-to-Sequence Relevance Models." arXiv:2403.07654, 2024.

Radford, A., Narashiman, K., Salimans, T., and Sutskever, I. 2018. "Improving Language Understanding by Generative Pre-Training." OpenAI, 2019.

Ren, S., Deng, Y., He, K., and Che, W. 2019. "Generating natural language adversarial examples through probability weighted word saliency." *In Proceedings of the 57th Annual Meeting of the Association for Computational Linguistics (ACL)*, 1085-1097.

Sen, J. 2024. "The FGSM Attack on Image Classification Models and Distillation as its Defense." In Nanda et al. (eds), *Advances in Distributed Computing and Machine Learning (ICADCML 2024)*, 1015: 347-360. Lecture Notes in Networks and Systems, Springer, Singapore.

Sen, J. and Dasgupta, S. 2023. "Adversarial Attacks on Image Classification Models: FGSM and Patch Attacks and their Impact." In Sen, J. and Mayer, J. (eds), *Information Security and Privacy in the Digital World: Some Selected Topics*, IntechOpen, London, UK.

Sen, J., Sen, A., and Chatterjee, A. 2023. "Adversarial Attacks on Image Classification Models: Analysis and Defense." In *Proceedings of the*

10th International Conference on Business Analytics and Intelligence (ICBAI 2023), Bangalore, India.

Sen, J. and Waghela, H. 2025. "Text-Based Adversarial Attacks and Defense", In Sen, J. (ed) *Data Privacy: Techniques, Applications, and Standards*, IntechOpen, London, UK.

Szegedy, C., Zaremba, W., Sutskever, I., Bruna, J., Erhan, D., Goodfellow, I. J., and Fergus, R. 2014. "Intriguing Properties of Neural Networks." In *Proceedings of the International Conference on Learning Representations (ICLR)*. arXiv: 1312.6199.

Vitorino, J., Maia, E., and Praca, I. 2024. "Adversarial Evasion Attack Efficiency against Large Language Models." arXiv Preprint arXiv:2406.08050.

Waghela, H., Sen, J., and Rakshit, S. 2025. "Saliency Attention and Semantic Similarity-Driven Adversarial Perturbation." In *Data Science and Applications. ICDSA 2024*, Nanda, S. J. et al. (eds), 1237: 461–471. Lecture Notes in Networks and Systems, Springer, Singapore.

Waghela, H., Sen, J., Rakshit, S., and Dasgupta, S. 2024a. "Adversarial Text Generation with Dynamic Contextual Perturbation." In *Proceedings of the 2024 IEEE CALCON 2024*, 1–6. IEEE.

Waghela, H., Sen, J., and Rakshit, S. 2024b. "Adaptive Meta-Learning for Robust Ensemble Defense against Adversarial Attacks." In *Proceedings of the International Conference BAMS-ORSI 2024*.

Waghela, H., Sen, J., and Rakshit, S. 2024c. "Adversarial Resilience in Image Classification: A Hybrid Approach to Defense." In *Proceedings of the 2024 International Conference on Innovation and Intelligence for Informatics, Computing, and Technologies (3ICT 2024)*, 419–426.

Waghela, H., Sen, J., Rakshit, S., and Dasgupta, S. 2024d. "Adversarial Robustness through Dynamic Ensemble Learning." In *Proceedings of the 2024 IEEE Silchar Subsection Conference (SILCON 2024)*, 1–6.

Waghela, H., Sen, J., and Rakshit, S. 2024e. "Robust Image Classification: Defensive Strategies against FGSM and PGD Adversarial Attacks." In *Proceedings of the IEEE Asian Conference on Intelligent Technologies (ACOIT 2024)*, 1 – 7.

Waghela, H., Sen, J., and Rakshit, S. 2024f. "Refining BERT Adversarial Attacks with Projected Gradient Descent." In *Proceedings of the IEEE 4th Asian Conference on Innovations in Technology (ASIANCON 2024)*, 1-7.

Waghela, H., Rakshit, S., and Sen, J. 2024g. "A Modified Word Saliency-Based Adversarial Attack on Text Classification Models." In *Computational Intelligence and Data Analytics*, Frery, A. C. et al. (eds),

371–382. Lecture Notes in Data Engineering and Communications Technologies, 236. Springer.

Wang, W. Y. 2017. “Liar, Liar Pants on Fire: A New Benchmark Dataset for Fake News Detection.” In *Proceedings of the 55th Annual Meeting of the Association for Computational Linguistics*, 2: 422-426.

Williams, A., Nangia, N., and Bowman, S. 2018. “A Broad-Coverage Challenge Corpus for Sentence Understanding through Inference.” In *Proceedings of the 2018 Conference of the North American Chapter of the Association for Computational Linguistics: Human Language Technologies*, 1:1112-1122. Dataset: https://huggingface.co/datasets/nyu-mll/multi_nli

Yelp Dataset: https://huggingface.co/datasets/Yelp/yelp_review_full

Zang, Y., Qi, F., Liu, C., Liu, W., Zhang, Q., Liu, H., and Huang, X. 2020. “Word-level Textual Adversarial Attacking as Combinatorial Optimization.” In *Proceedings of the 58th Annual Meeting of the Association for Computational Linguistics (ACL)*, 6066-6080.

Zhang, X., Zhao, J., and LeCun, Y. 2015. “Character-Level Convolutional Networks for Text Classification.” In *Proceedings of the 29th International Conference on Neural Information Processing Systems*, 1: 649-657. Retrieved from: https://huggingface.co/datasets/wangrongsheng/ag_news

Zhao, J., Chen, Y., and Li, X. 2022. “Word-Level Textual Adversarial Attack Method Based on Differential Evolution Algorithm.” *In Proceedings of 2022 International Conference on Cloud Computing, Big Data and Internet of Things (3CBIT)*, 29-34.

CHAPTER 8

COMPREHENSIVE ANALYSIS AND DEFENSE STRATEGIES AGAINST ADVERSARIAL ATTACKS ON IMAGE CLASSIFICATION MODELS

Introduction

The proliferation of machine learning models, particularly deep neural networks, across a wide array of application domains has led to unprecedented breakthroughs in tasks such as image recognition, natural language processing, and autonomous decision-making. Despite these successes, a growing body of research has revealed that these models are inherently vulnerable to a class of inputs known as adversarial examples. These are inputs that appear virtually indistinguishable from legitimate data to human observers but are manipulated in subtle ways to cause the model to make incorrect predictions (Szegedy et al., 2014). The presence of such vulnerabilities raises fundamental questions about the robustness, reliability, and generalizability of modern machine learning systems.

What is particularly disconcerting is the observation that adversarial examples tend to fool a wide variety of models, even those trained on different datasets or possessing distinct architectural characteristics. This universality suggests that adversarial susceptibility is not an artifact of specific training conditions or model configurations, but rather a symptom of deeper, systemic flaws in the learning process itself. Initially, several hypotheses were put forward to explain this phenomenon, including the high degree of non-linearity in deep models, under-regularization, and limited robustness due to insufficient model averaging. However, these explanations lacked a unifying framework and could not fully account for the consistent failure patterns observed across different models.

A significant theoretical advancement was provided by Goodfellow et al. (Goodfellow et al., 2015), who argued that adversarial examples are not necessarily a result of deep models being overly non-linear. Instead, they demonstrated that the linearity inherent in high-dimensional models could itself be sufficient to produce adversarial behavior. This insight marked a paradigm shift in understanding adversarial vulnerability: even simple linear approximations in high-dimensional input spaces can be exploited to craft effective perturbations. Furthermore, their work introduced adversarial training, a technique wherein the model is trained not only on clean inputs but also on their adversarial counterparts, as a form of regularization, akin to dropout (Srivastava et al., 2014). This approach improved model robustness while simultaneously enhancing generalization under certain conditions.

The practical implications of adversarial attacks are particularly serious in mission-critical applications where human safety is at stake. For instance, in the domain of autonomous vehicles, deep learning models are deployed to identify road signs, detect pedestrians, and interpret the driving environment (NVIDIA). An adversarial attack that leads to the misclassification of a stop sign as a speed limit sign could result in disastrous outcomes (Ciresan et al., 2012; Huang et al., 2011; Biggio et al., 2013; 2024; Anjos et al., 2011; Fogla & Lee, 2006). Such scenarios highlight the urgent need to rigorously evaluate and fortify machine learning models against adversarial threats.

Beyond traditional pixel-level perturbations, more sophisticated attack methodologies have emerged. One such approach involves the use of adversarial patches, carefully designed patterns that, when overlaid onto any part of an input image, cause the model to misclassify the entire image (Brown et al., 2017). Unlike example-specific perturbations, these patches are input-agnostic, making them highly transferable and practical for real-world exploitation. Their potential to deceive models across a variety of inputs significantly elevates the threat level and necessitates more comprehensive defense strategies.

This chapter investigates the nature, consequences, and countermeasures of adversarial attacks in the context of image classification tasks using deep neural networks. It focuses specifically on two prominent forms of attacks: the *Fast Gradient Sign Method* (FGSM), a gradient-based technique that produces minimal but effective input perturbations; and the adversarial patch, a spatially localized yet input-independent form of attack. The chapter evaluates how these techniques undermine classification accuracy, even for models that perform exceptionally well on unperturbed datasets. It also explores potential defense mechanisms, with a focus on defensive distillation, a strategy wherein a model is trained using softened outputs of a previously trained "teacher" network, thereby smoothing the decision boundaries and enhancing robustness.

The key contributions of this work are summarized as follows:

Conceptual Clarification and Attack Taxonomy: The chapter provides an in-depth discussion of adversarial attacks in deep learning, introducing FGSM and patch attacks within a broader taxonomy of threat models and perturbation techniques.

Empirical Analysis of Vulnerabilities: Experimental evaluations are presented to demonstrate the extent to which deep image classifiers are vulnerable to both gradient-based and spatially invariant attacks, underlining the fragility of current models in adversarial settings.

Defense through Knowledge Distillation: The concept of defensive distillation is introduced as a practical countermeasure. Its effectiveness is assessed in defending against FGSM attacks, offering insight into its utility and limitations.

The rest of the chapter is organized as follows. The *Related Work* section surveys related work, placing the current research within the context of adversarial machine learning literature and highlighting key contributions from prior studies. The section titled *Background Theories* lays out the theoretical foundations underlying adversarial examples and introduces the architectural elements of pre-trained image classification models. The section *FGSM and Patch Attack Results* presents detailed experimental results of FGSM and patch attacks, along with their quantitative impact on model accuracy. The section titled *Defensive Distillation Method* describes the defensive distillation method, including its algorithmic implementation and training regime. The section *Experimental Results of Defensive Distillation* provides a comparative evaluation of model performance before and after distillation under adversarial conditions. The *Conclusion and Future Works* section concludes the chapter key takeaways and proposes future directions for research, including ensemble defenses, certifiable robustness, and real-time attack detection systems.

Related Work

Over the past decade, the rise of deep learning has revolutionized numerous domains, particularly in image classification, natural language processing, and autonomous systems. However, alongside these advancements, there has emerged a growing awareness of the vulnerability of deep learning models to adversarial inputs, carefully crafted data points designed to deceive neural networks while appearing benign to human observers (Ciresan et al., 2012; Eykholt et al, 2018). These perturbations, often imperceptible to the human eye, can drastically alter the output of a classifier. A range of optimization-based strategies has been developed to systematically generate such adversarial instances, including box-constrained L-BFGS optimization (Szegedy et al., 2014), the Fast Gradient Sign Method (FGSM) (Goodfellow et al., 2015), DeepFool (M-Dezfooli et al., 2016), and Projected Gradient Descent (PGD) (Madry et al., 2018). Although these attacks frequently modify only a small portion of the input image or adjust pixel values minimally, their effects on the output can be substantial.

Some techniques aim to perturb only a localized or particularly salient region of the image. For instance, *Jacobian-based saliency map attacks* (JSMA) (Papernot et al., 2016) selectively modify a few pixels that are deemed most influential to the classifier's output, while localized patch attacks (Sharif et al., 2016) embed a visually distinct pattern at a fixed location to override the model's decision logic. These approaches exemplify the diversity of attack surfaces within image classification models and highlight the necessity of understanding both gradient-based and spatially localized adversarial mechanisms.

The foundational work by Szegedy et al. played a pivotal role in unveiling the nature and severity of adversarial vulnerability in deep networks (Szegedy et al., 2014). Their experiments using the L-BFGS method revealed a set of consistent and surprising properties:

i. The L-BFGS optimizer reliably identifies adversarial examples that are misclassified by neural networks.

ii. Such examples are nearly indistinguishable from the original images to a human observer, even within complex datasets like ImageNet (Deng et al., 2009).

iii. The same adversarial input often fools a diverse range of classifiers, even when those classifiers are trained independently on disjoint subsets of the training data.

iv. Adversarial perturbations were shown to degrade the performance of shallow classifiers such as softmax regression, further emphasizing that this is not an issue exclusive to deep models.

v. Significantly, their study proposed that incorporating adversarial examples into the training process could act as a regularization mechanism, improving the robustness and generalization of neural networks.

Building on these findings, researchers such as Eykholt et al. extended the study of adversarial attacks to the physical world (Eykholt et al., 2018). They demonstrated that simple, real-world manipulations, like placing stickers or printed patterns on street signs, could effectively mislead computer vision models used in autonomous driving systems. Their results suggest that adversarial threats are not limited to digital environments and can manifest in ways that compromise the safety and reliability of AI systems in practical settings.

These studies collectively indicate that despite their impressive performance on conventional test sets, modern classifiers often fail to internalize the fundamental principles underlying class semantics. Instead, they rely heavily on superficial correlations within the training data. As a result, when exposed to inputs that lie outside the data distribution or are deliberately crafted to exploit model weaknesses, these classifiers can yield highly erroneous predictions. This challenge is exacerbated in *convolutional neural networks* (CNNs), where feature similarity is frequently assessed via Euclidean distance. Such distance-based measures can be misleading in high-dimensional perceptual spaces, especially when minimal input perturbations lead to radically different outputs in the network's latent space.

Importantly, these issues are not exclusive to deep networks. Even linear classifiers can exhibit adversarial vulnerability under specific conditions. Despite extensive research, no model architecture has thus far demonstrated immunity to adversarial perturbations without sacrificing accuracy on clean inputs. This trade-off between robustness and accuracy remains one of the central challenges in adversarial machine learning.

A significant line of research has focused on developing defensive strategies to counteract adversarial attacks, particularly those involving small perturbations. Some of the most influential works in this area are summarized below:

Madry et al. developed an adversarial training framework based on PGD attacks, targeting models trained on MNIST and CIFAR-10 datasets (Madry et al., 2018). Their formulation framed adversarial robustness as a saddle-point optimization problem, and PGD was employed as a strong adversary to train robust models. Their adversarially trained classifiers achieved an accuracy of 89% on adversarial test cases, representing a significant milestone in robust learning.

Papernot et al. introduced a novel attack strategy based on understanding the input-output behavior of deep networks, which led to the design of saliency-based perturbations (Papernot et al., 2016). Their method succeeded in generating adversarial examples that humans still classified correctly, while the model failed. The attack boasted a 97% success rate while altering just 4.02% of the input features. Additionally, they proposed a difficulty measure for assessing class-wise vulnerability and suggested targeted defenses against saliency-based perturbations.

Tramèr et al. investigated black-box adversarial attacks, where perturbations are crafted without access to model internals (Tramer et al., 2018). They found that these attacks are especially dangerous when transferred from surrogate models. To combat this, they introduced ensemble adversarial training, a strategy that incorporates adversarial examples generated from multiple models into the training data. This approach significantly improved robustness, particularly on challenging benchmarks like ImageNet.

Dong et al. proposed a benchmark framework to systematically evaluate adversarial robustness (Dong et al., 2020). Their study highlighted three important insights: (i) adversarial training is one of the most effective defense mechanisms across different threat models, (ii) robustness curves provide a nuanced understanding of model behavior under attack, and (iii) randomization-based defenses exhibit increased resistance in query-limited black-box scenarios.

Chen et al. conducted a comprehensive analysis of existing defense mechanisms (Chen et al., 2022). They classified defense strategies into four categories: (i) gradient masking, (ii) adversarial training, (iii) input transformation, and (iv) adversarial detection. Their comparative evaluation revealed key trade-offs and outlined future research directions for constructing more reliable and scalable defenses.

Recent developments in adversarial machine learning have substantially advanced the formulation of both attack and defense strategies by leveraging semantic similarity measures, context-aware perturbation techniques, and ensemble-based robustness mechanisms. A notable body of work led by Waghela, Sen, Rakshit, and their collaborators (Waghela et al., 2024a–g; Waghela et al., 2025; Sen, 2024; Sen & Dasgupta, 2023; Sen & Waghela, 2025; Sen et al., 2023; Koley et al., 2024) has played a pivotal role in shaping this dynamic research landscape. These studies introduce innovative adversarial methodologies that integrate linguistic saliency, attention-guided perturbation, contextual embeddings from transformer-based models such as BERT, and semantic similarity constraints to generate adversarial examples that are not only effective but also linguistically coherent and contextually meaningful. On the defense side, this body of work presents several ensemble-based and meta-learning approaches that enhance model robustness against a wide spectrum of adversarial attacks. These include hybrid defense architectures that combine dynamic ensembling with perturbation-aware training, applicable across both natural language and image modalities. Collectively, these contributions represent a holistic advancement in adversarial machine learning, balancing attack success rates with semantic plausibility and advancing defense systems that generalize effectively across diverse datasets, model families, and task settings.

Several other works have contributed incremental and orthogonal improvements to this domain, ranging from certified defenses and robust optimization frameworks to ensemble modeling and adversarial data augmentation (Gu & Rigazio, 2015; Chalupka et al., 2015; Dong et al., 2020; Chen et al., 2022; Pestana et al., 2021; Li et al., 2022; Yuan et al., 2021; Xu et al., 2021).

In conclusion, the landscape of adversarial machine learning has rapidly evolved from identifying vulnerabilities to developing increasingly sophisticated defenses. While no single solution has emerged as universally effective, the combination of robust training strategies, attack-aware evaluation protocols, and system-level integration of defenses offers a promising path toward safer and more reliable deep learning systems.

Background Theories

This section provides the essential theoretical foundations needed to understand the adversarial attacks and deep learning architectures discussed throughout this chapter. It introduces the key concepts of adversarial perturbations and the Fast Gradient Sign Method (FGSM), a seminal attack strategy, followed by brief architectural overviews of three widely used *convolutional neural network* (CNN) models: ResNet-101, AlexNet, and RegNetY 400MF. Understanding both the nature of adversarial manipulation and the structure of the targeted models is critical for interpreting how these attacks compromise model performance.

***Adversarial Attacks*:** Adversarial attacks have emerged as a significant concern in the domain of deep learning. These attacks are designed to subtly modify an input, such as an image, in a way that causes a trained model to misclassify it, even though the modified input appears virtually identical to the original from a human perspective. For example, a classifier that correctly identifies an image of a goldfish may, after the addition of a small adversarial perturbation, mislabel it as a completely different object, even though the image remains clearly recognizable as a goldfish to the human eye.

The central premise of adversarial attacks is the *fragility of high-dimensional decision boundaries* in deep networks. These boundaries are susceptible to manipulation through gradient-based optimization, which identifies directions in input space that lead to maximal changes in the model's output. This vulnerability raises profound concerns about the trustworthiness and reliability of neural networks, especially in safety-critical applications.

This concept bears a conceptual resemblance to the functioning of *Generative Adversarial Networks* (GANs), where a generator attempts to produce samples that fool a discriminator. In adversarial image attacks, a similar goal is pursued: to deceive the target classifier (analogous to the discriminator) using imperceptibly modified inputs. However unlike GANs, the perturbations in adversarial attacks are often not intended to create entirely new samples but to exploit weaknesses in the decision surface of a given pre-trained model.

***Fast Gradient Sign Method (FGSM)*:** One of the earliest and most influential adversarial attack techniques is the FGSM, proposed by Goodfellow et al. (Goodfellow et al., 2015). FGSM is a *white-box* attack method that uses gradient information from the model to construct adversarial inputs in a computationally efficient manner. It operates by computing the gradient of the model's loss function with respect to the input image and then perturbing the image in the direction of the gradient's sign. The goal is to increase the loss function, thereby nudging the model toward incorrect classification.

The FGSM method is formally defined as:

$$adv_x = x + \varepsilon * sign(\nabla_x J(\theta, x, y)) \tag{8-1}$$

In (8-1), adv_x is the adversarial image generated, x is the original input image, y is the true class label, ε is the small scalar hyperparameter that controls the magnitude of the perturbation (commonly referred to as the attack strength), θ represents the parameters of the model, $J(\theta, x, y)$ is the loss function (e.g., categorical cross-entropy), and ∇_x denotes the gradient with respect to the input image.

The FGSM attack proceeds in three distinct steps:

1. Forward Propagation: The model computes the loss value based on its prediction and the ground-truth label.
2. Gradient Computation: The gradient of the loss is calculated with respect to each pixel of the input image.
3. Perturbation Application: The input is modified by moving each pixel in the direction of the gradient's sign, scaled by the magnitude ε.

Unlike traditional gradient descent in model training, where gradients guide weight updates to reduce the loss, FGSM reverses this logic, using gradients to *increase* the loss by directly modifying the input. Importantly, these changes are small enough to remain invisible to the human eye, yet sufficient to cause a significant shift in the network's prediction. FGSM serves as a foundational building block for more advanced adversarial attacks such as PGD (Madry et al., 2018), BIM (Kurakin et al., 2017), and MIM (Dong et al., 2018), and continues to be widely used in adversarial research for its simplicity and effectiveness.

***ResNet-101 Architecture*:** ResNet-101 is part of the Residual Network family of deep learning models, which revolutionized CNN architectures by introducing the concept of residual connections or skip connections (He et al., 2016). With 101 layers, ResNet-101 belongs to the category of ultradeep CNNs capable of learning complex hierarchical features. The skip connections in ResNet enable the model to learn identity mappings, allowing gradients to flow more smoothly during backpropagation and mitigating the vanishing gradient problem that plagues deep networks.

The architecture of ResNet consists of stacked residual blocks, each containing convolutional layers and shortcut connections that bypass one or more layers. These residual pathways allow the network to learn residual functions, i.e., differences from the identity, which simplifies optimization and accelerates convergence. ResNet-101 has demonstrated state-of-the-art performance across multiple vision tasks, including image classification, object detection, and semantic segmentation.

In practical settings, ResNet-101 is often used in transfer learning scenarios. A model pre-trained on a large dataset such as ImageNet can be fine-tuned on smaller, task-specific datasets, drastically reducing training time while retaining high accuracy. Due to its robust architecture and performance, ResNet-101 is a frequent target of adversarial attacks in robustness studies.

***AlexNet Architecture*:** AlexNet marked a significant turning point in the evolution of deep learning for computer vision. It won the *ImageNet Large Scale Visual Recognition Challenge* (ILSVRC) in 2012 by a substantial margin, demonstrating the power of deep convolutional networks on large-scale image datasets (Krizhevsky et al., 2017). The model comprises eight layers: five convolutional layers followed by three fully connected layers. Key innovations included the use of ReLU (Rectified Linear Unit) activations for non-linearity, dropout regularization to combat overfitting, max-pooling layers for spatial downsampling, and local response normalization (LRN) to enhance generalization.

AlexNet's success catalyzed widespread adoption of CNNs in academic and industrial applications. Although it has since been surpassed by more advanced architectures like VGG, ResNet, and DenseNet, AlexNet remains historically important and is still used as a benchmark model in adversarial research due to its relatively shallow depth and well-understood behavior.

***RegNetY 400MF Architecture*:** RegNetY 400MF belongs to the RegNet family of efficient convolutional neural networks designed for scalable performance across a range of computing budgets (Radosavovic et al., 2020). The "400MF" suffix refers to the model's approximate computational complexity (400 million FLOPs), placing it in the mid-range of the RegNet spectrum. RegNet models are characterized by regular, rule-based design patterns that optimize trade-offs between model accuracy and computational efficiency.

One of the distinguishing features of RegNetY variants is the inclusion of SE (Squeeze-and-Excitation) blocks, which enable channel-wise attention by recalibrating feature maps based on their importance. This improves representational power with minimal additional cost. RegNetY 400MF is suitable for tasks such as image classification, object detection, and semantic segmentation, and is particularly favored for deployment in resource-constrained environments due to its compactness.

Like ResNet-101, RegNetY 400MF supports transfer learning, enabling it to be fine-tuned on domain-specific datasets after being pre-trained on a large corpus like ImageNet. Its balance between efficiency and performance makes it a versatile candidate for studying adversarial robustness, especially in scenarios that demand both speed and accuracy.

FGSM and Patch Attack Results

This section presents a detailed evaluation of the effects of two prominent adversarial attack strategies, *Fast Gradient Sign Method* (FGSM) and adversarial patch attacks, on three well-known *convolutional neural network* (CNN) models pre-trained on the ImageNet dataset: ResNet-101, AlexNet, and RegNetY 400MF. The models used in these experiments were sourced from the PyTorch torchvision library, which provides standardized, pre-trained architectures for reproducible benchmarking. The analysis is conducted using selected images from the ImageNet validation set.

Baseline Performance without Adversarial Perturbations: Before investigating the robustness of the models under adversarial conditions, it is important to establish their baseline performance. Given the complexity of the ImageNet dataset, which includes 1000 object categories, model evaluation based solely on Top-1 accuracy can be misleading. Due to semantic overlap and visual ambiguity among classes, models might predict a label that is technically incorrect but still semantically reasonable. For this reason, the Top-5 accuracy metric, measuring whether the ground truth label appears within the top five predicted categories, is widely adopted in ImageNet-based evaluations.

Table 8-1. Top-1 and Top-5 Error Rates on ImageNet Dataset

Metric	ResNet-101	AlexNet	RegNetY 400MF
Top-1 Error Rate	13.30%	28.06%	18.72%
Top-5 Error Rate	2.16%	9.90%	3.76%

The classification error rates (Top-1 and Top-5) for the three CNN models (ResNet-101, AlexNet, and RegNetY 400MF) are summarized in Table 8-1. The ResNet-101 model exhibits the lowest error rates among the three, demonstrating superior generalization and feature extraction capabilities, likely due to its deeper architecture and residual learning framework.

After the overall evaluation of the three models on the ImageNet dataset, a closer inspection of specific instances within the dataset is conducted. Images corresponding to the indices 7, 16, 20, and 27 are randomly selected for detailed analysis. These images are associated with the classes "goldfish," "tiger shark," "hammerhead," and "electric ray," respectively. The classification performance of each model on these selected samples is examined to gain further insight into model behavior on individual examples.

Table 8-2. The ResNet-101 Classification Output for Selected Images

Image Index	True Label	Predicted Class (Top-5)	Confidence Scores
7	**Goldfish**	**Goldfish** Tench Flamingo Black Swan Terrapin	0.2372 0.1076 0.0555 0.0497 0.0485
16	**Tiger Shark**	**Tiger Shark** Electric Ray Great White Shark Hammerhead Stingray	0.8774 0.0782 0.0053 0.0045 0.0039
20	**Hammerhead**	**Hammerhead** Tiger Shark Electric Ray Great White Shark Gar	0.7204 0.2165 0.0244 0.0147 0.0043
27	**Electric Ray**	**Electric Ray** Stingray Loggerhead Leatherback Turtle Dugong	0.7381 0.1179 0.1033 0.0143 0.0090

Table 8.2 presents the classification outcomes of the ResNet-101 model for the four selected images. The results indicate consistently high classification accuracy, with confidence scores exceeding 90% for the true class in most cases, except for the image labeled "tiger shark." In this context, *confidence* denotes the probability assigned by the model to a particular class. For example, when the model correctly identifies an image as belonging to the "goldfish class," it assigns a confidence score of 0.9996, reflecting a 99.96% probability that the image corresponds to that class.

Figure 8-1 depicts the classification outcomes produced by the ResNet-101 model for the four selected images. For each image, the input is shown on the left, while the right side presents the model's top five predicted classes along with their corresponding confidence scores. These confidence levels are visually represented using horizontal bar graphs.

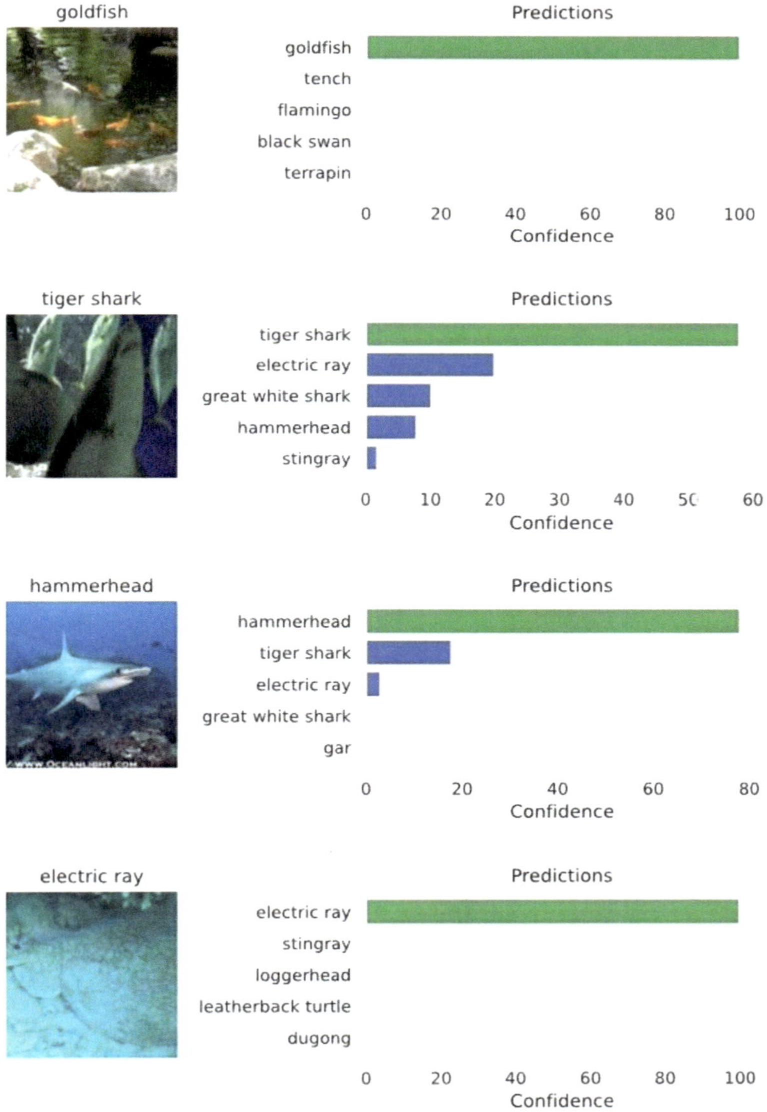

Figure. 8-1. The classification of images by the ResNet-101 model.

Classification Under the FGSM Attack: Following the evaluation of the three CNN architectures on image classification tasks using the ImageNet dataset, attention is turned to the effects of adversarial attacks on these models. The initial analysis focuses on the Fast Gradient Sign Method (FGSM) with an *epsilon* (ε) value of 0.02. This specific value corresponds to a pixel perturbation of approximately 1 within the standard 0-255 range (i.e., in the 8-bit color space), resulting in changes that are nearly imperceptible to the human eye. The performance of the ResNet-101 model under the FGSM attack with $\varepsilon = 0.02$ is summarized in Table 8-3, with a corresponding visual representation provided in Figure 8-2.

Table 8-3. The ResNet-101 Classification Output for Selected Images Under FGSM attack with $\varepsilon = 0.02$

Image Index	True Label	Predicted Class (Top-5)	Confidence Scores
7	**Goldfish**	Hippopotamus Lakeside Terrapin Tench Beaver	0.2372 0.1076 0.0555 0.0497 0.0485
16	**Tiger Shark**	Electric Ray Stingray Hammerhead Killer Whale Dugong	0.8774 0.0782 0.0053 0.0046 0.0039
20	**Hammerhead**	Tiger Shark Electric Ray **Hammerhead** Coral Reef Stingray	0.7204 0.2166 0.0244 0.0147 0.0043
27	**Electric Ray**	Loggerhead Leatherback **Electric Ray** Conch Stingray	0.7381 0.1179 0.1038 0.0143 0.0090

Even with minimal perturbation, the attack significantly distorts model predictions, often pushing the true class out of the Top-1 or even Top-5 list.

To assess sensitivity to increasing levels of noise, ε was varied from 0.01 to 0.10. The error rates for each model under these conditions are presented in Tables 8-4 through 8-6.

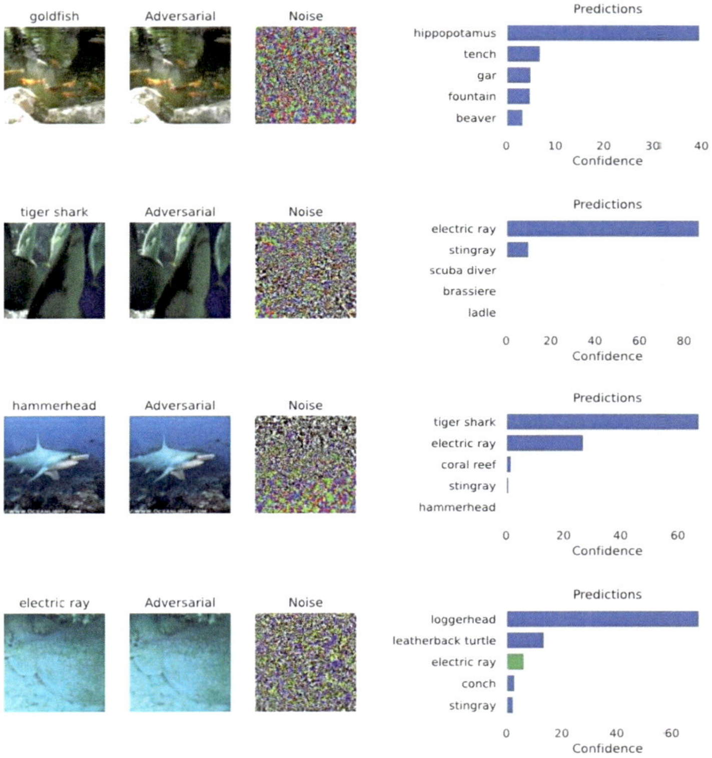

Figure. 8-2. Classification results of the ResNet-101 model when subjected to an FGSM attack with $\varepsilon = 0.02$.

Table 8-4. Classification Performance of ResNet-101 Model Under the FGSM Attack with Varying Epsilon Values

Noise Level (ε)	Top-1 Error (%)	Top-5 Error (%)
0.01	77.18	33.34
0.02	87.10	48.78
0.03	90.50	55.62
0.04	91.58	58.98
0.05	92.02	60.82
0.06	92.20	61.60
0.07	92.02	61.96
0.08	91.88	62.16
0.09	91.66	61.84
0.10	91.06	61.80

Table 8-5. Classification Performance of AlexNet Model Under the FGSM Attack with Varying Epsilon Values

Noise Level (ε)	Top-1 Error (%)	Top-5 Error (%)
0.01	79.04	44.16
0.02	92.28	65.30
0.03	96.36	75.92
0.04	98.02	81.78
0.05	98.80	85.84
0.06	99.10	88.34
0.07	99.24	89.98
0.08	99.34	91.02
0.09	99.38	92.18
0.10	99.48	92.84

Table 8-6. Classification Performance of RegNetY 400MF Model Under the FGSM Attack with Varying Epsilon Values

Noise Level (ε)	Top-1 Error (%)	Top-5 Error (%)
0.01	89.56	53.12
0.02	95.12	66.16
0.03	96.42	71.44
0.04	96.80	73.98
0.05	97.00	75.30
0.06	97.08	75.68
0.07	96.74	75.88
0.08	96.68	76.04
0.09	96.50	75.86
0.10	96.24	75.72

These results indicate a sharp degradation in performance across all models as ε increases. ResNet-101 reaches a Top-1 error of 92.20% and Top-5 error of 61.60% at $\varepsilon = 0.06$. AlexNet suffers more severely, with Top-1 error peaking at 99.48% and Top-5 error at 92.84%. RegNetY 400MF shows moderate resilience but still exhibits 97.08% Top-1 error at its worst. Overall, while all models are vulnerable, ReNet-101 demonstrates comparatively better robustness against FGSM perturbations.

***Classification Under Adversarial Patch Attack*:** As mentioned in the *Introduction* section, an alternative attack method on image classification models involves the use of adversarial patches (Brown et al., 2017). In this attack, the strategy is to manipulate a small portion of the image to take on a specific form and appearance, rather than the FGSM's approach of making slight pixel changes. This manipulation aims to deceive the classification model and compel it to predict a predetermined class. In practical scenarios, this type of attack presents a more significant threat than FGSM. For example, consider an autonomous vehicle network that receives real-time images from a camera. To trick the vehicle into misidentifying an automobile as a pedestrian, another driver could print and attach a particular pattern on the rear of the vehicle.

To replicate the adversarial patch attack on the same four images previously evaluated under the FGSM attack, the procedure begins with the random selection of five distinct images to serve as adversarial patches. These include: (i) a saltshaker, (ii) a soap dispenser, (iii) a digital clock, (iv) a piggy bank, and (v) a toaster. To examine the impact of patch size on the classification accuracy, each patch image is tested in three different dimensions: (i) 32*32, (iii) 48*48, and (iii) 64*64 pixels. The patches are depicted in Figure 8-3.

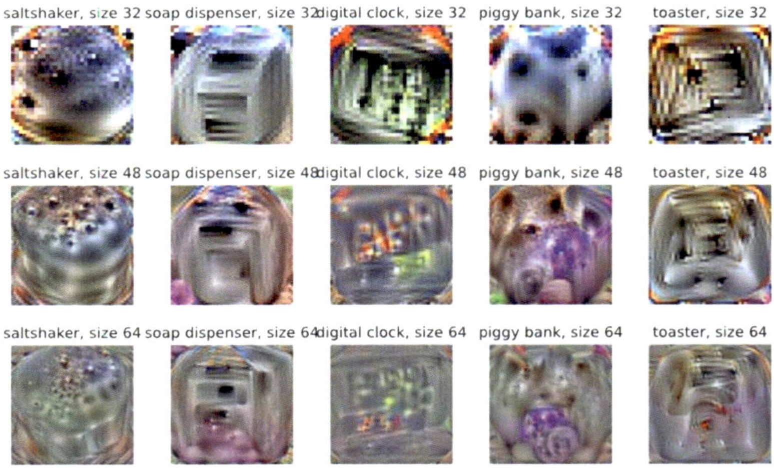

Figure. 8-3. The five images selected as adversarial patches: (i) saltshaker, (ii) soap dispenser, (iii) digital clock, (iv) piggy bank, and (v) toaster. Each patch is evaluated in three sizes: 32*32, 48*48, and 64*64.

Table 8-7. Classification Accuracy of the ResNet-101 Model Under Patch Attack- Top 1 Accuracy

Image Class	Top 1% Accuracy		
	Patch: 32*32	Patch: 48*48	Patch: 64*64
Saltshaker	72.52	96.26	99.34
Soap Dispenser	16.47	78.51	92.65
Digital Clock	55.35	96.79	99.37
Piggy Bank	78.03	95.54	99.17
Toaster	48.69	90.48	98.58

Table 8-8. Classification Accuracy of the ResNet-101 Model Under Patch Attack-Top 5 Accuracy

Image Class	Top 5% Accuracy		
	Patch: 32*32	Patch: 48*48	Patch: 64*64
Saltshaker	90.25	99.79	99.99
Soap Dispenser	61.76	95.77	99.25
Digital Clock	94.11	99.95	100.00
Piggy Bank	92.27	99.59	99.98
Toaster	72.02	98.12	99.93

The performance of the ResNet-101 model, measured in terms of Top-1 and Top-5 accuracy for varying patch sizes and images, is summarized in Table 8-7 through 8-12. Here, accuracy denotes the proportion of instances where the model assigns the highest confidence score to the target class corresponding to the patch.

Table 8-9. Classification Accuracy of the AlexNet Model Under Patch Attack- Top 1 Accuracy

Image Class	Top 1% Accuracy		
	Patch: 32*32	Patch: 48*48	Patch: 64*64
Saltshaker	16.85	54.84	86.40
Soap Dispenser	7.61	17.27	52.05
Digital Clock	25.70	69.95	94.99
Piggy Bank	1.32	79.58	96.70
Toaster	48.89	90.48	98.58

Table 8-10. Classification Accuracy of the AlexNet Model Under Patch Attack-Top 5 Accuracy

Image Class	Top 5% Accuracy		
	Patch: 32*32	Patch: 48*48	Patch: 64*64
Saltshaker	23.99	62.95	93.69
Soap Dispenser	25.97	77.38	91.37
Digital Clock	34.77	83.49	93.33
Piggy Bank	37.00	81.82	94.24
Toaster	48.89	90.48	98.58

Table 8-11. Classification Accuracy of the RegNetY 400MF Model Under Patch Attack- Top 1 Accuracy

Image Class	Top 1% Accuracy		
	Patch: 32*32	Patch: 48*48	Patch: 64*64
Saltshaker	23.99	62.95	93.69
Soap Dispenser	25.97	77.38	91.37
Digital Clock	34.77	83.49	93.33
Piggy Bank	37.00	81.82	94.24
Toaster	48.89	90.48	98.58

Table 8-12. Classification Accuracy of the RegNetY 400MF Model Under Patch Attack- Top 5 Accuracy

Image Class	Top 5% Accuracy		
	Patch: 32*32	Patch: 48*48	Patch 64*64
Saltshaker	48.51	81.75	99.03
Soap Dispenser	51.13	90.65	98.24
Digital Clock	64.18	95.92	99.28
Piggy Bank	59.41	92.72	98.71
Toaster	72.02	98.12	99.93

Figures 8-4 through 8-6 present the performance of the three classification models under a patch attack using a 64*64 "piggy bank" patch, as this configuration produced the highest accuracy among all tested patch images. To avoid repetition, results for the other patch types and sizes are not shown.

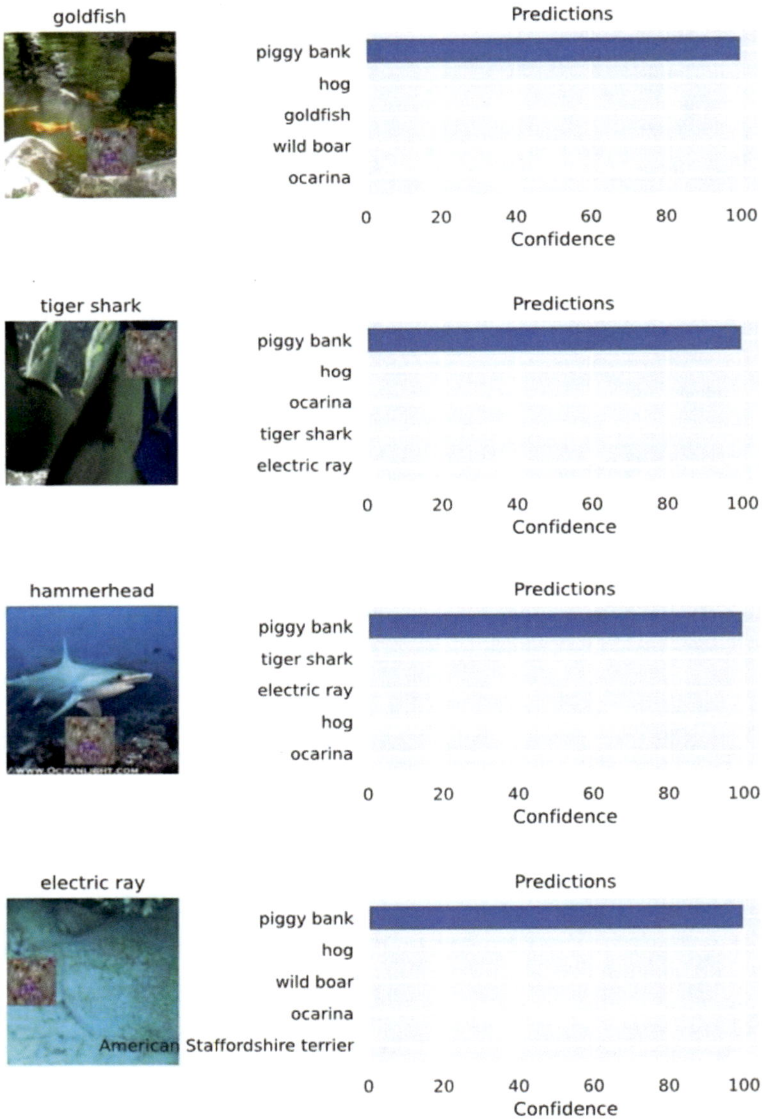

Figure. 8-4. Classification results of the ResNet-101 under the patch attack with a "Piggy Bank" patch of size 64*64 pixels

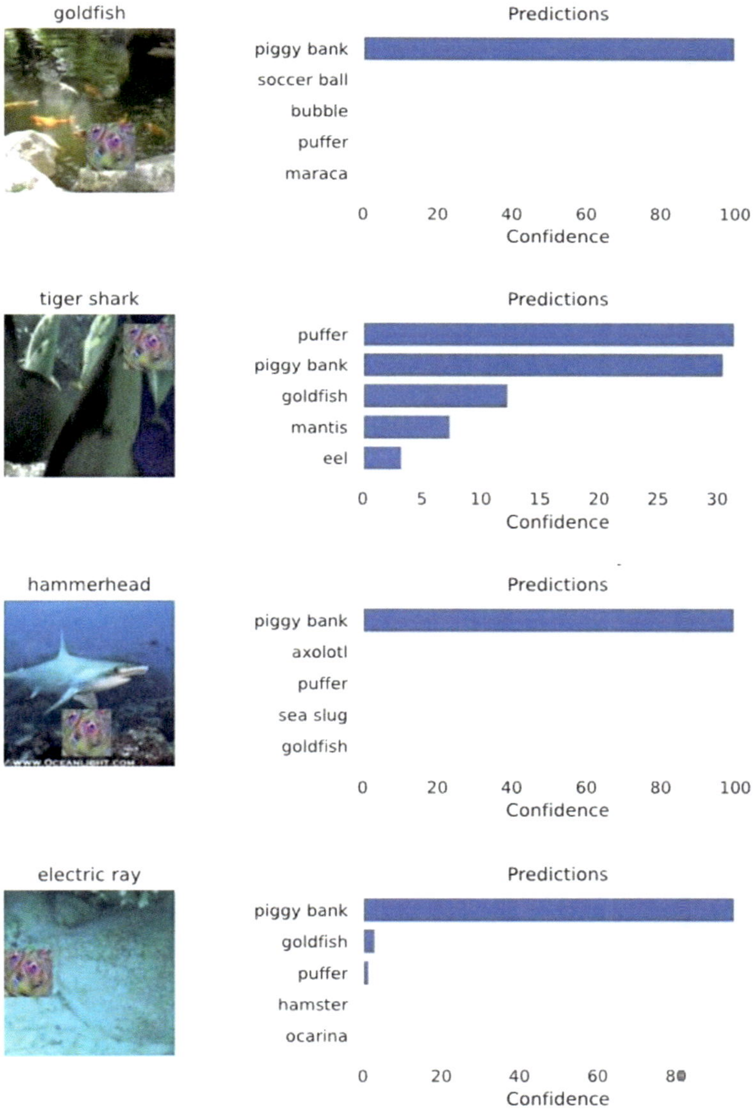

Figure. 8-5. Classification results of the AlexNet under the patch attack with a "Piggy Bank" patch of size 64*64 pixels

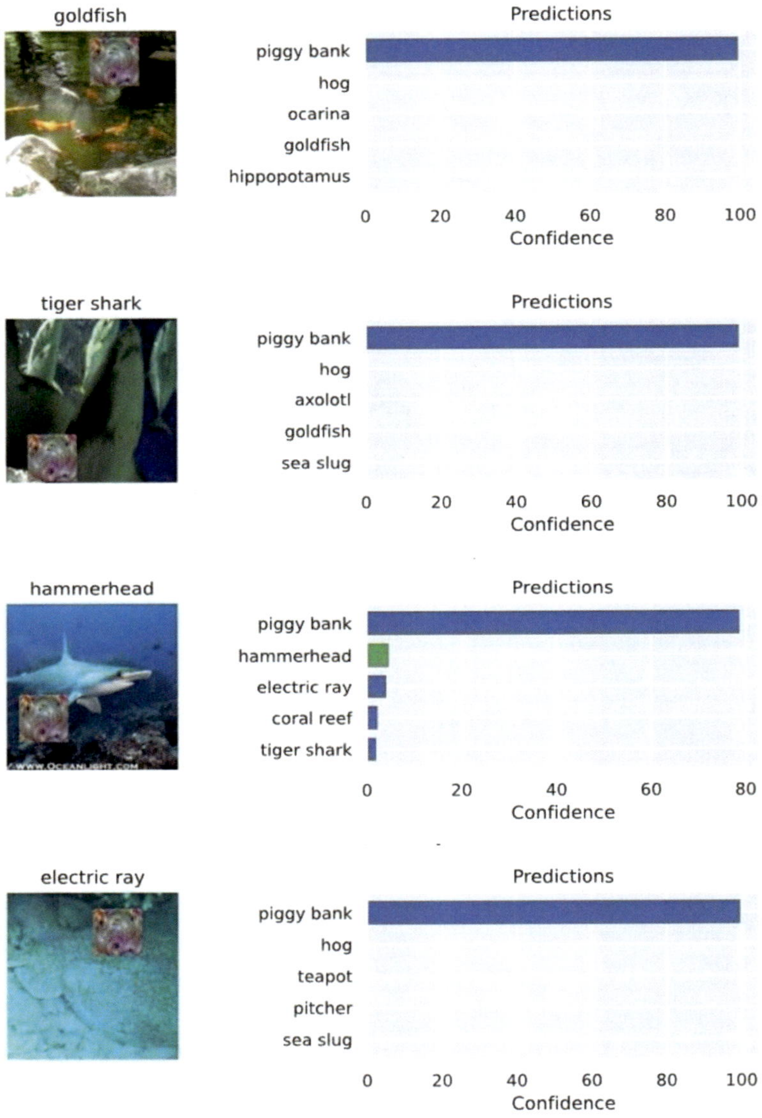

Figure. 8-6. Classification results of the RegNetY 400MF model under the patch attack with a "Piggy Bank" patch of size 64*64 pixels.

The experimental results clearly demonstrate that adversarial patch attacks severely degrade the classification across all three evaluated models. Among the various patch images tested, the "toaster" patch consistently induced the most detrimental effects, leading to significant misclassifications regardless of the model architecture. Furthermore, the impact of the attack was found to escalate with the increasing patch size. Specifically, the 64*64 patch dimension resulted in the most pronounced performance degradation for all three models, highlighting a strong correlation between patch size and attack effectiveness.

Defensive Distillation Method

Knowledge distillation is a model compression technique originally developed to facilitate the training of a compact Deep Neural Network (DNN) by transferring the learned knowledge from a larger, more complex model, often referred to as the *teacher*, to a smaller, more efficient model, called the *student*. This approach was first conceptualized by Ba & Caruna (Ba & Caruna, 2014), and later formalized by Hinton et al. in a seminal paper (Hinton et al., 2014). The key motivation behind distillation is to enable the deployment of deep learning models on resource-constrained devices, such as smartphones, embedded systems, or edge computing platforms, where computational and memory capacities are limited. By leveraging the soft predictions (probability distributions) generated by the teacher model, the student model is trained to approximate the same behavior using significantly fewer parameters, thus achieving faster inference and reduced resource consumption without a substantial loss in performance.

In a novel extension of this idea, Papernot et al. introduced defensive distillation, not just as a method for compression, but as a robust defense mechanism against adversarial attacks (Papernot et al., 2016b). Unlike conventional distillation, which focuses on transferring general knowledge between different architectures, defensive distillation aims to improve the resilience of a neural network against input perturbations deliberately crafted to mislead the model. In this defensive paradigm, the knowledge extracted from a DNN is utilized to retrain the same or similar architecture with modified learning objectives, ultimately reducing the model's susceptibility to adversarial manipulation.

The core intuition is grounded in the observation that adversarial examples exploit large gradients of the loss function with respect to input features, allowing small, often imperceptible, perturbations to drastically alter the network's prediction. Defensive distillation seeks to mitigate this vulnerability by suppressing the magnitude of these gradients (Papernot et al., 2016a). When the gradients are small, an adversary must introduce much larger changes to the input to produce a successful attack, thereby increasing the robustness of the model. This suppression is achieved through a two-phase training process: first, a teacher model is trained using conventional supervised learning; then, the student model is trained on the softened output probabilities (also known as soft targets) produced by the teacher, rather than on hard class labels.

A key element in this process is the introduction of a temperature parameter in the softmax layer, which controls the smoothness of the output distribution. The softmax function, commonly used in classification tasks, converts raw logits into a normalized probability distribution over the class labels. When a higher temperature (e.g., 2, 5, or even 10) is used, the output distribution becomes softer, i.e., more uniform across classes. Conversely, a low temperature (close to 1 or below) produces sharper distributions, where the predicted class dominates the others significantly.

During the training of the student model, the soft targets generated by the teacher model at a high temperature are used as the learning objective. This helps the student to capture nuanced inter-class relationships that are not evident from one-hot encoded labels alone. By learning from these smoothed probability distributions, the student network develops smoother decision boundaries that are inherently more robust to minor perturbations in the input space, a property that makes it harder for adversarial examples to successfully cross classification thresholds.

Moreover, this process helps the student model to generalize better to unseen and noisy inputs, as it learns not only to classify but also to model the uncertainty and similarity between classes. As a result, the final distilled model can serve as a hardened substitute for the original teacher model. Experimental studies have shown that such models exhibit greater resistance to gradient-based attacks like FGSM and PGD, which rely on exploiting abrupt changes in the model's loss landscape.

In summary, defensive distillation represents a promising technique at the intersection of model compression and adversarial robustness. By smoothing class boundaries and diminishing input gradient sensitivity, it empowers DNNs to operate more securely in adversarial environments. However, subsequent research has also identified potential limitations, such as diminished effectiveness against more sophisticated or adaptive attacks, prompting the exploration of hybrid techniques that combine distillation with other defense mechanisms, such as input preprocessing, adversarial training, and robust optimization strategies. As the adversarial arms race continues, distillation remains a foundational concept in designing secure and efficient machine learning systems.

Experimental Results of Defensive Distillation

To evaluate the efficacy of the defensive distillation method in mitigating adversarial attacks, an extensive set of experiments was conducted using the well-known MNIST dataset (LeCun & Cortes, 1998), which consists of 60,000 grayscale images of handwritten digits. This dataset offers a suitable benchmark for assessing the impact of adversarial perturbations, particularly those generated using the Fast Gradient Sign Method (FGSM), as well as for evaluating the defense capabilities of the distilled models.

An image classification model based on a convolutional neural network (CNN) architecture was designed and implemented for the experiments. From the total dataset, 50,000 samples were randomly selected for training, while the remaining 10,000 samples were reserved for testing. The architecture of the CNN model is described as follows:

- *Convolutional Layer 1*: Accepts single-channel grayscale input and produces 32 feature maps using a 3×3 kernel with a stride of 1. The ReLU activation function is employed to introduce non-linearity.
- *Convolutional Layer 2*: Takes the output from the previous layer (32 channels) and produces 64 feature maps using a 3×3 kernel and a stride of 1. ReLU activation is again applied.
- *Dropout Layer 1*: Applies 2D dropout with a dropout probability of 0.25 to prevent overfitting.
- *Dropout Layer 2*: Applies a more aggressive 2D dropout with a probability of 0.5.
- *Fully Connected Layer*: Flattens the output of the previous layer (9216 dimensions) and maps it to 128 units using the ReLU activation function.

The model was trained using the *Adam* optimizer with a learning rate of 0.0001. The optimizer's beta parameters were configured as (0.9, 0.999), controlling the exponential moving averages of the gradients and squared gradients for adaptive learning rate adjustment. The negative log-likelihood function served as the loss criterion, ensuring robust classification learning.

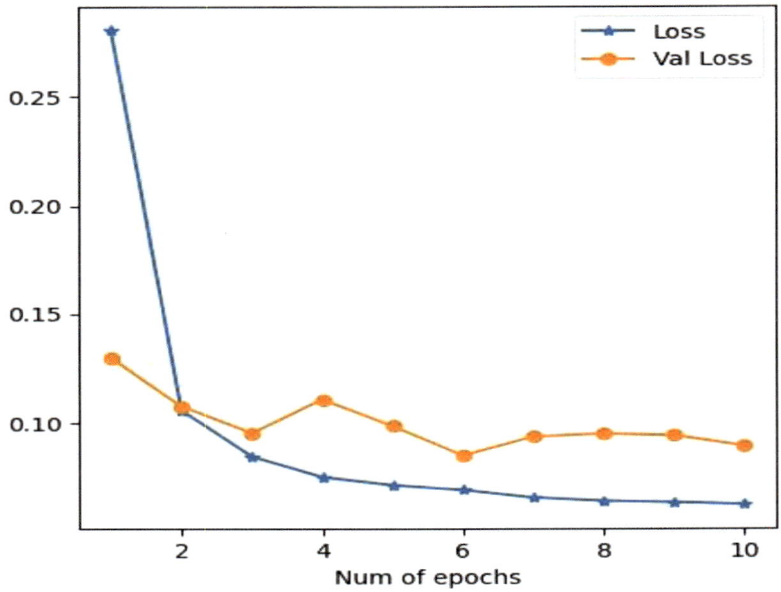

Figure. 8-7. Training and validation loss trends over successive epochs for the image classifier model.

To manage the learning rate dynamically, a ReduceLROnPlateau scheduler was integrated into the training process. This scheduler monitored the validation loss and reduced the learning rate when improvements plateaued. The mode was set to "min", and the learning rate was reduced by a factor of 0.1 if the validation loss did not improve for three consecutive epochs. The network was trained for over 10 epochs. The training and validation loss curves, presented in Figure 8-7, demonstrate the convergence behavior of the classifier.

Effect of FGSM Attack on Baseline Classifier: To examine the vulnerability of the trained model to adversarial perturbations, the FGSM attack was applied using varying values of the epsilon parameter (ε), which controls the intensity of the noise introduced into the input images. The selected values were: 0.000, 0.007, 0.010, 0.020, 0.030, 0.050, 0.100, 0.200, and 0.300. These values allow the evaluation of both subtle and aggressive perturbations.

Table 8-13 summarizes the classification accuracy of the CNN model under the FGSM attack for different ε values. As expected, the model exhibited high accuracy (96.98%) in the absence of perturbations. However, as ε increased, the performance significantly deteriorated. Notably, at ε = 0.3, the accuracy dropped dramatically to just 27.27%, indicating the model's high susceptibility to adversarial noise.

Table 8-13. Impact of the FGSM Attack on the Classification Accuracy of the Image Classifier Model

Epsilon	No. of Correctly Classified Cases	Total No of Cases	Classification Accuracy
0.000	9698	10000	0.9698
0.007	9650	10000	0.9650
0.010	9625	10000	0.9625
0.020	9585	10000	0.9585
0.030	9525	10000	0.9525
0.050	9366	10000	0.9366
0.100	8556	10000	0.8556
0.200	5405	10000	0.5405
0.300	2727	10000	0.2767

These results are further visualized in Figure 8-8, which shows the degradation in accuracy as a function of ε.

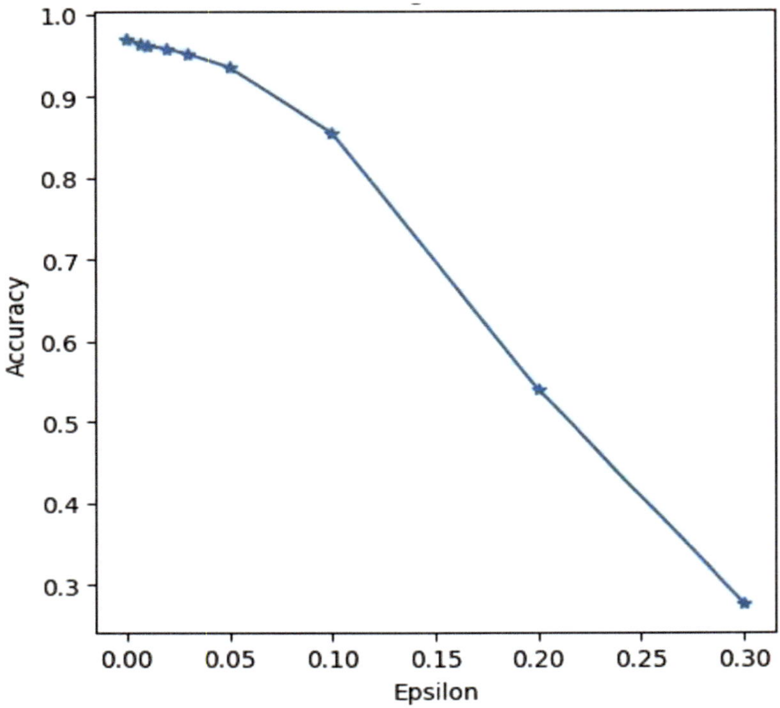

Figure. 8-8. Effect of the FGSM attack on the image classifier accuracy across varying noise levels.

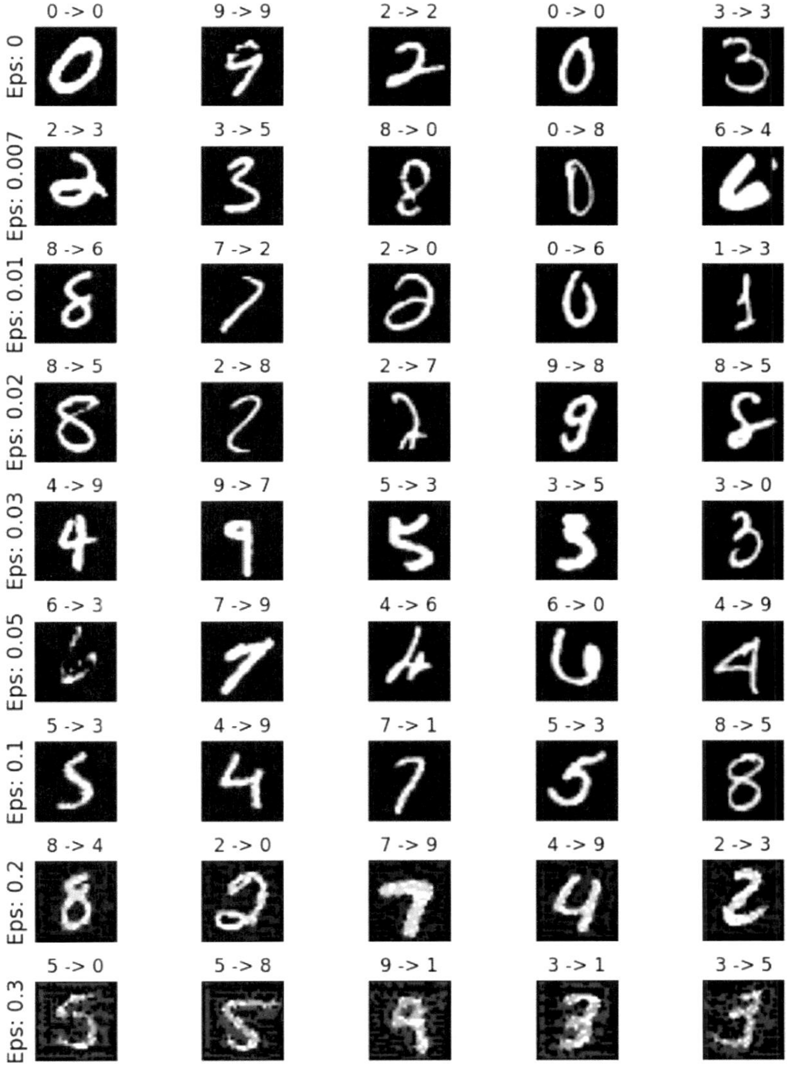

Figure. 8-9. Classification outcomes for selected images under varying noise levels of the FGSM attack.

Examples of perturbed images at various noise levels are provided in Figure 8-9, illustrating how minor modifications can lead to incorrect classifications.

***Enhancing Model Robustness through Defensive Distillation*:** To counteract the vulnerabilities exposed by the FGSM attack, the defensive distillation technique was employed. In this approach, the soft targets generated by a high-temperature softmax function were used to train a distilled version of the original network. The temperature was set to 100 during the distillation process, producing smoother output distributions that retain more information about inter-class relationships. These soft labels were then used to retrain the same network architecture on the original training data.

The distilled model was trained under the same conditions as the original, using the Adam optimizer and learning rate scheduler. The evolution of training and validation loss during distillation is shown in Figures 8-10, indicating stable convergence and generalization performance.

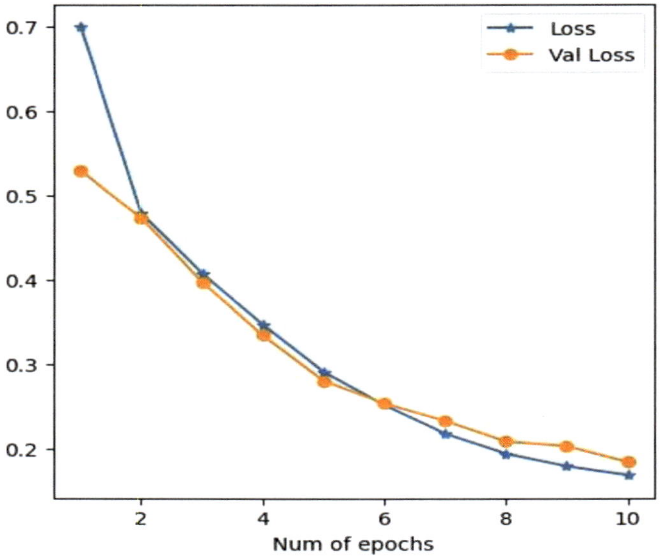

Figure. 8-10. Training and validation loss curves across epochs during the training of the distilled network.

To assess the effectiveness of the distilled model in resisting adversarial inputs, the same set of ε values was used to generate FGSM adversarial examples. The classification performance of the distilled model is shown in Table 8-14. The results clearly indicate substantial improvements in robustness: even at a high perturbation level of $\varepsilon = 0.3$, the accuracy remained at 91.11%, a stark contrast to the 27.27% achieved by the undistilled model under the same conditions. Figure 8-11 illustrates this resilience graphically, showing only minor degradation in accuracy as ε increases.

Table 8-14. Impact of the FGSM Attack on the Classification Accuracy of the Distilled Classifier Model

Epsilon	No. of Correctly Classified Cases	Total No of Cases	Classification Accuracy
0.000	9291	10000	0.9291
0.007	9275	10000	0.9275
0.010	9265	10000	0.9265
0.020	9275	10000	0.9275
0.030	9246	10000	0.9246
0.050	9216	10000	0.9216
0.100	9211	10000	0.9211
0.200	9131	10000	0.9131
0.300	9291	10000	0.9111

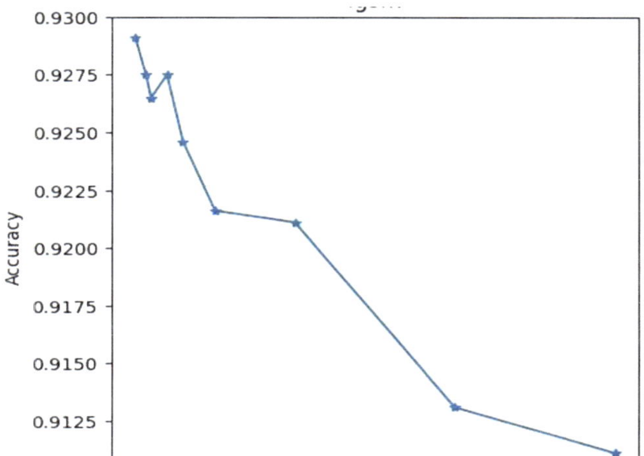

Figure. 8-11. Classification accuracy of the distilled network under FGSM attack across varying noise levels.

The experimental findings demonstrate that defensive distillation serves as an effective method for enhancing the adversarial robustness of deep learning models. While the original CNN model showed significant vulnerability to FGSM attacks, the distilled network maintained a high degree of classification accuracy even under substantial adversarial perturbations. These results substantiate the hypothesis that knowledge distillation, by softening class boundaries and minimizing gradient sensitivity, can effectively counteract gradient-based attacks such as FGSM. This positions defensive distillation as a valuable and practical defense strategy in the broader landscape of adversarial machine learning.

Conclusion and Future Work

Adversarial attacks represent a critical vulnerability in modern deep learning systems, especially those deployed in high-stakes applications such as autonomous vehicles, surveillance, and medical imaging. This study has explored two representative forms of such attacks, Fast Gradient Sign Method (FGSM) and the adversarial patch, and demonstrated their capacity to significantly degrade the performance of a CNN-based image classifier trained on the MNIST dataset. Even minimal perturbations, imperceptible to the human eye, were found to cause severe misclassification in the absence of any defense mechanism. This highlights a fundamental flaw in the robustness of neural network models and reinforces the need for proactive defensive strategies.

To address this vulnerability, the study incorporated *defensive distillation*, a technique that leverages knowledge distillation at elevated temperatures to enhance the robustness of the model. The results were promising. When the distilled model was subjected to the same FGSM attack that caused a drastic performance drop in the original model, it retained a remarkably high classification accuracy, even at perturbation levels where the original network's accuracy had dropped by more than 60%. This clearly demonstrates the efficacy of the distillation-based defense approach in mitigating adversarial risks.

Several important conclusions can be drawn from the experimental analysis conducted in this study:

Effectiveness of FGSM: The FGSM attack proved to be an efficient and scalable method for generating adversarial examples. As shown through systematic variation of the epsilon parameter, even small perturbations can cause dramatic reductions in classifier accuracy, making FGSM a useful benchmark for testing model robustness.

Limitations of Traditional CNNs: The unprotected CNN model, despite achieving nearly 97% accuracy on clean MNIST data, was highly susceptible to adversarial noise. This disparity between nominal and adversarial performance is concerning and indicative of a gap in model generalization under adversarial settings.

Robustness of Defensive Distillation: Defensive distillation, when implemented correctly with temperature scaling and soft targets, significantly enhances model resilience. Even under aggressive perturbations, the distilled model maintained accuracy levels above 91%, illustrating that distillation introduces valuable regularization and smooths the decision boundaries.

Trade-offs in Robustness vs. Accuracy: One noteworthy observation is that while the original model had slightly higher accuracy on clean data, the distilled model sacrificed minimal nominal accuracy in exchange for a substantial gain in robustness. This indicates that with careful tuning, distillation may offer a balanced solution without compromising clean-data performance.

Future Research Directions: While this work has laid the groundwork for understanding and defending against FGSM-based adversarial attacks using defensive distillation, it opens several avenues for further investigation:

Extension to More Complex Datasets and Architectures: Future work can extend the current analysis to more challenging datasets such as CIFAR-10, CIFAR-100, and ImageNet, and to more complex architectures like ResNet, EfficientNet, or Vision Transformers (ViT). The performance of defensive distillation under high-dimensional and more abstract feature spaces needs thorough evaluation.

Combination with Other Defenses: Defensive distillation can be integrated with other robust training approaches such as adversarial training, input denoising, randomized smoothing, or certified defenses. An ensemble of defense strategies may offer layered protection and be more resilient against adaptive adversaries.

Adaptive and Transferable Attacks: The robustness of the distilled model against *adaptive attacks*, which are specifically designed to circumvent known defense mechanisms, is yet to be explored. Moreover, the *transferability* of adversarial examples across different model architectures and defense strategies remains an open challenge.

Defense-Aware Attack Algorithms: As attackers become more sophisticated, future research must anticipate attack methods that are explicitly tuned to exploit the characteristics of defense mechanisms like distillation. Developing benchmark suites for evaluating defense-aware adversarial strategies is essential for stress-testing current methods. In particular, the *Carlini-Wagner* (CW) attack has emerged as one of the most potent examples of defense-aware adversarial techniques, effectively bypassing a range of defenses, including defensive distillation. Multiple studies have shown that distilled models, despite initial success against simple gradient-based attacks like FGSM, remain highly vulnerable to CW attacks due to their ability to optimize adversarial perturbations in a targeted, low-distortion manner (Athalye & Carlini, 2018; Athalye et al., 2018; Carlini & Wagner, 2018; 2017a; 2017b; 2016; McCarthy et al., 2023; Xu et al., 2017). Future work should focus on rigorously assessing the robustness of distillation-based defense under CW-style attacks and exploring adaptive countermeasures that can mitigate such threats. This includes the design of novel training paradigms and optimization constraints that explicitly account for attack awareness and model adaptability.

Explainability and Robustness Auditing: Integrating explainable AI (XAI) techniques to interpret how and why a model resists or succumbs to adversarial perturbations can enhance transparency. Saliency maps and gradient-based interpretation tools can be used to audit robustness and guide defensive improvements.

Dynamic Temperature Scaling: Instead of using a fixed temperature during distillation, future work could explore adaptive or layer-wise temperature tuning to better balance information compression and generalization. This may provide finer control over the soft label distributions used for training the student network.

Generalization to other Modalities: The principles of defensive distillation can be generalized to other data modalities such as text, audio, and time-series data. Investigating its applicability and limitations across diverse machine learning domains could broaden its impact and usability.

Robustness Certification: Another promising direction involves coupling distillation with certified robustness techniques that provide formal guarantees against adversarial perturbations within specific bounds. This would be particularly valuable in regulatory or mission-critical scenarios.

In summary, this study emphasizes the urgent need to fortify machine learning models against adversarial threats and validates the use of defensive distillation as an effective method for enhancing robustness. While the results are encouraging, the dynamic and evolving nature of adversarial machine learning necessitates continued research into more generalizable, scalable, and adaptive defense strategies. Developing robust AI systems that perform reliably not just under ideal conditions but also in adversarial and uncertain environments will remain a key research priority in the coming years.

References

Anjos A. and Marcel, S. 2011. "Counter-measures to Photo Attacks in Face Recognition: A Public Database and a Baseline." In *Proceedings of the 2011 International Joint Conference on Biometrics (IJCB 2011)*, 1-7. IEEE.

Athalye A. and Carlini, N. 2018. "On the Robustness of the CVPR 2018 White-Box Adversarial Example Defenses." arXiv Preprint arXiv: 1804.03286.

Athalye, A., Carlini, N., and Wagner, D. 2018. "Obfuscated Gradients Give a False Sense of Security: Circumventing Defenses to Adversarial Examples." arXiv Preprint arXiv:1802.00420.

Ba, J. and Caruana, R. 2014. "Do Deep Nets Really Need to be Deep?" *Advances in Neural Information Systems*, 2654-2662.

Biggio, B., Corona, I., Maiorca, D., Nelson, B., Srndic, N., Laskov, P., Giacinto, G., and Roli, F. 2013. "Evasion Attacks against Machine Learning at Test Time." In H. Blockeel et al. (eds) *Machine Learning and Knowledge Discovery in Databases. ECML PKDD 2013*. Lecture Notes in Computer Science, 8190: 387-402 Springer, Berlin, Heidelberg, Germany.

Biggio, B., Fumera, G., and Roli, F. 2014. "Pattern Recognition Systems Under Attack: Design Issues and Research Challenges." *International Journal of Pattern Recognition and Artificial Intelligence*, 28(7): 1460002.

Brown, T. B., Mane, D., Roy, A., Abadi, M., and Gilmer, J 2017. "Adversarial Patch." In *Proceedings of the 31st Conference on Neural Information Processing Systems (NIPS'17)*.

Carlini, N. and Wagner, D. 2018. "Audio Adversarial Examples: Targeted Attacks on Speech-to-Text." arXiv Preprint arXiv:1801.01944.

Carlini, N. and Wagner, D. 2017a. "Towards Evaluating the Robustness of Neural Networks." In *Proceedings of the 2017 IEEE Symposium on Security and Privacy (S&P 2017)*, 39-57.

Carlini, N. and Wagner, D. 2017b. "Adversarial Examples are Not Easily Detected: Bypassing Ten Detection Methods." *In Proceedings of the 10th ACM Workshop on Artificial Intelligence and Security (AISec 2017)*, 3-14.

Carlini, N. and Wagner, D. 2016. "Defensive Distillation is Not Robust to Adversarial Examples." arXiv Preprint arXiv:1607.04311.

Chalupka, K., Perona, P., and Eberhardt, F. 2015. "Visual Causal Feature Learning." In *Proceedings of the 31st Conference on Uncertainty in Artificial Intelligence*, 181-190. AUAI Press.

Chen, Y., Zhang, M., Li, J., and Kuang, X. 2022. "Adversarial Attacks and Defenses in Image Classification: A Practical Perspective." In *Proceedings of the 7th International Conference on Image, Vision and Computing (ICIVC 2022)*, 424-430.

Ciresan, D., Meier, U., Masci, J., and Schmidhuber, J. 2012. "Multi-Column Deep Neural Network for Traffic Sign Classification." *Neural Networks*, 32 (August 2012): 333-338.

Deng, J., Dong, W., Socher, R., Li, L-J., Li, K., and F-Fei, L. 2009. "ImageNet: A Large-scale Hierarchical Image Database." In *Proceedings of 2009 IEEE Conference on Computer Vision and Pattern Recognition (CVPR 2009)*, 248-255. IEEE Press.

Dong, Y., Fu, Q-A., Yang, X., Pang, T., Su, H., Xiao, Z., and Zhu, J. 2020. "Benchmarking Adversarial Robustness on Image Classification." In *Proceedings of the IEEE/CVF Conference on Computer Vision and Pattern Recognition (CVPR 2020)*, 13-19.

Dong, Y., Liao, F., Pang, T., Su, H., Zhu, J., Hu, X., and Li, J. 2018. "Boosting Advesarial Attacks with Momentum." In *Proceedings of 2018 IEEE/CVF Conference on Computer Vision and Pattern Recognition*, 9185-9193.

Eykholt, K., Evtimov, I., Fernandes, E., Li, B., Rahmati, A., Xiao, C., Prakash, A., Kohno, T., and Song, D. 2018. "Robust Physical-World Attacks on Deep Learning Visual Classification." In *Proceedings of the IEEE/CVF Conference on Computer Vision and Pattern Recognition (CVPR 2018)*, 1625-1634. IEEE Press.

Fogla, P. and Lee, W. 2006. "Evading Network Anomaly Detection Systems: Formal Reasoning and Practical Techniques." In *Proceedings of the 13th ACM Conference on Computer and Communications Security*, 59-68. ACM.

Goodfellow, I. J., Shlens, J., and Szegedy, C. 2015. "Explaining and Harnessing Adversarial Examples." *International Conference on Learning and Representations (ICLR 2015)*, Poster Track.

Gu, S. and Rigazio, L. 2015. "Towards Deep Neural Network Architectures Robust to Adversarial Examples." In the *International Conference on Learning and Representations (ICLR'15)*, Poster Track.

He, K., Zhang, X., Ren, S., and Sun, J. 2016. "Deep Residual Learning for Image Recognition." In *Proceedings of the 2016 IEEE Conference on Computer Vision and Pattern Recognition (CVPR)*, 770-778.

Hinton, G., Vinyals, O., and Dean, J. 2014. "Distilling the Knowledge in a Neural Network." In *Deep Learning and Representation Learning Workshop, NIPS 2014*. arXiv:1503.02531, 2014.

Huang, L., Joseph, A. D., Nelson, B., Rubinstein, B. I. P., and Tygar, J. D. 2011. "Adversarial machine learning," In *Proceedings of the 4th ACM Workshop on Security and Artificial Intelligence*, 43-58.

Koley, A., Satpati, P., Choudhary, I., and Sen, J. 2024. "An Investigation on the Efficiency of Some Text Attack Algorithms." In *Proceedings of the IEEE North Karnataka Subsection Flagship International Conference (NKCon 2024)*, 1–8.

Krizhevsky, A., Sutskever, I., and Hinton, G. 2017. "ImageNet Classification with Deep Convolutional Networks." *Communications of the ACM*, 60(6): 84-90.

Kurakin, A., Goodfellow, I. J., and Bengio, S. 2017. "Adversarial Machine Learning at Scale." In *the International Conference on Learning Representations (ICLR 2017)*, Poster Track.

LeCun, Y. and Cortes, C. 1998. "The MNIST Database of Digits." https://www.kaggle.com/datasets/hojjatk/mnist-dataset.

Li, C., Fan, C., Zhang, J., Li, C., and Teng, Y. 2022. "A Block Gray Adversarial Attack Method for Image Classification Neural Network." In *Proceedings of 2022 IEEE 24th International Conference on High Performance Computing & Communications (HPCC'22)*, 1682-1689.

M.-Dezfooli, S.-M., Fawzi, A., and Frossard, P. 2016. "Deepfool: A Simple and Accurate Method to Fool Deep Neural Networks." *In Proceedings of 2016 IEEE Conference on Computer Vision and Pattern Recognition (CVPR 2016)*, 2574-2582. IEEE.

Madry, A., Makelov, A., Schmidt, L., Tsipras, D., and Vladu, A. 2018. "Towards Deep Learning Models Resistant to Adversarial Attacks." In *the International Conference on Learning Representations (ICLR 2018)*, Poster Track.

McCarthy, A., Ghadafi, E., Andriotis, P., and Legg, P. 2023. "Defending against Adversarial Machine Learning Attacks Using Hierarchical Learning: A Case Study on Network Traffic Attack Classification." *Journal of Information Security and Applications*, 72 (c), 2023.

NVIDIA, Solutions for Self-Driving Cars, 2023. Available online at: https://www.nvidia.com/en-us/self-driving-cars (Accessed on May 9, 2023)

Papernot, N., McDaniel, P., Jha, S., Fredrikson, S. M., Celik, Z. B., and Swami, A. 2016a. "The Limitations of Deep Learning in Adversarial Settings." In *Proceedings of the 1st IEEE European Symposium on Security and Privacy*, 372-387.

Papernot, N., McDaniel, P., Wu, X., Jha, S., and Swami, A. 2016b. "Distillation as a Defense to Adversarial Perturbations against Deep Neural Networks." In *2016 IEEE Symposium on Security and Privacy (S & P 2016)*, 582-597.

Pestana, C., Akhtar, N., Liu, W., Glance, D., and Mian, A. 2021. "Adversarial Attacks and Defense on Deep Learning Classification Models Using YCbCr Color Images." In *Proceedings of the International Joint Conference on Neural Networks (IJCNN 2021)*, 1-9.

Radosavovic, I., Kosaraju, R. P., Girshick, R., He, K., and Dollár, P. 2010. "Designing Network Design Spaces." In *Proceedings of 2020 IEEE/CVF Conference on Computer Vision and Pattern Recognition (CVPR)*, 10425-10433.

Sen, J. 2024. "The FGSM Attack on Image Classification Models and Distillation as its Defense." In Nanda et al. (eds), *Advances in Distributed Computing and Machine Learning (ICADCML 2024)*, 1015: 347-360. Lecture Notes in Networks and Systems, Springer, Singapore.

Sen, J. and Dasgupta, S. 2023. "Adversarial Attacks on Image Classification Models: FGSM and Patch Attacks and their Impact." In Sen, J. and Mayer, J. (eds), *Information Security and Privacy in the Digital World: Some Selected Topics*, IntechOpen, London, UK.

Sen, J., Sen, A., and Chatterjee, A. 2023. "Adversarial Attacks on Image Classification Models: Analysis and Defense." In *Proceedings of the 10th International Conference on Business Analytics and Intelligence (ICBAI 2023)*, Bangalore, India.

Sen, J. and Waghela, H. 2025. "Text-Based Adversarial Attacks and Defense", In Sen, J. (ed) *Data Privacy: Techniques, Applications, and Standards*, IntechOpen, London, UK.

Sharif, M., Bhagavatula, S., Bauer, L., and Reiter, M. K. 2016. "Accessorize to a Crime: Real and Stealthy Attacks on State-of-the-Art Face

Recognition." In *Proceedings of the 2016 ACM SIGSAC Conference on Computer and Communications Security*, 1528–1540. ACM Press.

Srivastava, N., Hinton, G., Krizhevsky, A., Sutskever, I., and Salakhutdinov, R. 2014. "Dropout: A Simple Way to Prevent Neural Networks from Overfitting," *The Journal of Machine Learning Research*, 15(1): 1929-1958.

Szegedy, C., Zaremba, W., Sutskever, I., Bruna, J., Erhan, D., Goodfellow, I. J., and Fergus, R. 2014. "Intriguing Properties of Neural Networks." In the *International Conference on Learning Representations (ICLR 2014)*, Poster Track.

Tramer, F., Kurakin, A., Papernot, N., Goodfellow, I., Boneh, D., McDaniel, P. 2018. "Ensemble Adversarial Training: Attacks and Defenses." In the *International Conference on Learning Representations (ICLR 2018)*, Poster Track.

Waghela, H., Sen, J., and Rakshit, S. 2025. "Saliency Attention and Semantic Similarity-Driven Adversarial Perturbation." In *Data Science and Applications. ICDSA 2024*, Nanda, S. J. et al. (eds), 1237: 461–471. Lecture Notes in Networks and Systems. Springer, Singapore.

Waghela, H., Sen, J., Rakshit, S., and Dasgupta, S. 2024a. "Adversarial Text Generation with Dynamic Contextual Perturbation." In *Proceedings of the 2024 IEEE CALCON 2024*, 1–6. IEEE.

Waghela, H., Sen, J., and Rakshit, S. 2024b. "Adaptive Meta-Learning for Robust Ensemble Defense against Adversarial Attacks." In *Proceedings of the International Conference BAMS-ORSI'24*, December 12–14, 2024. IIT Bombay, Mumbai, India.

Waghela, H., Sen, J., and Rakshit, S. 2024c. "Adversarial Resilience in Image Classification: A Hybrid Approach to Defense." In *Proceedings of the 2024 International Conference on Innovation and Intelligence for Informatics, Computing, and Technologies (3ICT'24)*, 419–426. Sakhir, Bahrain.

Waghela, H., Sen, J., Rakshit, S., and Dasgupta, S. 2024d. "Adversarial Robustness through Dynamic Ensemble Learning." In *Proceedings of the 2024 IEEE Silchar Subsection Conference (SILCON'24)*, 1–6, Agartala, India, November 15 – 17, 2024.

Waghela, H., Sen, J., and Rakshit, S. 2024e. "Robust Image Classification: Defensive Strategies against FGSM and PGD Adversarial Attacks." In *Proceedings of the IEEE Asian Conference on Intelligent Technologies (ACOIT 2024)*, 1 – 7, September 6–7, 2024. Kolar, Karnataka, India.

Waghela, H., Sen, J., and Rakshit, S. 2024f. "Refining BERT Adversarial Attacks with Projected Gradient Descent." In *Proceedings of the IEEE*

4th Asian Conference on Innovations in Technology (ASIANCON 2024), 1-7, August 24–25, 2024.

Waghela, H., Rakshit, S., and Sen, J. 2024g. "A Modified Word Saliency-Based Adversarial Attack on Text Classification Models." In *Computational Intelligence and Data Analytics*, Frery, A. C. (eds), 371–382. Lecture Notes in Data Engineering and Communications Technologies, 236. Springer.

Xu, W., Evans, D., and Qi, Y. 2017. "Feature Squeezing Mitigates and Detects Carlini/Wagner Adversarial Examples." arXiv Preprint arXiv: 1705.10686.

Yuan, H., Li, S., Sun, W., Li, Z., Steven, X. 2021. "An Efficient Attention-based Image Adversarial Attack Algorithm with Differential Evolution on Realistic High-resolution Image." In *Proceedings of 2021 IEEE/ACIS 20th International Fall Conference on Computer and Information Science (ICIS Fall'21)*, 115-120.

CHAPTER 9

EFFECTIVE DEFENSIVE STRATEGIES FOR FGSM AND PGD ADVERSARIAL ATTACKS IN IMAGE CLASSIFICATION

Introduction

The proliferation of deep learning has revolutionized the field of computer vision, enabling machines to interpret and understand visual information with unprecedented accuracy. *Convolutional Neural Networks* (CNNs), in particular, have emerged as the cornerstone of this transformation, powering applications such as image classification, object detection, facial recognition, medical diagnostics, and autonomous navigation. Fueled by massive labeled datasets, increased computational capabilities, and refined neural architectures, CNN-based image classifiers have achieved performance levels that often surpass human benchmarks. These advancements have facilitated the widespread integration of deep learning systems into real-world applications, many of which are safety-critical and demand high reliability.

Despite their success, deep learning models remain acutely vulnerable to adversarial attacks, strategically crafted inputs designed to deceive neural networks into making incorrect predictions. These adversarial examples introduce minimal and often imperceptible perturbations to the input data, yet they can cause significant misclassification errors. The subtlety of such attacks, combined with their effectiveness, presents a formidable challenge to the security and trustworthiness of machine learning systems. This vulnerability is particularly concerning in domains where incorrect predictions can have serious consequences. For instance, in autonomous vehicles, a misclassified stop sign could lead to unsafe driving behavior. In medical imaging, slight perturbations to a diagnostic scan could lead to incorrect identification of disease states, affecting treatment decisions and patient outcomes.

Among the numerous adversarial attack techniques developed, two methods stand out due to their effectiveness and widespread use: the *Fast Gradient Sign Method* (FGSM) (Goodfellow et al., 2015) and *Projected Gradient Descent* (PGD) (Madry et al., 2018). FGSM, a single-step gradient-based approach, generates adversarial examples by computing the sign of the gradient of the loss function with respect to the input data. The perturbation, although small, is strategically aligned to maximize the model's prediction error. Its simplicity and computational efficiency have made it a standard method for evaluating model robustness. PGD extends this idea by applying iterative gradient updates constrained within a perturbation budget. This multi-step approach enables the generation of more potent adversarial examples and is considered one of the strongest first-order adversarial attacks. The iterative nature of PGD allows it to exploit vulnerabilities in neural networks more effectively, making it a benchmark for evaluating the strength of defensive mechanisms.

The emergence of such powerful attack strategies has motivated the development of a broad spectrum of defense techniques aimed at preserving the integrity of machine learning models in adversarial settings. These defense mechanisms can be broadly categorized into four primary classes: (i) adversarial training, (ii) input preprocessing, (iii) model architecture modification, and (iv) adversarial input detection. *Adversarial training* involves incorporating adversarial examples into the training process, thereby improving the model's resilience to similar attacks (Carmon et al., 2019; Goodfellow et al., 2015; Gowal et al., 2021a; Gowal et al., 2021b; Madry et al., 2018; Sehwag et al., 2022; Tramer et al., 2018; Wang et al., 2020; Wong & Kolter, 2018; Zhang et al., 2019). *Input preprocessing* techniques attempt to cleanse adversarial noise from the data before classification, often through filtering, denoising, or transformation strategies (Buckman et al., 2018; Cohen et al., 2019; Das et al., 2017; Gong & Wang, 2023; Guo et al., Liao et al., 2018; Meng et al., 2017; Prakash et al., 2018; Xie et al., 2018; Xu et al., 2018). *Modifying the architecture* of neural networks to enhance robustness includes innovations such as robust activation functions or architecture-level redundancy (Cohen et al., 2019; Gowal et al., 2021a; Lecuyer et al., 2019; Pang et al., 2019; Paul & Chen, 2022; Raghunathan et al., 2018; Wong & Kotler, 2018; Xie et al., 2019; Xie et al., 2020; Zoran et al., 2020). Finally, *adversarial input detection* schemes aim to identify potentially malicious inputs before they can influence the model's decision-making process (Carlini & Wagner, 2017a; Dathathri et al., 2019; Feinman et al., 2017; Grosse et al., 2016; Lee et al., 2018; Lu et al., 2017; Ma et al., 2018; Meng & Chen, 2017; Metzen et al., 2017; Roth et al., 2019; Samangouei et al., 2018).

Each of these defense strategies presents trade-offs. While adversarial training can improve robustness against known attacks, it is computationally intensive and may not generalize well to unseen perturbations. Preprocessing techniques offer a lightweight layer of protection but may compromise input fidelity or introduce new vulnerabilities. Architectural modifications often require redesigning or retraining models, which can hinder practical deployment. Detection methods, although useful, are frequently circumvented by adaptive attacks and may suffer from false positives. Thus, there remains a pressing need for defenses that are both effective and computationally feasible, particularly in applications where latency and accuracy are critical.

Addressing these challenges, the current study explores a hybrid defense strategy that combines adversarial training with a convolutional autoencoder-based preprocessing module. The convolutional autoencoder serves as a front-end denoising filter that reconstructs clean images from adversarial inputs, thereby neutralizing perturbations before classification. This dual-defense approach aims to enhance model robustness without substantially compromising accuracy or efficiency. The framework is implemented using the Visual Geometry Group 16 layers (VGG16) CNN architecture and evaluated on the MNIST and Fashion-MNIST datasets, which are standard benchmarks in the adversarial robustness literature.

The methodology involves generating adversarial examples using FGSM and PGD attacks, training the VGG16 model on both clean and adversarial inputs, and integrating a convolutional autoencoder to preprocess perturbed images. The autoencoder is trained to reconstruct clean images from adversarially corrupted inputs, thereby mitigating the attack's effects. By combining these two complementary defense mechanisms, one at the training level and one at the input level, the framework seeks to improve classification accuracy under adversarial conditions and generalize across varying levels of perturbation.

This chapter aims to offer a comprehensive examination of the threat posed by gradient-based adversarial attacks and the design of effective countermeasures using neural reconstruction techniques. In addition to presenting the empirical results of the proposed defense scheme, the chapter provides a critical perspective on the broader implications of adversarial robustness in AI systems. Emphasis is placed on the applicability of these defenses in real-world scenarios, the computational trade-offs involved, and potential avenues for enhancing scalability and generalization.

The chapter is organized as follows. The *Related Work* offers an overview of existing adversarial attack strategies and corresponding defense mechanisms. The *Proposed Methodology* section details the design and implementation of the convolutional autoencoder-based defense framework. The section *Experimental Results* presents empirical evaluations conducted on benchmark datasets under various adversarial conditions. Finally, the chapter concludes with the *Conclusion and Future Work section.*

Related Work

The intersection of adversarial machine learning and deep learning security has become a critical research frontier in recent years, driven by increasing awareness of the vulnerabilities that *deep neural networks* (DNNs) exhibit under adversarial conditions. The rapid expansion of deep learning in real-world applications has heightened the urgency to understand and mitigate these vulnerabilities. Existing literature offers a wide spectrum of research contributions on both adversarial attack methodologies and corresponding defense strategies. This section provides a thematic synthesis of foundational and recent works in this domain, focusing on the evolution of adversarial attacks, the development of defense mechanisms, and the challenges that continue to shape this dynamic research landscape.

***Adversarial Attacks on Deep Learning Models*:** The concept of adversarial examples was formally introduced by Goodfellow et al., who proposed the *Fast Gradient Sign Method* (FGSM) as an efficient single-step attack that perturbs the input data along the gradient of the model's loss function (Goodfellow et al., 2015). This work not only highlighted the brittleness of deep models to subtle perturbations but also initiated a broad inquiry into the reliability of machine learning models in adversarial environments. Despite its simplicity, FGSM remains a foundational method for evaluating model robustness.

Building on this idea, Madry et al. introduced the *Projected Gradient Descent* (PGD) attack, which extends FGSM through iterative refinement within a constrained perturbation boundary (Madry et al., 2018). PGD is now widely regarded as one of the most powerful first-order adversarial attacks and is frequently employed as a benchmark in adversarial defense evaluations. The theoretical rigor and empirical effectiveness of PGD have made it a cornerstone in the study of robust optimization.

Beyond these canonical methods, numerous other attack strategies have emerged, targeting different facets of model behavior and application contexts. For instance, *attention-guided adversarial attacks* on image captioning systems have demonstrated how attention mechanisms can be exploited to generate more effective and semantically precise adversarial examples (Li et al., 2024). While highly effective, these attacks often come with increased computational overhead due to their optimization complexity.

Studies focusing on domain-specific vulnerabilities, such as those affecting medical image analysis systems, have revealed how model architecture choices, training data characteristics, and domain constraints can exacerbate susceptibility to adversarial manipulation (Bortsova et al., 2021). Even minute perturbations in diagnostic images have been shown to cause critical misclassifications, underscoring the urgency of developing domain-aware defense mechanisms.

Recent work by Li et al. proposed the *Block Gray Adversarial Attack* (BGAA), a structured attack that perturbs specific regions of an image using constrained color transformations (Li et al., 2022). BGAA achieves high attack success rates while maintaining imperceptibility, further illustrating the adaptability of adversarial methods to exploit model sensitivities.

Critiques of detection-based defenses have also highlighted key limitations in current adversarial detection strategies. Notably, Carlini and Wagner demonstrated that many detection techniques can be circumvented by adaptive attacks, thereby challenging the efficacy of standalone detection systems (Carlini & Wagner, 2017a; 2017b).

Defensive Mechanisms against Adversarial Perturbations: In response to the proliferation of attack methods, various defensive strategies have been proposed, each aiming to enhance the resilience of machine learning models to adversarial perturbations. These defenses can be broadly categorized into training-based methods, input transformation techniques, architectural modifications, and detection mechanisms.

Adversarial training remains one of the most widely adopted and empirically validated defense strategies. By augmenting training datasets with adversarially perturbed samples, models can learn to generalize better in the presence of attacks. While effective, this approach is computationally intensive and often fails to defend against novel or more sophisticated attack variants.

Defensive distillation, introduced as an alternative to adversarial training, seeks to reduce a model's sensitivity to input perturbations by training a secondary model on soft probabilities generated by a teacher network (Papernot et al., 2016). This process smooths the decision boundaries and enhances robustness. However, subsequent research has shown that distillation-based defenses may be ineffective against stronger or adaptive adversaries.

Another emerging line of research explores the adversarial robustness of *multimodal architectures*, particularly those combining visual and textual modalities. Cui et al performed a comprehensive evaluation of how such systems respond to adversarial perturbations targeting either or both modalities (Cui et al., 2023). This analysis offers valuable insights into the unique vulnerabilities of multimodal fusion networks used in tasks such as image captioning and visual question answering. While the work presents an in-depth investigation of attack effects on selected multimodal models, its generalizability is somewhat constrained by the specificity of the attack types and architectures considered.

Ensemble-based training, wherein adversarial examples are generated across multiple models and incorporated into the training pipeline, has also shown promise (Tramer et al., 2018). This technique increases the diversity of adversarial training data, potentially improving generalization. Nevertheless, the added computational burden poses scalability challenges for deployment in time-sensitive or resource-constrained settings.

Biologically inspired defenses present a novel and less conventional line of research (Garcia-Porras et al., 2023). These approaches draw from principles observed in natural systems, such as robustness through redundancy and hierarchical processing. While conceptually intriguing, their effectiveness varies across datasets and attack types, and further empirical validation is required to assess their practicality in operational environments.

Tensor decomposition-based defenses, such as the Tensorshield framework (Entezari & Papalexakis, 2022), aim to separate clean image structures from adversarial noise using multi-dimensional signal representations. These techniques have demonstrated potential in preserving classification accuracy while removing perturbations, although they may be sensitive to the statistical properties of the input domain.

A defense strategy proposed by Li and Cao introduces a *sparse denoising mechanism* that utilizes both image label information and pixel-level guidance to selectively remove adversarial perturbations while preserving critical features necessary for classification (Li & Cao, 2022). Experimental results indicate that this targeted denoising approach can enhance the robustness of image classifiers across multiple types of adversarial attacks.

Several studies have examined the limitations of *gradient obfuscation* as a defense strategy (Athalye et al., 2018). While some models appear robust due to masked or distorted gradients, adaptive attacks can often circumvent such defenses, exposing the need for truly gradient-aware robustness rather than superficial obfuscation.

Chen et al. carried out a broad evaluation of adversarial vulnerabilities in image classification models, taking into consideration a range of attack techniques, including both gradient-based and optimization-driven methods (Chen et al., 2022). The authors compare the impact of these attacks across different datasets and model architectures, reinforcing the urgent need for effective defenses. The work also provides a comparative assessment of defense strategies, such as adversarial training, defensive distillation, and input preprocessing, and highlights their respective advantages and limitations in practical settings.

Recent advances in adversarial machine learning have introduced sophisticated techniques for both crafting and defending against adversarial examples. A significant contribution to this evolving field has been made by Waghela, Sen, Rakshit, and their collaborators (Waghela et al., 2024a–g; Waghela et al., 2025; Sen, 2024; Sen & Dasgupta, 2023; Sen & Waghela, 2025; Sen et al., 2023; Koley et al., 2024). Their work explores context-aware perturbation methods that incorporate linguistic saliency, semantic similarity, and attention-based mechanisms using transformer-based embeddings (e.g., BERT) to generate more effective and semantically coherent adversarial inputs. On the defense front, they propose ensemble and meta-learning strategies that enhance robustness by combining dynamic ensembling with perturbation-aware training.

Input Preprocessing and Architectural Enhancements: Several defenses operate at the input level, transforming data before it reaches the classifier. *Feature squeezing*, for instance, reduces the complexity of input data through bit-depth reduction or spatial smoothing, making it more difficult for adversarial perturbations to survive preprocessing (Xu et al., 2018).

However, these transformations can sometimes degrade legitimate inputs or prove ineffective against carefully designed attacks.

GAN-based defenses involve training generative models to reconstruct clean versions of adversarial examples (Liu et al., 2020). By leveraging the generative capacity of adversarial networks, these methods attempt to restore the original data distribution. While promising, they often suffer from instability during training and require fine-tuning to generalize across datasets.

Neural fingerprinting introduces a novel approach where distributional signatures are learned to distinguish between clean and adversarial inputs (Dathathri et al., 2018). This method relies on capturing subtle statistical shifts in feature distributions. Although potentially effective, its robustness may be limited by the variability and complexity of real-world data.

Randomized smoothing provides a certifiable form of robustness by adding Gaussian noise to inputs and averaging model predictions over multiple noisy samples (Cohen et al., 2019). This technique offers probabilistic guarantees under certain assumptions but may be computationally expensive, especially for high-resolution images.

Another line of work explores *density-based representations* for differentiating between natural and adversarial inputs by analyzing pixel intensity distributions (Huang et al., 2021). These methods attempt to exploit inherent differences in the data structure introduced by adversarial perturbations. Though effective in some cases, they can be dataset-dependent and sensitive to noise.

Sequential attention mechanisms have also been employed to enhance model robustness by encouraging models to focus on relevant regions of an image over time (Zoran et al., 2020). This temporal processing approach has been shown to improve both accuracy and resilience under attack, offering a promising direction for integrating attention-based robustness into CNN architectures.

Finally, comprehensive surveys and meta-analyses, such as those by Ren et al., have systematically categorized adversarial threats and countermeasures, highlighting persistent challenges such as transferability, adaptiveness of attacks, and the lack of universal defenses (Ren et al., 2020).

Summary of Research Landscape: Despite notable progress, no single defense mechanism has emerged as universally effective across all attack vectors and datasets. The integration of autoencoder-based preprocessing with adversarial training, as explored in this chapter, builds upon these foundational insights. By combining complementary defense strategies, one operating at the data level and the other at the model training level, this approach aims to offer a practical and effective solution for improving image classification robustness under adversarial conditions.

Data and Methodology

This chapter presents a comprehensive methodology that integrates adversarial attack generation, classification model design, and a defense framework based on a convolutional autoencoder. The process follows a modular sequence: dataset preparation, model development, adversarial perturbation generation, defense implementation, and evaluation of robustness. The complete pipeline for implementing and evaluating the adversarial defense strategy is outlined in Figure 9-1. The figure illustrates the sequential steps, including data preprocessing, model design, attack generation, model training, and performance evaluation. In the following, each component of the methodology is discussed in detail.

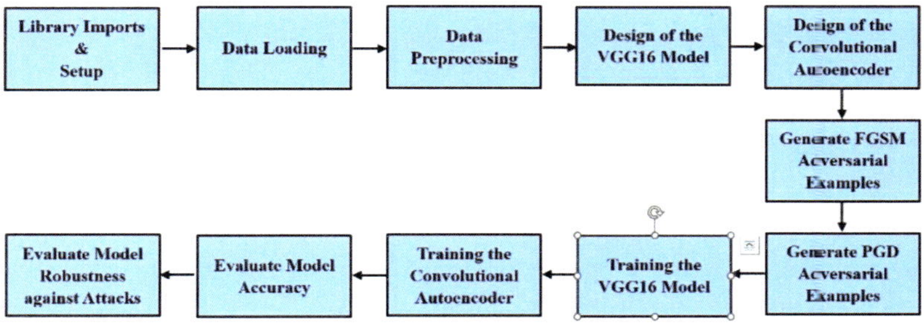

Figure. 9-1. The workflow of the proposed adversarial defense framework. The process begins with data preparation and model design, followed by the generation of adversarial examples using FGSM and PGD. The VGG16 classifier and the convolutional encoder are trained independently, and the system is finally evaluated based on classification accuracy and robustness against adversarial perturbation.

Computational Environment and Software Framework: The experimental framework is implemented using *Python 3.10* with *PyTorch* as the primary deep learning library. PyTorch is chosen for its flexibility in model design and dynamic computation graph support, making it suitable for research-focused experimentation. Auxiliary libraries include *NumPy* for numerical operations, *Matplotlib* and *Seaborn* for visualization, and *Torchvision* for standardized dataset handling and transformation pipelines.

The experiments are conducted on a system equipped with a GPU (NVIDIA RTX 3060), which significantly accelerates the training and adversarial generation processes. GPU support is particularly essential for training convolutional autoencoders and for executing iterative attacks such as PGD.

Dataset Description and Loading: Two standard benchmark datasets are employed in this study: *MNIST* (Lecun et al., 1998) and *Fashion-MNIST* (Xiao et al., 2017).

- *MNIST*: This dataset consists of 70000 grayscale images of handwritten digits (0-9), split into 60000 training and 10000 test samples. Each image is 28*28 pixels in size.
- *Fashion-MNIST*: A drop-in replacement for MNIST, this dataset contains grayscale images of 10 fashion categories (e.g., T-shirts, shoes, bags). It has the same structure as MNIST, offering a more complex classification challenge due to higher intra-class similarity.

To prepare the datasets for input into the *VGG16 architecture* (Simonyan & Zisserman, 2015), all images are resized from 28*28 to 32*32 pixels. This resizing is crucial because the original VGG16 network, designed for ImageNet-scale data, expects larger spatial dimensions. Further, all pixel values are normalized to the [0, 1] range using min-max scaling and then converted into PyTorch tensors.

Data augmentation techniques such as *random rotations* and *horizontal flips* are deliberately avoided to maintain consistency in the attack surface and to isolate the impact of adversarial perturbations without introducing natural variability.

Data Partitioning and Batch Processing: Each dataset is divided into a training set and a validation set. Specifically, 50,000 images are used for training and 10,000 for validation. Efficient data loading is ensured through PyTorch's *DataLoader* utility, with a batch size of 64, enabling parallel data processing.

Architecture and Design of the VGG16 Classifier: The image classification model is based on a modified VGG16 architecture, which is known for its simplicity and strong performance on image-based tasks. The VGG16 model consists of a sequence of VGGBlocks, each comprising two convolutional layers followed by batch normalization and max pooling.

The key architectural features include the following:

- 3*3 *Convolution Kernels*: These allow fine-grained feature extraction while keeping parameter count manageable.
- *Batch Normalization*: It stabilizes gradients and accelerates convergence by normalizing intermediate outputs.
- *Max Pooling (2*2)*: It reduces spatial resolution and controls overfitting by downsampling feature maps.
- *Dropout*: It is applied in the *fully connected layers* to prevent co-adaptation of neurons and enhance generalization.
- *ReLU Activations*: Introduce non-linearity, enabling the model to learn complex decision boundaries.

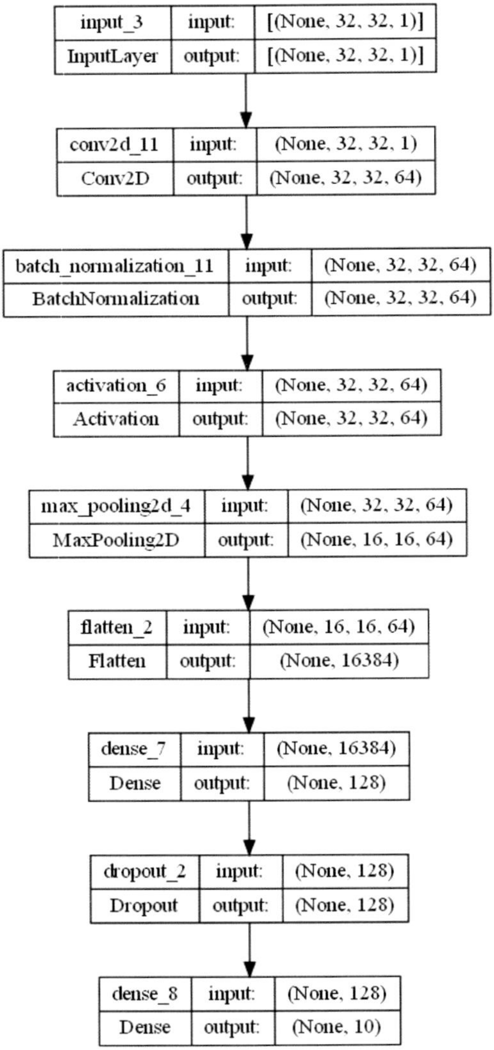

Figure. 9-2. The architecture of the VGG16-based classification model. The diagram illustrates one representative Conv2D layer, batch normalization, activation, and max pooling.

The model has two dense layers at the end, and a final softmax output layer maps the feature representations to class probabilities. Figure 9-2 presents a simplified view of the VGG16-based classifier. Highlighting one representative convolutional block, followed by the core dense layer responsible for final classification.

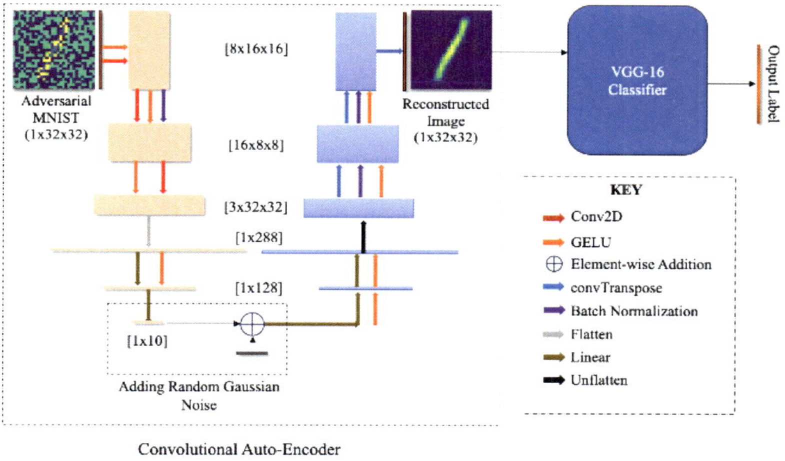

Figure. 9-3. The architecture of the convolutional autoencoder used for reconstructing adversarial images. The encoder compresses the perturbed input into a latent representation through a series of convolutional layers, GELU activations, and batch normalization. A Gaussian noise is added in the latent space to enhance generalization. The decoder reconstructs the input using transposed convolutions and normalization, producing a denoised image. The denoised image is then fed into the VGG16 classifier for final prediction.

Design of the Convolutional Autoencoder: To enhance robustness, a *convolutional autoencoder* is integrated into the pipeline as a preprocessing defense mechanism. The architecture of the autoencoder is exhibited in Figure 9-3. The autoencoder consists of the following:

- *Encoder*: Three convolutional layers reduce the spatial dimensions while increasing the depth of feature maps. The GELU (Gaussian Error Linear Unit) activation function is used in place of ReLU for smoother gradient flow (Hendrycks & Gimpel, 2023). *Gaussian noise* is added to the latent representation to improve generalization and robustness.
- *Latent Bottleneck*: A compressed, dense representation of the input, which captures the essential structure of the image while excluding high-frequency adversarial noise.

- *Decoder*: Fully connected layers and transposed convolutional layers sequentially reconstruct the input image. *Batch normalization* and *GELU* are used post-layer, and a *sigmoid activation* caps the pixel values in the [0, 1] range to match original data characteristics.

The autoencoder is trained using *Mean Squared Error* (MSE) loss to minimize reconstruction error between clean and adversarial images, thereby learning to suppress adversarial noise.

Adversarial Attack Generation: To evaluate the robustness of the classification model and the effectiveness of the defense mechanism, two adversarial attack methods are implemented:

- *Fast Gradient Sign Method (FGSM)*: This technique perturbs the input image in the direction of the gradient of the loss with respect to the input. The perturbation is scaled by a small factor (*epsilon*), resulting in subtle but strategically crafted changes that significantly affect model predictions.
- *Projected Gradient Descent (PGD)*: An iterative enhancement of FGSM, PGD introduces multiple small perturbations (*step size* α) at each iteration. After each step, the perturbed image is projected back into the ε-ball centered at the original input to ensure bounded distortion. This method is known for producing stronger and more transferable adversarial examples.

Both attacks are implemented in white-box settings, assuming full access to the model's architecture and gradients.

Model Training Procedure: The VGG16 classifier is trained on clean images from the MNIST and Fashion-MNIST datasets. The model is optimized using the *Adam* optimizer (Kingma & Ba, 2015) with a learning rate of 0.001 and a batch size of 64. Training proceeds for 50 epochs with an *early stopping* criterion (Prechelt, 2002) employed to halt training when the validation loss ceases to improve. Hence, it prevents overfitting and promotes generalization.

The convolutional autoencoder is trained using adversarial examples generated by both FGSM and PGD. The objective is to reconstruct the original clean images from their adversarially perturbed versions. The training process minimizes the *Mean Squared Error* (MSE) over 100 epochs between the original and reconstructed images. This enables the autoencoder to act as a filter that removes adversarial noise.

To promote robustness, a mix of FGSM and PGD adversarial examples is used in each training epoch, exposing the autoencoder to a diverse set of perturbation patterns.

Evaluation Metrics and Defense Robustness Assessment: Two key performance metrics are used to evaluate the models:

- *Classification Accuracy*: Defined as the ratio of correctly predicted instances to the total number of inputs, accuracy is computed separately for clean images, adversarial examples (without defense), and reconstructed images (after autoencoder). This provides a baseline measure of model vulnerability under attack.
- *Defense Effectiveness*: The efficacy of the autoencoder-based defense is measured by comparing the classification accuracy before and after the application of the autoencoder on adversarial samples. A significant recovery in accuracy post-reconstruction indicates a successful defense mechanism.

Results Visualization and Analysis: The experimental results are analyzed by comparing classification accuracy on clean and adversarial datasets, both with and without the defense mechanism in place. Accuracy trends are plotted against varying perturbation strengths (ε-values), illustrating the resilience of the model under different levels of adversarial attacks. These visualizations highlight the improved robustness achieved by integrating the convolutional autoencoder into the classification pipeline.

Experimental Results

To evaluate the effectiveness of the proposed adversarial defense framework, a comprehensive set of experiments was carried out on the MNIST and Fashion-MNIST datasets using a high-performance computing environment. All experiments were conducted on the Kaggle platform, utilizing an NVIDIA Tesla P100 GPU. This GPU is equipped with 3584 CUDA cores, 16 GB of HBM2 memory, and offers a memory bandwidth of 732 GB/s. The hardware is further supported by Intel Xeon CPUs with 4 to 8 cores. This infrastructure ensured efficient training and evaluation of deep models, particularly under resource-intensive adversarial conditions.

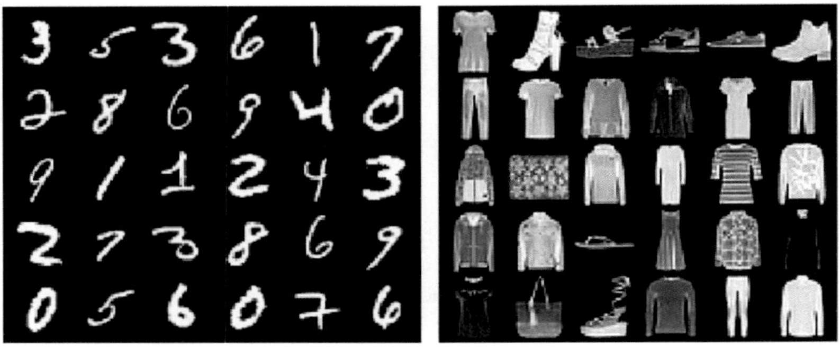

Figure. 9-4. Representative sample images randomly selected from (a) the MNIST dataset (left) and (b) the Fashion-MNIST dataset (right).

The datasets used, MNIST and Fashion-MNIST, are widely recognized benchmarks in image classification research. The MNIST dataset comprises grayscale images of handwritten digits (0–9), while Fashion-MNIST contains grayscale images of fashion articles such as shirts, trousers, and shoes. Each dataset consists of 60,000 training images and 10,000 test images, all sized 28*28 pixels. These were resized to 32*32 pixels to match the input requirements of the VGG16 model. Figure 9-4 shows sample images randomly selected from both datasets, providing visual context for the classification tasks.

Baseline Performance under Adversarial Conditions: The first phase of experimentation involved evaluating the baseline VGG16 model without any defensive measures in place. Adversarial samples were generated using two widely studied attack methods: the Fast Gradient Sign Method (FGSM) and Projected Gradient Descent (PGD). Both attacks were implemented with varying noise intensities, denoted by ε (epsilon), to examine the model's robustness across a spectrum of adversarial perturbations.

Table 9-1. Classification Accuracy of the VGG16 Model under FGSM Attack at Varying Noise Levels on MNIST and Fashion-MNIST Test Sets

Noise Level (ε)	Accuracy on MNIST	Accuracy on MNIST Fashion
0.00	0.9909	0.9077
0.10	0.9077	0.4746
0.20	0.8248	0.3767
0.30	0.7278	0.2951
0.40	0.5753	0.2435
0.50	0.4139	0.1887
0.60	0.2621	0.1405
0.70	0.1611	0.0960
0.80	0.0994	0.0696
0.90	0.0714	0.0499
1.00	0.0528	0.0444

Table 9-1 presents the classification accuracies of the VGG16 model under FGSM attacks for different ε values on both datasets. The results clearly indicate a steep decline in classification accuracy with increasing perturbation strength. On the MNIST dataset, the accuracy drops from 99.09% at ε = 0.00 to just 5.28% at ε = 1.00. A similar, albeit more dramatic, degradation is observed on the Fashion-MNIST dataset, where the accuracy falls from 90.77% to only 4.44%. The graphical representation in Figure 9-5 illustrates these trends, highlighting the high sensitivity of the model to adversarial noise.

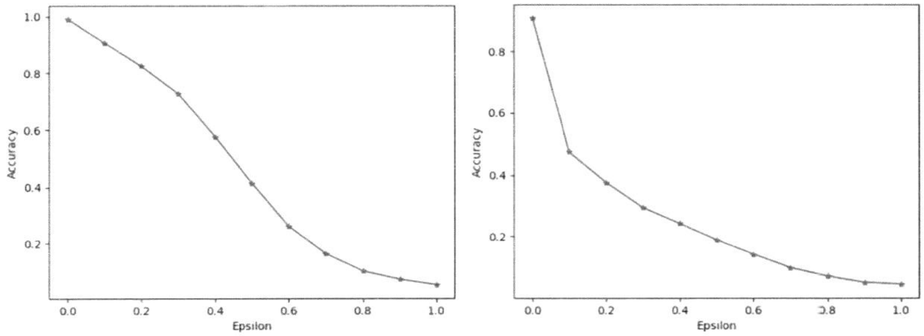

Figure. 9-5. Test accuracy of the VGG16 model under FGSM attack across different perturbation levels on **(a)** MNIST dataset (left) and **(b)** Fashion-MNIST dataset (right).

Table 9-2. Classification Accuracy of the VGG16 Model under PGD Attacks at Varying Noise Levels on MNIST and Fashion-MNIST Test Sets

Noise Level (ε)	Accuracy on MNIST	Accuracy on MNIST Fashion
0.00	0.9927	0.9603
0.05	0.6135	0.3153
0.10	0.1725	0.2947
0.15	0.0420	0.2946
0.20	0.0181	0.2943
0.25	0.0135	0.2949
0.30	0.0122	0.2956
0.35	0.0121	0.2956
0.40	0.0126	0.2948

The PGD attack, known for its iterative nature and stronger impact, was then employed to test the model's resilience further. The classification accuracies obtained under PGD attacks are tabulated in Table 9-2, with visual summaries provided in Figure 9-6. The results reveal that PGD is significantly more destructive than FGSM. On MNIST, the accuracy drops to under 2% for $\varepsilon \geq 0.20$, indicating a near-complete failure of the classifier to cope with the attack. On Fashion-MNIST, the accuracy consistently hovers around 29.4% beyond $\varepsilon = 0.10$, showing that PGD can induce substantial misclassification while retaining some minimal residual performance.

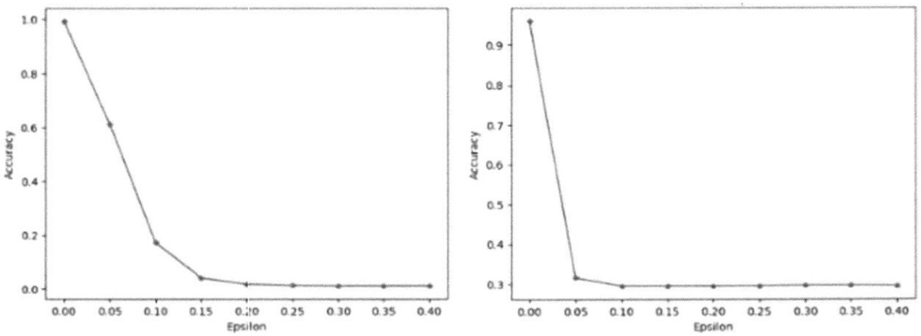

Figure. 9-6. Test accuracy of the VGG16 model under PGD attack across different perturbation levels on **(a)** MNIST dataset (left) and **(b)** Fashion-MNIST dataset (right).

Evaluation of the Defense Performance with Convolutional Autoencoder: To counteract these attacks, a convolutional autoencoder was employed as a preprocessing defense module. The autoencoder was trained to learn mappings from adversarially perturbed images back to their clean counterparts. Its performance was assessed based on the quality of reconstructions, training convergence, and, most importantly, the classification accuracy of the downstream VGG16 model after passing inputs through the autoencoder.

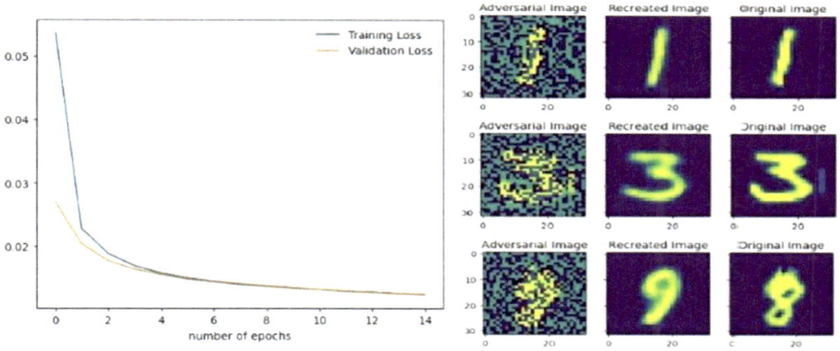

Figure. 9-7. (a) Training and validation loss curves of the autoencoder trained on FGSM-generated adversarial samples from the MNIST dataset (left). **(b)** Some adversarial images created using FGSM and their corresponding reconstructions by the autoencoder (right).

The training and validation loss curves for the autoencoder, when trained on FGSM adversarial samples, are shown in Figures 9-7(a) and 9-8(a) for MNIST and Fashion-MNIST, respectively. These plots demonstrate stable convergence, indicating that the autoencoder effectively learned to denoise adversarial samples. Figures 9-7(b) and 9-8(b) display the visual outcomes of this process, showcasing side-by-side comparisons of original, adversarial, and reconstructed images. The reconstructions are perceptually close to the clean images, suggesting successful mitigation of adversarial perturbations.

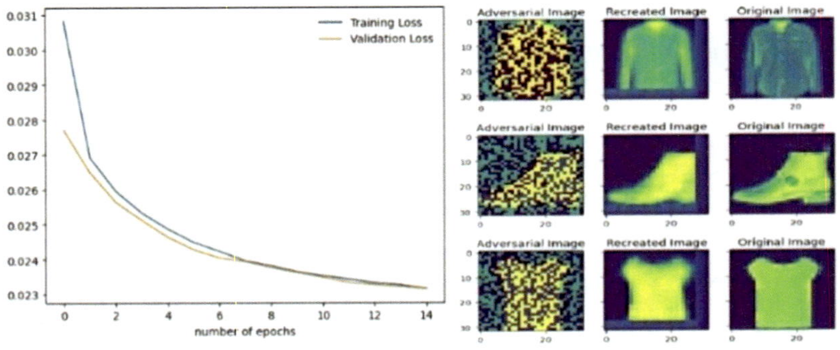

Figure. 9-8. (a) Training and validation loss curves of the autoencoder trained on FGSM-generated adversarial samples from the Fashion-MNIST dataset (left). **(b)** Some adversarial images created using FGSM and their corresponding reconstructions by the autoencoder (right).

The classification results after applying the autoencoder defense to FGSM-attacked data are presented in Table 9-3. The improvements in accuracy are substantial. For instance, at $\varepsilon = 0.80$, the MNIST accuracy improves from 9.94% (without defense) to 87.92% (with defense). Similarly, on the Fashion-MNIST dataset, the accuracy rises from 6.96% to 69.88%. These improvements confirm that the autoencoder can significantly restore the model's predictive capability even under severe adversarial distortion. Notably, the defense introduces only a negligible inference-time overhead, with processing times consistently in the range of 0.0003 seconds per image, making it suitable for real-time applications.

Table 9-3. Test Accuracy of the VGG16 Model on the MNIST and Fashion-MNIST under FGSM with Autoencoder-Based Defense

Noise Level (ε)	Test Acc on MNIST	Time for defending an attack (s)	Test Acc on MNIST Fashion	Time for defending an attack (s)
0.00	0.9569	0.003	0.7479	0.003
0.10	0.9372	0.0003	0.7063	0.0003
0.20	0.9309	0.0003	0.6582	0.0003
0.30	0.9198	0.0003	0.6652	0.0003
0.40	0.8945	0.0003	0.6652	0.0003
0.50	0.8695	0.0003	0.6558	0.0003
0.60	0.8609	0.0003	0.6703	0.0003
0.70	0.8629	0.0003	0.6866	0.0003
0.80	0.8792	0.0003	0.6988	0.0003
0.90	0.7527	0.0003	0.7175	0.0003
1.00	0.3571	0.0003	0.4605	0.0003

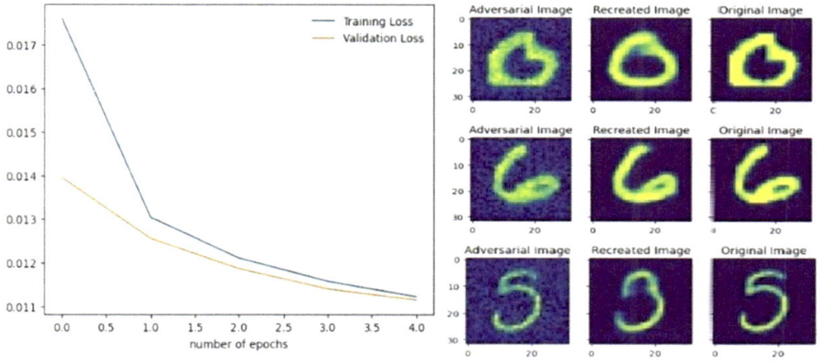

Figure. 9-9. (a) Training and validation loss curves of the autoencoder trained on PGD-generated adversarial samples from the MNIST dataset (left). **(b)** Some adversarial images created using PGD and their corresponding reconstructions by the autoencoder (right).

The same methodology was extended to address PGD attacks. The training and validation losses during the learning process are illustrated in Figures 9-9a and 9- 10a, while the sample reconstructions for MNIST and Fashion-MNIST are shown in Figures 9b and 10b, respectively. As with FGSM, the visual outputs demonstrate that the autoencoder successfully removes perturbations and preserves image semantics.

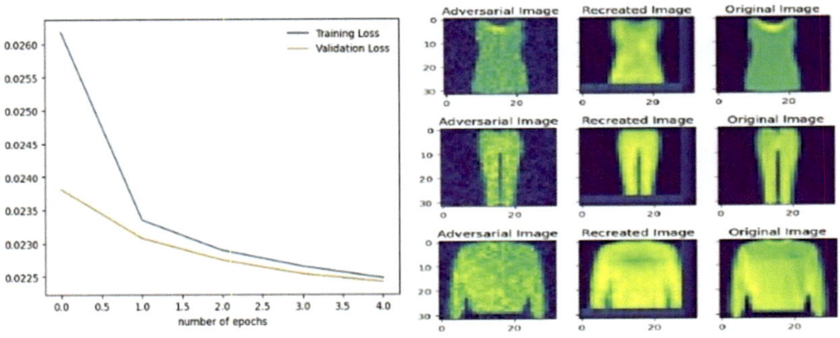

Figure. 9-10. (a) Training and validation loss curves of the autoencoder trained on PGD-generated adversarial samples from the Fashion-MNIST dataset (left). **(b)** Some adversarial images created using PGD and their corresponding reconstructions by the autoencoder (right).

Table 9-4. Test Accuracy of the VGG16 Model on MNIST and Fashion-MNIST under PGD Attack with Autoencoder-Based Defense

Noise Level (ε)	Test Acc on MNIST	Time for defending an attack (s)	Test Acc on MNIST Fashion	Time for defending an attack (s)
0.00	0.9203	0.0012	0.7049	0.0012
0.05	0.9342	0.0012	0.7112	0.0012
0.10	0.9318	0.0012	0.7023	0.0012
0.15	0.9298	0.0012	0.7011	0.0012
0.20	0.9123	0.0012	0.7022	0.0012
0.25	0.9108	0.0012	0.7031	0.0012
0.30	0.9028	0.0012	0.7002	0.0012
0.35	0.9021	0.0012	0.7010	0.0012
0.40	0.9023	0.0012	0.7024	0.0012

The corresponding classification accuracies post-defense for PGD attacks are shown in Table 9-4. Once again, the results underscore the effectiveness of the defense mechanism. On the MNIST dataset, the classification accuracy is elevated to over 90% across various ε values, even reaching 93.42% at ε = 0.05. For the Fashion-MNIST dataset, the defended accuracy remains consistently above 70%, indicating that the autoencoder generalizes well across different types of inputs and adversarial patterns. The time required to process each input remains around 0.0012 seconds, confirming the low computational cost of the defense scheme.

Comparative Insights and Observations: A comparative analysis of Tables 9-1 through 9-4 reveals several key insights:

- *FGSM vs. PGD*: PGD, due to its iterative updates, exerts a more aggressive impact on classification performance than FGSM. However, the proposed autoencoder defense remains effective across both attack types, demonstrating generalizability.
- *Dataset Sensitivity*: The Fashion-MNIST dataset appears more vulnerable to adversarial attacks than MNIST, particularly under FGSM. This could be attributed to the higher intra-class variability and more complex textures in fashion items compared to digits.
- *Defense Robustness*: The convolutional autoencoder can maintain high accuracy across varying perturbation strengths, which is particularly valuable in real-world deployments where the nature and intensity of attacks may vary unpredictably.
- *Efficiency*: With sub-millisecond processing latency, the defense mechanism is not only effective but also computationally efficient, a critical requirement for applications in embedded systems, autonomous vehicles, and real-time surveillance.

The experimental evaluation demonstrates that the proposed convolutional autoencoder significantly enhances the robustness of deep image classifiers against adversarial perturbations, without introducing substantial computational overhead. Through extensive empirical analysis, it has been shown that the model can restore classification accuracy to a high degree under both FGSM and PGD attacks on two distinct benchmark datasets. The results affirm the viability of the proposed defense strategy and suggest promising avenues for future research involving adaptive autoencoders, multimodal adversarial training, and hybrid defense frameworks combining reconstruction and detection.

Conclusion

This study investigated the application of a convolutional autoencoder-based preprocessing strategy as a defense mechanism against adversarial perturbations generated by *Fast Gradient Sign Method* (FGSM) and *Projected Gradient Descent* (PGD) attacks. Experimental evaluation was conducted using the MNIST and Fashion-MNIST datasets in conjunction with a VGG16 classifier. The results underscore the efficacy of the proposed approach in significantly enhancing model resilience, as the autoencoder successfully reconstructed adversarially corrupted inputs and mitigated the effects of both first-order (FGSM) and iterative (PGD) adversarial attacks. The preprocessing step introduced by the autoencoder effectively restored much of the classification accuracy lost due to adversarial manipulations, affirming its potential as a lightweight and effective defense mechanism within the adversarial machine learning landscape.

The defense was found to be particularly effective against FGSM attacks by correcting input-level distortions in near real-time and significantly reducing adversarial impact on prediction performance. Against more advanced attacks like PGD, which involve iterative optimization for crafting perturbations, the autoencoder demonstrated robust performance by filtering out imperceptible noise patterns while preserving critical image features required for accurate classification. These results validate the use of autoencoders not only as anomaly detectors but also as input transformation agents that can sanitize adversarial inputs before classification.

Despite these promising outcomes, several challenges and limitations were identified. The incorporation of the autoencoder into the classification pipeline introduces non-trivial computational overhead. The training process, especially when extended to account for a variety of attack types, demands significant time and computational resources. Furthermore, the defense performance was evaluated on relatively simple datasets. Its generalizability to more complex, high-resolution datasets remains uncertain and necessitates further study.

To build upon this work and advance the field of adversarial robustness, several promising directions for future research are identified:

1. *Generalization to Diverse and Complex Datasets*: Evaluating the defense strategy on more diverse and challenging datasets, such as CIFAR-10, SVHN, CelebA, and ImageNet, is essential to understand its scalability and effectiveness in real-world scenarios. High-dimensional and color image datasets may introduce new vulnerabilities and computational constraints that require adaptation of the current architecture.
2. *Extension to Stronger and Adaptive Attacks*: The current evaluation is limited to FGSM and PGD attacks. Future studies should consider more powerful attack strategies such as the Carlini & Wagner (CW) attack, DeepFool, AutoAttack, and other adaptive or white-box attacks that dynamically respond to specific defense mechanisms.

Analyzing failure cases against such advanced attacks can offer critical insights for designing more robust countermeasures.

3. *Hybrid and Ensemble Defense Architectures*: Future work can explore the integration of autoencoders with other defense techniques, such as adversarial training, feature squeezing, defensive distillation, randomized smoothing, and certified defenses, to develop ensemble models that provide layered security. Such hybrid strategies may offer complementary strengths and address the limitations of any single defense approach.
4. *Theoretical Analysis of Robustness Guarantees*: A formal, mathematical analysis of the defense strategy's robustness bounds is crucial. Leveraging theoretical tools such as Lipschitz continuity, manifold learning, and robustness certificates can help assess the provable effectiveness of the autoencoder under varying threat models and perturbation budgets.
5. *Optimization of Computational Efficiency*: Reducing the computational complexity of the autoencoder remains a critical area for further research. Investigating techniques such as model pruning, quantization, knowledge distillation, and lightweight encoder-decoder networks could allow for faster inference and more efficient deployment on edge devices and embedded systems.
6. *Domain Adaptation and Transfer Learning*: In practical applications, defense models often need to operate across varying data distributions. Research into transfer learning-based autoencoders or domain adaptation techniques could improve robustness in cross-domain scenarios and enable better performance with minimal retraining.
7. *Real-Time and Resource-Constrained Deployment*: Deploying adversarial defenses in latency-sensitive environments such as autonomous driving, robotics, and medical imaging requires real-time performance. Evaluating the practicality of the autoencoder defense under such operational constraints will offer valuable feedback on its deployability and necessary architectural optimizations.
8. *Multimodal Defense Extensions*: With the growing prevalence of multimodal learning systems involving image, text, and speech inputs, future studies can investigate the extension of autoencoder-based defenses to multimodal or cross-modal adversarial examples. Defending against joint perturbations in image-text or image-audio data will be vital for robust real-world AI systems.

9. *Explainability and Interpretability of Defense Behavior*: Understanding how the autoencoder modifies adversarial inputs and why certain perturbations are neutralized more effectively than others remain a key open problem. Leveraging *explainable AI* (XAI) techniques can help visualize latent representations and identify vulnerable regions in the input space.
10. *Continuous Adaptation to Evolving Threats*: As adversarial techniques evolve, static defense mechanisms may become obsolete. Future research should investigate adaptive defenses that evolve in response to adversarial trends, possibly using meta-learning or reinforcement learning frameworks to adjust the defense strategy in real time.
11. *Robustness Against Black-Box and Transfer Attacks*: Evaluating the effectiveness of the proposed defense against black-box attacks, where the attacker has no access to model internals, as well as transfer attacks, where adversarial examples are generated from surrogate models, will shed light on the applicability of the defense mechanisms in security-critical applications.
12. *Benchmarking Frameworks and Open-Source Toolkits*: To foster reproducibility and standardization in adversarial robustness research, the development of comprehensive benchmarking frameworks and open-source libraries for evaluating autoencoder-based defenses across attack scenarios is essential. Establishing standardized protocols for defense evaluation will enable more rigorous comparison across methods.

In conclusion, while the convolutional autoencoder demonstrates strong potential as a pre-processing defense mechanism against adversarial image perturbations, its full capabilities and limitations remain an open and fertile area of research. Bridging the gap between experimental promise and real-world applicability will require coordinated efforts across algorithmic development, theoretical analysis, system optimization, and robust evaluation methodologies. Through such multi-faceted research endeavors, the vision of deploying resilient AI systems capable of operating safely in adversarial environments can be progressively realized.

References

Athalye, A., Carlini, N., and Wagner, D. 2018. "Obfuscated Gradients Give a False Sense of Security: Circumventing Defenses to Adversarial Examples." arXiv Preprint arXiv: 1802.0040.

Bortsova, G., Gonzalez-Gonzalo, C., Wetstein, S. C., Dubost, F., Katramadas, I., Hogeweg, L., Liefers, B., van Ginneken, B., Pluim, J. P. W., Veta, M., Sanchez, C. I., de Bruijne, M. 2021. "Adversarial Attack Vulnerability of Medical Image Analysis Systems: Unexplored Factors." *Medical Image Analysis*, 73(102141).

Buckman, J., Roy, A., Raffel, C., and Goodfellow, I. 2018. "Thermometer Encoding: One Hot Way to Resist Adversarial Examples." *In Proceedings of the International Conference on Learning Representations (ICLR 2018)*.

Carlini, N. and Wagner, D. 2017a. "Adversarial Examples are not Easily Detected: Bypassing Ten Detection Method." In *Proceedings of the 10th ACM Workshop on Artificial Intelligence and Security (AISec 2017)*, 3-14.

Carlini, N. and Wagner, D. 2017b. "Towards Evaluating the Robustness of Neural Networks," In *Proceedings of the 2017 IEEE Symposium on Security and Privacy (S&P)*, pp. 39-57.

Carmon, Y., Raghunathan, A., Schmidt, L., Liang, P., and Duchi, J. C. 2019. "Unlabeled Data Improves Adversarial Robustness." In *Proceedings of the 33rd International Conference on Neural Information Processing Systems (NeurIPS 2019)*, 11192-11203.

Chen, Y., Zhang, M., Li, J., and Kuang, X. 2022. "Adversarial Attacks and Defenses in Image Classification: A Practical Perspective." In *Proceedings of the 7th International Conference on Image, Vision and Computing (ICIVC'22)*, 424-430.

Cohen, J., Rosenfeld, E., and Kolter, Z. 2019. "Certified Adversarial Robustness via Randomized Smoothing." In *Proceedings of the 36th International Conference on Machine Learning (ICML 2019), PMLR* 97: 1310-1320.

Cui, X., Aparcedo, A., Jang, Y. K., and Lim, S-N. 2023. "On the Robustness of Large Multimodal Models against Image Adversarial Attacks." arXiv Preprint arXiv:2312.03777.

Das, N., Shanbhogue, M., Chen, S-T., Hohman, F., Chen, L., Kounavis, M. E., Chau, D. H. 2017. "Keeping the Bad Guys Out: Protecting and Vaccinating Deep Learning with JPEG Compression." arXiv Preprint arXiv:1705.02900.

Dathathri, S., Zheng, S., Yin, T., Murray, R. M., and Yue, Y. 2018. "Detecting Adversarial Examples via Neural Fingerprinting." arXiv Preprint arXiv:1803.03870.

Entezari, N. and Papalexakis, E. E. 2022. "Tensorshield: Tensor-based Defense against Adversarial Attacks on Images." In *Proceedings of the 2022 IEEE Military Communications Conference (MILCOM 2022)*, 999-1004.

Feinman, R., Curtin, R. R., Shintre, S., Gardner, A. B. 2017. "Detecting Adversarial Samples from Artifacts." arXiv Preprint arXiv:1703.00410.

Garcia-Porras, O., Salazar-Colores, S., Moya-Sanchez, E. U., and A. Sanchez-Perez, A. 2023. "Adversarial Attack versus a Bio-inspired Defensive Method for Image Classification." In Mata-Rivera M. F. et al. (eds.) *Telematics and Computing, Communications in Computer and Information Science*, 1906: 533-547, Springer, Cham.

Gong, Z. and Wang, W. 2023. "Adversarial and Clean Data are Not Twins." In *Proceedings of the 6th International Workshop on Exploiting Artificial Intelligence Techniques for Data Management (aiDM 2023)*, 1-5.

Goodfellow, I. J., Shlens, J., and Szegedy, C. 2015. "Explaining and Harnessing Adversarial Examples." In *International Conference on Learning Representations (ICLR'15)*, Poster Track.

Gowal, S., Qin, C., Uesato, J., Mann, T., and Kohli, P. 2021a. ''Uncovering the Limits of Adversarial Training against Norm-Bounded Adversarial Examples." arXiv Preprint arXiv:20210.03593.

Gowal, S., Rebuffi, S-A., Wiles, O., Stimberg, F., Calian, D. A., and Mann, T. 2021b. "Improving Robustness Using Generated Data." In *Proceedings of the 33rd International Conference on Neural Information Processing Systems (NeurIPS 2021)*

Grosse, K., Papernot, N., Manoharan, P., Backes, M., and McDaniel, P. 2016. "Adversarial Perturbations against Deep Neural Networks for Malware Classification." arXiv Preprint. arXiv: 1606.04435.

Guo, C., Rana, M., Cisse, M., van der Maaten, L. 2018. "Countering Adversarial Images Using Input Transformations." arXiv Preprint arXiv:1711.00117.

Hendrycks, D. and K. Gimpel, K. 2023. "Gaussian Linear Units (GELUs)." arXiv Preprint arXiv:1606.08415v5.

Huang, Y.-T., Liao, W.-H., and C.-W. Huang, C.-W. 2021. "Defense Mechanism against Adversarial Attacks Using Density-based Representation of Images." In *Proceedings of the 25th International Conference on Pattern Recognition (ICPR)*, 3499-3504.

Kingma, D. P. and Ba, J. 2015. "Adam: A Method for Stochastic Optimization." In *Proceedings of the International Conference on Learning Representations (ICLR 2015).*

Koley, A., Satpati, P., Choudhary, I., and Sen, J. 2024. "An Investigation on the Efficiency of Some Text Attack Algorithms." In *Proceedings of the IEEE North Karnataka Subsection Flagship International Conference (NKCon 2024)*, 1–8.

Lee, K., Lee, K., Lee, H., and Shin, J. 2018. "A Simple Unified Framework for Detecting Out-of-Distribution Samples and Adversarial Attacks." In *Proceedings of the 32nd International Conference on Neural Information Processing Systems (NIPS 2018)*, 7167-7177.

Lecun, Y., Bottou, L., Bengio, Y., and Haffner, P. 1998. "Gradient-based Learning Applied to Document Recognition." In *Proceedings of the IEEE*, 86(11): 2278-2324.

Lecuyer, M., Atlidakis, V., Geambasu, R., Hsu, D., and Jana, S. 2019. "Certified Robustness to Adversarial Examples with Differential Privacy." In *Proceedings of 2019 IEEE Symposium on Security and Privacy (IEEE S&P, 2019)*, 656-672.

Li, C., Fan, C., Zhang, J., Li, C., and Teng, Y. 2022. "A Block Gray Adversarial Attack Method for Image Classification Neural Network." In *Proceedings of the 24th International Conference on High Performance Computing & Communications; 8th International Conference on Data Science & Systems; 20th International Conference on Smart City; 8th International Conference on Dependability in Sensor, Cloud & Big Data Systems & Applications (HPCC/DSS/SmartCity/DependSys)*, 1682-1689.

Li, J., Ni, M., Dong, Y., Zhu, T., Liu, W. 2024. "AICAttack: Adversarial Image Captioning Attack with Attention-based Optimization." arXiv Preprint arXiv: 2402.11940.

Li, M. and Cao, C. 2022. "Defense against Adversarial Attacks Using Image Label and Pixel Guided Sparse Denoiser." In *Proceedings of the 7th International Conference on Big Data Analytics (ICBDA 2022)*, 253-258.

Liao, F., Liang, M., Dong, Y., Pang, T., Hu, X., Zhu, J. 2018. "Defense against Adversarial Attacks Using High-Level Representation Guided Denoiser." In *Proceedings of 2018 IEEE/CVF Conference on Computer Vision and Pattern Recognition (CVPR 2018)*, 1778-1787.

Liu, S., Shao, M., and Liu, X. 2020. "GAN-based Classifier Protection against Adversarial Attacks." *Journal of Intelligent & Fuzzy Systems: Applications in Engineering and Technology*, 39(5): 7085-7095.

Lu, J., Issaranon, T., Forsyth, D. 2017. "SafetyNet: Detecting and Rejecting Adversarial Examples Robustly." In *Proceedings of 2017 IEEE International Conference on Computer Vision (ICCV 2017)*, 446-454.

Ma, X., Li, B., Wang, Y., Erfani, S. M., Wijewickrema, S., Schoenebeck, G., Song, D., Houle, M. E., and Bailey, J. 2018. "Characterizing Adversarial Subspaces Using Local Intrinsic Dimensionality." In *Proceedings of the International Conference on Learning Representations (ICLR 2018)*.

Madry, A., Makelov, A., Schmidt, L., Tsipras, D., and Vladu, A. 2018. "Towards Deep Learning Models Resistant to Adversarial Attacks." In *the International Conference on Learning Representations (ICLR 2018)*, Poster Track.

Meng, D. and Chen, H. 2017. "MagNet: A Two-Pronged Defense against Adversarial Examples." In *Proceedings of the 2017 ACM SIGSAC Conference on Computer and Communications Security (CCS 2017)*, 135-147.

Metzen, J. D., Genewein, T., Fischer, V., and Bischoff, B. 2017. "On Detecting Adversarial Perturbations." In *Proceedings of the International Conference on Learning Representations (ICLR 2017)*.

Pang, T, Xu, K., Du, C., Chen, N., and Zhu, J. 2019. "Improving Adversarial Robustness via Promoting Ensemble Diversity." In *Proceedings of the 36th International Conference on Machine Learning (ICML 2019)*, PMLR, 97, 2019.

Papernot, N., McDaniel, P., Wu, X., Jha, S., and Swami, A. 2016. "Distillation as a Defense to Adversarial Perturbations against Deep Neural Networks." In *Proceedings of IEEE Symposium on Security and Privacy (SP 2016)*, 582-597.

Paul, S. and Chen, P-Y. 2022. "Vision Transformers are Robust Learners." In *Proceedings of the 36th Association for the Advancement of Artificial Intelligence Conference on Artificial Intelligence (AAAI 2022)*, 36(2), AAAI Technical Tracks 2.

Prakash, A., Moran, N., Garber, S., DiLillo, A., Storer, J. 2018. "Deflecting Adversarial Attacks with Pixel Deflection." In *Proceedings of the 2018 IEEE/CVF Conference on Computer Vision and Pattern Recognition (CVPR 2018)*, pp 8571-8580.

Prechelt, L. 2002. "Early Stopping- But When?" In: Orr, G. B. et al, (eds) *Neural Networks: Tricks of the Trade*. Lecture Notes in Computer Science, 1524: 55-69.

Raghunathan, A., Steinhardt, J., and Liang, P. 2018. "Certified Defenses against Adversarial Examples." *In Proceedings of the International Conference on Learning Representations (ICLR 2018)*.

Ren, K., Zheng, T., Qin, Z., and Liu, X. 2020. "Adversarial Attacks and Defenses in Deep Learning." *Engineering*, 6(3): 346-360.

Roth, K., Kilcher, Y., and Hofmann, T. 2019. "The Odds are Odd: A Statistical Test for Detecting Adversarial Examples." In *Proceedings of the 36th International Conference on Machine Learning (ICML 2019)*, PMLR 97, 2019.

Samangouei, P., Kabkab, M., and Chellapa, R. 2018. "Defense-GAN: Protecting Classifiers against Adversarial Attacks Using Generative

Models." In *Proceedings of the 6th International Conference on Learning Representations (ICLR 2018)*.

Sehwag, V., Mahloujifar, S., Handina, T., Dai, S., Xiang, C., Chiang, M., and Mittal, P. 2022. "Robust Learning Meets Generative Models: Can Proxy Distributions Improve Adversarial Robustness? In *the International Conference on Learning Representations (ICLR 2022)*, Poster Track.

Sen, J. 2024. "The FGSM Attack on Image Classification Models and Distillation as its Defense." In Nanda et al. (eds), *Advances in Distributed Computing and Machine Learning (ICADCML 2024)*, 1015: 347-360. Lecture Notes in Networks and Systems, Springer, Singapore.

Sen, J. and Dasgupta, S. 2023. "Adversarial Attacks on Image Classification Models: FGSM and Patch Attacks and their Impact." In Sen, J. and Mayer, J. (eds), *Information Security and Privacy in the Digital World: Some Selected Topics*, IntechOpen, London, UK.

Sen, J., Sen, A., and Chatterjee, A. 2023. "Adversarial Attacks on Image Classification Models: Analysis and Defense." In *Proceedings of the 10th International Conference on Business Analytics and Intelligence (ICBAI 2023)*, Bangalore, India.

Sen, J. and Waghela, H. 2025. "Text-Based Adversarial Attacks and Defense." In Sen, J. (ed) *Data Privacy: Techniques, Applications, and Standards*, IntechOpen, London, UK.

Simonyan, K. and Zisserman, A. 2015. "Very Deep Convolutional Networks for Large-scale Image Recognition." In *the International Conference on Learning Representations (ICLR)*, Poster Track.

Tramer, F., Kurakin, A., Papernot, N., Goodfellow, I., Boneh, D., and P. McDaniel, P. 2018. "Ensemble Adversarial Training: Attacks and Defenses." In *Proceedings of* the *International Conference on Learning Representation (ICLR'18)*.

Waghela, H., Sen, J., and Rakshit, S. 2025. "Saliency Attention and Semantic Similarity-Driven Adversarial Perturbation." In *Data Science and Applications. ICDSA 2024*, Nanda, S. J. et al. (eds), 1237: 461–471. Lecture Notes in Networks and Systems, Springer, Singapore.

Waghela, H., Sen, J., Rakshit, S., and Dasgupta, S. 2024a. "Adversarial Text Generation with Dynamic Contextual Perturbation." In *Proceedings of the 2024 IEEE CALCON 2024*, 1–6. IEEE.

Waghela, H., Sen, J., and Rakshit, S. 2024b. "Adaptive Meta-Learning for Robust Ensemble Defense against Adversarial Attacks." In *Proceedings of the International Conference BAMS-ORSI 2024*.

Waghela, H., Sen, J., and Rakshit, S. 2024c. "Adversarial Resilience in Image Classification: A Hybrid Approach to Defense." In *Proceedings of the 2024 International Conference on Innovation and Intelligence for Informatics, Computing, and Technologies (3ICT 2024)*, 419–426.

Waghela, H., Sen, J., Rakshit, S., and Dasgupta, S. 2024d. "Adversarial Robustness through Dynamic Ensemble Learning." In *Proceedings of the 2024 IEEE Silchar Subsection Conference (SILCON 2024)*, 1–6.

Waghela, H., Sen, J., and Rakshit, S. 2024e. "Robust Image Classification: Defensive Strategies against FGSM and PGD Adversarial Attacks." In *Proceedings of the IEEE Asian Conference on Intelligent Technologies (ACOIT 2024)*, 1 – 7.

Waghela, H., Sen, J., and Rakshit, S. 2024f. "Refining BERT Adversarial Attacks with Projected Gradient Descent." In *Proceedings of the IEEE 4th Asian Conference on Innovations in Technology (ASIANCON 2024)*, 1-7.

Waghela, H., Rakshit, S., and Sen, J. 2024g. "A Modified Word Saliency-Based Adversarial Attack on Text Classification Models." In *Computational Intelligence and Data Analytics*, Frery, A. C. et al. (eds), 371–382. Lecture Notes in Data Engineering and Communications Technologies, 236. Springer.

Wang, Y., Zou, D., Yi, J., Bailey, J., Ma, X., and Gu, Q. 2020. "Improving Adversarial Robustness Requires Revisiting Misclassified Examples." In *Proceedings of the International Conference on Learning Representations (ICLR 2020)*.

Wong, E. and Kotler, J. Z. 2018. "Provable Defenses against Adversarial Examples via the Convex Outer Adversarial Polytope." In *Proceedings of the 35th International Conference on Machine Learning (ICML 2018)*, PMLR 80, 2018.

Xiao, H., Rasul, K., and Vollgraf, R. 2017. "Fashion-MNIST: A Novel Image Dataset for Benchmarking Machine Learning Algorithms." arXiv Preprint arXiv:1708.07747.

Xie, C., Tan, M., Gong, B., Wang, J., Yuille, A. L., Le, Q. V. 2020. "Adversarial Examples Improve Image Recognition." In *Proceedings of the 2020 IEEE/CVF Conference on Computer Vision and Pattern Recognition (CVPR 2020)*, 816-825.

Xie, C., Wang, J., Zhang, Z., Ren, Z., and Yuille, A. 2018. "Mitigating Adversarial Effects through Randomization." In *Proceedings of the International Conference on Learning Representations (ICLR 2018)*.

Xie, C., Wu, Y., van der Maaten, L., Yuille, A. L., and He, K. 2019. "Feature Denoising for Improving Adversarial Robustness." In *Proceedings of 2019 IEEE/CVF Conference on Computer Vision and Pattern Recognition (CVPR 2019)*, 501-509.

Xu, W., Evans, D., and Qi, Y. 2018. "Feature Squeezing: Detecting Adversarial Examples in Deep Neural Networks." In *Proceedings of Network and Distributed Systems Security Symposium (NDSS 2018)*.

Zhang, H., Yu, Y., Jiao, J., Xing, E. P., Ghaoui, L. E., and Jordan, M. I. 2019. "Theoretically Principled Trade-off between Robustness and Accuracy." In *Proceedings of the 36th International Conference on Machine Learning (ICML 2019), PMLR 97*, 2019.

Zoran, D., Chrzanowski, M., Huang, P.-S., Gowal, S., Mott, A., and Kohli, P. 2020. "Towards Robust Image Classification Using Sequential Attention Models." In *Proceedings of IEEE/CVF Conference on Computer Vision and Pattern Recognition (CVPR 2020)*, 9480–9489.

CHAPTER 10

HYBRID DEFENSE STRATEGIES FOR ENHANCING ADVERSARIAL ROBUSTNESS IN IMAGE CLASSIFICATION

Introduction

In recent years, image classification has become a cornerstone of intelligent visual computing, with deep learning techniques propelling advancements across various domains such as autonomous driving, healthcare imaging, surveillance, facial recognition, and digital content moderation. These applications demand not only high accuracy but also robustness and reliability, especially in safety-critical scenarios. For instance, in autonomous vehicles, a real-time image classifier must correctly identify road signs and obstacles under varying environmental conditions; in medical diagnostics, a deep learning system must accurately classify radiological scans to assist in clinical decision-making. In such contexts, even a single misclassification could lead to catastrophic outcomes.

The success of deep learning in image classification is largely attributed to the development of *convolutional neural networks* (CNNs), such as AlexNet (Krizhevsky et al., 2017), VGGNet (Simonyan & Zisserman, 2015), ResNet (He et al., 2016), and DenseNet (Huang et al., 2017), which have consistently achieved state-of-the-art results on benchmark datasets like CIFAR-10 (Krizhevsky, 2008) and ImageNet (He et al., 2016). These models excel at automatically learning hierarchical feature representations from raw pixel data, thereby eliminating the need for manual feature engineering and offering superior generalization across diverse visual categories. Their performance, scalability, and accessibility have cemented their place in modern computer vision pipelines.

Despite these impressive achievements, a critical vulnerability of deep neural networks has come to light: their susceptibility to *adversarial examples*, inputs intentionally perturbed in a manner that causes the model to produce incorrect predictions, while appearing virtually unchanged to the human eye. The *Fast Gradient Sign Method* (FGSM), introduced by Goodfellow et al. (Goodfellow et al., 2015), first demonstrated how gradient-based perturbations could be used to mislead classifiers. Building upon this, *Projected Gradient Descent* (PGD) was proposed by Madry et al. (Madry et al., 2018) as a more powerful iterative attack that constrains adversarial noise within a defined norm-ball. These perturbations, though imperceptible, can significantly degrade model performance and pose severe security risks. For example, altering a few pixels in a stop sign image could cause a classifier to mislabel it as a speed-limit sign, compromising road safety; similarly, adversarial perturbations in medical images may lead to misdiagnoses.

The field of *adversarial machine learning* has thus evolved to address these vulnerabilities. A wide range of defense strategies has been proposed, generally falling into three broad categories:

- *Adversarial training*, where the model is trained on both clean and adversarial examples, allowing it to learn more robust decision boundaries (Madry et al., 2018);
- *Input transformations*, which apply preprocessing steps such as random resizing, JPEG compression, or noise injection to distort adversarial perturbations (Pestana et al., 2021; Zhang et al., 2021); and
- *Model regularization* techniques such as *defensive distillation* (Papernot et al., 2016), gradient smoothing, and adversarial logit pairing are designed to reduce the model's sensitivity to small perturbations.

Each of these approaches offers specific advantages. *Adversarial training* is among the most widely used and empirically validated defenses, particularly effective against first-order attacks like FGSM and PGD. However, it is computationally expensive and often limited in generalizability to attacks not encountered during training. *Input transformation techniques* are lightweight and model-agnostic, making them suitable for deployment during inference, but their effectiveness may vary across attack types. *Regularization methods*, while theoretically appealing, may involve delicate hyperparameter tuning and sometimes lead to reduced performance on clean data.

Despite significant progress, none of these standalone defense methods provides comprehensive resilience against the diverse and evolving landscape of adversarial attacks. As Carlini and Wagner demonstrated, even state-of-the-art detection-based defenses can be bypassed through carefully crafted attacks that exploit their assumptions and weaknesses (Carlini & Wagner, 2017). In this adversarial arms race, *adaptive and hybrid strategies* have emerged as a promising alternative.

Hybrid defense strategies aim to combine complementary mechanisms, most commonly adversarial training and input transformations, to develop multi-layered defenses that balance robustness, accuracy, and computational feasibility. The core idea is to leverage the strengths of each method while mitigating its individual weaknesses. For instance, adversarial training equips the model with resistance to known attack patterns through exposure during training, whereas input transformations act as a preprocessing filter during inference to disrupt adversarial noise that might bypass the trained defenses. This layered defense strategy has been shown to enhance both robustness and generalization, offering resilience not only to white-box and black-box attacks but also to adaptive adversaries (Sen & Dasgupta, 2023; Sen et al., 2023; Waghela et al., 2024e).

This chapter presents a comprehensive framework for enhancing adversarial robustness in image classification by integrating *adversarial training with input transformation techniques*. The proposed hybrid defense method utilizes FGSM and PGD during training to generate adversarial samples, while simultaneously applying random resizing, JPEG compression, and Gaussian noise injection to disrupt perturbations during both training and inference. The defense is implemented and evaluated on benchmark datasets using the ResNet-18 architecture, with a focus on performance under varying attack strengths and perturbation budgets.

By demonstrating how adversarial training and input transformations can be synergistically combined, this chapter contributes to the growing body of research focused on developing resilient, secure, and trustworthy deep learning models for image classification. The hybrid framework discussed here offers both a conceptual roadmap and practical implementation guidance for researchers and practitioners working to fortify AI systems against adversarial threats.

The rest of the chapter is organized as follows. The section titled *Related Work* provides an in-depth survey of existing adversarial attack methods and the spectrum of defense strategies proposed in the literature, including hybrid techniques. The section *Hybrid Defense Strategy* outlines the conceptual and architectural design of the proposed defense framework, detailing how adversarial training and input transformations are systematically integrated. The section *Implementation Details* presents the technical workflow, including code-level descriptions of each defense module and training procedure. The section *Performance Evaluation* discusses the empirical evaluation of the hybrid strategy, highlighting its effectiveness through comparative accuracy metrics, ablation studies, and convergence plots. Finally, the section *Conclusion and Future Work* reflects on the broader implications of this work, summarizes key insights, and identifies open research questions and future directions.

Related Work

The increasing deployment of deep learning models in real-world applications has brought heightened attention to their vulnerability to adversarial attacks, carefully crafted perturbations designed to deceive neural networks while remaining imperceptible to human observers. This susceptibility poses a significant threat to the reliability and security of AI-driven systems, particularly in domains such as autonomous navigation, medical imaging, and security analytics. Consequently, a substantial body of research has emerged to characterize the nature of these attacks and to develop corresponding defense mechanisms aimed at improving adversarial robustness.

The foundational work by Goodfellow et al. introduced the concept of *adversarial examples* and proposed the *Fast Gradient Sign Method* (FGSM), a gradient-based technique for generating perturbations that can mislead neural networks (Goodfellow et al., 2015). This work demonstrated that even simple, linear perturbations, when aligned with the gradient of the loss function, could significantly impair model performance. FGSM has since become a baseline attack in the adversarial machine learning literature, sparking interest in both attack development and robust defense strategies. In the literature, researchers have proposed several approaches and techniques for forecasting the daily prices of stocks and index values of various sectors of the economy. Neural network-based approaches are the most popular among these propositions.

Building upon this foundation, Madry et al. proposed a *robust optimization framework* that incorporated *Projected Gradient Descent* (PGD) into the training process. PGD, an iterative variant of FGSM, applies small-step perturbations repeatedly, with projections back into the allowable perturbation space, thereby producing stronger adversarial examples

(Madry et al., 2018). Their approach, now considered a gold standard in adversarial training, showed that exposure to adversarial examples during training could substantially improve robustness. However, the method is computationally intensive and can overfit to specific attack patterns, limiting its generalization to adaptive or unseen attack strategies.

Recognizing the challenge of creating generalizable defenses, Carlini and Wagner evaluated the effectiveness of ten contemporary detection-based methods and introduced new attack techniques capable of bypassing them (Carlini & Wagner, 2017). Their work underscored a critical insight: many defense methods, particularly those based on input anomaly detection, are brittle when facing adaptive adversaries. This led to a shift in the community toward designing *robust learning paradigms* rather than relying solely on post hoc detection.

One such learning-centric method is *defensive distillation*, introduced by Papernot et al. (Papernot et al., 2016). By training a student model on the softened outputs of a pre-trained teacher network, this approach aimed to reduce sensitivity to input perturbations. Although it initially showed promise, subsequent research revealed that it was ineffective against stronger, more adaptive attacks, such as the Carlini-Wagner attack, thus limiting its standalone utility.

Expanding on hybrid strategies, Waghela et al. examined the effectiveness of FGSM and PGD attacks in image classification tasks and introduced an *autoencoder-based defense*, wherein adversarial inputs are reconstructed into their clean counterparts before classification (Waghela et al., 2024e). Their results indicated that input reconstruction techniques can serve as viable preprocessing defenses, though their reliance on the reconstruction quality and sensitivity to high-frequency perturbations remains a limitation.

In another direction, Pestana et al. explored the role of color space in adversarial defense by training models on *YCbCr images*, showing that such representations can offer improved robustness against certain attacks (Pestana et al., 2021). While promising, the applicability of this strategy is largely domain-specific and requires further validation across diverse datasets and attack types.

Li et al. examined defense strategies in the context of *medical imaging*, comparing classification-based and detection-based mechanisms (Li et al., 2021). Their findings highlighted the complementary strengths of combining detection and classification for enhanced robustness. However, the study primarily focused on conventional adversarial scenarios, leaving open questions about the efficacy of such hybrid systems under emerging, more complex attack patterns.

A distinct category of research investigates *image reconstruction and restoration* as defense mechanisms. Zhang et al. proposed an approach that reconstructs input images before classification, mitigating adversarial noise (Zhang et al., 2021). Although this method improves resilience, it is sensitive to the fidelity of the reconstruction pipeline and may fail against perturbations that affect global semantic features.

Domain-specific defenses have also emerged. Spasiano et al. evaluated adversarial threats in infrared imaging systems, emphasizing the need for customized defense strategies tailored to non-RGB modalities (Spasiano et al., 2022). Similarly, Shi et al. and Xu et al. proposed methods for *hyperspectral image classification*, incorporating attention mechanisms to mitigate adversarial effects (Shi et al., 2024; Xu et al., 2020). Their findings, though promising, raise questions about generalizability beyond specialized data types.

Learning-based defenses have taken a novel turn with techniques such as *Adversarials-1*, introduced by Worzyk and Kramer, which trains models using adversarial examples as a regularization mechanism (Worzyk & Kramer, 2018). Likewise, *attention-based defenses*, including *attention transfer* (Li et al., 2021) and *salient feature extraction* (Chen et al., 2022), seek to enforce robust feature learning by focusing on parts of the input space most relevant for classification.

The progress in adversarial machine learning has led to the development of increasingly sophisticated attack and defense techniques, integrating concepts such as semantic similarity, dynamic perturbation, and ensemble-based robustness. A body of work by Waghela, Sen, Rakshit, and their collaborators (Waghela et al., 2024a–g; Waghela et al., 2025; Sen, 2024; Sen & Dasgupta, 2023; Sen & Waghela, 2025; Sen et al., 2023; Koley et al., 2024) has substantially enriched this research domain. These studies propose advanced adversarial methods that are both context-sensitive and semantically aware, leveraging saliency-guided perturbations, attention-based architectures, BERT-style embeddings, and lexical similarity metrics to craft high-quality adversarial samples that retain linguistic coherence. On the defense side, the authors introduce a range of hybrid and ensemble-based frameworks, including meta-learning strategies, to enhance model robustness across modalities. These defense mechanisms are designed to generalize across tasks and adversarial scenarios, offering scalable protection for both text and vision systems. Collectively, this body of work represents a comprehensive and integrative approach that advances both the efficacy of adversarial attacks and the adaptability of defenses, with a strong emphasis on semantic fidelity, cross-domain applicability, and architectural generalization.

Recent survey efforts, such as the comprehensive review by Xu et al., have attempted to categorize adversarial attacks and defenses across modalities, including images, graphs, and text (Xu et al., 2020). These reviews have highlighted key limitations in existing methods, namely, the trade-off between robustness and accuracy, high computational costs, and lack of adaptability to unseen attacks.

Overall, these studies collectively reveal a pattern: while many individual defense techniques offer partial robustness, none alone provides complete protection against the broad and evolving spectrum of adversarial threats. *Input transformations*, such as those explored by Zhang et al. (Zhang et al., 2021) and Waghela et al. (Waghela et al., 2024e), are simple to deploy but can be bypassed by transformation-aware attacks. *Adversarial training*, as demonstrated by Madry et al. (Madry et al., 2018), remains one of the most effective strategies, yet is costly and susceptible to attack-specific overfitting.

Given these challenges, the development of *hybrid defense frameworks* that integrate multiple defense modalities has gained momentum. The proposed approach in this chapter, detailed in *Hybrid Defense Strategy*, builds upon this trend by combining adversarial training with input transformation techniques to construct a multi-layered, adaptive defense mechanism. Through this combination, the defense can learn robust representations while simultaneously disrupting adversarial perturbations at the input level.

As demonstrated in the *Performance Results* section, such a hybrid strategy can offer superior resilience to adversarial attacks compared to standalone methods. Moreover, the *Implementation Details* section outlines how this strategy can be practically realized within standard deep learning workflows, using models like ResNet-18 (He et al., 2016) and datasets such as CIFAR-10 (Krizhevsky, 2008).

In summary, the growing sophistication of adversarial attacks necessitates the adoption of comprehensive, multifaceted defense strategies. This chapter contributes to that effort by synthesizing prior insights into a unified framework that improves adversarial robustness without sacrificing generalization or performance on clean data.

Hybrid Defense Strategy

The vulnerability of deep neural networks to adversarial perturbations necessitates the development of robust, multifaceted defense mechanisms capable of generalizing across a diverse range of attack vectors. To this end, the proposed framework adopts a *hybrid defense strategy* that synergistically combines two complementary techniques, *adversarial training* and *input transformations*, to improve the adversarial resilience of image classification models. The goal of this hybrid methodology is to enhance robustness without significantly sacrificing classification accuracy on clean data, thereby addressing one of the central trade-offs in adversarial defense research.

Input Transformation as a Pre-emptive Defense Layer: Input transformations serve as the first line of defense by modifying images prior to their ingestion by the neural network. These transformations are designed to degrade or eliminate adversarial noise while preserving essential semantic content needed for accurate classification. The underlying principle is that many adversarial perturbations are sensitive to small alterations in input distribution. By introducing randomness or compression artifacts, these transformations can effectively neutralize certain adversarial effects.

In the proposed framework, the following transformation techniques are incorporated:

- *Random Resizing and Cropping*: This transformation introduces spatial variability by altering the scale and aspect ratio of the input images before cropping them to the desired size. The transformation disrupts the spatial consistency that adversarial perturbations often rely on, thereby reducing their effectiveness across different image configurations.
- *JPEG Compression*: Compression is widely used in image processing pipelines and introduces quantization noise that can blur or eliminate high-frequency adversarial signals. JPEG compression is effective at suppressing perturbations that operate in the pixel space while maintaining sufficient image quality for human and machine interpretation.

- *Gaussian Noise Injection*: This transformation adds small, randomly sampled Gaussian noise to each pixel in the input image. The added noise interferes with finely tuned adversarial perturbations by introducing stochasticity, thereby forcing the model to focus on more robust and generalizable features.

These transformations are applied both during training and inference, ensuring consistent exposure of the model to perturbation-resilient inputs throughout its lifecycle. When applied in conjunction with adversarial training, the input transformations form a layered defense architecture, one that seeks to disrupt adversarial noise at the input level and reinforce robustness at the representational level.

Although computationally lightweight compared to adversarial training, the effectiveness of input transformations depends on several factors, including the nature of the perturbation and the sensitivity of the model to input variations. Therefore, the selection and tuning of these transformations must strike a balance between noise suppression and preservation of classification-relevant features.

Adversarial Training for Robust Feature Learning: Adversarial training represents a direct strategy to harden the model against adversarial attacks by explicitly incorporating adversarial examples into the learning process. By exposing the model to such perturbed instances during training, it learns to recognize and correct for adversarial patterns, thereby improving its robustness at inference time.

The adversarial training component in this framework utilizes two widely studied first-order attack methods: *Fast Gradient Sign Method* (FGSM) and *Projected Gradient Descent* (PGD). FGSM generates adversarial examples by applying a one-step perturbation in the direction of the gradient of the loss function with respect to the input. PGD extends this approach iteratively, applying multiple small steps followed by projection into a constrained norm-ball to keep the perturbation within acceptable bounds.

The adversarial training pipeline involves the following stages:

- *Adversarial Example Generation*: During each training iteration, adversarial examples are created on-the-fly using the PGD algorithm. This involves computing the gradient of the loss function with respect to the input, applying a step in the gradient direction, and projecting the result back into the allowed perturbation space.

The process is repeated for a fixed number of iterations, with hyperparameters such as step size (α), number of iterations, and perturbation budget (ε) tuned to achieve a balance between attack strength and computational feasibility.

- *Dataset Augmentation and Training*: The training set is augmented with both clean and adversarial samples. The model is trained to minimize a composite loss function that accounts for both types of inputs. This dual-exposure encourages the model to develop robust feature representations capable of handling both unperturbed and maliciously altered data.
- *Hyperparameter Optimization*: A grid search or heuristic-based optimization is performed over key parameters, namely, the PGD step size, number of iterations, and perturbation norms. The objective is to achieve maximum robustness with minimal degradation in clean-data accuracy. Special care is taken to prevent overfitting to specific adversarial patterns, thereby enhancing generalization to unseen attacks.

While adversarial training is known to be one of the most effective defense strategies, it incurs additional computational overhead and may slightly reduce model accuracy on clean data. However, when combined with input transformations, this limitation is mitigated, and the model benefits from both *robust learning* and *resilient input preprocessing*.

Integrated Training Pipeline: The core strength of the proposed hybrid defense strategy lies in the seamless integration of adversarial training and input transformations within a unified training pipeline. This integration ensures that the classifier is exposed not only to clean and adversarial data but also to transformed variants of both. The training procedure is structured as follows:

1. *Preprocessing*: Every input image is subjected to a combination of input transformations: random resizing and cropping, JPEG compression, and Gaussian noise addition. These transformations are applied stochastically to introduce variability and suppress deterministic attack patterns.
2. *Adversarial Example Generation*: Transformed images are passed through the PGD attack routine to generate adversarial versions that reflect both transformation-invariant and perturbation-sensitive distortions.
3. *Model Training*: The model is trained on a batch composed of clean images, transformed images, and adversarially perturbed images.

The loss function is computed over this combined batch to ensure that the classifier learns to maintain accuracy across a diverse spectrum of input conditions.

4. *Evaluation and Validation*: After training, the model is evaluated on separate sets of clean and adversarially attacked test images. Performance metrics include classification accuracy, Robustness under varying attack budgets, and the convergence behavior. Detailed results are presented and analyzed in the *Performance Results* section.

This integrated approach introduces a moderate computational burden due to the generation of adversarial examples and the execution of transformation operations. However, optimizations such as parallel processing, GPU acceleration, and batch-level caching can substantially reduce training time.

Trade-offs and Design Considerations: As with any robust learning strategy, the hybrid defense approach involves several trade-offs. While adversarial training enhances resilience, it may cause minor reductions in performance on clean inputs. Conversely, input transformations can sometimes alter semantically important features, leading to marginal misclassifications. The combined strategy, however, aims to minimize these limitations by distributing the burden of defense across complementary mechanisms.

An additional consideration is *attack generalizability*. Many defenses are tuned to resist specific attack types, such as FGSM (Goodfellow et al., 2015) or PGD (Madry et al., 2018), but fail against others, e.g., C&W (Carlini & Wagner, 2017) and DeepFool (Moosavi-Dezfooli et al., 2016). The use of *first-order attacks* during training, combined with transformation-based input preprocessing, improves generalization to a broader class of attacks, a key design objective of this hybrid framework.

In conclusion, the proposed methodology establishes a *robust, layered defense architecture* that leverages the strengths of adversarial training and input transformation in a unified, scalable pipeline. By addressing both model and input vulnerabilities, this hybrid strategy represents a comprehensive solution to the problem of adversarial robustness in image classification. Its practical implementation and empirical evaluation are discussed in detail in the subsequent sections on *Implementation Details* and *Performance Results*.

Implementation Details

To operationalize the proposed hybrid defense framework for adversarial robustness in image classification, an integrated system, referred to as *Adversarial Defense via Resizing and Transformation* (ADRT), has been implemented. As shown in Figure 10-1, the system comprises four principal components:

1. Input Transformation
2. Adversarial Sample Generation
3. Model Training, and
4. Performance Evaluation

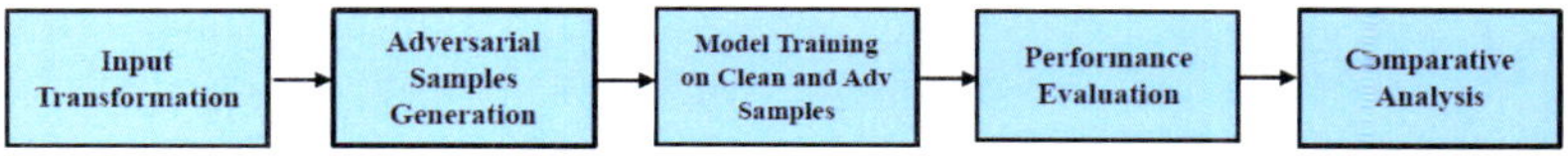

Figure. 10-1. The block diagram of the proposed hybrid adversarial defense pipeline illustrating the sequential flow: input transformation, adversarial sample generation, model training on both clean and adversarial data, performance evaluation, and comparative analysis.

Each module plays a distinct yet interdependent role in enhancing the classifier's resilience to adversarial attacks. The implementation is carried out using the *PyTorch* deep learning framework due to its flexibility, dynamic computation graph, and robust support for custom operations.

```
import torch
import torchvision.transforms as transforms

def random_resizing(image, min_scale=0.8, max_scale=1.2):
    scale = torch.FloatTensor(1).uniform_(min_scale, max_scale).item()
    resize_transform = transforms.Resize((int(image.size(1) * scale), int(image.size(2) *
    return resize_transform(image)

def jpeg_compression(image, quality=75):
    transform = transforms.Compose([
        transforms.ToPILImage(),
        transforms.Resize((image.size(1), image.size(2))),  # Resize to original size afte
        transforms.ToTensor()
    ])
    return transform(image)

def add_noise(image, noise_factor=0.1):
    noise = torch.randn_like(image) * noise_factor
    return torch.clamp(image + noise, 0.0, 1.0)
```

Figure. 10-2. Python code snippets for image preprocessing functions: random resizing and cropping, JPEG compression, and Gaussian noise injection.

Input Transformation Module: This module applies a sequence of stochastic and deterministic transformations to incoming images. The implementation of these transformation functions is illustrated in Figure 10-2. The primary objective is to introduce variability and degrade potential adversarial noise, thereby increasing the diversity and resilience of the training and inference pipelines. Drawing on prior work that demonstrated the effectiveness of input preprocessing in mitigating adversarial perturbations (Goodfellow et al., 2015; Waghela et al., 2024e; Zhang et al., 2021), this module leverages three techniques:

- ***Random Resizing and Cropping***: This operation introduces spatial variability by resizing the image based on a random scale factor drawn from a predefined range (e.g., 0.9-1.1). Cropping is subsequently applied to restore the image to its original dimensions. This spatial inconsistency effectively disrupts fixed-location adversarial patterns, making the perturbations less effective across variations.
- ***JPEG Compression Simulation***: Compression artifacts introduced by JPEG encoding are simulated using PIL-based tensor-to-image transformations. The image is converted to a PIL object, re-encoded at a specific quality level, and then reconverted to a tensor. This simulates real-world compression scenarios and degrades high-frequency adversarial noise that may otherwise bypass the model's defense.
- ***Gaussian Noise Injection***: Controlled Gaussian noise is added to the transformed image to further reduce the influence of subtle perturbations. The noise is sampled with a specified standard deviation (noise factor), and pixel values are clamped to remain within the valid range [0, 1], ensuring no loss of visual integrity.

These transformations are applied both during training and inference, ensuring consistent model exposure to perturbed yet semantically intact inputs. The primary goal is to enhance the model's generalization by simulating real-world distortions and making it more robust to imperceptible perturbations introduced by adversarial attacks.

Adversarial Sample Generation Module: Following the input transformations, adversarial examples are generated to simulate worst-case attack conditions during training. This module utilizes FGSM and PGD attacks for adversarial sample generation. However, this work has used PGD due to its stronger attack capability.

The PGD algorithm is implemented with the following configurable parameters:

- *Model*: The target neural network to be attacked.
- *Input Images*: Clean images post-transformation.
- *True Labels*: Ground-truth labels corresponding to each input.
- *Epsilon* (ε): The maximum permissible perturbation per pixel.
- *Step Size* (α): The magnitude of perturbation applied per iteration.
- *Number of iterations*: Total attack steps for convergence.

```
def pgd_attack(model, images, labels, eps=0.03, alpha=0.01, iters=40):
    adv_images = images.clone().detach() + 0.001 * torch.randn_like(images)
    adv_images = adv_images.to(images.device)
    adv_images.requires_grad = True

    for _ in range(iters):
        outputs = model(adv_images)
        model.zero_grad()
        loss = torch.nn.CrossEntropyLoss()(outputs, labels)
        loss.backward()
        adv_images = adv_images + alpha * adv_images.grad.sign()
        adv_images = torch.clamp(adv_images, 0, 1)
        adv_images = torch.min(torch.max(adv_images, images - eps), images + eps).detach_()
        adv_images.requires_grad = True

    return adv_images
```

Figure. 10-3. Python code for the PGD adversarial attack generation function.

An example implementation of the PGD-based attack routine is shown in Figure 10-3. In the PGD routine, each input image is initialized with a small amount of random noise to avoid starting from a potentially robust region. The algorithm iteratively adjusts the input by computing the gradient of the cross-entropy loss with respect to the input pixels and updating the image in the direction that maximizes this loss. After each step, the adversarial image is projected back into the ℓ_∞-ball centered around the original image and clamped to the valid pixel intensity range.

The use of PGD ensures that the adversarial samples generated are strong and effective in misleading the classifier, thereby preparing the model to better resist such attacks during deployment.

Model Training Module: Model training is conducted using a combination of clean, transformed, and adversarially perturbed images to enable the network to generalize across both natural and adversarial distributions. The architecture employed for classification is ResNet-18 (He et al., 2016), initialized from scratch with weights trained over the target dataset, e.g., CIFAR-10 (Krizhevsky, 2009).

```
import torch.optim as optim
import torch.nn as nn
import torchvision.models as models

# Load model (e.g., ResNet50)
model = models.resnet50(pretrained=False, num_classes=10).to(device)
optimizer = optim.Adam(model.parameters(), lr=0.001)
criterion = nn.CrossEntropyLoss()

# Training loop
num_epochs = 10

for epoch in range(num_epochs):
    model.train()
    for images, labels in train_loader:
        images, labels = images.to(device), labels.to(device)

        # Apply input transformations
        images_transformed = random_resizing(images)
        images_transformed = jpeg_compression(images_transformed)
        images_transformed = add_noise(images_transformed)

        # Generate adversarial examples
        adv_images = pgd_attack(model, images_transformed, labels)

        # Combine clean and adversarial examples
        combined_images = torch.cat([images, adv_images], dim=0)
        combined_labels = torch.cat([labels, labels], dim=0)

        # Forward pass
        outputs = model(combined_images)
        loss = criterion(outputs, combined_labels)

        # Backward and optimize
        optimizer.zero_grad()
        loss.backward()
        optimizer.step()

    print(f'Epoch [{epoch+1}/{num_epochs}], Loss: {loss.item():.4f}')
```

Figure. 10-4. Training loop combining clean and adversarial samples for model robustness enhancement.

The training workflow comprises the following key steps:

- *Initialization*: The ResNet-18 model is initialized with output dimensions matching the number of classes in the dataset. The training is performed on a GPU-enabled device. The Adam optimizer is used for weight updates, with a typical learning rate of 0.001. The loss function is set to *CrossEntropyLoss*, suitable for multi-class classification tasks.
- *Batch Processing*: For each training epoch, the dataset is processed in mini-batches. Input transformations are first applied to each batch, followed by the generation of adversarial examples using the PGD routine. Clean and adversarial images are concatenated to form a unified batch, with the corresponding ground-truth labels duplicated.
- *Forward and Backward Propagation*: The composite batch is passed through the model, and predictions are obtained. The total loss- computed across both clean and adversarial samples- is used to perform gradient *backpropagation*. Weight updates are applied via the optimizer, and gradients are reset at each step to prevent accumulation.

The overall training loop, including data preparation, attack generation, and gradient-based learning updates, is shown in Figure 10-4. This process enables the model to simultaneously learn from natural variations and adversarial perturbations, improving its robustness without sacrificing classification accuracy under standard conditions.

Performance Evaluation Module: The final component evaluates the trained model's performance on both clean and adversarial test datasets. Evaluation is conducted using a dedicated routine that quantifies the model's classification accuracy under different conditions.

Key aspects of the evaluation phase include:

- *Evaluation Mode Activation*: The model is set to evaluation mode, disabling dropout and batch normalization updates to ensure consistent inference behavior.
- *Gradient-Free Inference*: To conserve computational resources, gradient tracking is disabled using *torch.no_grad()*. This is suitable for inference-only workflows and accelerates the evaluation process.
- *Accuracy Calculation*: The model processes test data in batches, outputting class probabilities or logits. Predicted classes are determined using *argmax* over the output vector. Classification

accuracy is computed as the ratio of correctly predicted instances to the total number of samples processed.

```
def evaluate_model(model, test_loader):
    model.eval()
    correct = 0
    total = 0

    with torch.no_grad():
        for images, labels in test_loader:
            images, labels = images.to(device), labels.to(device)

            # Test on clean images
            outputs = model(images)
            _, predicted = torch.max(outputs.data, 1)
            total += labels.size(0)
            correct += (predicted == labels).sum().item()

            # Generate adversarial examples for testing
            adv_images = pgd_attack(model, images, labels)
            outputs_adv = model(adv_images)
            _, predicted_adv = torch.max(outputs_adv.data, 1)
            correct += (predicted_adv == labels).sum().item()
            total += labels.size(0)

    print(f'Test Accuracy: {100 * correc ↓ (2 * total):.2f}%')
```

Figure. 10-5. Evaluation function for measuring model accuracy under clean and adversarial conditions.

The evaluation routine that computes classification accuracy across clean and adversarial test sets is exhibited in Figure 10-5. The evaluation is conducted over two test scenarios: (i) unmodified clean data and (ii) adversarially perturbed data generated using PGD or FGSM. This dual-mode evaluation provides a comprehensive view of the model's ability to generalize and withstand adversarial manipulations.

Performance Evaluation

To evaluate the efficacy of the proposed hybrid defense mechanism, comprising input transformation and adversarial training, comprehensive experiments were conducted using the ResNet-18 model trained on the CIFAR-10 dataset. The implementation and experimentation were carried out on the Kaggle computing platform equipped with an NVIDIA Tesla

P100 GPU, which features 3,584 CUDA cores, 16 GB HBM2 memory, and 732 GB/s memory bandwidth, in conjunction with a multi-core Intel Xeon processor.

Dataset and Preprocessing: The CIFAR-10 dataset, a standard benchmark for image classification, comprises 60,000 color images of 32×32 pixels, uniformly distributed across 10 classes. To enhance the model's generalization capability and resistance to perturbations, a series of preprocessing techniques was applied:

- *Random Cropping with Padding*: Each image was padded by 4 pixels, and a 32*32 region was randomly cropped, thereby enabling spatial variance during training.
- *Random Horizontal Flipping*: Images were flipped horizontally with a 50% probability to introduce orientation invariance.
- *Tensor Conversion*: Images were converted from PIL format to PyTorch tensors with pixel values normalized to the [0,1] range.
- *Channel Normalization*: Pixel intensities for RGB channels were normalized using class-specific mean and standard deviation values derived from the CIFAR-10 dataset.

Input Transformation Effectiveness: To isolate the contribution of input transformation, the ResNet-18 classifier was initially trained on clean CIFAR-10 images without any defensive preprocessing. Under this setup, FGSM and PGD attacks were launched on the model.

When exposed to the FGSM attack with a perturbation magnitude of $\varepsilon = 1/255$, the classifier achieved an accuracy of 85%. However, after applying input transformations such as resizing, JPEG compression, and Gaussian noise injection, accuracy improved to 89%, indicating that transformation-based defenses can mitigate the impact of simple adversarial perturbations. Likewise, under a PGD attack with a step size of $\alpha = 2/255$, the classifier's accuracy improved from 88% to 91.70% following the input transformations. These results validate the contribution of transformation-based defenses in shielding models from minor but structured perturbations.

Adversarial Training with FGSM: Subsequent experiments examined the resilience of the model when trained with adversarial examples generated via FGSM. The ResNet-18 model was trained for 45 epochs using a dataset augmented with both clean and adversarially perturbed images. The training and test loss curves for this setup are shown in Figure 10-6, demonstrating stable convergence across epochs.

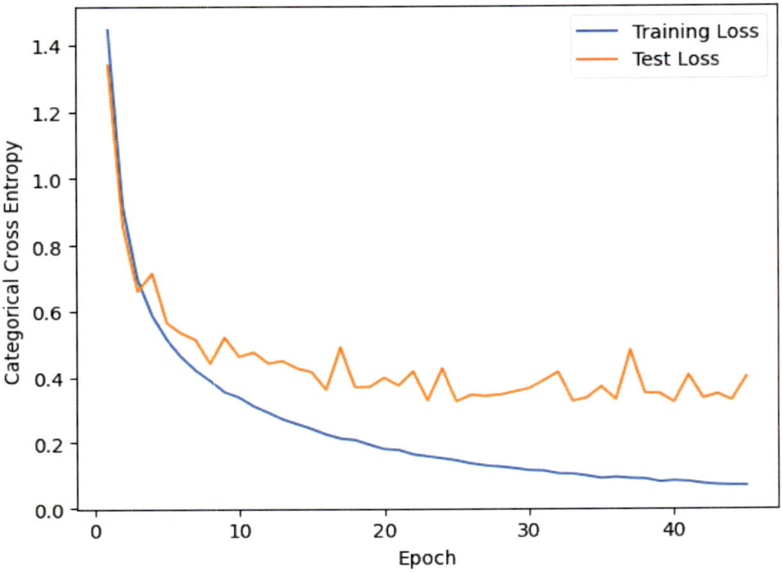

Figure. 10-6. Epoch-wise training loss and test loss of the ResNet-18 model on clean CIFAR-10 images.

Table 10-1. Classification Accuracy of the ResNet-18 Model on Clean CIFAR-10 and FGSM-Generated Adversarial Images.

Noise Level (ε)	Accuracy on Clean Images	Accuracy on FGSM-Adversarial Images
0.00	0.9601	0.9601
0.10	0.5801	0.9296
0.20	0.2473	0.9175
0.30	0.2173	0.9125
0.40	0.1702	0.9087
0.50	0.1401	0.9023
0.60	0.1202	0.9020
0.70	0.1019	0.8987
0.80	0.0920	0.8743
0.90	0.0514	0.8432

When subjected to FGSM attacks of varying intensities, the accuracy degradation was considerably lower for the adversarially trained model, as shown in Table 10-1. Even with perturbations as high as $\varepsilon = 0.9$, the classifier maintained an accuracy above 84%, highlighting the robustness imparted by adversarial training. Furthermore, Figure 10-7 illustrates example misclassifications under the FGSM attack, showcasing the visual subtlety of perturbations.

Figure. 10-7. Examples of incorrect predictions made by the ResNet-18 model under FGSM attack with a perturbation level of $\varepsilon = 1/255$.

Adversarial Training with PGD: In a similar configuration, the model was retrained with adversarial examples generated using the PGD attack. This multi-step, iterative attack is considered a stronger adversarial method due to its cumulative perturbation over several iterations.

The ResNet-18 model was again trained for 45 epochs, achieving a test accuracy of 91% on adversarially perturbed samples. Training and validation losses, as depicted in Figure 10-8, show effective convergence despite the adversarial complexity introduced by PGD. The performance across various PGD step sizes (α) is summarized in Table 10-2. As α increases, a gradual decline in classification accuracy is observed, although the model continues to perform above 88%, even at $\alpha = 10/255$. These results substantiate the strength of PGD-based adversarial training in handling iterative attacks.

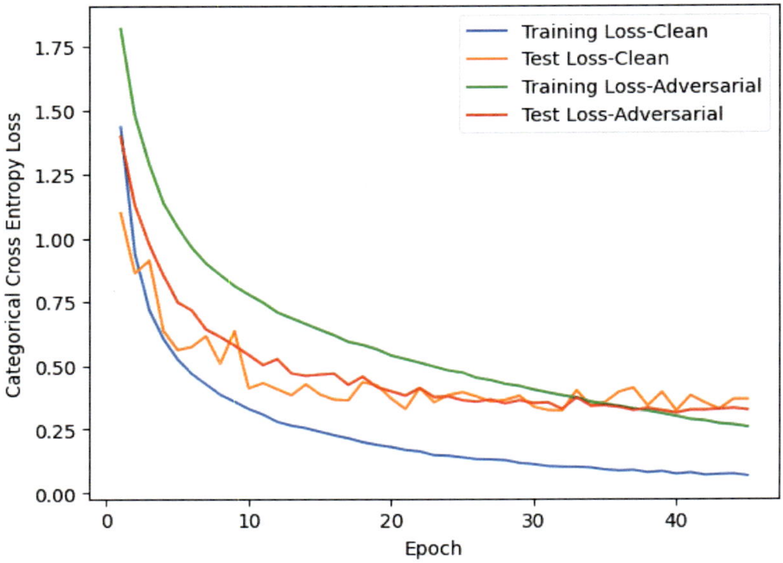

Figure. 10-8. Epoch-wise training loss and test loss of the ResNet-18 model on clean and FGSM-perturbed CIFAR-10 images.

Table 10-2. Classification Accuracy of the ResNet-18 Model Under PGD Attack with Varying Step Sizes (α) on the CIPHER-10 Test Set.

Step Size (α)	Accuracy on PGD-Adversarial Images
1/255	91.70
2/355	91.30
3/355	91.20
4/255	91.10
5/255	90.76
6/255	90.20
7/255	89.20
8/255	89.15
9/255	89.03
10/255	88.34

Comparative Loss Analysis: To comprehensively evaluate training behavior, loss trajectories for models trained under three different setups: clean data, FGSM-adversarial data, and PGD-adversarial data, are visualized together in Figure 10-9. All models demonstrated consistent convergence, confirming that adversarial training does not significantly impair training stability. Notably, adversarially trained models maintained competitive test losses despite the added complexity.

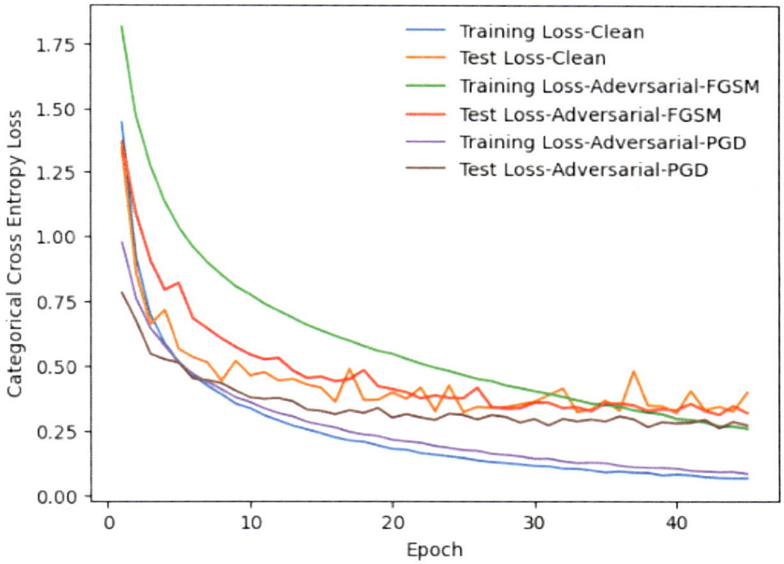

Figure. 10-9. Epoch-wise training loss and test loss of the ResNet-18 model on clean and adversarial samples generated by FGSM and PGD attacks.

Table 10-3. Ablation Analysis of the ResNet-18 Classifier on CIFAR-10 Images Under FGSM Attack ($\alpha = 0.1$) with and without Input Transformation and Adversarial Training.

Method	Accuracy
Clean Image	0.9601
Clean Image +FGSM (ε=0.1)	0.5801
Transformed Image + FGSM (ε=0.1)	0.8814
Transformed Image + Adversarial Training + FGSM (ε=0.1)	0.9296

Ablation Study: To assess the individual and combined contributions of input transformation and adversarial training, an ablation analysis was performed. As illustrated in Table 10-3, the baseline model trained solely on clean data and attacked with FGSM ($\varepsilon = 0.1$) achieved a mere 58.01% accuracy. When input transformation was incorporated, accuracy improved to 88.14%. The best performance, 92.96%, was achieved when both input transformation and adversarial training were employed together.

This synergistic effect clearly demonstrates the strength of the hybrid defense framework in mitigating adversarial threats.

In summary, the experimental results reinforce the effectiveness of the hybrid defense strategy. Input transformations offer lightweight, preprocessing-based robustness, while adversarial training equips the model with enhanced resistance against both simple and iterative perturbations. The fusion of these techniques achieves a resilient architecture capable of preserving classification performance even in the presence of substantial adversarial manipulations.

Conclusion and Future Work

The growing prevalence of adversarial threats to deep learning models, particularly in the domain of image classification, has sparked widespread concern in the machine learning research community. This chapter addressed this pressing issue by proposing and evaluating a hybrid defense framework that combines *input transformation techniques* with *adversarial training* to enhance the adversarial robustness of convolutional neural networks. Using the ResNet-18 architecture trained on the CIFAR-10 dataset, we demonstrated how this integrated approach significantly improves model resilience against both single-step and iterative attacks, specifically FGSM and PGD.

The input transformation component, incorporating random resizing, JPEG compression, and Gaussian noise injection, plays a critical role in disrupting adversarial patterns during both training and inference. These transformations act as lightweight preprocessing defenses that can degrade the effectiveness of small, imperceptible perturbations without substantially altering the semantic content of the image. Simultaneously, adversarial training, particularly with robust attacks such as PGD, exposes the model to perturbed samples during training, enabling it to learn more generalized and stable feature representations. Experimental results validated the efficacy of this hybrid defense, with performance improvements observed across a range of perturbation intensities and adversarial conditions.

Beyond improving classification accuracy under attack, the hybrid strategy offers a scalable and practical framework that balances computational complexity with robustness. By conducting an ablation analysis, we also highlighted the individual and collective contributions of each defense component, thereby reinforcing the argument for a layered approach to adversarial defense.

Future Research Directions: While the hybrid defense framework presented in this chapter shows promising results, it also opens several avenues for future investigation. Below are some potential directions that could guide subsequent research and innovation in this domain.

Adaptive Input Transformations: The current approach relies on fixed transformation parameters, such as Gaussian noise intensity or compression quality. Future research could focus on developing *adaptive transformation strategies* that learn optimal transformation parameters in a data-driven or attack-aware manner. This would allow the defense mechanism to dynamically adjust to the type and severity of an incoming attack.

Adversarial Training with Diverse Attacks: This chapter employed FGSM and PGD as representative attacks for adversarial training. Expanding the attack set to include more sophisticated techniques, such as DeepFool (Moosavi-Dezfooli et al., 2016), Carlini and Wagner (Carlini & Wagner, 2017), or AutoAttack (Croce & Hein, 2020), can make the training process more comprehensive and prepare the model for a broader adversarial landscape. Training with *ensembles of attacks* may provide better generalization to unseen perturbations.

Cross-Architecture Generalization: While ResNet-18 was used as the primary backbone in this study, it would be beneficial to explore the performance of the proposed hybrid defense on other architectures, such as VGG (Simonyan & Zisserman, 2015), DenseNet (Huang et al., 2017), Vision Transformers (ViTs) (Dosovitskiy et al., 2025), or EfficientNet (Tan & Le, 2019). Understanding the *transferability and generalizability* of the defense framework across model families can lead to more robust deployments in diverse real-world scenarios.

Defense Against Physical-World Attacks: Most adversarial research, including this work, assumes a digital input setting. However, real-world adversarial attacks may involve *physical perturbations* such as printed adversarial images or sensor interference. Extending the hybrid defense strategy to handle such physical-world scenarios remains an open and challenging area of research.

Certified Robustness and Theoretical Guarantees: One limitation of empirical defenses like adversarial training is the lack of formal guarantees on robustness. Future work could incorporate *certified defense mechanisms* or robustness verification tools that provide theoretical bounds on adversarial perturbations under which the model is *provably safe*. Hybrid frameworks could be augmented with such methods to balance empirical performance and theoretical rigor.

Efficiency-Aware Robust Training: Adversarial training is computationally intensive and can significantly slow down the training process. Research is needed on *efficient adversarial training algorithms*, including curriculum-based training, selective adversarial sampling, and lightweight surrogate models. These can make robust training feasible for large-scale models and datasets.

Robustness-Accuracy Trade-off Optimization: A recurring theme in adversarial defense research is the trade-off between robustness and clean-data accuracy. Future studies could aim to develop *optimization strategies* or *multi-objective loss functions* that explicitly balance robustness with standard performance, possibly by leveraging reinforcement learning or neural architecture search (Sener & Koltun, 2018; Zhang et al., 2019).

Explainability and Visualization of Robust Models: Understanding how and why robust models resist adversarial perturbations remains a relatively unexplored field. Developing tools for *visualizing the decision boundaries*, saliency maps, and internal representations of adversarially trained networks can aid in diagnosing failure cases and improving model transparency.

In summary, this chapter has introduced a practical and effective hybrid strategy for adversarial defense in image classification, grounded in empirical evaluations and reinforced by theoretical considerations. As the arms race between attack and defense techniques continues to evolve, the insights and methodologies presented here offer a strong foundation upon which more robust, adaptive, and intelligent defense mechanisms can be built.

References

Carlini, N. and Wagner, D. 2017. "Adversarial Examples are not Easily Detected: Bypassing Ten Detection Methods." In *Proceedings of the 10th ACM Workshop on Artificial Intelligence and Security (AISec 2017)*, 3-14.

Chen, R., Chen, J., H. Zheng, H., Q. Xuan, Z. Ming, W. Jiang, and C. Cui, "Salient feature extractor for adversarial defense on deep neural networks." *Information Sciences*, 600: 118-143.

Croce, F. and Hein, M. 2020. "Reliable Evaluation of Adversarial Robustness with an Ensemble of Diverse Parameter-Free Attacks." In *Proceedings of the 37th International Conference on Machine Learning (ICML 2020)*, PMLR 119: 2206-2216.

Dosovitskiy, A., Beyer, L., Kolesnikov, A., Weissenborn, D., Zhai, X., Unterhiner, T., Dehghani, M., Minderer, M., Heigold, G., Gelly, S., Uszkoreit, J., and Houlsby, N. 2025. "An Image is Worth 16x16 Words: Transformers for Image Recognition." In *Proceedings of the International Conference on Learning Representations (ICLR 2025)*, Oral Track.

Goodfellow, I. J., Shlens, J., and Szegedy, C. 2015. "Explaining and Harnessing Adversarial Examples." In the *International Conference on Learning Representations (ICLR 2015)*, Poster Track.

He, K., Zhang, X., Ren, S., and Sun, J. 2016. "Deep Residual Learning for Image Recognition." In *Proceedings of the IEEE Conference on Computer Vision and Pattern Recognition (CVPR 2016)*, 770-778.

Huang, G., Liu, Z., van der Maaten, L., Weinberger, K. Q. 2017. "Densely Connected Convolutional Networks. " In *Proceedings of the 2017 IEEE Conference on Computer Vision and Pattern Recognition (CVPR 2017)*, 2261-2269.

Koley, A., Satpati, P., Choudhary, I., and Sen, J. 2024. "An Investigation on the Efficiency of Some Text Attack Algorithms." In *Proceedings of the IEEE North Karnataka Subsection Flagship International Conference (NKCon 2024)*, 1–8.

Krizhevsky, A. 2009. "Learning Multiple Layers of Features from Tiny Images." Technical Report, University of Toronto. https://www.cs.toronto.edu/~kriz/learning-features-2009-TR.pdf.

Krizhevsky, A., Sutskever, I., and Hinton, G. E. 2017. "ImageNet Classification with Deep Convolutional Neural Networks." *Communications of the ACM*, 60(6): 84-90.

Li, X., Pan, D., and Zhu, D. 2021. "Defending against Adversarial Attacks on Medical Imaging AI System, Classification or Detection?" In

Proceedings of the IEEE 18th International Symposium on Biomedical Imaging (ISBI 2021), 1677-1681.

Li, Z., Feng, C., Wu, M., Yu, H., Zheng, J., and Zhu, F. 2021. "Adversarial Robustness via Attention Transfer." *Pattern Recognition Letters*, 146: 172-17.

Madry, A., Makelov, A., Schmidt, L., Tsipras, D., and Vladu, A. 2018. "Towards Deep Learning Models Resistant to Adversarial Attacks." In the *International Conference on Learning Representations (ICLR 2018)*, Poster Track.

Moosavi-Dezfooli, S-M., Fawzi, A., and Frossard, P. 2016. "DeepFool: A Simple and Accurate Method to Fool Deep Neural Networks." In *Proceedings of the 2016 IEEE Conference on Computer Vision and Pattern Recognition (CVPR 2016)*, 2574-2582.

Papernot, N., McDaniel, P., Wu, X., Jha, S., and Swami, A. 2016. "Distillation as a Defense to Adversarial Perturbations against Deep Neural Networks." In *Proceedings of the IEEE Symposium on Security and Privacy (S&P 2016)*, 582-597.

Pestana, C., Akhtar, N., Liu, W., Glance, D., and Mian, A. 2021. "Adversarial Attacks and Defense on Deep Learning Classification Models Using YCbCr Color Images." In *Proceedings of the International Joint Conference on Neural Networks (IJCNN 2021)*, 1-9.

Sen, J. 2024. "The FGSM Attack on Image Classification Models and Distillation as its Defense." In Nanda et al. (eds), *Advances in Distributed Computing and Machine Learning (ICADCML 2024)*, 1015: 347-360. Lecture Notes in Networks and Systems, Springer, Singapore.

Sen, J. and Dasgupta, S. 2023. "Adversarial Attacks on Image Classification Models: FGSM and Patch Attacks and their Impact." In Sen, J. and Mayer, J. (eds), *Information Security and Privacy in the Digital World: Some Selected Topics*, IntechOpen, London, UK.

Sen, J., Sen, A., and Chatterjee, A. 2023. "Adversarial Attacks on Image Classification Models: Analysis and Defense." In *Proceedings of the 10th International Conference on Business Analytics and Intelligence (ICBAI 2023)*, Bangalore, India.

Sen, J. and Waghela, H. 2025. "Text-Based Adversarial Attacks and Defense." In Sen, J. (ed) *Data Privacy: Techniques, Applications, and Standards*, IntechOpen, London, UK.

Shi, C., Dang, Y., Fang, L., Lv, Z., and Zhao, M. 2022. "Hyperspectral Image Classification with Adversarial Attack." *IEEE Geoscience and Remote Sensing Letters*, 19 (5510305): 1-5.

Sener, O. and Koltun, V. 2018. "Multi-task Learning as Multi-objective Optimization." In *Proceedings of the 32nd International Conference on Neural Information Processing Systems (NIPS 2018)*, 525-536.

Shi, C., Liu, Y., Zhao, M., Pun, C-M., Miao, Q. 2024. "Attack-invariant Attention Feature for Adversarial Defense in Hyperspectral Image Classification." *Pattern Recognition*, 145(109955), 2024.

Simonyan, K. and Zisserman, A. 2015. "Very Deep Convolutional Networks for Large-Scale Image Recognition." In *Proceedings of the International Conference on Learning Representations (ICLR 2015)*, Poster Track.

Spasiano, F., Gennaro, G., and Scardapane, S. 2022. "Evaluating Adversarial Attacks and Defences in Infrared Deep Learning Monitoring Systems." In Proceedings of the *International Joint Conference on Neural Networks (IJCNN 2022)*, 1-6.

Tan, M. and Le, Q. 2019. "EfficientNet: Rethinking Model Scaling for Convolutional Neural Networks." In *Proceedings of the 36th International Conference on Machine Learning (ICML 2019)*, PMLR, 97:6105-6114.

Waghela, H., Sen, J., and Rakshit, S. 2025. "Saliency Attention and Semantic Similarity-Driven Adversarial Perturbation." In *Data Science and Applications. ICDSA 2024*, Nanda, S. J. et al. (eds), 1237: 461–471. Lecture Notes in Networks and Systems, Springer, Singapore.

Waghela, H., Sen, J., Rakshit, S., and Dasgupta, S. 2024a. "Adversarial Text Generation with Dynamic Contextual Perturbation." In *Proceedings of the 2024 IEEE CALCON 2024*, 1–6. IEEE.

Waghela, H., Sen, J., and Rakshit, S. 2024b. "Adaptive Meta-Learning for Robust Ensemble Defense against Adversarial Attacks." In *Proceedings of the International Conference BAMS-ORSI 2024*.

Waghela, H., Sen, J., and Rakshit, S. 2024c. "Adversarial Resilience in Image Classification: A Hybrid Approach to Defense." In *Proceedings of the 2024 International Conference on Innovation and Intelligence for Informatics, Computing, and Technologies (3ICT 2024)*, 419–426.

Waghela, H., Sen, J., Rakshit, S., and Dasgupta, S. 2024d. "Adversarial Robustness through Dynamic Ensemble Learning." In *Proceedings of the 2024 IEEE Silchar Subsection Conference (SILCON 2024)*, 1–6.

Waghela, H., Sen, J., and Rakshit, S. 2024e. "Robust Image Classification: Defensive Strategies against FGSM and PGD Adversarial Attacks." In *Proceedings of the IEEE Asian Conference on Intelligent Technologies (ACOIT 2024)*, 1 – 7.

Waghela, H., Sen, J., and Rakshit, S. 2024f. "Refining BERT Adversarial Attacks with Projected Gradient Descent." In *Proceedings of the IEEE*

4th Asian Conference on Innovations in Technology (ASIANCON 2024), 1-7.

Waghela, H., Rakshit, S., and Sen, J. 2024g. "A Modified Word Saliency-Based Adversarial Attack on Text Classification Models." In *Computational Intelligence and Data Analytics*, Frery, A. C. et al. (eds), 371–382. Lecture Notes in Data Engineering and Communications Technologies, 236. Springer.

Worzyk, N. and Kramer, O. 2018. "Adversarials-1: Defending by Attacking." In *Proceedings of the International Joint Conference on Neural Networks (IJCNN 2018)*, 1-8.

Xu, H., Ma, Y., Liu, H. C., Deb, D., Liu, H., Tang, J-L., and Jain, A. K. 2020. "Adversarial Attacks and Defenses in Images, Graphs and Text: A Review." *International Journal of Autonomous Computing*, 17(2): 151–178.

Xu, Y., Du, B., and Zhang, L. 2021. "Self-attention Context Network: Addressing the Threat of Adversarial Attacks for Hyperspectral Image Classification." *IEEE Transactions on Image Processing*, 30: 8671-8685.

Zhang, S., Gao, H., and Rao, Q. 2021. "Defense against Adversarial Attacks by Reconstructing Images." *IEEE Transactions on Image Processing*, 30: 6117-6129.

Zhang, H., Yu, Y., Jio, J., Xing, E., El Ghaoui, L., and Jordan, M. 2019. "Theoretically Principled Trade-off between Robustness and Accuracy." In *Proceedings of the 36th International Conference on Machine Learning (ICML 2019)*, PMLR 97:7472-7482.

Zhou, M., Wang, L., Niu, Z., Zhang, Q., Zheng, N., and Hua, G. 2024. "Adversarial Attack and Defense in Deep Ranking." *IEEE Transactions on Pattern Analysis and Machine Intelligence*, 46(8): 5306-5324.

INDEX